MIRROR HATE

By the same author:

Arthur Griffith and Non-Violent Sinn Féin
The Young Ireland Movement
Irish Issues in New Zealand Politics

Mirror Hate

The convergent ideology of Northern Ireland
paramilitaries, 1966-1992

RICHARD DAVIS
Professor of History
University of Tasmania

Dartmouth

Aldershot • Brookfield USA • Singapore • Sydney

Published by
Dartmouth Publishing Company Limited
Gower House
Croft Road
Aldershot
Hants GU11 3HR
England

Dartmouth Publishing Company
Old Post Road
Brookfield
Vermont 05036
USA

British Library Cataloguing in Publication Data
Mirror Hate: Convergent Ideology of
Northern Ireland Paramilitaries, 1966-92
I. Title
322.4209416

Library of Congress Cataloging-in-Publication Data
Davis, Richard P.
    Mirror Hate : the convergent ideology of Northern Ireland
paramilitaries, 1966-92 / Richard Davis.
        p.   cm.
    Includes bibliographical references and index.
    ISBN 1-85521-558-6 : $59.95 (Approx.)
    1. Northern Ireland–History–1969- 2. Paramilitary forces-
-Northern Ireland–History–20th century. 3. Propaganda–Northern
Ireland–History–20th century. 4. Irish unification question.
I. Title.
DA990.U46D38   1994
941.5082–dc20   94-27123
                                                                      CIP

ISBN 1 85521 558 6

Contents

Preface

This monograph developed from discussions with the late John Whyte, the doyen of Northern Ireland analysts, who was also good enough to read the early drafts. I have greatly benefited from his advice. Other scholars who have read drafts in whole or part are Paul Bew, Ronnie Buchanan, Ian Breward, Bill Bostock, Gary Easthope, Bishop Richard Hanson, David Wilson, Alan O'Day. I have also received valuable assistance from Bishop Edward Daly, Frs Raymond Murray, Denis Faul and Des Wilson, Eamon Phoenix, Christopher McGimpsey, R.D.C. Black, David Harkness, Conor Cruise O'Brien, and many others. I am most indebted to the Institute of Irish Studies, Queen's University, Belfast, under the Directorship of Ronnie Buchanan, where I was a research associate 1981-82 and a fellow 1985-86. While the two major figures in the story, Gerry Adams and the Rev. Ian Paisley, exhibited a mirrored reaction in their lack of response to my request for an interview, I received enormous support and encouragement from the staff of the Linen Hall Library, whose collection of the literature of the Northern Ireland Troubles, currently under the direction of Robert Bell, forms the basis for this work. I am grateful to the Blackstaff Press for permission to publish stanzas from John Hewitt's 'The Anglo-Irish Accord' from Frank Ormsby, ed. (1981), *The Collected Poems of John Hewitt*. I should also like to thank the University of Tasmania for granting me sufficient overseas leave to spend in aggregate over two years of the current Troubles in Belfast. In the final stages of production the editorial work of Simon Harris, Lynn Rainbird and my wife Marianne have been invaluable.

Introduction

To most people living outside Northern Ireland the Anglo-Irish Agreement of November 1985 appeared an eminently sensible compromise designed to end nearly two decades of intermittent strife. The 60 per cent unionist majority in the Province was assured a continued link with Britain, while the identity and interests of the nationalist 40 per cent minority was guaranteed by a regular conference of representatives of the British and Irish governments. Provision was also made for the supersession of the Anglo-Irish Conference by a devolved Northern Irish government based on agreement between the unionist and nationalist communities. Furthermore, increased co-operation between the British and Irish governments in the defeat of terrorism was foreshadowed.

The Provisional IRA, the apparent source of most violence and disorder in the province, was naturally indignant. Little anticipated by the outside world, and probably the British and Irish ministers responsible for the Accord, was the hostility and violent reaction of the Protestant majority.

To the amazement of the uninitiated, unionist representatives, both elected and self-appointed, proceeded to emulate Provisional republicans in the fervour of their hatred for the government of Margaret Thatcher and their threats of a gory outcome. The People's Democracy (PD) march from Belfast to Derry in early 1969, which then evoked loyalist violence, was appropriated by the latter in January 1986, but symbolically reversed in direction. Boycotts of Westminster, local authorities and rates closely followed traditional Sinn Féin tactics. Unionist 'integrationists' accused their 'devolutionist' rivals of seeking a Unilateral Declaration of Independence (UDI) as a form of 'Protestant Sinn Féin'. Mob attacks on the Royal Ulster Constabulary and their families reinforced the Provisional selective assassination of the security forces. Loyalist protest demonstrations moreover drew off police to the cities, thus reducing pressure on the Provisionals in country districts. Strikes and threats to 'make Ulster ungovernable' dovetailed neatly with Provisional rhetoric and action. All in all, response to the Anglo-Irish Agreement appeared to confirm the hostile stereotype of the Irish, regardless of faction, being universally addicted to mindless violence and mayhem. The Northern Ireland poet, John Hewitt, seeing both sides 'slave to and victim of this mirror hate' sought plaintively 'a neutral sod' where all could debate 'without intemperate speech.'

The suggestion that the apparently polarised 'two nations' of Northern Ireland have in fact much in common is certainly not new. John Morley, in his *Life of Gladstone*, assimilated perfervid Orange rhetoric with the 'florid violence' of the Fenians.[1] Recent journalism abounds with references to unionism and republicanism as 'mirror images' of each other. Danger lies in the imprecision of the term. The concept, however, is useful. A systematic search for conscious or unconscious convergence between ostensibly opposed traditions may deepen understanding of the real issues at stake and lead to a sharpening of terminology as a tool for dissipating old myths.

The present study is based on the excellent collection of pamphlets and periodicals garnered since the onset of the present Troubles in 1968 by the Linen Hall Library, Belfast. Many books have been based on interviews with rival Northern Ireland leaders, the best being Padraig O'Malley's *The Uncivil Wars*. Yet newspaper files are unrivalled for the detection of shifting ground, inconsistency, and revealing give-aways. Though loosely categorised as propaganda, aimed variously at potential supporters and the outside world, the ephemera of the Ulster Troubles expose many deeply held convictions. Here the emphasis is on the smaller weeklies, usually more extreme than the daily press speaking for more conventional organisations. Yet, as Sarah Nelson and Dervla Murphy argue, most militants were 'not that different' from the general population. Unionist reaction to the Agreement, when many highly educated Protestants were unable to dissociate from the melodramatic assertions of inveterate hardliners, endorses this conclusion. It is therefore dangerous and irresponsible to dismiss the more outrageous statements cited below as mere eccentric curiosities.

If the 'mirror-image' thesis is sustainable, it must be capable of separation into manageable, if not always totally watertight, compartments. First, there is identically *patterned opposition*. Loyalist gables inscribed with FTP ('Fuck the Pope') clearly mirror nationalist counterparts sporting FTQ ('Fuck the Queen'). Secondly, *direct borrowing* of symbols or tactics frequently occurs across sectarian lines. The loyalist Derry to Belfast march of January 1986 is a good example which also includes an element of patterned opposition. Third comes *calculated antagonism*, which sometimes obscures agreement on fundamentals. A characteristic incident was the loyalist one-day strike of 3 March 1986 against the Anglo-Irish Agreement. While Protestant areas remained grimly closed, with the skeletal remains of burnt-out cars as a savage warning to strike-breakers, in Catholic districts, despite power cuts, ostensibly carefree shoppers created a carnival atmosphere. The fourth, and most important, variant of the mirror image is unconscious *cultural convergence*. This can be detected in anti-British feeling, always simmering beneath the surface, which welled up in the 'loyalist' community after the Accord. Finally, we find *antithetical interpretation*, where the same event, person or statement is interpreted in totally different senses on the two sides.

Analysis of 'extremist' political ephemera since the 1960s demonstrates the extent to which 'mirrored' arguments have crossed the apparently impassable divide. The first chapter introduces the main contesting groups against a backdrop of some significant events since 1966. Chapter two discusses the relevant periodicals. Three surveys the attitude of republicans and loyalists to a history which both acknowledge as fundamental to their respective positions. The fourth chapter analyses the Roman Catholic Church, embattled on two flanks, and compares its situation with that of the Protestant Churches. This discussion leads in chapter five to the all-important issue of separate versus integrated education. After education, the sixth section examines violence and brings the British security forces into the debate. In seven, social and economic disputation is scoured for republican-unionist convergence. The eighth chapter traces the conflict to the Third and Fourth Worlds, especially Southern Africa, where apparently divergent precedents are drawn to boost the Northern Ireland controversy. The conclusion seeks an explanation for the symbiotic 'mirror hate' of the major contestants.

Many arguments are derived from the Irish Revolutionary period, 1916-21. This culminated in independence for the 26 Counties of what is now the Irish Republic, while the Six Counties of Northern Ireland obtained a parliament under Westminster control. The present 'Ulster Troubles' have already resulted in the scrapping of the Northern Ireland parliament, which for fifty years maintained unbroken unionist rule, and the more recent establishment of an international Agreement endorsing the Irish identity of the nationalist minority. The unfinished period since 1968 can therefore be considered a 'second Irish revolution'. If the Downing Street Declaration of 15 December 1993, between the Irish Taoiseach, Albert Reynolds, and the British Prime Minister, John Major, leads eventually to a form of Irish unity by agreement, the second revolution will be great indeed. Though the final outcome of this revolution is uncertain, it is clear that, despite the wishes of many loyalists, the old unionist-dominated Stormont parliament will never be re-established.

Notes

1.   Morley, John (1908), *Life of William Ewart Gladstone*, Vol. 2, London: Edward Lloyd, 418.

1 Background of antagonism: plantation and division

The conflict in Northern Ireland, like similar apparently intractable divisions in Belgium, Bosnia, Azerbeijan and Sri Lanka, is of particularly long provenance. Ireland, though subjected to various Celtic invasions which left a pre-Celtic people in a state of semi-subservience similar to the pre-Aryan Indians, never succumbed to Rome. The Vikings after the ninth century were contained and absorbed; not until 1169 did the Normans appear as a new and apparently all-powerful invader. Yet the Normans, and the English kings their suzerains, were unable before 1603 to destroy completely the independence of the old Gaelic chieftains. Over the centuries the latter had alternately submitted conditionally and rebelled; culturally they assimilated their conquerors and reduced effective English power to the Pale, a thirty-mile-deep strip between Dublin and Drogheda. Ironically the last great Gaels to challenge the might of the Tudor monarchy were the O'Neills and O'Donnells of Ulster.

The surrender of the O'Neill and the O'Donnell in 1603 and their flight to Spain six years later paved the way for the epoch-making plantation of Ulster in the reign of James I. To prevent a Gaelic resurgence the plantation strategy, already attempted with little success in other parts of Ireland, was applied. The government of James I assigned O'Neill and O'Donnell lands to 'Undertakers' from Scotland or England. These were charged with introducing a reliable tenantry to replace the rebellious Irish, thus assimilating Ireland with England and Scotland. Contemporaneously there was extensive unofficial migration of lowland Scots to the north-eastern Irish counties of Down and Antrim. The plantations further west were not very successful in replacing the poorer Irish with English and Scots, but in Antrim and Down a new Protestant population was created.

Though religious differences originally played no part in the strife between Gaels and English in Ireland, the Tudor acceptance of Protestantism in the sixteenth century was not endorsed by either the Gaelic Irish or the Norman descendants in Ireland, who both remained true to traditional Catholicism. Thus the potent catalyst of religion, especially in Ulster, was added to national antagonism. During the seventeenth century a series of wars and rebellions left the land and political control of Ireland in the hands of a Protestant (understood then as Anglican) upper class, while outside Ulster the lower classes on the land were almost invariably Catholic. In North-East Ulster the incomplete plantations and the Scottish migrations brought an explosive amalgam of local Presbyterian and Anglican majorities confronting large groups of resentful unassimilated Catholics.

In the eighteenth century, the penal laws against Catholicism were gradually relaxed, and, assisted by the advocacy of Henry Grattan, the Irish parliament gained a modicum of independence from Britain and moved slowly towards admitting Catholics to its body. But in Ulster tensions between Catholics and Protestants intensified. The Orange Order (originally mainly Anglican, later Presbyterian) was established in 1795 after a territorial clash between Catholic and Protestant religious factions. The Order proved useful to the British government in putting down the 1798 rebellion of the United Irishmen. One of their leaders, Theobald Wolfe Tone, had lobbied vigorously for French Revolutionary assistance, and aspired to create a non-sectarian Ireland independent of Britain. The failure of the '98 Rebellion and the subsequent merging in 1800 of the Protestant-dominated Irish parliament with that of the United Kingdom of Great Britain and Ireland, introduced an era of fitful resistance. Daniel O'Connell's successful movement for Catholic Emancipation in 1829, which enabled Catholics to sit in the United Kingdom parliament, strengthened the resolve of the Anglicans and Presbyterians in North-East Ulster. They determined to preserve the link with Britain to avoid being swamped in a Catholic-majority independent Ireland. Once rivals, Anglicans and Presbyterians began to emphasise their common 'Protestant' links. The economic growth of the city of Belfast, especially in linen manufacture and later shipbuilding, while the rest of Ireland stagnated economically, emphasised differences attributed by some to Protestant initiative. Yet the migration, especially during the famine years of 1845-49, of Catholics to West Belfast and other city enclaves occasioned a tradition of periodic sectarian riot and mayhem, intensifying in the second half of the nineteenth century. Meanwhile, in the south O'Connell, unsuccessful in his efforts to secure repeal of the Act of Union, alienated the Young Irelanders, inspired by the Protestant journalist, Thomas Davis. In 1848, these Young Irelanders, led by William Smith O'Brien, a Protestant landlord of ancient Irish stock, attempted a hopeless insurrection in the midst of a famine which decimated the Irish population. Some survivors established the secret Fenian movement whose Rising failed in 1867 but it spawned an Irish Republican Brotherhood (IRB) which continued into the twentieth century. In the 1870s and 1880s a constitutionalist Home Rule party, led by Charles Stewart Parnell, persuaded W.E. Gladstone's Liberal government to introduce a limited Irish Home Rule bill in 1886. This created a storm of Orange and unionist opposition in Ulster; the bill was rejected by the House of Commons and its 1893 successor by the House of Lords. Ulster Protestant fury reached a crescendo in 1911-14, when a Liberal-Irish Home Rule majority emasculated the power of the House of Lords to ensure the passage of limited Irish self-government in the latter year. Northern Protestant and Irish nationalists, and their private armies, the Ulster and Irish Volunteers, appeared on the verge of conflict when World War I intervened in August 1914.

The Irish Revolution and partition

The truce proved temporary. Irish nationalists and Ulster unionists joined the British Army in large numbers to resist Germany. Meanwhile, a minority of extreme nationalists, despairing of a Home Rule Act certain to be amended to give the Northern Protestants a virtual veto over their inclusion in a future self-governing Ireland, staged an unsuccessful but ultimately decisive rebellion in Easter Week 1916. The revolt was attributed to Sinn Féin, originally a passive resistance movement established in 1905 by the brilliant journalist, Arthur Griffith, who emphasised Irish language, culture and industrial protection.

Catholic Ireland was rapidly converted from moderate constitutional nationalism to apparent republicanism by the executions of the rebel leaders of 1916, who included Padraic Pearse and the socialist thinker, James Connolly. But Northern Protestants, many of whose leaders were members of wartime coalition governments, had the clout to resist their own inclusion in a self-governing Ireland. The militant Sinn Féiners, under the leadership of a 1916 commander, Eamon de Valera, annihilated their constitutionalist opponents in the post-war general election of December 1918. An Irish Assembly was set up and defended by the Irish Republican Army (IRA) directed by Michael Collins. Meanwhile, intransigent Ulster Unionist MPs held the North-East. During the Irish War of Independence (1919-21), the Lloyd George coalition government determined on partition. Led by Sir Edward Carson, the Ulster Unionists ensured that partition gave them the six counties of Ulster, where they had a two-to-one majority, rather than the full nine counties of the historical Province where their bare majority might soon be at risk.[1]

The Ulster Catholic minority was dumbfounded by a settlement, cunningly imposed by Lloyd George on Irish negotiators. Pliable after the savageries of guerrilla war, the Irish plenipotentiaries were persuaded that the Six County statelet could be made unviable by a Boundary Commission. Initially, the Catholic minority in Northern Ireland refused to recognise their new parliament, theoretically subordinate to Westminster. This nationalist minority negotiated unsuccessfully with the new Irish Free State, established by the Treaty in December 1921. The Free State incorporated the remaining twenty-six Irish counties, one of which was Donegal, the most northerly county in Ireland. The Civil War in the south between the supporters of the Treaty, signed by Griffith and Collins, and opponents, inspired by de Valera, lessened the impact of northern nationalist action. The Unionist government of Northern Ireland at Stormont under Sir James Craig (later Lord Craigavon), J.M. Andrews, Sir Basil Brooke (later Lord Brookeborough), Terence O'Neill, J.D. Chichester-Clark and Brian Faulkner ruled without a break from 1922 till its suspension in 1972. During this period the Unionists at every election capitalised on the constitutional threat to the State, emphasising continued activity by the IRA, claiming succession from the 1919-21 insurgents. On the other hand, Catholics complained of discrimination in housing, services and jobs. Many of these complaints have been found to be well justified.[2] The perpetual Special Powers Act, allowing the suspension of civil liberties, and the B Specials, a part-time Protestant police auxiliary, were particularly loathed by Catholics. Though children educated at their partly subsidised schools almost equalled Protestant children in numbers, Catholic emigration was heavier, thus preserving the two-to-one balance. Statements by Unionist prime ministers that they presided over 'a Protestant Parliament and a Protestant State' and that they refused to employ Catholics on principle[3] suggested that Catholic emigration was part of their strategy.

Modernising attempts in the 1960s

By the 1960s, however, it appeared that a new era had dawned in Northern Ireland. Educational reforms in post-war Britain extended to Northern Ireland. A new tertiary-educated Catholic leadership confronted the would-be modernising prime minister, Terence O'Neill, who sought to liquidate the divisive legacy of his predecessor Lord Brookeborough by integrating Catholics in the general community. O'Neill broke new ground by visiting Catholic schools and posing for photographs with the Catholic Primate, Cardinal Conway. But critics have maintained that his government, encouraging industrial development in the Protestant east and establishing a new university in Protestant Coleraine, rather than Catholic Derry, did nothing for the material interests of the minority. O'Neill was also unable to overcome the local 'zero sum game' in which the smallest concession to Catholics appeared a sellout to Protestants.

O'Neill's well-meaning efforts were doomed by a revival of the same loyalist intransigence which had blocked moderate Home Rule bills before 1914. The Rev. Ian Paisley was heir to a long line of nineteenth-century Protestant clerics, such as Henry Cooke, Thomas Drew and Hugh Hanna, whose charismatic anti-Catholic rhetoric had provoked a sequence of savage sectarian riots in nineteenth-century Belfast. While Cooke, Drew and Hanna represented mainstream Anglicanism and Presbyterianism, Paisley belonged to the Ulster tradition of breakaway fundamentalist Protestant sectarianism. Born in 1926, Paisley was ordained in 1945 by his Independent Baptist father; in 1951 young Ian established his own 'Free Presbyterian' Church, with himself as perpetual moderator. His combination of spectacular anti-Catholicism and anti-Establishment unionist populism detonated the sensitive Northern Ireland atmosphere of 1966. Originally appearing a crude and archaic exhibitionist, Paisley eventually emerged as the voice of Northern Ireland Protestantism. As early as 1967 he cited a public opinion poll according him the support of 31 per cent of the Northern Irish population.

The Vietnam War, which mobilised radical European youth, the Second Vatican Council's ecumenism, which convinced Bible Protestants that a sellout by established Protestant Churches was imminent, and the fiftieth anniversary of the Irish Easter Week Rising in 1966, all worked to destroy the precarious balance which the optimistic O'Neill hoped to establish in his modernised Northern Ireland. In 1966 all the insecurities of ultra-Protestants, fearful of a world likely to leave them an isolated enclave in a Catholic sea, surfaced in Ian Paisley's dramatic rhetoric. Even the new sexual permissiveness, symbolised by the mini-skirt, was answered by Paisley's insistence that the scriptural way was 'bend the knee not bare the knee'. His new *Protestant Telegraph* provided salutory sublimation for Puritans by depicting the sexual perversities of the Roman Catholic confessional.

In such an atmosphere, Captain O'Neill's conciliatory gesture of exchanging visits with Séan Lemass, the Irish Taoiseach, or Prime Minister, appeared an act of extreme provocation leading inevitably to bitter Paisleyite demonstrations. Paisley suffered the strategic martyrdom of a short gaol sentence for a demonstration against the ecumenical tendencies of the official Presbyterian Church. His march incited a riot when entering the Cromac Square in the Catholic Markets area of Belfast. Though Paisley could flirt with violence and withdraw unscathed, his rhetoric was too intoxicating for some. An organisation calling itself the UVF after Carson's Ulster Volunteer Force, which had resisted the the third Home Rule Bill after 1912, mounted attacks on Catholics and killed two. Gusty Spence, later to be converted to more ecumenical thinking, and four others, one of whom blamed Paisley for his predicament, were sentenced to life imprisonment. As Spence said later, 'at that time the attitude was that if you couldn't get an IRA man you should shoot a Taig [Catholic]'.[4] On the other side, the triumphalist celebration of the fiftieth anniversary of the 1916 Rising, so different from the low-key acknowledgement of the event twenty-five years later, raised the expectations of Northern nationalists and the hackles of their unionist counterparts.

The current Troubles begin

1966 is regarded by some as the first year of the Northern Ireland Troubles; others prefer 1969, when riots in Derry and Belfast on 12 August led to the deployment of British troops on an increasing scale. But Northern Ireland first impressed itself on the world's notice, via the television camera, in the second half of 1968, that year of world-wide student protest. On 29 January 1967 the Northern Ireland Civil Rights Association (NICRA) was formed to oppose discrimination, gerrymandering, the B Specials and the Special Powers Act, while insisting on the principle of 'one man one vote' in local elections. The now virtually disarmed IRA played a large part in NICRA's formation, but as many others—Protestants, Catholics, trade unionists and communists—joined, the movement became too conservative for some of the new radicals who hoped to provoke the authorities into over-reaction. NICRA's significance lay in its insistence on reforms within the British system, not a demand for union with the Irish Republic.

In June 1968 a young Nationalist MP, Austin Currie, engaged in a protest occupation of a house at Caledon, near Dungannon, from which a Catholic family had been evicted to make way for an unmarried Protestant woman. Currie, a lorry driver's son who had obtained a history degree through scholarships, was a classic example of the new educated Catholic leadership. He persuaded NICRA to participate in a march from Coalisland to Dungannon against housing discrimination. Despite the reluctance of some NICRA leaders to demonstrate on the streets, the march went ahead and was challenged by a counter-demonstration organised by Paisley. Worse was to come. Violence broke out at demonstrations in Derry (5 October) and Armagh (30 November) when members of Paisley's Ulster Constitutional Defence Committee (UCDC) and its paramilitary Ulster Protestant Volunteers (UPV) violently challenged NICRA. At Derry, where demonstrations had been banned, Catholic MPs like Gerry Fitt and Austin Currie were batoned by members of the Royal Ulster Constabulary (RUC) in full view of TV cameras. Seventy-seven people were injured. The police used water-cannon. Citizens in the Catholic Bogside area set up barricades and challenged them. As Purdie demonstrates, NICRA, reluctantly dragged into the protest by the more radical Derry Citizens Action Committee, after 5 October became a mass movement overnight and transformed the politics of Northern Ireland. On the other side Paisley emerged as the defender of a beleaguered Protestant Ulster.[5]

Many Protestants saw the issue in simplistic terms: (NI)CRA = IRA. The UCDC and UPV policy was therefore 'to confront the enemy at every possible opportunity.' When students, lecturers and graduates at Queen's University, such as Bernadette Devlin and Michael Farrell, formed the People's Democracy (PD),[6] the *Protestant Telegraph* insisted that it was a synonym for the IRA's Republican Clubs, intended to create 'disturbance, riot and bloodshed in Belfast.'[7] The almost moribund IRA, through its Wolfe Tone Clubs, did play a leading role initiating NICRA. But PD, with republican sentiments and some Protestant members, for a time filled the vacuum left by IRA lethargy since its unsuccessful 1956-62 'border campaign', and provided a focus for Catholic aspirations. The more moderate NICRA halted its operations when O'Neill on 9 December announced a package of reforms, including a Londonderry Commission instead of the notoriously gerrymandered city council, and fair housing allocations. O'Neill also sacked his hardline minister, William Craig. PD, influenced by Michael Farrell's Young Socialist Alliance, determined to challenge the Northern Ireland government's will to stand up to extremists, or force the British government to intervene. A marathon march from Belfast to Derry, emulating Martin Luther King's 1966 Selma to Montgomery walk in Alabama, began on 1 January 1969.[8]

The march, in Northern Ireland circumstances, was as provocative as Paisley's invasion of Cromac Square in 1966 because it attempted to cross traditional Protestant territory. Ciaran McKeown, a Queen's University student leader who claims to have unilaterally authorised the title 'People's Democracy', was totally opposed to the march. He blamed Farrell's Young Socialists, who, claiming to unite the Protestant and Catholic working classes, unleashed 'a murderous phase of sectarianism' and destroyed the gains of the civil rights movement.[9] Prime Minister O'Neill, admitting that NICRA had achieved reforms 'which would otherwise have taken years to wring from a reluctant government', was also scathing about Paisley. Only the extreme Protestant reaction ensured world publicity for what began as 'a pathetic, bedraggled, left-wing, long-haired walk.'[10] The march certainly helped to achieve O'Neill's downfall. Harassed along the way, sometimes by B Specials in mufti, it eventually encountered the hideous violence of Paisleyites at Burntollet Bridge, not far from Derry. Attendant police did nothing to assist the marchers. Young men and girls, some wearing 'the provocative mini-skirt', were brutally stoned and battered with wooden clubs. Bernadette Devlin, herself knocked down, beaten and kicked, vividly described the 'hordes of screaming people wielding planks of wood, bottles, laths, iron bars, crowbars, cudgels studded with nails'.[11] The *Protestant Telegraph* played down the attack, concentrating on the subsequent Catholic stoning of a Protestant rally at the Londonderry Guildhall.[12] In fact, members of the RUC were guilty of misconduct in rampaging through the Catholic Bogside, where barricades were erected and the scene set for a major conflagration later in the year.

O'Neill called a general election in February 1969 to strengthen his hand against unionist extremists. He failed to secure the election of sufficient liberal unionists; indeed O'Neill, appropriately challenged for the seat of Bannside by both Ian Paisley and Michael Farrell, was nearly beaten by the former. John Hume of Derry, a constitutional nationalist, and several other new Catholic leaders were elected at this time. The bombing of Belfast water and power installations, attributed to the IRA but in fact the work of Protestant extremists, possibly linked with Paisley's church,[13] 'quite literally', O'Neill lamented, 'blew me out of office.' He had the satisfaction of piloting 'one man one vote' in local elections through the Northern Ireland parliament before resigning on 28 April.[14] O'Neill's cousin and successor, James Chichester-Clark, at first tried to reassure the Paisleyites but 'Chi-Chi' ultimately found it impossible to reconcile the demands of successive British governments for reform with the conservatives of his party.

Enter the British Army

Tension, especially in Derry, mounted despite the 'false calm'[15] after Chichester-Clark's accession to the prime ministership. The traditional Orange marching season culminates in the 12 July celebration of King William III's 1690 Protestant victory at the Boyne, and the 12 August commemoration of the Londonderry Apprentice Boys who, in 1689, closed the city gates against King James II's Catholic army at the beginning of an epic siege. The defeatist Governor Lundy has provided a contemptuous synonym for weak-kneed Protestants ever since. In 1969 this sensitive festival brought violence to a new peak. In Derry the Apprentice Boys march led to 'The Battle of the Bogside' when Catholics, defending themselves behind barricades with petrol bombs, resisted the incursions of the RUC and B Specials, using CS gas for the first time in the British Isles. For her part in the contest, Bernadette Devlin, elected MP for Mid-Ulster in April, was sentenced to six months' imprisonment. In Belfast, Catholic riots, intended to take the heat off nationalists in Derry, provoked massive Protestant incursions into the border areas between the Catholic Falls and the Protestant Shankill Roads. Large numbers of Catholic, and some Protestant, families were burnt out and forced to evacuate.[16] The RUC and B Specials ran amok through Catholic areas where the IRA was at last galvanised into action. Five Catholics and one

Protestant were killed. The British Labour government of Harold Wilson sent British soldiers to Belfast and Derry to support the civil power in response to Chichester-Clark's request. The RUC and B Specials were withdrawn.[17] Though it is said to be a myth that British troops were introduced to protect embattled Catholics,[18] Bernadette Devlin herself had demanded British police to replace the RUC during the Belfast to Derry march of January 1969.[19] Initially, many Catholics showered the soldiers with drinks, meals and invitations home, sometimes in the areas most hostile to the British Army a few months later. According to soldiers' accounts, the girls were exceptionally friendly and many marriages took place: 'We felt like knights in shining armour, like Sir Galahad. We were the do-gooders.' By 1973 British soldiers were spat at by attractive girls.[20] Conor Cruise O'Brien suggests paradoxically that Catholics may have simultaneously welcomed the support of the British Army and the Provisional IRA against rampaging Protestants.[21]

In the early days of British Army intervention there were serious clashes with the Protestant community. On 10 October 1969 the publication of the Hunt Report, recommending the replacement of the B Specials by an Ulster Defence Regiment (UDR) under British Army control, led to Protestant riots causing the first death of a member of the security forces, an RUC constable.

The IRA split and the rise of the Provisionals

The UDR as a local Army auxiliary force was born in January 1970, almost simultaneously with its great enemy, the Provisional IRA (PIRA). In the riots of August 1969 the current IRA leadership had been caught unprepared with only six firearms, as Catholic graffiti, 'IRA = I Ran Away', indicated. This dereliction, and conservative dislike for the pacifist and socialistic stance of the modernised IRA, had led to a split in December 1969. According to Seán MacStiofain, subsequently the Provisional chief of staff, the real target of the IRA Marxists 'was not sectarianism, but religion as such'.[22] Other issues were the old IRA's desire to retain Stormont, to end the traditional parliamentary abstention policy, and to form a broad National Liberation Front with other groups.

By early 1970 both the military IRA wing and its Sinn Féin political support body had disintegrated into rival sections. The 'Provisionals' originally took the name in hope of endorsement by a reunited IRA, but later encouraged association with the 'Provisional' government of Easter Week 1916. To avoid outflanking by the Provisionals, the Officials (OIRA) conducted a counter-productive campaign of violence which included the shooting of Northern Ireland Senator Jack Barnhill, in December 1971, the assassination of a Catholic soldier on leave in his Derry home, and the Aldershot bombing of February of 1972 which killed six cleaners and a Catholic chaplain.[23] The Officials soon afterwards declared a ceasefire, which served as a disguise for continued operations until Cathal Goulding, the chief of staff in Dublin, scaled them down. In 1975 and 1977 there were shootouts between OIRA and PIRA in which about sixteen were killed. According to a British soldier, 'the unofficial order was to keep off the streets and let them get on with it ... and it was really satisfying to see those bastards gone.'[24] More intra-republican violence resulted from the 1974 split from OIRA of the Irish Republican Socialist Party (IRSP), to which Bernadette Devlin McAliskey briefly adhered, and its military wing, the Irish National Liberation Army (INLA). The Officials converted themselves into a constitutionalist Workers' Party (WP), which has had considerable success in elections in the Irish Republic but little in Northern Ireland. Despite WP denials, a shadowy OIRA persisted, but never dominated the political movement.[25] Most general references to the IRA in subsequent pages denote PIRA, often known in Catholic areas as the 'Ra'.

In 1970 the Officials still controlled important areas of Catholic Belfast, such as the Lower Falls area, the scene of rioting in April. Ironically, the infant Provisionals at this time tried to calm the Catholic rioters.[26] On 18 June a British general election resulted in the defeat of Harold Wilson's Labour government. Paisley, who had just won O'Neill's old seat in Stormont, now obtained a Westminster seat also. He incensed Nationalists at Stormont by quoting the 1647 Presbyterian *Westminster Confession of Faith* which depicted the pope as the 'man of sin'. Ted Heath's Conservatives were pledged to continue Labour's Northern Ireland policy, but events soon suggested that the 'softly softly' policy of Home Secretary James Callaghan, accused by loyalists of appeasing the Catholic minority, had ended.[27] At the end of June, the Provisionals, still relatively weak, with a membership of about 1,500, had their baptism of fire defending, against rioting Protestants, St Matthew's Catholic Church in the isolated Short Strand Catholic enclave of Belfast. Three Protestants and one PIRA man were killed.[28] A few days later, on 3 July, the honeymoon between the British Army, which had failed to intervene in the Short Strand, and Catholics finally ended with a 34-hour curfew and a rough arms search in the Lower Falls. Subsequent riots and action by OIRA left five dead and hundreds of residents suffering the after-effects of high dosages of CS gas. The search was spectacularly divisive. Nevertheless, tacit co-operation between Army and IRA over the maintenance of order in Catholic areas continued until the spring of 1971.[29]

After the riots of October 1969, loyalist self-help associations sprang up. They mirrored the Catholic community organisations which maintained the 'no-go' areas in Belfast and Derry and paved the way for the Provisionals. A founder member of the Shankill Defence Association was John McKeague, unsuccessfully prosecuted for the bombs that brought down O'Neill. McKeague, however, was arrested for rioting on 5 October 1969, and sentenced to three months in prison.[30] Once close to Paisley, McKeague fell out with the latter and was driven from his organisation in 1971. A British sergeant detected an almost collusive pattern to Protestant and Catholic riots in the New Lodge area to the north of the Shankill Road: 'It tended to be one side rioting against the security forces, then there'd be a calm, and then the other side would riot against the security forces.' Both sides 'had a sort of mutual respect' and would riot for about eighteen hours before going home for tea.[31]

The moderate response: Alliance and the SDLP

1970 also saw the formation of two important political parties which were to work towards middle-ground co-operation. In May, Alliance, a moderate unionist party, led by a Catholic, Oliver Napier, attempted to bridge the sectarian divide. Of greater significance was the merging of the Civil Rights, old Nationalist, and Republican Labour MPs in Stormont to form a united opposition Social Democratic and Labour Party (SDLP) in August 1970. Its original leader was Gerry Fitt (now Lord Fitt), the veteran Republican Labour MP for West Belfast in Westminster. Fitt, bloodied but unbowed after the Derry 1968 confrontation and as unpopular with Provisionals as with loyalists, held the leadership until 1979. John Hume, a Derry teacher and civil rights activist, was from the start the most effective member and, after Fitt's resignation, leader. Hume represented the new tertiary-educated Catholic politician, while Fitt, a former seaman, typified the older working-class activist. As the Provisionals advocated abstention and boycott until 1982, when they obtained a third of the nationalist vote, the SDLP could always reasonably claim to represent the

Catholic community. Its socialist and non-sectarian pretensions declined on the departure of members such as Gerry Fitt, Paddy Devlin and the Protestant Ivan Cooper. In the 1990s the SDLP has nominated some Protestant candidates in local elections.

The shock of internment: August 1971

The Provisionals, however, held the initiative in the Catholic community, commencing with 153 explosions in their 1970 bombing campaign against economic targets. The strategy was partly defensive in that the British Army was forced away from Catholic areas to defend the central business area.[32] British Army authorities were still negotiating with PIRA leaders shortly before the reprisal killing of the first British soldier by the Provisionals. Chichester-Clark, after the counter-productive gesture of declaring war on the Provisionals, resigned the prime ministership to the more astute Brian Faulkner in March 1971. The SDLP responded to the shooting of Derry Bogsiders by withdrawing from Stormont to establish a rival assembly at Dungiven. Faulkner's first tentative approach to power-sharing, the offer of committee chairmanships, was thus rejected. Against an all-out PIRA offensive, the Faulkner government persuaded the British government to adopt on 9 August the traditional expedient of internment without trial.

The arrests proved counter-productive. A trial sweep warned the suspects and poor intelligence led to the arrest of some wrong people. Experimental interrogation on eleven suspects, using techniques such as forcing the victims to stand spreadeagled against a wall for days,[33] resulted in Britain's condemnation by the European Court of Human Rights in 1979 for 'inhuman and degrading' treatment, just short of formal torture. Protestants were generally ignored in the arrests. To the entire nationalist community, 9 August 1971 became a day of infamy annually celebrated. Violence escalated rapidly: 1972 with 468 deaths was by far the worst year of the Troubles.

Anti-establishment unionism: UDA and DUP

Republican violence was paralleled by loyalist violence. The first six assassinations before the end of 1971 were the work of the IRA, but in 1972 Protestant paramilitaries began killing Catholics, often at random.[34] In September 1971 the diverse Protestant defence associations were united in the Ulster Defence Association (UDA) by Harding Smith of Woodvale (a rival of McKeague of Shankill). This grouping claimed 25,000 members in 1971, and in the following

year may have had 40,000.[35] Sometimes parading menacing
phalanxes of masked men on Belfast streets, the UDA soon
outnumbered other loyalist paramilitaries like the UVF; the UDA
became the extreme loyalist answer to the Provisionals, adopting
their tactics and propaganda. For example, in December 1971 a
loyalist bomb at McGurk's Catholic bar in North Queen Street,
Belfast, killed fifteen. Both Protestant and Catholic paramilitaries
hooded their victims before execution, sometimes following
interrogation with torture in what the Protestants called 'the
romper room'. The homosexual John McKeague is credited with
initiating the rompering tactic by carving up a young boy. Between
1975 and 1977, the Protestant paramilitary horror reached its
ultimate atrocity in the ritualistic slashing to death of nineteen
Catholics by the 'Shankill Butchers'. The Provisionals complained
that the 'Butchers' barely stopped short of cannibalism in 'gouging
out the eyes of their victims, cutting off their noses, inflicting the
stigmata of our Lord on their hands and feet; filling gouged-out eye
sockets with rosary beads'.[36] Although never convicted of these
crimes, the leader of the 'Butchers', Lennie Murphy, in 1982
suffered 'a curiously ecumenical death' when 'fingered' by
Protestant paramilitary colleagues for disposal by the PIRA. In the
same year, McKeague was eliminated by INLA. Early in June 1973,
the Ulster Freedom Fighters (UFF) emerged as an assassination
group whose relationship with the UDA paralleled that of the IRA
with the legalised Sinn Féin.[37]

The UDA disclaimed the influence of Protestant clergy. On the 29
September 1971 Paisley's Protestant Unionist Party was disbanded
to form a new Democratic Unionist Party (DUP) as a more tightly
organised constituency party. On 5 October, Stormont MPs Paisley,
his allied Free Presbyterian minister, the Rev. William Beattie,
Desmond Boal, and John McQuade formally joined; on 30 October
a public meeting was held at the Ulster Hall. Boal wanted a party
conservative on constitutional issues but radical on social policy.
He broke with Paisley in 1974. Some former Irish Labour supporters
may have joined in Belfast, but Paisley obtained considerable
support in rural areas. He modified the religious thrust of his
message for political advantage. Recruiting was slow in 1972 but
the Border Poll, discussed below, and elections of 1973 generated
enthusiasm. Branches were formed throughout the north in 1974,
enabling the first party convention to be held in November. March
1975 saw the appointment of full-time staff.[38]

The political organisations in 1971 made interesting approaches
across the sectarian divide. In July the Officials met representatives

of the ultra-loyalist UVF to consider a common policy against anticipated internment. In October the DUP, to the UDA's annoyance, held a secret meeting with the SDLP, again emphasising internment but also considering quotas on Stormont committees and urgent policies on unemployment.[39] There was much unionist concern when Paisley on 25 November suggested that apart from the theocratic nature of the southern Irish State there would be no fundamental objection to Irish unity.[40] Paisley also fell foul of the Orange Order, which refused to appoint Free Presbyterian chaplains. He patronised the Independent Orange Order.[41]

The bloodiest Sunday

In 1972 events outran political theory. On 30 January British soldiers fired on a demonstrating crowd in Derry, killing thirteen. Television showed Fr Edward Daly, soon to be Bishop of Derry and a strong opponent of the IRA, frantically trying to extricate a dying man from a hail of British bullets. Catholic anger exploded. In the Irish Republic the British Embassy was burned by a furious mob. The new 'Bloody Sunday' passed into nationalist memory as one of the greatest of all British atrocities in Ireland. But loyalist opinion exhibited patterned opposition. On TV McKeague demanded 'one, two, three, many more Bloody Sundays'.[42] The resultant Widgery Tribunal's Report was denounced by nationalists as a whitewash. It admitted that none of the deceased or wounded had been 'shot whilst handling a firearm or bomb' but suspected that some had been involved in such activities earlier. There was 'no reason to suppose that the soldiers would have opened fire if they had not been fired upon first.'[43]

Vale Stormont, *ave* truce talks

After Bloody Sunday, violence became its own rationale. The Officials' reprisal bombing of Aldershot army camp, William Craig's threatening Vanguard rally in Ormeau Park, the loyalist blasting of the Abercorn Restaurant in Belfast, and the Provisionals' Donegall Street explosion, which killed six and wounded 147, made Northern Ireland a universal byword for death and destruction. On 24 March the first phase of the Ulster Troubles ended with the suspension of Stormont and the imposition of direct Westminster rule for the first time since 1921. The government of Brian Faulkner gave way to that of the Conservative secretary of state for Northern Ireland, William Whitelaw. This was the logical outcome of the Labour government's decision to send in troops to deal with the August 1969 riots, but Harold Wilson had hesitated before taking the final step. In the nine months before the ending of Stormont 80 Catholics and 38 Protestants were killed. The reaction of loyalists to the abolition of Stormont, regarded as their basic guarantee of security, was intense. A strike was called and the UDA reorganised. 'Sold down the river!' cried its paper.[44] A feud between Harding Smith of Woodvale and McKeague of the Shankill ended with the latter being forced out of UDA ranks to form a new Protestant paramilitary, the Red Hand Commandos.[45] The former minister, Craig, inspired by the 1965 action of Ian Smith's regime in Rhodesia, talked of a UDI for Northern Ireland. In early 1972 he formed the Vanguard Unionist Party with its own paramilitary Vanguard Service Corps. After much aggressive political activity as Vanguard leader, Craig's support evaporated and in February 1978 he crept back to the Ulster or 'Official' Unionist Party (OUP). On the other side the Provisionals effectively undermined a peace group, Catholic Women Together movement.

What was Whitelaw to do? Trying a flexible response he made a truce with the Provisionals, and flew MacStiofain and other leaders, including the young West Belfast republican, Gerry Adams, to London. They found little common ground. The truce collapsed in June over a clash between Catholic tenants and Protestant squatters in the new Lenadoon housing estate in South-West Belfast. Fatefully, Whitelaw conceded special category status to political prisoners after a hunger strike by Provisionals, including the well-known Billy McKee. Later in the year Lord Diplock's Report, which Paisley claimed to have anticipated,[46] recommended non-jury courts for political offences. British horror of Provisional violence was balanced by an early willingness to negotiate with Provisional leaders.

The torment of terror, 1972

After the truce, the Provisional press celebrated extensive use of the new car bomb.[47] On 21 July, or 'Bloody Friday', the Provisionals exploded no less than 26 bombs in the heart of Belfast, killing eleven and injuring many more. PIRA blamed the police for the deaths, claiming that adequate thirty-minute warnings had been given. They failed to mention their simultaneous hoax warnings.[48]

Whitelaw now responded to the repeated loyalist demand that the Catholic no-go areas in Belfast and Derry be demolished. Loyalist no-go areas had been set up in protest, a good example of direct borrowing. Clearance of barricades was achieved in Operation Motorman on 31 July. Anticipating resistance amounting to full-scale war the Army trundled up its heavy armour—but met no opposition, MacStiofain pointing out that the IRA would have been disadvantaged in such an encounter.[49] Catholics now found themselves exposed to the sectarian reprisals of Protestant paramilitary squads who could drive into the ghettoes and take vengeance almost with impunity. Dillon and Lehane have argued that at this time more civilians were killed by Protestant murder gangs and bombs than by the Provisionals.[50]

The depths of Northern Irish misery were plumbed in 1972. Some people lived huddled together in their ghettoes, never daring to set foot in the city centre. Evening outings were hazardous. The middle-classes, relatively secure in quiet areas of the city, learned to shun public places. Such conditions were rapid breeding grounds for fear and paranoia which spread quickly through the increasingly divided communities. Gradually, violence was reduced to what Home Secretary Reginald Maudling tactlessly referred to as an 'acceptable level'. The death toll was never again to rise to the 1972 peak. Belfast city centre was cordoned off, cars prohibited and all shoppers bodily checked on entry. Citizens learned to accept rigorous security precautions and the omnipresence of police and soldiers armed to the teeth with the most ferocious modern weapons; controls outraging dignity and self-respect in other western countries were accepted meekly.

Mirage in the desert: towards power-sharing

After the horrors of 1972 came the apparently hopeful experiment in 1973 and 1974 of power-sharing, equally abhorred by most Protestant leaders and PIRA. The latter used every propagandist device to destroy the credibility of their power-sharing community rivals, the SDLP. PIRA carried the bombing campaign to England where public opinion polls were already showing an increasing desire to be rid of Northern Ireland. The Provisionals also worked to persuade the Catholic community to boycott three important electoral polls held in 1973.

At the Border Poll of 8 March 1973 41.5 per cent did in fact abstain, leaving only 57 per cent to vote positively for unionism. This implied not a comfortable two to one majority, but potentially something like four to three, a very different picture. In late April came the first 'one man one vote' elections for the new local authorities after their reorganisation in 1972. The unionist ngs won 297 of the total 526 seats. Paisley's DUP started ly with thirteen seats, a figure which was to rise to 77 in the lections of 1977, and again dramatically to 142 in 1981. On tholic side the SDLP established itself by acquiring 83 of the total 103 positions won by advocates of united Ireland.[51] In June there followed elections to a new assembly for Northern Ireland based on Whitelaw's power-sharing white paper of March 1973. The object was to establish a consensus government based on proportional representation.

Whitelaw almost achieved the impossible. The elections gave Faulkner's Official Unionists (22), Alliance (8) and the SDLP (19) together a comfortable majority in the 78-seat Assembly. Opposition groupings like Craig's Vanguard, Paisley's DUP and other unionists (27) vociferously opposed any truck with the SDLP enemy. But the reality was less promising. Faulkner's group was too small and unreliable on both power-sharing with the SDLP and the 'Irish dimension' with its Council of Ireland linking North and South.

Heath and Whitelaw persisted. At the Sunningdale Conference, 6-9 December 1973, an agreement was hammered out between the government, an accommodating Fine Gael-Labour coalition in the Irish Republic, and a power-sharing team of Faulkner unionists, SDLP, and Alliance. The Irish government was later accused, by a negotiating member, Conor Cruise O'Brien, of pushing the Irish dimension too hard. According to Longford and McHardy, it was Heath who forced on the unwilling unionists a Council of Ireland, far in advance of what the southern government was prepared to accept.[52] Brian Faulkner was given no concessions which might have enabled him to sell the agreement to the unionist population.[53]

Ulster Workers exultant: the swamping of Sunningdale

On 1 January 1974 Faulkner took office as chief minister of a power-sharing executive of unionists working with SDLP members such as John Hume, Gerry Fitt, Austin Currie, and the Alliance leader, Oliver Napier. The timing of the British general election of February, which saw Heath defeated by Harold Wilson's Labour, was unfortunate. It enabled the anti-power-sharing unionists to win an early trial of strength by carrying all the Northern Ireland seats save Fitt's West Belfast. The legitimacy of the new Northern Ireland administration was totally undermined. The Wilson government, though it adopted a bi-partisan approach to power-sharing, lacked enthusiasm for its implementation. In May the intimidation of the Ulster Workers' Council (UWC) strike brought the Province to a standstill. It threatened to cut off electrical power which, amongst other deprivations, would have stopped electric sewerage and engulfed the whole community, rich and poor, in a sea of excrement. The executive, without adequate support from the British Army, had no alternative but resignation on 28 May. The loyalists were naturally exultant. There is truth in the contention of Downey, who believed power-sharing feasible, that the executive was 'dead before the official obsequies', failing, not because of the UWC strike, but because of faulty construction.[54] According to Paul Foot, 'increasingly powerful political forces inside MI5 and their colleagues in Army Intelligence and Information' organised defiance.[55] Ironically, public opinion polls in the 1980s still showed an apparent majority for political power-sharing.[56]

The loyalist community, despite its victory, was far from united. The paramilitaries berated the politicians for leaving the hard work to them. Ciaran McKeown detected a grudging sympathy for the Provisionals: 'the Loyalists were increasingly sure that their main function in life was not to murder Catholics simply to keep middle-class unionists in power.'[57] Disillusionment with Britain led some loyalists to flirt with nationalist symbols, such as the legendary hero Cuchulain, adapted for Ulster purposes. On the republican side there was a tendency for the Officials and Dublin-based Provisionals to see the UWC action as a prelude to non-sectarian working-class unity, but the Northern Provisionals had no such illusions.[58]

Back to the drawing board: the Locust Decade

After the collapse of Sunningdale came locust years of missed opportunities. Constitutional ideas like Northern Ireland Secretary Merlyn Rees's convention and James Prior's 'rolling devolution' were negated by the increasing intransigence of the unionists assisted symbiotically by the terrorist and propagandist activity of the Provisionals and their junior partners. Could tougher direct rule provide a military solution? Might the new Peace People undermine the revolutionaries from within? Was 'Ulsterisation', replacing British soldiers by local UDR troops and police as in Vietnam, the answer? Might it end the vicious circle where British soldiers, called in to end violence, by their presence encouraged more violence? Could the Churches effect reconciliation?

The urgency was undeniable. There were 275 and 297 deaths from sectarian or political violence in 1975 and 1976 respectively, making them the worst years of the Troubles after 1972. The conflict was brought home to Northern Ireland's partners in the eternal triangle. Loyalists bombed Dublin in May 1974; republican explosions killed five in Guildford in October and nineteen in Birmingham in November. The British police forced the conviction of innocent people: by 1991 the 'Guildford Four' and the 'Birmingham Six' had been released at last , leaving the British reputation for justice in tatters. In Northern Ireland reconciliation attempts failed. Rees's Constitutional Convention, to allow Ulster groups to decide their own destinies, proved abortive. The election in July 1975 produced an assembly containing 47 delegates opposing, and only 31 supporting, the principle of power-sharing. This disappointing contrast to the election of June 1973 suggested that Sunningdale had driven the communities further apart. The final Convention, disbanded by Rees in March 1976, reported intransigently against power-sharing of the Sunningdale variety, demanded straight majority rule, and provided a basis for future unionist rhetoric. Paisley's paper inconsistently criticised the Catholic majoritarianism of Bishop Lucey of Cork.[59]

Feakle and the ceasefire

A hopeful sign was the meeting on 10 December 1974 of a group of liberal Protestant clerics, led by the Rev. William Arlow of the Church of Ireland, with Provisional leaders at Feakle, Co. Clare.[60] PIRA agreed to a truce or ceasefire, which was never formally ended but petered out in early 1976. Merlyn Rees believed that the ceasefire had lasted effectively until August 1975. He denied that any deal was done with the Provisionals; however, there were numerous contacts between government officials and representatives of Provisional Sinn Féin. The latter set up seven 'incident centres' to co-operate with the government in monitoring the ceasefire. Arlow claimed that Rees had assured the Provisionals that a negative report by the Northern Ireland Convention would lead to the withdrawal of the British Army. Rees flatly denied this.[61] Instead, he used the PIRA lull to phase out internment. In March he ended special category status for political offenders and on 1 May 1976 appointed the vigorous Kenneth Newman as head of the RUC.

According to Bishop and Mallie, the ceasefire, always opposed by the Northern Provisional leadership, brought PIRA 'the closest it has yet been to collapse and defeat.' It ended the dominance of the Dublin leadership of Dáithí O'Conaill and Ruairí O'Brádaigh

(MacStiofain had already lost influence) and elevated the younger Northerners, Gerry Adams, Danny Morrison and Martin McGuinness to effective command.[62] The Provisional ceasefire towards the security forces never ended general violence. In 1975-76, while straight sectarian killings, like those of the Shankill Butchers, persisted, bloody, quasi-religious, disputes between the UVF and UDA were paralleled by similar conflicts between OIRA and IRSP, the latter partly backed by PIRA.[63]

The Peace People: hopes dashed

On 10 August 1976, a Provisional, driving on the Andersonstown Road, was shot by the Army and his car killed three young children. Not long before, the Provisionals had assassinated Christopher Ewart-Biggs, the British ambassador to the Irish Republic. Two Catholic women from West Belfast, Mrs Betty Williams and Mairead Corrigan, aunt of the dead children, working with the journalist and early civil rights activist, Ciaran McKeown, established the movement later known as the Peace People. Rallies, attracting both Catholics and Protestants, culminated in a gathering of 25,000 on 28 August at Ormeau Park in East Belfast, opposite Paisley's Martyrs Memorial Church. Clergy of many denominations joined in, Cardinal Conway walking in the Boyne and Armagh rallies. From the outset the Peace People had to face the unrelenting hostility of the Provisionals who could not tolerate such a challenge in their own areas. While a rally in the Protestant Shankill passed off successfully, the Falls rally was attacked by republican sympathisers in 'another Burntollet'. McKeown 'saw the distressing sight of hatred in the faces of quite young women, as they gripped Mairead', who was scratched and had some hair pulled out.[64] Loyalists in general were no more supportive: Paisley's journal claimed that 'the Roman tail can be seen to be wagging the verminous peace dog'.[65] The UDA, despite rumours of a death threat to McKeown, was not totally unfriendly,[66] while John McKeague actually praised the Peace People's conduct.[67] Sadly, the moderate parties, Alliance and the SDLP, disliked the Peace People's disdain for party politics and desire to build support from grass roots. According to McKeown, the Churches even looked askance at his emphasis on total non-violence and rejection of the notion of a just war: 'I could not imagine Jesus of Nazareth looking down the sights of a rifle to kill anyone for any reason whatsoever'.[68]

The Peace People, like Terence O'Neill in the 1960s, were ultimately unable to please both religious communities simultaneously. Some of the initial publicity, grants from foundations culminating in the Nobel Peace Prize, which Betty Williams insisted on keeping for herself, and visits to sympathetic communities abroad, gave rise to strong criticism. Though hoping to break Helder Camara's 'spiral of violence' with the tactics of Gandhi and Martin Luther King, the Peace People were unable to gain a serious hearing for the ideas of McKeown who wanted the replacement of the personality cult by hard, disciplined work from individuals. In May 1977 the Peace People bravely resisted UDA intimidation during an unsuccessful loyalist strike. Nevertheless, the acceptance of honours from Elizabeth II on her Jubilee visit to Northern Ireland in August irritated many Catholics. When its founding members split up in 1980, the Peace People became dependent upon the energy of Steve McBride, who later joined Alliance. From their East Belfast 'Peace House' they published a monthly, *Peace by Peace*, into the 1980s, and organised non-sectarian sport and youth camps. But their dramatic days were over. The assistance to disillusioned or intimidated guerrillas leaving the country, though a threat to the Provisional power-base, helped in reducing violence. The UDA claimed that the Peace People were used by PIRA to infiltrate agents overseas.[69]

Diplock judges and protesting politicals

When internment without trial was phased out by Rees it was replaced by measures recommended by Lord Diplock's Report of December 1972. This advised no-jury courts and the easier admissibility of confession evidence in place of intimidated or biased jurors. The Irish Republic used similar methods. Diplock court convicts were, following the Gardiner Report of January 1975,[70] denied the political status granted by Whitelaw after a hunger strike in 1972.

The Provisionals were determined to win a psychological tug-of-war with the government. Equally violent loyalist paramilitary prisoners also strove to maintain their political status,[71] retained by all those convicted before March 1976. Loyalist arguments were identical to those of the Provisionals.[72] On 16 September 1976, a Provisional, Ciaran Nugent, convicted for hijacking a van, resisted the new regime by going 'on the blanket' and rejecting prison clothing. He served the whole of his $3^1/_2$ year sentence in this painful manner, being soon joined by others.[73]

Forceful confessions

Thus in the 1970s, the British authorities retaliated with a series of punitive measures designed to force the gaoled republicans and loyalists, whose protests were in a lower key, to accept criminalisation. The measures were well publicised by the indefatigable Catholic chaplains Fathers Denis Faul and Raymond Murray, whose stream of pamphlets documented every aspect of the ill-treatment of their community, inside and outside prison.[74] Such material was not read by unionists, conditioned to regard it as typical republican propaganda. The European Human Rights Commission and Amnesty International refused to endorse political status for republican and loyalist prisoners. The Faul and Murray exposure of pre-sentence brutality, especially in *The Castlereagh File*, were, however, supported by T.P. Coogan's *On the Blanket*, Peter Taylor's *Beating the Terrorists*,[75] an Amnesty International Report in 1978 and the government's own *Bennett Report* of 1979. There emerged a cycle of interrogation, criminalisation, protest, punishment, and reinforced protest. Beating and degradation, plus official punishments like loss of remission, limited exercise and restricted visiting became almost commonplace. Loyalists, no less than republicans, continued to denounce the system. The UVF unequivocally condemned convictions based on confessions extracted by brutality and welcomed the *Bennett Report*.[76] Even Paisley's paper, while ridiculing the suggestion that 'any mad dog of a papist rascal' found guilty had been forced to sign a confession, condemned the treatment of loyalists: 'Thanks to Diplock the spiral of injustice dictates that once in Long Kesh the rules are to keep you in.' Under the Diplock system, he believed that Provisional suspects were favoured, while loyalists were imprisoned for trivial offences.[77] Meanwhile, prison protest effectively undermined the Peace People; McKeown's compromise advocacy of 'emergency status', instead of political status, was unpopular with members from a unionist background and encouraged division.[78]

The dirty protest

The blanket protest escalated into 'dirty protest' in March 1978. Prisoners refused access to toilets if not in prison uniform rejected the alternative of buckets to slop into.[79] The result was a 'no wash' protest ending in the smearing of excrement on the cell walls to dissipate the stench. The protest amongst the men in the Maze was followed by the women in Armagh Prison after similar conflict with prison authorities. The prisoners maintained, with the support of chaplains like Fr Murray at Armagh, that the dirty protest was not a Promethean defiance of bourgeois convention. It was, they claimed, a response to outrageous punishment. With women prisoners, adequate sanitary facilities became a privilege for good behaviour. To the authorities the sufferings were purely voluntary. Some loyalist prisoners conducted a clean blanket protest, but rejected the dirty protest. 'After all, even the savages in darkest Africa observe their toilet instincts, and what animal fouls its own nest?'[80] The loyalist prisoners, demanding segregation from the republicans, were, however, equally hostile to the prison authorities. Their clean blanket protest was yet another example of direct tactical borrowing.[81] Loyalists left the actual shooting of prison officers to the Provisionals.

Violence declines: PIRA regroups

Nationalists complained bitterly, not only of the Diplock 'spiral of injustice', but of the deaths in Catholic areas from plastic bullets, which had replaced the less lethal rubber bullets for crowd control, and several examples of what appeared to be 'stakeouts', or deliberate shootings of republican activists by the security forces. These complaints were documented in detail by the tireless Frs Faul and Murray. Nevertheless, the tough Mason-Newman regime seemed to be paying dividends. As the Callaghan Labour Government was dependent on the votes of Ulster Unionist MPs for survival, sheer repression appeared the only feasible option. There was a dramatic fall from 297 deaths in 1976 to 111 in 1977, and in 1978 to 81, the lowest since 1970. Deaths rose again in 1979 to 113, and then dropped further to 75. Belfast citizens could now leave their homes at night more confidently than for many years. In response, the PIRA in 1977 scrapped its formal battalions, Upper Falls, Lower Falls, East Belfast, etc., replacing them with a small cell system, suggested by Martin McGuinness as much less penetrable by informers. The system, corresponding to that of the nineteenth-century IRB and other revolutionary organisations, was never universally implemented but did achieve a rough distinction between the IRA personel who controlled Catholic areas and the élite Active Service Units which carried out bombings and assassinations.[82]

By May 1979, however, most Unionist MPs had tired of the Callaghan Labour Government, which was also deserted by Gerry Fitt. In November, Fitt resigned from the SDLP, relinquishing the leadership to John Hume. Callaghan was resoundingly beaten in the British general election by the Conservatives led by Margaret Thatcher who was to dominate Northern Ireland politics until her resignation in 1990. Humphrey Atkins (May 1979 to September 1981) replaced Roy Mason as Northern Ireland Secretary. The long-term failure of the latter to find a solution for Northern Ireland was underlined in May by Brigadier J.M. Glover's 'Ministry of Defence Document 37' which considerably boosted Provisional morale when they secured a copy.[83] Accepting the Provisionals as genuinely working-class, Glover acquitted them of being 'mindless hooligans'. The report depicted them as self-financing with money to last five years and virtually unbeatable in the foreseeable future. *An Phoblacht* rejoiced that 'BOMB ON is the message from the nationalist people to the IRA'.

Bomb on they did. On 27 August the war hero and last viceroy of India, Earl Mountbatten of Burma, and three of his party were blown up in Co. Sligo in the Irish Republic, while eighteen British soldiers died from explosions at Warrenpoint in Northern Ireland. Plans for Pope John Paul II's visit to Northern Ireland were cancelled and the Pope's subsequent call for peace at Drogheda in the Irish Republic was bluntly rejected by PIRA. PIRA's paper boasted that 1979 was the worst year for the security forces since 1973, with 28 British, 10 UDR, 14 RUC, and 9 warders killed.[84] Margaret Thatcher had clearly not inherited a vanquished PIRA from James Callaghan.

Thatcher and Atkins confronted not only the revived PIRA but a difficult constitutional situation. Though somewhat inhibited by the failure of a second loyalist strike in 1977 and the DUP's polling of less than a third of the votes obtained by the Official Unionists in the May 1979 general election, Paisley was buoyed by triumph in the European elections of June. With nearly 30 per cent of Northern Ireland first preferences, Paisley topped the poll ahead of John Hume of the SDLP and John Taylor of the Official Unionists. Together they won the three seats of Northern Ireland voting as a single constituency. With some plausibility Paisley could now claim status as the authentic voice of Protestant Ulster. Moderation also appeared on the decline in the Irish Republic. The Coalition government, containing Drs Garret FitzGerald and Conor Cruise O'Brien, both much hated by the Provisionals, had been defeated in 1977 by Jack Lynch's Fianna Fail. In late 1979 Lynch was edged out as Taoiseach by Charlie Haughey. In 1970 the latter had been accused, but not convicted, of running arms to the infant Provisionals. In reality, Haughey was now as much abhorred as his political rivals by PIRA and in late 1980 began a series of talks between British and Irish leaders which ultimately culminated in the Anglo-Irish Agreement of 1985.

Protest by hunger strike

The failure of the the 'dirty protest' led to the use of the ultimate weapon of prison protest, the hunger strike. The tactic was well established in Ireland and other countries; two republicans had already died on hunger strike in the 1970s. In late 1980 loyalist prisoners with characteristic convergence went on hunger strike alongside republicans, not, they claimed, for political status but for 'special category status'. Ironically, the loyalist prisoners, usually so critical of the clerically dominated republicans, allowed themselves to be talked out of their design by Canon William Arlow, of Feakle fame, after a mere five days. The Provisionals were scornful of such lack of determination.[85] Their strikers were subsequently to resist an emissary from the Pope himself.

Initially, however, the republican hunger strike also ended in late 1980 when the authorities appeared to have accepted five demands (own clothes, free association, restored remission, no labour, educational facilities) which were held to constitute political status. On 1 March 1981 the Provisional commander in the Maze Prison, Bobby Sands, began a new hunger strike. There was division in the Roman Catholic hierarchy between English prelates, like Cardinal Hume, who repeated the traditional condemnation of death by hunger striking as suicide, and Cardinal Tomás O'Fiaich of Armagh, who, with most of his Irish colleagues, maintained that death, being an indirect result of a refusal to take food during a protest, was not self-destruction. To loyalists, however, such an argument was 'semantic gobbledegook'.[86] Despite rejection of the suicide argument, most Irish Catholic clerics were opposed to the strategy of hunger strike.

The death of convict Sands, MP

The Sands protest riveted world attention when, in mid-strike, he was elected at a by-election on 9 April 1981 MP for Fermanagh-South Tyrone to replace the dead nationalist MP, Frank Maguire. The SDLP constitutional nationalists did not attempt to split the vote, while the Sands campaign received wider support from people like Bernadette Devlin (now MacAliskey). Those hoping to save Sands's life with their votes were disappointed when Margaret Thatcher refused concessions and Sands was allowed to die on 5 May, after rejecting an appeal from the Pope's envoy. His huge funeral with full PIRA military honours at Belfast's Milltown cemetery two days later achieved international headlines. At the end of May a *Sunday Times* survey of 64 foreign newspaper editors found that 36 favoured immediate British withdrawal from Northern Ireland or Irish unity, that five wanted Britain to remain to keep the peace, while only one supported Mrs Thatcher.[87] There was, apart from the usual backing of the pro-Provisional American NORAID, much expatriate Irish enthusiasm in countries like Australia and New Zealand.[88]

International interest waned after the high-point of Sands's death and had almost evaporated by 3 October when the strike, after ten deaths, was finally called off. Opponents of the strike claimed that outside Provisional leadership was manipulating the Maze prisoners into a deadly protest for propagandist reasons. It is now clear that it was the prisoners themselves and not the somewhat embarrassed leadership, headed by Gerry Adams, which insisted on maintaining the protest. Sands, whose reading of Frantz Fanon, Che Guevara and Camilo Torres was intensified by the bad Irish history of Leon Uris's *Trinity*, saw himself in the blood sacrificial role of Padraic Pearse, leader of the Easter Week Rising of 1916.[89] Sands's prison essays, poems and hunger strike diary, smuggled out on toilet paper, encapsulate the dirty protest, the hunger strike, degrading searches, the sense of Irish republican tradition, and love of the Gaelic language.[90] It was the intoxicating power of the Irish republican ethos rather than pressure from the outside leadership which persuaded striker after striker to sacrifice their lives in the most painful manner. As Padraig O'Malley puts it: 'The prisoners did what they were supposed to do. Their actions, ultimately, were not the actions of autonomous individuals but rather a reflexive embrace of the way in which political prisoners throughout Irish history were presumed to have behaved.'[91]

The families of prisoners were a different matter. In May there had been controversy over the alleged pressure by the family of Raymond McCreesh to keep him on hunger strike when he was too disoriented to decide for himself.[92] It, however, proved possible, when the striker became incapable of making a conscious decision, for his next of kin to sign for injections inhibiting further fasting. On 31 July Mrs Catherine Quinn, 'unable to watch her son writhing in agony, signed for medical intervention.'[93] Once the injections had taken effect it was impossible for a striker to continue. Three further deaths followed, but the end was in sight. On 20 August a striker was signed off the protest by his wife. A month later a mother warned her son that as she was not going to let him die, he should abandon the protest immediately to save his eyesight and general health.[94] By the beginning of October, the families of five of the remaining six hunger strikers announced that they would authorise medical treatment when entitled to do so, thus ending the hunger strike after 217 days. A statement was issued complaining that the strikers had been undermined by the Catholic hierarchy aided by the SDLP and the Irish government of Garret FitzGerald.[95] Fr Denis Faul became the republican scapegoat *par excellence* for the failure to obtain the five demands. He had coordinated the anti-strike families, after failing to talk Sands out of his strike.[96] But, almost immediately the strike had ended, the new Northern Irish Secretary, James Prior, announced prison reforms approximating the demands. Shortly afterwards, despite complaints about British inflexibility, the men on the blanket were at last wearing their own clothes while loyalists denounced the sellout.

The legacy of ten dead hunger strikers

Margaret Thatcher had certainly toughed it out and won a technical victory which helped to build her legend of invincibility, soon reinforced by further victories over General Galtieri's Argentina in 1982 and Arthur Scargill's British miners in 1984-85. But commentators who see the 1981 hunger strikes as a major watershed in the Northern Ireland Troubles are correct. Virtually all important developments in the 1980s can be traced to the legacy of Sands and his colleagues. Although technically defeated, the Provisionals were immediately strengthened in membership, money and morale. Bobby Sands's election victory in Fermanagh-South Tyrone, followed by the retention of the seat in August with an increased majority by Owen Carron, turned the Provisionals from barren election boycotts. Danny Morrison, editor of *An Phoblacht*, declared the new policy as the Armalite rifle in one hand and the ballot-box in the other. When elections were held for James Prior's new 'rolling devolution'[97] Northern Ireland Assembly in October 1982, Provisional Sinn Féin won an awe-inspiring 10.1 per cent of the vote compared with only 18.8 for the SDLP. The possibility, equally unwelcome to both British and Irish Governments, that Sinn Féin would overtake the SDLP in the Catholic community led to initiatives intended to boost the latter, such as the New Ireland Forum in 1984 and the Anglo-Irish Agreement in 1985.

The hardening of loyalists

The hunger strike had also a profound effect on the loyalist community, almost enabling Paisley's more extreme DUP to oust the less flamboyant Official Unionists as the majority party of the Protestant community. While Sands sought recognition as a reincarnation of Padraic Pearse, Paisley was equally concerned to revive the spirit of Edward Carson in his own person. Paisley's 'Carson Trail' rallies between 9 February and 28 March began before Sands refused food. On the day of Sands's funeral Paisley held his own service at the Cenotaph beside the City Hall, where he attributed the hunger strike to the bloodthirsty machinations of the Church of Rome.[98] Paisley's evocation of the ferocious spirit of Protestant anti-strike graffiti was rewarded in the local elections of May 1981. For the first and only time the DUP marginally outpolled the Official Unionists (26.6 to 26.5 per cent). On 2 September, Paisley called for a 'Third Force', on the lines of the old B Specials; two months later he claimed between 15,000 and 20,000 members. Paisley capitalised on the post-hunger strike assassination (14 November) by PIRA of the Rev. Robert Bradford, MP, a vociferous advocate of ruthless measures against terrorists. Declaring that 'law and order has collapsed completely', Paisley's journal cried, 'mobilise or capitulate',[99] and organised, with Official Unionist participation, a 'Day of Action' on 23 November. If the security forces failed in their job, Paisley promised to exterminate the IRA. Loyalist momentum, however, was not maintained. The Third Force petered out, while the UDA turned against the 'self-centred politicians' who had manipulated them in the 1970s.[100] Paisley, a passionate opponent of homosexuality, was embarrassed when a former political associate and Tara paramilitary leader, William McGrath, was gaoled in late 1981 for sexual interference with inmates under his care at the Kincora Boys' Home in Belfast. At the by-election in March 1982 for Bradford's seat of South Belfast, the DUP's candidate, the Rev. William McCrea, was beaten into third place behind the Official Unionist, the Rev. Martin Smyth, head of the Orange Order, and a moderate Alliance candidate. The UDA's attempt to emulate Sinn Féin by going political failed badly when its leading theorist, John McMichael, achieved only 576 votes in a constituency of 66,219.

British and republican violence

Despite increasing support after the hunger strikes, PIRA had logistical problems in the first half of 1982; anti-terrorist security was improving in the Republic, which set an important precedent in March 1984 by extraditing INLA's Dominic McGlinchey to Northern Ireland. In 1982 Ulster's age of the 'supergrass' began; by November the 'shoot-to-kill' squads of the Army or RUC disposed of known republicans with minimal formality. Though even Paisley condemned supergrasses, they posed a serious problem to all paramilitaries, especially after October 1983 when the chief justice accepted their evidence without corroboration.

. On the left, moreover, PIRA had to contend with the adventurism of INLA, whose actions like the Ballykelly pub bomb (sixteen killed in December 1982) and the Darkley church shooting of three members of a Pentecostalist congregation (21 November 1983) were denounced by Gerry Adams. PIRA persisted with dramatic 'propaganda by deed'. An attempt to assassinate the Northern Ireland chief justice, Lord Lowry, failed in March 1982, but weapons such as Russian RPG rockets and M-60 machine guns were produced in attacks on the security forces. About 42 of the latter were killed by PIRA in 1982. There were also spectaculars like the Maze breakout of September 1983 (nineteen Provisionals made good their escape), the July 1982 nail bombs in London which killed ten soldiers (including bandsmen), and the pre-Christmas 1983 Harrods bomb (five killed, eighty wounded). The latter was not authorised by the PIRA army council.

PIRA's Armalite and ballot-box policy

Danny Morrison's Armalite and ballot-box strategy, put to the 1981 Provisional Sinn Féin Ard Fheis, saw the ballot hand emerging triumphant after the elections for James Prior's Northern Ireland Assembly in October 1982. Both the SDLP and Provisional Sinn Féin, approaching its share of the Catholic vote, were committed to boycotting this attempt at 'rolling devolution', intended to delegate increasing power as Northern Ireland parties learned to co-operate. Gerry Adams, Danny Morrison, Owen Carron, Martin McGuinness, and Jim McAllister were elected. The Adams strategy had clearly succeeded; at the Sinn Féin Ard Fheis later in the month, the old Provisional plan for a federated Ireland, disliked by northerners, was dropped. At the next Ard Fheis in November 1983, the veteran southern-based leaders O'Brádaigh and O'Conaill withdrew, allowing Adams to be elected Sinn Féin president. In 1986 the old guard, rejecting the abandonment of Sinn Féin's policy of parliamentary abstention in the Republic, split off to form Republican Sinn Féin. Sinn Féin's greater political emphasis was indicated by an attempt, totally unsuccessful, to phase out kneecapping for community punishment.

Politics and the New Ireland Forum

The British general election of June 1983 saw a further Sinn Féin advance to 13.4, as opposed to 17.9 per cent for the SDLP. The split vote reduced nationalist representation to Hume in Derry and Adams in West Belfast. The gap between Sinn Féin and the SDLP was closing further. Before the election two bishops, Edward and Cahal Daly, had questioned the morality of a Sinn Féin vote; six months later the primate, Cardinal O'Fiaich, suggested that a vote for the peaceful proposals of Sinn Féin was legitimate. The SDLP, in some desperation, had campaigned on Garret FitzGerald's New Ireland Forum. FitzGerald's Fine Gael-Labour coalition played box and cox with Charlie Haughey's Fianna Fail in the Irish Republic. FitzGerald, victorious in 1981, lost office in February 1982 but regained it in November of the same year.

While unionists boycotted the New Ireland Forum, nationalists boycotted Prior's new Northern Ireland Assembly. The New Ireland Forum report of May 1984 suggested complete Irish unity, a federal Ireland, recently discarded by Sinn Féin which was not admitted to the discussions, or Irish-British joint sovereignty over Northern Ireland. None of these alternatives attracted the unionist parties which had rejected the Forum. The SDLP needed a more potent policy. But unconscious convergence became more apparent when the Republic's abortion referendum of September 1983 (passed by 67 to 33 percent) was paralleled in February 1984 by the impotent Northern Ireland Assembly's twenty-to-one resolution against extending British liberalised abortion laws to the province. Paisley and other unionists were in virtual agreement with the philosophy of Irish bishops whose insistence on the Republic's anti-abortion amendment to the Constitution was regarded as a blow to Irish unity.

Paisley's DUP had not, however, achieved the supersession of the Official Unionists as Northern Ireland's major party. Despite the DUP's 0.1 percent win over the Official Unionists in the 1981 municipal elections the pace was not maintained in 1982 and 1983. The DUP slipped from 26.6 to 23 and then to 20 per cent at the

Assembly and Westminster elections. As an individual, Paisley in the European elections of June 1984 polled a resounding best of 33.6 per cent first preferences, 12 per cent ahead of the Official Unionists. Hume of the SDLP, on the other hand, declined 2.5 per cent from his 1979 vote, while Danny Morrison of Sinn Féin almost held his party's percentage in 1983 with 13.3.

The Anglo-Irish Agreement, November 1985

Margaret Thatcher roughly rejected the three main options of the 1984 New Ireland Forum in an over-reactive Out, Out, Out press conference, but talks continued between the British and Irish governments. Something had to be done to prevent the undermining of the SDLP by the politically resurgent Sinn Féin. The 1985 marching season had seen violent clashes between loyalists and the RUC in Portadown and Castlewellan. They were to prove a portent. The battle-lines were drawn well in advance. An *ad hoc* alliance was forged between the OUP and the DUP. Loyalists bitterly complained that they had been excluded from discussions they were determined in any case to block.

The Anglo-Irish Agreement, signed at Hillsborough by Garret FitzGerald and Margaret Thatcher on 15 November 1985, established a joint conference on Northern Ireland with a permanent secretariat. It recognised the right of the Northern Ireland majority to remain in the union, while accepting the Irish identity of the minority. The Provisionals, and the Irish opposition leader, Haughey, insisted that the agreement was a sellout which would 'copper-fasten' partition. Loyalists were equally insistent on the sellout, but for diametrically opposed reasons, asserting that the British government was treacherously forcing Ulster into the Irish Republic. An Irish police football team, playing in Derry, ran the gauntlet of loyalists attacking them as the agents of a foreign power and republicans condemning them as British collaborators. Such incidents thus provided a classic example of mirrored antithetical interpretation. The Provisionals continued to demonstrate that their Armalites were no ornaments, while the loyalists moved from rhetorical violence to bashings, burnings and bullets in the streets.

Loyalist oratory employed images, once directed towards Rome, against the British government. Margaret Thatcher was portrayed as a 'tin foil cutty' and a 'modern Jezebel' hugging the viper FitzGerald to her bosom. The secretary of state, Tom King, became a 'Judas' and 'King Rat'. Paisley promised resistance to the death and an aftermath 'too horrible to contemplate' if the Agreement were not abandoned.

In the joint OUP-DUP alliance for resistance, James Molyneux found it hard to match the panache of his charismatic colleague. But Paisley himself struggled to keep ahead of his own extremists. An appeal to the courts against an alleged abandonment of sovereignty predictably failed. At a loyalist protest gathering on 23 November outside the City Hall, the *Belfast Newsletter* calculated 203,000 demonstrators, the *Irish Times* only 30,000. Some UDA units in uniform participated. Unionist MPs then resigned their seats to force a *de facto* referendum, reminiscent of 1974. Though polling 418,000 on 23 January 1986 against the Agreement they lost Newry-Armagh to the SDLP deputy-leader, Seamus Mallon. This was due to a swing of about 7 per cent away from Sinn Féin. The violence of the loyalist reaction had increased the popularity of the Agreement amongst nationalists.

After the by-elections came the one-day strike of 3 March. Memories of 1974 were revived by power cuts, UDA road blocks, and very considerable intimidation. Molyneux later regretted that he had been pressured into co-operating with the strike. The RUC was attacked by one side for its failure to keep the roads open, while roughs on the other harassed police wives and families. A boycott by unionist councillors, originally directed against Sinn Féin representatives, developed into a protest against the Anglo-Irish Agreement. Portadown, home of a new militant loyalist organisation, the Ulster Clubs, again proved a flash-point. The British and Irish governments, despite domestic political threats to both Thatcher and FitzGerald, refused to suspend the Agreement; PIRA's selective assassination, calculated to keep loyalist anger at boiling point, continued inexorably. The hope of 'talks about talks', if not talks themselves, was soon dashed. Loyalists justified their refusal to negotiate while the Agreement was in force by the SDLP's mirrored refusal to enter the Northern Ireland Assembly established by Prior.

The Unionist constitutional opposition flags while violence mounts

Despite their bluster, the loyalist leaders had failed to shake the resolve of the Thatcher government on the Agreement. The defeat of Prime Minister Garret FitzGerald in the Irish Republic's general election on 19 February 1987 made no difference; the new prime minister, Charles Haughey, persisted with the Accord, despite his strictures in opposition. When Thatcher's government itself was triumphantly re-elected on 11 June, the Unionists, who lost Enoch Powell's seat to the SDLP, had less chance of overturning the Agreement by frontal assault. Their internal stresses intensified. The DUP's continued alliance with the OUP was unpopular with many supporters. The boycott of the British government by local councils began to wear thin, while the Methodist Church advised working within the Agreement and itself entered talks with the Catholics. However, Catholics themselves became disillusioned with the Agreement. Diplock Courts were not given three judges as the Irish Republic demanded, and the Republic's new extradition law of 1987 seemed inadequate to Britain. Catholics were still two and a half times more likely than Protestants to be unemployed as discrimination quietly persisted.

Violence, moreover, was not reduced by the Agreement. With 93 killed in the Troubles in 1987, the year proved the worst since 1981. Both republicans and loyalists were involved. Internal INLA feuding at the beginning of the year resulted in twelve deaths and the emergence of yet another republican paramilitary group, the Irish People's Liberation Organisation (IPLO). The IRA suffered one of its most serious setbacks at Loughgall on 8 May when SAS (Special Air Services) marksmen killed seven of its operatives and an innocent bystander in a morally dubious 'stakeout' which led to rioting in Catholic areas. On 8 November the IRA appeared to have destroyed its credibility at Enniskillen. A bomb, for which it apologised, killed 11 and injured 63. As usual the initial horror was soon absorbed. Killings continued on both sides. The UDA's deputy leader, John McMichael, author of a plan for devolved government with power-sharing between Catholics and Protestants, was assassinated by an IRA booby trap bomb on 22 December 1987. The UDA's assassination wing, the UFF, also patronised by McMichael, had eliminated a number of Catholics during the year.

Horrendous events in early 1988 fuelled further escalation of an apparently unending conflict. On 6 March three PIRA operatives, Mairead Farrell, Sean Savage and Daniel McCann, were killed at Gibraltar by the SAS. Farrell had taken a leading role in the 'dirty protest' at Armagh women's prison. Investigation demonstrated that all three were unarmed and were not then detonating a bomb, though they undoubtedly intended to lay one later. Moreover, the Provisionals were shot repeatedly on the ground to finish them off. While the official inquest in September found little amiss, there were a number of demands for further inquiry. The Northern Irish Catholic community was aghast, but worse was to come. At the Gibraltar Provisionals' funerals in Belfast on 16 March, Michael

Stone, a loyalist later sentenced to life imprisonment for six murders,[101] attacked the mourners with grenade and gun, killing three before capture. At the subsequent interment of one of Stone's victims, Kevin Brady, the crowd attacked, in their car in full view of TV, two Signals' corporals, Robert Howes and Derek Wood. After a savage beating both were finally shot dead by PIRA. The frightening polarisation of the communities was demonstrated by the UDA's *Ulster* which, seeing the 'sub-humans at a so-called Christian funeral rip the bodies of two soldiers apart' portrayed Stone as an almost Christ-like figure who had 'changed the whole perspective of the War in Ulster' by a courageous and self-sacrificing attempt to kill the top Provisionals.[102]

Gibraltar and its aftermath did indeed set the pattern for the following years. Not only was there a marked increase in republican and loyalist violence, but the British Government's efforts to combat it raised increasing concern about the erosion of civil rights in Northern Ireland. Gibraltar, especially when publicised by the award-winning TV documentary, *Death on the Rock*, dramatically epitomised the dangers of shoot-to-kill, currently exposed by the long-running Stalker affair. In most suspicious circumstances John Stalker, Deputy Chief Constable, Manchester, had been taken off an inquiry into a shoot-to-kill episode in Armagh in 1982.[103] Further examples of stakeouts were to follow in the next years. Even non-political criminals with dummy guns were ruthlessly gunned down in West Belfast in January 1990 and two teenage joyriders, male and female, were shot dead in the same nationalist area.[104] The issue of police brutality and false conviction surfaced again. There were still demands for videos of interrogations at Castlereagh Barracks. In 1991 the High Court in Belfast awarded £47,500 of damages to prisoners in the Maze who were beaten up by warders after their 1983 escape attempt. In England the mid-1970s convictions of the Guildford Four (19 October 1989), the Birmingham Six (14 March 1991) and the Maguire Seven (26 June 1991) were quashed. On the other side, the historian Robert Kee, who had agitated for the release of the Guildford Four and the Maguire Seven,[105] also helped to secure the reopening of the case of a UDR Four. Such cases demonstrated that police had used strong-arm tactics to extort confessions, fabricated them and concealed other evidence vital to the defence. British authorities came badly out of these affairs. The reopening of suspect cases had long been stalled, while Lord Denning regretted the abandonment of capital punishment, which would have eliminated the tiresome complaints of the

Birmingham Six.[106] The government stonewalled on the accusations of its former intelligence officer, Colin Wallace. Wallace, himself convicted of murder on dubious evidence, complained of misinformation and 'dirty tricks' in the 1970s, including a cover-up on the security forces involvement in the Kincora Boys' Home case.[107] In July a Panorama TV documentary found that minimum force had not been used in seven recent Army shootings and in two cases the suspects had been finished off. Of greatest concern was the accumulating evidence that there had been collusion between the security forces and the Protestant paramilitaries, who were supplied with evidence of republican activists to facilitate their assassinations. The Stevens Inquiry of 1990 into such collusion led to a number of prosecutions, one of the most revealing being that of Brian Nelson, a UDA man recruited by British Intelligence. There was, however, no sign of an end to violence as the 1980s passed into the 1990s.

In many ways the situation in the early 1990s appeared to have returned to carnage reminiscent of some of the worst periods of the 1970s. Although the death rates were not nearly so horrific, republican and loyalist extremists vied with each other in stepping up violence. 1991 saw 94 Troubles-related killings in Northern Ireland. The IRA returned to major city centres, in both the Province and England, producing alarm and chaos with firebombs directed at large stores. Communication systems such as the Belfast-Dublin rail link and the London underground were regularly disrupted, inspiring the Peace Train protest.[108] The UFF in retaliation attempted, not so successfully, to firebomb Dublin and the Irish Republic in general. The dreary round of tit-for-tat assassinations was also renewed. On the republican side PIRA was joined in its ruthlessness by the Irish People's Liberation Organisation (IPLO), the INLA breakaway, and even the old Official IRA saw three of its members gaoled in early 1992 for hijacking a lorry. On the loyalist side most killings were the work of the UDA's UFF auxiliary, effectively supported by the UVF, which had its own Protestant Action Force (PAF). Loyalist apologies for slaying Protestants mistaken for Catholics were matched by the now ritualistic excuses of the IRA. The politics of the last atrocity were kept alive. PIRA proxy bombings forced victims to drive explosives-laden cars into security force targets. UVF actions included the shooting of two girls in a mobile shop outside Craigavon.[109] After the Provisionals had killed eight Protestants in a minibus at Teebane on 17 January 1992, UFF operatives, shouting 'Remember Teebane', sprayed with bullets a bookmakers shop on the Ormeau Road and killed five more people. British Army reinforcements were steadily moved into Northern Ireland and there were renewed calls for internment, which had escalated violence in 1971. Sinn Féin leaders, like Gerry Adams, tried to distance themselves partly from PIRA, claiming that the latter had no organic links with Sinn Féin.[110] The chances of Sinn Féin being admitted to the negotiating table decreased with every violent incident, despite Adams' insistence that there had already been many instances of negotiation with the IRA in arms. Kneecapping for community offences by both republicans and loyalists, for women as well as men, aroused the ire of Peter Benenson, founder of Amnesty International. Once again PIRA promised to drop it for all but very serious offences.

A new generation was taking over the struggle in the 1990s. Margaret Thatcher resigned as British Prime Minister on 22 November 1990 and Charlie Haughey, accused in 1970 of supplying arms to the infant Provisionals, finally resigned as Fianna Fail leader and Taoiseach at the end of January 1992. A few days later, on 15 February 1992, the 'Officials' experienced yet another split. Failing by a few votes to persuade the WP Ard Fheis to abandon its Official IRA:New Agenda split and Stalinist past, the leader, Proinsias de Rossa formed a new party, the New Agenda, later the Democratic Left, from five of the party's six TDs.[111] The deaths of Terence O'Neill (13 June 1990) and Dáithí O'Conaill, Chief of Staff of the original PIRA and later a member of dissident Republican Sinn Féin, symbolised the end of an era. Loyalists ridiculed the claim by Tom French, leader of the WP, that there were no links with OIRA.[112] Andy Tyrie and John McMichael had left the UDA stage and the new commander, Tommy Lyttle, lost their immunity from successful prosecution when sentenced to seven years' imprisonment on 3 July 1991. A few days earlier, Archbishop Cahal Daly, successsor to Tomás O'Fiaich of Armagh, received his cardinal's hat. Ian Paisley lost some of his authority to Peter Robinson, his only lieutenant who had retained independent authority in the DUP. Paisley's daughter Rhonda had likewise established her own position as a DUP leader in the Belfast City Council.

There were indications of positive change. After many setbacks the painfully slow progress of the constitutional parties to talks for an internal settlement was gathering momentum. The Fair Employment Tribunal registered the first successful complaint of a Catholic in October 1991 and the Catholic unemployment differential fell in the same year from two and a half to two in an area where unemployment was still over 14 per cent. Despite

Catholic hierarchical disapproval, the Integrated Education sector was increasing its influence in Northern Ireland. President Mary Robinson of the Irish Republic made Northern Ireland conciliation the cornerstone of her term of office and broke all precedents by visiting Belfast in February 1992. The British general election of April 1992, which returned the Government of John Major, saw no real drop in the Sinn Féin vote, steady at 10 per cent, after its campaign emphasising the ballot paper in one hand and a solution, not an Armalite, in the other. More significant was the fact that Gerry Adams lost his West Belfast seat to Dr Joe Hendron of the SDLP as a result of tactical voting by unionists.[113] The willingness of 3000 Protestants to vote for an SDLP candidate augured well for a power-sharing agreement, but the London IRA bombs which followed the election indicated that the ballot-box may now play a minor role to the Armalite in the Provisionals' future strategies.

In 1993 the IRA's continued militancy, confronted by a ruthless assassination campaign by the UFF, UVF and Red Hand Commandos, was highlighted by the slaughter of ten people by an IRA bomb at a fish shop on the Shankill Road on 23 October and the brutal UFF retaliatory shooting dead of seven people at a bar in Greysteel a week later. Meanwhile talks between Gerry Adams and John Hume of the SDLP helped an upsurge of opinion for peace to gather momentum. The Downing Street Declaration of Prime Minister John Major and Taoiseach Albert Reynolds on 15 December 1993 was hailed as a significant breakthrough. While in substance it went little beyond the the Anglo-Irish Agreement of 1985, the Declaration recognised that the people of Northern Ireland, not the people of Ireland as a whole, had the right to decide on national unity. But this was accompanied by a strong denial that Britain had any strategic or economic interest in Northern Ireland. It fell far short of Gerry Adams's demand that Britain would actively persuade unionists to agree to a United Ireland. Nevertheless there was scope for Sinn Féin to participate in peace talks, if the IRA abandoned violence.

The greatest significance of the Downing Street Declaration, as opposed to the Anglo-Irish Agreement, appears to lie in the reaction it evoked. Instead of the normal antithetical interpretation by unionists as a sellout to republicanism and by republicans as a total abandonment of Irish unity, a war-weary public forced a measured response. True, Ian Paisley was characteristically uncompromising in his denunciation of the Declaration and *An Phoblacht* was soon attacking Major's hypocrisy,[114] but moderate unionists were glumly acquiescent and Sinn Féin slow to reject it outright. Gerry Adams, while demanding the British Government's clarification and its persuasion of unionists into a united Ireland, appeared to admit that unionists could not be coerced. If such hints of compromise can be worked into an overall settlement, without violent splits in republican and loyalist ranks, the 'dreary steeples of Tyrone and Fermanagh' which to Winston Churchill had symbolised the integrity of an unending quarrel, and whose mirrored responses will be analysed in the following chapters, can at last be removed from world politics.

Notes

1. It was later argued that the Six County area in fact represented historical Ulster.
2. See Whyte, John (1990), *Interpreting Northern Ireland*, Oxford: Clarendon.
3. Farrell, Michael (1980, 1st ed. 1976), *Northern Ireland: The Orange State*, London: Pluto, 92, and Lyons, F.S.L. (1973), *Ireland Since the Famine*, London: Collins/Fontana, 725 (Brooke).
4. Dillon, Martin (1989), *The Shankill Butchers: A Case History of Mass Murder*, London: Hutchinson, xviii (C.C. O'Brien's Introduction).
5. Purdie, Bob (1990), *Politics in the Streets: The Origins of the Civil Rights Movement in Northern Ireland*, Belfast: Blackstaff, 156.
6. Arthur, Paul (1974), *The People's Democracy, 1968-1973*, Belfast: Blackstaff, 20-22.
7. *Protestant Telegraph* (PT), 19 October 1967 (NICRA); 7 September 1967 (confrontation); 19 October 1967 (PD).
8. Farrell, Michael (1980), *Northern Ireland: The Orange State*, 249.
9. McKeown, Ciaran (1984), *The Passion of Peace*, Belfast: Blackstaff, 47 and 53.
10. O'Neill, Terence (1972), *The Autobiography of Terence O'Neill*, London: Hart Davies, 110-112.
11. See PT, 2 August 1969; Devlin, Bernadette (1969), *The Price of My Soul*, London: Pan, 138-43; and Egan, Bowes and McCormack, Vincent (1969), *Burntollet*, Belfast: LRS, 40 for photo of battered girl in mini-skirt.
12. PT, 11 January 1969. The headline was 'RC Mob attacks a Protestant Rally'.
13. According to Insight's (1972) *Ulster*, Harmondsworth: Penguin, 79, 'the role of several influential adherents of the Free Presbyterian church is unclear'. See also Boulton, D. (1973), *The UVF, 1966-73*, Dublin: Torc, 104-5.
14. *Autobiography of Terence O'Neill*, 122, 125-6.
15. Devlin, *The Price of My Soul*, 199.
16. The Scarman Report calculated that 1,820 families fled their homes in Belfast between July and September 1969; 82.7 per cent of these were Catholic. See Farrell, *The Orange State*, 263.

17. Longford, Lord and McHardy, Ann (1981), *Ulster*, London: Weidenfeld and Nicholson, 113. Quotes McCann, Eamon (1981), *War and an Irish Town*, London: Pluto.

18. Downey, James (1983), *Them and Us: Britain and the Northern Question, 1969-1982*, Dublin: Ward River Press, 57-8.

19. Devlin, *The Price of My Soul*, 130. At the 'Battle of Bogside', she believed that Harold Wilson sent in the troops because he disliked the B Specials, not to help Faulkner (204).

20. Arthur, Max (1989, 1st ed. 1988), *Northern Ireland Soldiers Talking: 1969 to Today*, London: Sidgwick and Jackson, 7-15, 126, 163-4.

21. O'Brien, C.C. (1978), *Herod: Reflections on Political Violence*, London: Hutchinson, 42.

22. MacStiofain, Sean (1975), *Memoirs of a Revolutionary*, Great Britain [sic]: Gordon Cremonesi, 96.

23. *United Irishman* (UI), 3 March 1972, claimed that at least twelve officers were killed, but the information was suppressed.

24. Browne, Vincent, in *Magill*, April 1982. Arthur, Max, *Northern Ireland Soldiers Talking*, 123.

25. Browne, Vincent, in *Magill*, May 1982 and Downey, *Them and Us*, 102. Patterson, Henry (1989), *The Politics of Illusion: Republicanism and Socialism in Modern Ireland*, London: Hutchinson, 150-51.

26. Insight, *Ulster*, 204.

27. Arthur, Paul (1980) *Government and Politics in Northern Ireland*, London: Longman, 112. *Combat* (C) (4, 16) 78, rejected Callaghan, James (1973), *A House Divided: The Dilemma of Northern Ireland*, London: Collins, 'there never was a more biased book written'. PT, 12 November 1977, quoted the *Crossman Diaries* on the incompetence of the Labour Cabinet on Ulster. Denis Healey criticised Wilson and Callaghan who wished to side with the Catholics.

28. Hall, Michael (1988), *20 Years: A Concise Chronology of Events in Northern Ireland from 1968-1988*, Newtownabbey: Island Publications, 22; Flackes, W.D. and Elliott, Sydney (1989) *Northern Ireland: A Political Directory, 1968-88*, Belfast: Blackstaff, 228.

29. Clutterbuck, Richard (1973), *Protest and the Urban Guerrilla*, London: Cassell, 90.

30. Farrell, *The Orange State*, 265.

31. Arthur, *Northern Ireland Soldiers Talking*, 28.

32. Bishop, Patrick and Mallie, Eamonn (1988), *The Provisional IRA*, London: Corgi, 165.

33. See McGuffin, John (1973 and 1974), *Internment*, Tralee: Anvil, and *The Guineapigs*, Harmondsworth: Penguin.

34. Dillon, Martin and Lehane, Denis (1973), *Political Murder in Northern Ireland*, Harmondsworth: Penguin, 42.

35. Flackes and Elliott, *Northern Ireland: A Political Directory*, 272. By 1978 this had dropped to 10-12,000, partly due to the more restrictive policy of its leadership.

36. *Republican News* (RN), 30 August 1975.

37. Dillon and Lehane, *Political Murder in Northern Ireland*, 253, 277-8, 280; Dillon, *The Shankill Butchers: A Case Study of Mass Murder*, x

(C.C. O'Brien) 19-20; Kelley, Kevin (1982), *The Longest War: Northern Ireland and the IRA*, Dingle: Brandon, 238-9.

38. PT, 20 June 1981. See Smyth, Clifford (1987), *Ian Paisley: Voice of Protestant Ulster*, Edinburgh: Scottish Academy Press, 26-36.
39. Boulton, *The UVF*, 139 and 147.
40. *UDA News* (UDAN) (16) 1972; Boulton, 189.
41. PT, 17 April 1976, RN, 5 December 1971, claimed that Paisley was trying to break the link between the Orange Order and the Official Unionists.
42. Bell, Geoffrey (1976), *The Protestants of Ulster*, London: Pluto, 9.
43. Widgery, Lord (1972), *Report of the Tribunal appointed to inquire into the events of Sunday, 30 January 1972*, London: HM Stationery Office.
44. UDAN, (1, 3) 1972.
45. Boulton, *The UVF*, 153 and 161.
46. PT, 6 January 1973.
47. RN, 14 May 1972. It emphasised that towns outside Belfast could now be hit. See also MacStiofain, *Memoirs of a Revolutionary*, 243, for car-bomb strategy to make government difficult by attacking the economic structure, and to keep the British Army in the city away from nationalist areas.
48. Bishop and Mallie, *The Provisional IRA*, 232.
49. MacStiofain, *Memoirs of a Revolutionary*, 298-9. He pointed out that the static defence of no-go areas was contrary to the principles of guerrilla warfare.
50. Dillon and Lehane, *Political Murder*, 213.
51. McAllister, Ian (1977), *The Northern Ireland Social Democratic and Labour Party*, London: Macmillan, 125-6.
52. Longford and McHardy, *Ulster*, 158.
53. Downey, *Them and Us*, 129.
54. Downey, *Them and Us*, 128. See also Fisk, Robert (1975), *The Point of No Return: The Strike which broke the British in Ulster*, London: André Deutsch.
55. Foot, Paul (1990), *Who Framed Colin Wallace?*, London: Pan, 104.
56. *An Phoblacht* (AP), 5 June 1974. See *Irish Times* (IT) poll, 25 June 1982 (55 per cent in favour - 75% Catholic, 45% Protestant); UTV, 12 February 1982 (73% in favour).
57. McKeown, *The Passion of Peace*, 121.
58. C (1.28) 1974, 25 April 1984; RN, 15June 1974, 25 May 1974, 1 June 1974; AP, 31 May 1974. See also Fisk, Robert (1975), *The Point of No Return: The Strike which broke the British in Ulster*, 218-219; UI, 7.74. See Probert, Belinda (1978), *Beyond Orange and Green: The Northern Ireland Crisis in a New Perspective*, Dublin: Academy Press, 141-144.
59. PT, 22 May 1976.
60. Gallagher, E. and Worrall, S. (1982), *Christians in Ulster, 1968-1980*, Oxford: OUP, 1-2 and 99-102.
61. Rees, Merlyn (1985), *Northern Ireland: A Personal Perspective*, London: Methuen, 231. See also 217-249 and 319 for general discussion of the ceasefire.
62. Bishop and Mallie, *The Provisional IRA*, 275-86.

63. According to Easthope, Gary (1986, September), 'Religious War in Northern Ireland', *Sociology*, Oxford, 10, 3, the UDA and Provisional splits were equivalent to religious sectarianism.
64. McKeown, *The Passion of Peace*, 199-200.
65. PT, 26 February 1977.
66. *Ulster* (U), September 1976. McKeown, 194, for death threat.
67. C (4,22) 1979.
68. McKeown, *The Passion of Peace*, 176.
69. U, September 1978. *Peace by Peace* (PP), 16 and 29 October 1976 (Gandhi and Luther King), 25 March 1977 (King and Muldoon), 8 April 1977, 22 April 1977 (Camara), 20 May 1977 and 3 June 1977 (loyalist strike and Camara), 1 July 1977 (Muldoon room in Peace House), 26 August 1977 (Queen).
70. Political status allowed prisoners their own clothes and self-organisation. The Gardiner Report considered this destructive- of prison authority and the establishment of virtual terrorist universities. Women, not compelled to wear uniform, sometimes opted for militaristic black skirts and berets. Moreover, 'prisoner of war' status in gaol destroyed some of the credibility of the British government's efforts to claim 'normalisation' and 'an acceptable level of violence'. Gardiner also recommended the construction of the H-Block cells at the Maze Prison.
71. Loyalists paraded in gaol under commanders like Gusty Spence and celebrated the anniversary of the Somme with rousing orations, subsequently published by *Combat* or other loyalist periodicals.
72. According to the UVF *Combat*, 4, 1976: 'The very processes they are subjected to on arrest, starting with the arrest itself and ending in the Diplock courts, are political and are [as] far removed from the normal British practices and justice, as we are from the moon.'
73. Coogan, T.P. (1980), *On the Blanket: The H-Block Story*, Swords: Ward River Press, 79-83 for Nugent.
74. See for example Faul, Denis and Murray, Raymond (1980), *H-Block and its Background* (from *Doctrine and Life*, November 1980), and *Moment of Truth for Northern Ireland* (also from *Doctrine and Life*, March 1980).
75. Faul and Murray (1978), *The Castlereagh File: Allegations of RUC Brutality, 1976-1977*, n.p.; Coogan, *On the Blanket*, passim; Taylor, Peter (1980), *Beating the Terrorists*, Harmondsworth: Penguin, 105; PT, 18 April 1981.
76. C (4, 23) 1979. It claimed that the UVF had not contributed to the commission on the ground that it was not a public enquiry.
77. PT, 26 January 1974 and 4 September 1976.
78. McKeown, *The Passion for Peace*, 299-300, 304.
79. O'Malley, Padraig (1990), *Biting at the Grave: The Irish Hunger Strikes and the Politics of Despair*, Belfast: Blackstaff, 22.
80. U, July 1978. Paisley's journal, however, had no sympathy for prison protest.
81. *Combat* boasted in 1979 that two UVF men, Jim Watt and Alex Smith, had completed a year, C (4, 27) 1979. *An Phoblacht* noted that only ten

loyalists, compared to 400 republicans, protested and these were not backed from outside, AP, 22 December 1979.
82. Bishop and Mallie, *The Provisional IRA*, 322-3. By 1980 there was internal criticism of the cell system for delaying operations and inhibiting a wider membership, AP, 5 January 1980. *Fortnight*, No. 187, July-August 1982, 4-5, 'The Provos have second thoughts'.
83. AP, 19 May 1979.
84. AP, 5 January 1980.
85. AP, 13 and 20 December 1980.
86. U, September 1981.
87. *Sunday Times* (ST), 31 May 1981 (Phillip Knightley).
88. Eamonn O'Connor of Sydney was only dissuaded from continuing a sympathetic hunger-strike of 39 days to force Malcolm Fraser's Liberal government to take diplomatic action, by the personal intervention of Gerry Adams and the H- Block blanket men. AP, 5 and 9 September 1981.
89. O'Malley, *Biting at the Grave*, 47-56 and 64.
90. See Sands, Bobby (1990), *The Diary of Bobby Sands: The first seventeen days of Bobby's H-Block hunger-strike to the death*, Dublin: Republican Publications; Sands, Bobby (1984 reprint), *One Day in My Life*, Dublin: Mercier; Sands, Bobby (1982), *Skylark Sing Your Lonely Song: An Anthology of the Writings of Bobby Sands*, Dublin: Mercier; Sands, Bobby (1981), *Prison Poems* [Danny Morrison introduction] Dublin: Sinn Féin Publicity; Sands, Bobby (1981), *The Writings of Bobby Sands* [Gerry Adams Introduction], Dublin: Sinn Féin POW Department.
91. O'Malley, *Biting at the Grave*, 117.
92. Collins, Tom (1986), *The Irish Hunger Strike*, Dublin: White Island Book Company, 220-228, rejects this and the authenticity of a tape recording, purporting to demonstrate family pressure to maintain the strike, published by the *Sunday Times*, 24 May 1981.
93. AP, 12 September 1981.
94. AP, 3 October 1981.
95. AP, 10 October 1981 and Collins, *The Hunger Strike*, 602.
96. O'Malley, *Biting at the Grave*, 127.
97. Prior hoped to tempt Unionists to cooperate with the SDLP with the hope of increased local autonomy.
98. PT, 16 May 1981.
99. PT, 21 November 1981.
100. U, December 1981.
101. 3 March 1989.
102. *Ulster*, April 1988.
103. See Stalker, John (1988), *Stalker: Ireland, 'Shoot to Kill' and the 'Affair'*, London: Penguin. The 'Affair' was far from over when Stalker published his book. In early 1990 Stalker presented a document to the Home Office which purported to demonstrate that the Government had authorised the removal of Stalker from the RUC investigation through unfounded charges against him.
104. On 22 July 1991 a BBC Panorama programme surveyed 7 recent army shootings, concluded that minimum force had not been used and that

twice soldiers had finished off wounded suspects. The joyriders were
shot on 30 September 1990.
105. Kee, Robert (1986), *Trial and Error: The Maguires, the Guildford Pub Bombings and British Justice*, London: Hamish Hamilton.
106. 16 August 1990, apology in *Spectator*, 23 August 1990.
107. The British Armed Forces Minister, Archie Hamilton, admitted the disinformation campaign of Wallace in the 1970s. An inquiry was set up into Wallace's dismissal, 30 January 1990.
108. 19 July 1991 in London.
109. 8 April 1991, PIRA forced an RUC civilian worker to carry a bomb in a handbag to Beleek Police Station. It was defused unlike several carbombs. On 28 March 1991 UVF shot the girls.
110. 22 January 1992.
111. *Fortnight*, No. 305, April 1992, 28-9 and AP, 27 February 1992. The latter ridiculed the Workers' Party 'collapsing on its own contradictions' and branded the claims by de Rossa and others to have no knowledge of the Official IRA as hypocritical. The Official IRA issue had been brought to a head by the jailing of three members, two with Workers' Party links, on 6 January 1992.
112. *Loyalist*, March 1992.
113. AP, 16 April 1992 and *New Statesman*, 17 April 1992 (article by Robin Wilson, editor of *Fortnight*). The SDLP did well with 23.5% and four seats, while the DUP could only manage 13.1 as opposed to the OUP's 34.5% The attempt to run Conservatives in Northern Ireland achieved a mere 5.7%.
114. AP, 29 December 1993: 'for all the flowery language of the Downing Street Declaration, the British government will always put its interests before the wishes of the Irish people.'

2 The press of antagonism

Background

Terrorism, according to Robert Taber, popular with the Provisional IRA, is political theatre, designed not so much to physically defeat an established government, as to create a 'climate of collapse' which will force concession.[1] The periodicals spawned by a terrorist struggle are therefore a vital part of the action, not a mere accessory. They serve to mobilise and sensitise potential supporters, to answer the charges of opponents, to glorify the fallen heroes of the guerrilla struggle and to provide and advertise the political agenda of the guerrillas' open support group, if it exists. The periodicals have also to maintain and adapt the basic ideology of the armed struggle, while countering that of opponents, and answering their periodicals. Far from periodicals merely publicising terrorist actions, militant deeds often illustrate the essential message purveyed by revolutionary papers.

The Anglo-Irish War, 1919-21, provides an excellent example. Though most emphasis has been placed on the assassination policy of Michael Collins' famous 'squad' and the 'flying columns' in the country, these were supported by a prolific 'mosquito press' which did much to encourage British opposition to the war of reprisal in Ireland. The effectiveness of the *Irish Bulletin* in presenting the Irish case to the world press has been fully acknowledged. It is significant that the brilliant Irish journalist and founder of the original Sinn Féin, Arthur Griffith, emerged as the head of the Irish government after signing the Anglo-Irish Treaty in December 1921.[2]

Jimmy Vitty, librarian of the Linen Hall Library, Belfast, when proffered a civil rights pamphlet in 1968, made the inspired decision to preserve all material concerning the apparently short-term disturbances. Over the years the collection of pamphlets, handbills, posters and newspapers grew into a superb resource, the Northern Ireland Political Ephemera Collection. Now available on microfiche, the collection makes the Northern Ireland Troubles one of the best documented conflicts ever. In 1984 Robert Bell took over as supervisor from Jim Gracey, Paula Howard and John Killen, who had built up the initial collection.[3] Most Northern Ireland organisations, regardless of political ideology, were eager to immortalise their philosophies by supplying free copy to the Linen Hall Library. *An Phoblacht*, for example, pointed out that the 'unique and valuable' collection had a direct connection with the republican movement in that the United Irishman Thomas Russell had been the Linen Hall Library's first librarian.[4] This did not, however, prevent a PIRA man on the run on New Year's Day, 1994, leaving bombs in the Library and destroying part of the biographical section, though not the priceless Irish Collection.

Before the outbreak in 1968, the polarisation of Northern Irish society was exhibited by Belfast's three main dailies. The *Belfast News Letter*, Ireland's oldest surviving paper, founded in 1737, was committed to firm unionism.[5] The *Irish News*, established under the guidance of the Catholic Bishop of Down and Connor in 1891 to repudiate the Irish Home Rule leader, Parnell, after the latter's involvement in the celebrated O'Shea divorce case,[6] still maintains 'faith and fatherland' on its masthead. In 1982 the paper was taken over by the Fitzpatrick legal family from the less enterprising McSparrens. Under a new English editor, Nick Garbutt, the *Irish News* sought to transform itself from a glum information sheet for the Catholic ghetto to a modern vehicle of constitutional nationalism, interesting even to liberal Protestants. Advanced Irish republicans repudiate the paper as committed to the Catholic-based SDLP and dominated by the clergy.[7] The afternoon *Belfast Telegraph*, caters for both Catholic and Protestant readers with a milder and more tactful support of the British connection than the *News Letter*.[8] The faith and politics of each Northern Ireland householder can still be guaged with some accuracy from the tell-tale morning print protruding through the letter-box.

These Belfast dailies were supplemented by many provincial and politico-religious papers representing organisations ranging from the banned and occasionally active Official IRA's[9] *United Irishman*[10] to various periodicals associated with the Orange Order.

Summary of the political papers since 1966[11]

Long before the outbreak of the Troubles Paisley in 1955 began the anti-Romanist and anti-ecumenical monthly, the *Revivalist*. Free Presbyterian political progress, hindered by the antagonism of the mainstream dailies, necessitated Paisley's *Protestant Telegraph*,[12] published from 1966 to April 1982 when superseded by the short-lived *Voice of Ulster*. The latter was an attempt to shift focus from the fundamentalist preoccupations of the Free Presbyterian Church to the more political DUP. Like its predecessor emanating from the DUP headquarters at 296 Albertbridge Road, the *Voice* advertised itself as the official journal of the party. The *Voice of Ulster* petered out in late 1983, being partly replaced by the *DUP Voice*, East Antrim, 1985-86. Paisley's occasional cyclostyled sheet, the *Protestant Blu Print*, 1985-88, provided clippings antagonistic to Catholic, ecumenical, Irish republican and British opponents. The *New Protestant Telegraph* attempted to recreate the original formula, demonstrating the apparent timelessness of the Northern Ireland problem. Though the Protestant paramilitary organisations, spawned by the Troubles, published periodicals of their own, often critical of Paisley, the latter's journals remained the classic statement of militant Protestantism, and the most undeviating opponent of the revolutionary republican journals.

Readers of the early *Protestant Telegraph* might have anticipated the course of events when NICRA moved onto the streets in late 1968. The civil rights movement eventually published its own journal as did its more militant rival, People's Democracy (PD). Michael Farrell edited a succession of PD papers, the *Free Citizen* to 1971, the *Unfree Citizen* to 1975 and finally the *Socialist Republic*. He remained active in the movement until 1980. While the IRA was in the throes of disintegration and re-formation, PD acted as the authentic voice of republicanism in Northern Ireland; later, while affiliated to the Fourth (Trotskyist) International, it continued to support many positions of Provisional Sinn Féin, but criticised its superficial social analysis and sometimes counterproductive violence. According to the Provisionals, 'PD might have the right language, but they have no practice.'[13]

After the republican split in late 1969, Provisional Sinn Féin published *An Phoblacht* from Dublin on 31 January 1970 and the *Republican News*[14] from Belfast (first issue June 1970) as its two quality periodicals. They soon became weeklies. Meanwhile, a number of crudely produced news-sheets, such as the *Volunteer*, *Saoirse*, the *Ardoyne Freedom Fighters*, the *Tattler*, and the *Barricades Bulletin* (Falls) appeared in several areas.[15] These unsophisticated prints had no compunction about distributing ferocious drawings of 'touts' being kneecapped as a warning to their particular districts.[16] The arguments of the increasingly well-produced *An Phoblacht* and *Republican News* became sufficiently refined to attract several well-known Irish writers, such as Desmond Fennell, who shared some, though not all, of their philosophy. Controversy between the priorities of the Dublin-based *An Phoblacht*, under a number of different editors,[17] and *Republican News* in Belfast was symptomatic of the growing dissatisfaction of Northern Ireland-based militants with the initial Dublin-based leadership.[18] On 3 February 1979 the two papers were merged under the able Northern editor since 1975, Danny Morrison. In October 1982, Morrison handed over to Mick Timothy, the paper's southern correspondent, and became Sinn Féin Director of Publicity. On Timothy's death in January 1985 Rita O'Hare, an *An Phoblacht* journalist since her release in 1979 from three years' imprisonment in Limerick, took over. She had initially jumped bail in Belfast and the Irish courts had then refused to extradite her to Northern Ireland.[19] In 1990 O'Hare followed the arrested Morrison as Sinn Féin Director of Publicity, being herself succeeded as editor of *An Phoblacht* by Micheál Mac Donncha.[20] Numerous occasional pamphlets and other publications appeared, some for overseas consumption such as NORAID's *The Irish People*, New York, published after 1972.[21] According to Robert Bell, the Provisionals' bi-annual *Iris—the Republican Magazine* (first issue 1981) is 'the most sophisticated of the Irish propagandist magazines'. *Iris* was produced as an analytical journal with a special eye for visitors or overseas enquirers, for whom a sheaf of *An Phoblacht* backnumbers was inconvenient.[22]

Though soon ousted by the Provisionals as a significant force in Northern Ireland, the Officials continued to emulate, if not excel, their rivals in the proliferation of newspapers and pamphlets. This publication facility suggested that the Official IRA, declining after its indefinite ceasefire of 1972 and supposedly defunct in the 1980s, remained an essential source of illegal funds for the Workers' Party (WP), splitting the latter in 1992.[23] In 1980 the Officials' *United*

Irishman, evoking the name of Arthur Griffith's original Sinn Féin paper of 1899, was replaced by the *Northern People*, the *Irish People* catering since 1972 for the Officials' supporters in the Irish Republic. Sinn Féin was dropped from the title of the 'Workers' Party', which became fully constitutional, if ostensibly Marxist, in its objectives. Ironically, it was now, apart from its socialism, in many ways closer to Arthur Griffith's original non-violent Sinn Féin[24] than its Provisional rivals who continued to use the old nomenclature. Like the Provisionals, the Officials were supported by overseas journals. They also maintained 'theoretical' outlets, such as *Teoric* and *Workers Life* (after 1980), for longer articles. The 1970 editor of the *United Irishman*, Seamus O'Tuathail, was replaced after his internment in August 1971 by Eoin O'Murchú, who subsequently joined the Communist Party of Ireland (CPI).[25] A former psychology lecturer, Des O'Hagan, was apparently deposed as editor in 1977.[26] O'Hagan, however, remained a leading spokesman for the WP.

The WP, gathering a handful of seats in the Irish Dail as a more radical alternative to the lack-lustre Irish Labour Party, polled only feebly in Northern Ireland. It had numerous rivals on the left in the Six Counties. The IRSP, breaking from the Officials in 1974, established the inevitable news-sheets, *Saoirse* (after 1980) in Belfast and *The Starry Plough* in Dublin. Published infrequently, they were pallid reflections of *An Phoblacht* with INLA 'war news' and general articles. The pretensions of the organisation to a deeper socialist analysis than that of the Provisionals is belied by the *Starry Plough*. The Communist Party published from Dublin the *Irish Socialist* and from Belfast *Unity—For Working-Class Unity, Peace and Socialism*; it shares James Connolly with the Provisionals and advocates a united Ireland. The *Voice of Revolution: Marxist-Leninist weekly* from Dublin, which initially took the pro-Beijing line of the CPI (Marxist-Leninist), also appropriated Connolly. Furthermore, the unionist British and Irish Communist Organisation (BICO) produced a steady stream of papers and pamphlets from its headquarters in Athol Street, Belfast. Masterminded eventually by Brendan Clifford and the historian Dr Peter Brooke, author of the controversial history of the Irish Presbyterian Church,[27] BICO published the *Irish Communist* (1965), the *Communist* (containing articles on extra-Irish affairs, 1967) and the cyclostyled *Workers Weekly* (1972), plus a galaxy of cheaply produced pamphlets and reprints goading Irish nationalists by suggesting 'two nations' attitudes in the writings of a republican hero like Wolfe Tone and the nationalist poet Thomas

Moore.[28] BICO has recently been associated with the full integrationist unionists, working for the establishment of British political parties in Ireland. Communism, in the light of such activities, has been placed firmly on the back burner. BICO, seen by Robert Bell as less critical of the Protestant paramilitaries, is totally opposed to the Ulster devolutionist or 'Independent Ulster' line of the UDA.

The largest of the Protestant paramilitary groups, the UDA, and its smaller rivals, made full use of crude cyclostyled news-sheets. According to John Darby, these were, despite extremely poor production, 'if anything more numerous than the republican ones'.[29] In October 1971 the UDA brought out its raw weekly, the *UDA News*.[30] The more professional *Ulster Loyalist* between 1973 and 1977 was in turn replaced by the glossier monthly, *Ulster*, one of the most important papers of the Ulster Troubles.[31] Sam A. Duddy, editor of the *Ulster Loyalist*,[32] subsequently edited *Ulster*. The rival UVF, a smaller organisation but apparently more popular with graffiti writers in loyalist areas, produced its *Combat* in 1974, in the wake the effective loyalist challenge to British-inspired power-sharing. To Bob Purdie, quoted in the *Republican News*, 'Most loyalist newspapers are shoddy little rags, full of crude bigotry, and hollow braggadocio; *Combat*, in contrast, is well produced and *written with intelligence.*' However, there is evidence that readers found it 'too deep or hard to understand.'[33] There were various short-term or pseudonymous editors, while Billy Mitchell, alias 'Richard Cameron', was held responsible by opponents who talked of 'Billy's fortnightly liar.'[34] Earlier, the eccentric loyalist John McKeague produced, from 1970 to 1977, the *Loyalist News*.[35] McKeague's style is epitomised in his celebrated lines in a loyalist songbook for which he was unsuccessfully prosecuted:

> You've never seen a better Taig
> Than with a bullet in his back.

Although the *Loyalist News* originally purveyed an anti-Catholicism as vigorous as that of the *Protestant Telegraph*, and though his Red Hand Commandos claimed responsibility for 'several vicious sectarian murders',[36] McKeague subsequently softened his approach[37] and became a friend of the radical priest, Fr Desmond Wilson of Ballymurphy. Wilson made him one of the heroes of his ecumenical novel, *The Demonstration* (1982). According to the *Republican News*, the *Loyalist News* began to lose readers because of too many meetings with Provos and not enough hatred in the journal.[38] Wilson himself wrote a regular column for the strongly republican *Andersonstown News*[39] in which he denounced British militarism and the insensitivities of the Catholic hierarchy. Another surprising friend of Fr Wilson's was the maverick Sammy Smyth, assassinated in 1976,[40] several years before his counterpart, John McKeague, was shot in 1982. Smyth, also partly alienated from the UDA, published his own *Ulster Militant*, 1972-3, in which he declared that 'if you want a Protestant Ulster then you are going to have to put the R.C.s out of it.'[41] The somewhat less overtly political *Shankill Bulletin* was the regional equivalent to the *Andersonstown News*.

The 'mosquito' loyalist press used crude cartoons and rough verse in its anti-republican and anti-Catholic polemic. Paisley's publications sometimes adopted similar denigration of unionist opponents.[42] John Darby regards 'RAB' McCullough, a Shankill building site labourer, contributing to the *Loyalist News*, as the 'only significant loyalist cartoonist',[43] and comparable with the more sophisticated Oisin of the *Andersonstown News* and Cormac of *An Phoblacht*. The republican and loyalist cartoons reinforce the common view that republicans emphasise political differences, while loyalists concentrate on religion. Loyalist cartoonists stress confessional malpractice, priestly denunciation of birth control and the hypocrisy of celibacy. Crude draftsmanship and crude diction were essential to the message purveyed. The frequency of sexual innuendo supports American historian Richard Hofstadter's belief that 'anti-Catholicism is the pornography of the Puritan'.[44] On the republican side, despite occasional sexual innuendo, religious attacks on Protestantism are rare.[45] Paisley is a favourite subject for cartoonists like Oisin, but Protestantism as such is rarely lampooned. Kormski's 'Dog Collars', one of the few cartoons ridiculing clerics indiscriminately, appeared from late 1982 to early 1986 in the academically oriented *Fortnight*,[46] which strives to maintain impartiality.

In addition to the journals representing paramilitary organisations, republican and loyalist, the British security forces have also had their papers, such as the *Constabulary Gazette*, *Police Beat* and *Visor*. The first two are fairly unremarkable police journals, which do, however, carry some articles on wider aspects of the Troubles. *Visor*, published for British soldiers, attempted to raise morale with pin-ups, thus exciting the ridicule of their opponents. In 1982 it attracted the attention of the Equal Opportunities Commission for its use of naked women.[47] Cartoons and articles were directed mainly against republicans but sometimes also against loyalist militants. According to the *Andersonstown News*, *Visor* was 'the Brits' equivalent of *Loyalist News*.'[48]

On the constitutional or non-violent side there are a number of publications, but none, with the exception of Paisley's, of much account in the struggle. Significantly, the parties obtaining majority support in the unionist and nationalist communities, the OUP and the SDLP, have not placed much emphasis on regular propagandist journals either at home or abroad. To some extent this is because they are serviced by the major dailies, the Belfast, subsequently *Ulster News Letter* and the *Irish News* respectively. The SDLP made a marginally greater effort than the Official Unionists to maintain papers. The latter, in the initial issue of the *Unionist Clarion* in March 1976, admitted that it was not the first paper published by the Ulster Unionist Party, but that other attempts had failed through lack of interest. It likewise disappeared after its third issue.[49] To a certain extent, the *Orange Standard*, established in 1982, with articles by leaders such as the Orange Grand Master and Official Unionist MP after 1982, the Rev. Martin Smyth, represents respectable unionism. Like the Official Unionists, the SDLP admitted that it found distribution a problem militating against its early papers. Nevertheless, the SDLP brought out a modest *SDLP News* on 5 October 1972. In the following year it produced the more ambitious *Social Democrat*, which ran intermittently until 1984 before being replaced in 1986 by the *SDLP Newsline*. According to *An Phoblacht*, its rival's sporadic productions collapsed for want of buyers and sellers. The SDLP itself had admitted distribution problems.[50] Unlike the paramilitaries, the SDLP is at a disadvantage in having to raise money by legal means.[51] It endeavoured to repudiate both republican and loyalist extremists and all violence, while giving attention to social reform. However, its message that the Provisional struggle in Northern Ireland was not a war of national liberation[52] was more difficult to sell to enthusiasts at home and abroad than Provisional guerrilla actions. In countries like Australia and New Zealand, where the Provisionals actively propagate their views and periodicals, the SDLP is virtually unknown. The moderate unionist Alliance Party, despite the recent seepage of its votes,[53] has been more consistent than the OUP, DUP or SDLP in maintaining a regular paper, *Alliance*, since 1971. Its design and layout, however, as Robert Bell suggests, 'is a little dull', while its non-denominational membership renders topical its articles on subjects like integrated education.[54]

Smaller, more short-lived groups and their papers came and went. Closely associated with Craig's Ulster Vanguard was the UDA and a new body, led by Billy Hull and Hugh Petrie, the Loyalist Association of Workers (LAW). LAW petered out in 1973, merging with Craig and others, into the UWC whose strike in May 1974 ended the power-sharing experiment. The Loyalist Association of Workers published its journal *Law* in 1972-3, emphasising traditional Protestant and unionist demands rather than those of labour. The Vanguard Unionist Party published a few issues of *The United Ulsterman* in 1972 and 1973 and a brief *Vanguard Bulletin* in 1976 before Craig in the following year shocked his former allies by proposing what was virtually the power-sharing with the SDLP which he had resisted so strongly in 1974.

The Peace People maintained a regular paper, *Peace by Peace*. Resisting the second, unsuccessful, loyalist strike of 1977 *Peace by Peace* developed Ciaran McKeown's philosophy of non-violence based on the Sermon on the Mount, Mahatma Gandhi, Martin Luther King and Helder Camara.[55] The hope of a sympathiser that *Peace by Peace* might eventually replace the hopelessly sectarian *Irish News* and *Belfast News Letter* indicates the unrealistic expectations harboured by some for the Peace People.[56]

Circulation

What is the specific influence of these numerous papers? Do they really represent significant Northern Ireland opinion or can they be dismissed as the products of idealists or fanatics, totally ignored by the ordinary citizen? Unfortunately, as Dervla Murphy has pointed out, in Northern Ireland 'extremists are just that—extreme representatives of their respective communities. They are not another sort of human being.'[57] Circulation of the mosquito press is not a complete indication of influence. The outlets for distribution are different. Few bookshops or newsagents in Central Belfast publicly display *An Phoblacht*, *Combat* or *Ulster*. Many are sold by mail subscription, outside Catholic churches and Gaelic Athletic Association fixtures. Less orthodox means include pairs of newsboys (one selling, one keeping watch) in Belfast or republican criers on the steps of the General Post Office, Dublin (headquarters of the the 1916 Easter Week Rising). Loyalist purveyors accompany Orange parades, such as twelfth of July marches. The UDA's *Ulster* persistently advertised for distributors, often young boys. The agents of paramilitary groups are not anxious to open their circulation books to outside observers. When the organisations boast a high circulation for their journals, detailed statistics cannot be checked. As the main Catholic-nationalist daily, the *Irish News*, with 1989 sales of 42,439, and an estimated readership of 150,000, provides a rough yardstick for judging the assertions of the paramilitary press. Circulation, or readership, can be assumed to be about 3.5 times sales.[58]

The Provisional *Volunteer* maintained in 1970 that it had sold 2,500 copies, some abroad. In the following year its stablemate, the *Tattler*, claimed 8,000.[59] *An Phoblacht* asserted that it had a circulation of 20,000 in the Irish Republic on its inception in 1970. Its partner, *Republican News*, catered for the Six Counties with an initial run of 15,000. By 1973, *An Phoblacht* assessed a rise to 40,000 copies. In 1977 it claimed 63,000. *Republican News*, not to be outdone, asserted a readership of 60,000.[60] As circulation figures, rather than hard sales, these become more probable. However, in 1978 the *Republican News* was harassed by the authorities, who once confiscated 30,000 actual copies.[61] The paper acknowledged a decline to 16,000, with 3,000 abroad.[62] The united *An Phoblacht/Republican News*, printed in Dublin and stimulated by the hunger strikes of 1981, would, on its own figures, appear capable of increasing its circulation to 60,000 or 70,000 copies. Even 20,000 hard sales, reinforced by numerous free propaganda copies, would seem a high figure. The *Belfast Telegraph*, Northern Ireland's highest circulation daily, which sometimes achieved a readership of 59 per cent of the population, varied in sales between 219,874 in 1967 to 144,237 in 1986.[63] The latter result was symptomatic of the predicament of all Northern Ireland dailies, facing competition from television and British tabloids.[64] Moreover, in elections from 1982 and 1987, Provisional Sinn Féin polled between 65,000 and 102,000 votes, something more than one-third of the nationalist community which Frank Burton's study attributed to them in 1976.[65] Significantly, Peter O'Rourke, presenting the history of *An Phoblacht* and the *Republican News* in 1988 and 1990, did not specifically insist on circulation greater than 40,000 for the former and 30,000 for the latter in the 1970s. The *Andersonstown News*, a weekly with Provisional sympathies, also claimed 40,000 readers. In the United States, NORAID estimated a circulation of 10,000 for its *Irish People*.[66] O'Rourke was reticent on the details of his assertion that *An Phoblacht/Republican News* has the highest circulation in Ireland. Indeed, *An Phoblacht* may have suffered a decline proportionate to its electoral failure to obtain more than a 1.85 per cent vote in the Irish Republic and reduction to 10 per cent in the Six Counties.[67]

Political weeklies must surely share the general decline in newspaper readership. There were, however, few other outlets for Provisional propaganda; the *Irish News*, for example, refused in 1973 to publish Provisional communiques.[68] Thus the paramilitary papers were vital for influencing its voters, though not all electors necessarily read them at first hand. On the other side, *Ulster*, of the UDA, whose political fronts attracted few voters, asserted 13,000 copies in 1981 and in 1989 claimed a readership of 32,000, in more than twenty countries.[69] Paisley's *Protestant Telegraph* more moderately calculated a 7,000 circulation in 1981. McKeague's *Loyalist News*, said to be the most popular ultra-Protestant paper, was estimated at 10,000 copies. *Combat* in its earlier years advertised an incredible rise in circulation from 4,000 to 65,000.[70] The decline of the unionist *News Letter* to 44,483 in 1989 suggests caution. As the paramilitaries depended on sources of funds other than subscribers and advertisers, they could afford to give many copies away. Sinn Féin sympathisers, being more insulated from the British media, may have preserved a higher rate of nationalist newspaper readership.

Trials and tribulations

Circulation was always affected by the harassment of the paper's staff. As strong measures were often taken by the British and Irish Governments against Provisional and extreme Protestant publicity in the media, the ability of prohibited organisations to publish their papers is surprising. There was, however, a long tradition of underground publication in Ireland. The secret insurrectionary Fenian Brotherhood in the 1860s had put out their *Irish People* for a few years in the very shadow of Dublin Castle, the nerve centre of British administration in Ireland, while the bloodshed of the Anglo-Irish War had not checked the proliferation of Sinn Féin prints. Mosquito editors and their staff learned to survive every discouragement from the security forces. The device of an open, constitutional organisation, supportive of, but in theory distanced from, the guerrillas, was adopted by both loyalists and republicans. The republicans had persistently used Sinn Féin, originally a non-violent organisation, as the public mouthpiece of the IRA. The authorities oscillated between banning, legalising and partially silencing these supportive organisations. The papers emanating from them were often ambiguous. *An Phoblacht's* 'War News' of

PIRA assassinations and bombings, eerily contrasting with the increasingly sophisticated left-radical tone of the remainder of the paper, was paralleled not only by the IRSP *Starry Plough*, but by *Combat* and *Ulster*. These papers all emphasised the 'boys behind the wire'. While the *Starry Plough* followed *An Phoblacht's* format of opening with 'war news', and sometimes providing a front page photograph of a spectacular or horrific action, the loyalists by the 1980s grew more reticent, allowing the deeds of the UFF[71] and Protestant Action Force (PAF), the UVF equivalent, to follow, or be interspersed with, articles on a common Ulster cultural identity, and even the Gaelic language, themes difficult to reconcile with the realities of sectarian assassination. In the early 1970s periodicals such as the *Loyalist News*, the *Ulster Loyalist* and the *Ulster Militant* were less cautious in suggesting the need to eliminate not only large numbers of Catholics but many of their loyalist rivals. No details were spared of brutal murders by opponents on the other side of the sectarian divide, while each periodical strove to invest its paramilitaries with the most chivalrous and respectable intentions. Thus *Combat* talked of the issue being decided by a well-trained loyalist infantry, a far cry from the bestialities of the UVF-related 'Shankill Butchers',[72] while *An Phoblacht* depicted neatly uniformed PIRA men (and sometimes women) posing with Armalite rifles or sophisticated rocket launchers. Though Paisley's *Protestant Telegraph* avoided direct military representations, except in the days of the Third Force, 1981-2, the depiction of the opposition excited the most violent associations. Catholic priests, for example, were drawn in cartoons as thugs with guns. The mutually antagonistic stereotypes, which so concern educationalists and sociologists, are a stock-in-trade of these papers.

The security forces made some effort to prevent the effective dissemination of such publications. Until recently the loyalists have either experienced less harassment, or been less outspoken about it. Paisley claimed publicly in 1969 that the British Government had a plan for certifying him as insane, and in 1973 threatened that revealing documents would be released on his assassination by British forces, whom he alleged were being flown in from Germany to eliminate loyalist leaders.[73] No raids by the security forces on the Puritan Printing Press are recorded. As Paisley's support grew in the Protestant community, such actions would have been spectacularly counterproductive. The UDA headquarters, as in 1982, 1988, and 1989, were sometimes disrupted by raids for arms or other material,[74] but the attempt to pin terrorist charges on the leaders at first failed to stick, like those against the Sinn Féin publicists. Both UDA and UVF were included in the exceptionally stringent British broadcasting ban of October 1988. The UDA itself was outlawed only on 10 August 1992, following persistent demands from constitutional nationalists. In 1989, however, the UDA *Ulster* complained that two Special Branch raids in close proximity followed the pattern of harassment of loyalist printing which had developed early in the Ulster Troubles. *Ulster* insisted that the real object of the raids, which had included the arrest of the editor, was not to check terrorism but to disrupt a paper which was increasing its circulation and influence. Typically, the UDA organ complained that the security forces did nothing to inhibit the printers of *An Phoblacht*, then produced in Armagh.[75] The UDA leader, Tommy Lyttle, was arrested and charged with intimidation in 1990.[76] In 1992, the year of the formal ban on the UDA, a number of supportive newspapers sprang up, such as the *Freedom Fighter*, the *Loyalist* and the *Warrior*. The latter told of a destructive raid by the security forces on the Macosquin headquarters of the UDA front, the Ulster Democratic Party.[77]

Despite such incidents on the loyalist side republican papers suffered more. Seamus O'Tuathail, editor of the Officials' *United Irishman*, was lifted, possibly by accident, in the internment swoop on 9 August 1971.[78] The Officials ceased to be a threat to the government following their indefinite ceasefire of 1972, but the Provisional papers were subjected to intense police attention in both North and South. Internment caused the arrest of several members of *Republican News's* editorial board but considerably increased the paper's popularity and enabled it to be published weekly, instead of monthly. In 1974 Labour's Secretary of State, Merlyn Rees, lifted the ban on Provisional Sinn Féin to confirm his view in opposition, 'that those who supported the so-called political aims of the paramilitary groups should have freedom of expression and the opportunity to work through political channels.'[79] The *Republican News* editor, Sean McCaughey, in the same year established the enlarged paper in its first permanent office at 170 Falls Road and adopted a professional format. Further improvement of the paper under Danny Morrison after 1975 and the advent of the tougher Roy Mason as Secretary of State led to government action against it. While some of the earlier republican prints were so crude as to suggest their fabrication by the security forces as anti-Provisional propaganda, a well-produced and sophisticated newspaper could do much to dispel the 'mad bomber' image of the organisation. According to Morrison, Mason could have banned the paper under emergency legislation, but feared a comparison with South Africa and inconsistency with its criminalisation policy which refused recognition to political offences.[80] Raids on the *Republican News* office began on 15 December 1977 and continued till 27 April 1978, after which the paper was forced underground in different Belfast houses with a reduction in size from twelve to four pages. Morrison himself was arrested in September 1978 but released some weeks later, the charges of IRA membership having then failed to stick. Continuity of publication was maintained, but the harassment was an important factor in the amalgamation of *An Phoblacht* and *Republican News* in early 1979 and its publication from Dublin with Morrison as editor of the joint production. Like the UDA later, Morrison rejected Mason's claim that the sole object of the arrests and surveillance had been to seize IRA members. On the contrary, Morrison saw it as an attack on the paper itself, citing the destruction and confiscation of newspaper property, the timing of raids to coincide with days of going to press, interference with distributors, and the cutting of telex lines.[81] This bungled prosecution, according to Morrison, 'strengthened our position to such an extent that when the charges were dropped, we were all able to "go public."'[82] Previously the distinction between Sinn Féin and the IRA was something of a legal fiction; now the way was cleared for Sinn Féin to function as an open political party. Morrison, however, was arrested again in September 1979 and, after relinquishing the editorship, in 1990, again on a charge of IRA membership.[83] On the latter occasion Morrison was convicted.

Production of the paper in Dublin was not without its parallel hazards. Even before Morrison's tribulations, Eamonn Mac Thomais, editor of *An Phoblacht*, had been arrested by the Garda Special Branch and sentenced by a court under the Republic's emergency legislation to fifteen months imprisonment for PIRA membership, and the same term again shortly after his release in 1974.[84] With the amalgamation of *An Phoblacht* and *Republican News* in 1979 the production of the paper was first moved to Lurgan and, following further police raids, to Dublin.[85]

Close links between the IRA and Sinn Féin could always justify raids, but, as the *Irish Times* reporter David McKittrick pointed out, the Northern Ireland Secretary of State 'appears to take exception to the existence of a fairly well-produced Provisional Republican weekly newspaper.'[86] Without some regular and effective organ of opinion, the Provisional Armalite and ballot-box strategy laid down by Morrison would have been severely inhibited. The very efforts of the British and Irish governments to prevent the expression of the Provisional viewpoint prove this proposition.

Development of the major papers through the Ulster Troubles

By 1990 most of the main newspapers spawned by the Ulster Troubles had approximately twenty years of experience and development. The most notable were the Provisional *An Phoblacht*, the UDA's *Ulster* and Paisley's (or the DUP's) *Protestant Telegraph*. Other papers came and went, were absorbed into the major organs, or marginalised with their supportive organisations. The mainstream constitutional unionists and nationalists continued to be served by the major dailies, the Belfast *News Letter* and the *Irish News*. Paisley's DUP proved a special case. As a constitutional unionist party it received publicity in the *News Letter*, but Paisley's rhetorical violence and association with quasi-paramilitaries like the Ulster Protestant Volunteers at the start of the Troubles and the Third Force in the early 1980s, place him closer to the UDA and UVF.

The *Protestant Telegraph* in its various manifestations is of primary importance in an understanding of the Troubles. It differed in some notable ways from *An Phoblacht* and *Ulster*. The Provisional and UDA periodicals experienced many changes of policy and editors in twenty years. The *Protestant Telegraph* was, according to Boulton, the brainchild of Noel Doherty, a printer and Free Presbyterian who proved invaluable to Paisley in establishing the Puritan Printing Press, near Paisley's church on the Ravenhill Road, Belfast. Doherty in 1966 was also a link between Paisley's UPV and the UVF, but Paisley broke off relations when the UVF was outlawed. Doherty was later gaoled on explosives charges.[87] The *Protestant Telegraph*, always very much the mouthpiece of Ian Paisley, was remarkably constant in policy. Paisley's slow metamorphosis from the fanatical outsider to the most popular individual unionist leader was not reflected in any softening of his nineteenth-century anti-Romanism. The 1987 exposition by the *Protestant Blu Print*, edited by Paisley's daughter Cherith, of St Alphonsus Ligouri's position on oral sex is of a piece with the 1966 *Protestant Telegraph*'s depiction of Catholic confessionals as 'sin boxes leading to greater villainies between confessors and penitents.'[88] Ironically, the exposure in the 1990s of a number of sexual scandals and child abuse cases in the international Catholic Church have fuelled Paisley's long-term preoccupation. Paisley's paper could scarcely omit to mention Andrew Greeley's estimate of

100,000 young victims of priestly sex abuse, or similar problems in Canada. It gleefully advertised yet another edition of Maria Monks' *Awful Disclosures* of Montreal convent unchastity and murder in the 1830s. In the wake of Bishop Eamon Casey of Galway's admission of paternity in 1992, the *New Protestant Telegraph* revelled in a study showing that only 50 per cent of American priests practised celibacy.[89] Loyalists could hardly afford to throw stones after the sentence of William McGrath, once a preacher in Paisley's church, for raping the Kincora boys. But even the UDA's *Ulster*, which paraded its desire for an independent, non-sectarian Ulster, also wallowed one-sidedly in Catholic clerical unchastity.[90] Paisley's more secular lieutenant, Peter Robinson, persuaded him to replace the aggressively sectarian *Protestant Telegraph* with the more political, though short-lived, *Voice of Ulster*.[91]

The relatively haphazard publication record of Paisley's papers and those of the Protestant paramilitaries, with the partial exceptions of the UDA and UVF, contrasts with the efficiency of Provisional printing. *An Phoblacht, Ulster* and *Combat* have remained in continuous publication since the early 1970s, constantly upgrading their format, while the *Protestant Telegraph*, after being replaced briefly by the *Voice of Ulster*, regressed to the crudely cyclostyled *Protestant Blu Print*, 1985-88, before being continued by the *New Protestant Telegraph*. In reality the Paisley papers fulfilled a very different function from those of the paramilitaries. While the latter found orthodox publicity difficult to obtain, Paisley had innumerable channels for projecting his message: the proliferating Free Presbyterian churches, the European Parliament, Westminster and the various Stormont Assemblies, not to mention the media. His papers were not required to present a liberal image to the general public, but rather to keep his old fundamentalist constituency on its anti-Catholic toes. Like the paramilitaries, there were some concessions to modern progressive thought.[92] The *New Protestant Telegraph* and DUP campaigned on environmental issues, demanding the closure of Sellafield, more recycling, the end of flouridation. There were policies on equal pay for women and childcare relief. In 1993 women's issues topped the DUP conference agenda and Paisley's daughter Rhonda was appointed spokesperson for DUP women's issues. Even animal welfare was included.[93] Paisley's paper and the DUP, like Sinn Féin, opposed economic rationalism and welfare cuts. As Paisley said in parliament, 'closures and cutbacks to save money are not the answer to our social and economic ills.'[94]

Though rifts, problems with the security forces and internecine rivalries hampered them far more than they did Paisley's paternalistic editorial regime, republican and loyalist papers preserved more effective continuity. While the Provisionals provided full details of editors, and even internal disputes, the loyalists were more reticent, making more frequent use of pseudonyms. Their progress, however, was very similar in developing from three or four rough or cyclostyled sheets in the early 1970s to glossy monthlies or sixteen page two-toned prints in the 1990s.

The Provisionals began with the twins, *An Phoblacht* in Dublin and *Republican News* in Belfast. The former, edited for its first two years by Sean O'Brádaigh, brother of the Provisional Sinn Féin president (1970-83) Ruairí, was very much the mouthpiece of the Dublin-based leadership who dominated the movement till the late 1970s. Ruairí O'Brádaigh wrote the Eire Nua constitution which, with its federal structure allowing Protestant predominance in the North, became unpopular with Provisionals in the war zone. For a start, however, the division was not apparent. Jimmy Steele, who established the *Republican News* in mid-1970, was a traditionalist republican and celebrated gaol escapee of the 1940s. Steele played a leading role in the split with what became the Official IRA and established a conventional paper with a 'florid, romantic' style, very strong on claims for Provisional historical legitimacy.[95] A succession of short-term editors followed his early death. The last of these, Sean McCaughey (1974-5) was a supporter of Eire Nua and happy to identify with the Dublin leadership.[96] In 1975 a younger group, led by Danny Morrison (recently released from internment) and Tom Hartley ousted McCaughey. With Morrison as editor, Tom Hartley as manager and Gerry Adams contributing (originally from Long Kesh), *Republican News* was soon at loggerheads with *An Phoblacht*. The young northerners disliked the eighteen-month ceasefire imposed by Dublin and Eire Nua. They wished to develop a more socialistic and pragmatic policy, which led in 1982 to the contest of elections by Sinn Féin in the north and the abandonment of Eire Nua, in 1983 to Gerry Adams's replacement of O'Brádaigh as president of Sinn Féin, and in 1986 to the dropping of the policy of abstention from the Dail in the south and the resultant secession of O'Brádaigh and his supporters. As editor, Morrison, despite his lack of an IRA military background, greatly improved the quality and professionalism of *Republican News*, demonstrating a journalistic flair comparable to that of Arthur Griffith in the early years of the century. His appointment as editor of the combined *An Phoblacht/Republican News* (1979-82), was due partly to British harassment in Belfast, partly to the changing power balance between north and south, but also to his ability as a propagandist. With Gerry Adams and Martin McGuinness, Morrison, even in gaol, is one of the big three in the Provisional movement in the 1990s.

The editorship of Morrison and his successors saw important changes. The conservative green nationalism which had originally ridiculed the Marxism and interests abroad of the Officials became weekly more progressive.[97] Much space was now devoted to the overseas causes which attracted world liberal opinion: South Africa, Nicaragua, Chile and others. As Morrison said, 'I certainly don't think the republican movement has ever been insular: our thinking has always involved the lessons of other countries.'[98] Multinationals were attacked and a generally non-Marxist socialism purveyed. Many articles would not have been out of place in the *New Statesman*. As a sign of the times, the amalgamated *An Phoblacht/Republican News* dropped *An Phoblacht's* exclusive dating by Irish months. An Irish page continued, and was sometimes reinforced with Irish lessons, somewhat simplistic for readers who had studied Gaelic in the Irish Republic or in Catholic schools in the North. Nevertheless, Deasún Breathnach, the last editor of the unamalgamated *An Phoblacht*, gave up reading the new paper 'when the amount of matter published in the Irish language became a mere trickle.' It was, he considered, assisting the English 'by suppressing the Irish language' and assimilating its readers to Anglo-American culture.[99] The appointment of Rita O'Hare as editor after Mick Timothy (1982-5) was followed by an increase in the paper's size from twelve to sixteen pages and an improved coverage of social, political and economic issues in Ireland as a whole.[100] Such changes expressed the current emphasis on women's issues. Between 1985 and 1990, O'Hare certainly gave much space to rape centres, crêches and problems of female poverty, as well as the continued battle against the strip searching of women in Northern Ireland prisons. She herself was clear that 'unless women organize as women, they can't hope to make permanent gains.' O'Hare considered divorce, contraception and the discussion of abortion important.[101] Sinn Féin and *An Phoblacht* supported the Irish Republic's unsuccessful divorce referendum in 1986, but was more ambivalent on abortion and Catholic control of education. Though Danny Morrison personally opposed abortion,[102] and Gerry Adams admitted a reluctance to interfere with the Catholic Church's strong views on education,[103] *An*

Phoblacht's women writers did raise the possibility of dissent on such vital issues. Attacks on the Catholic bishops for their opposition to republican action formed a tradition dating back to the Fenians. The wheel had come a full circle from 1969, when the Provisionals split from the Officials on the ground that the latter had been distracted by side issues from pure republicanism. Only the grisly and persistent 'war news', and a smattering of Gaelic, provided proof of Provisional ideological purity.

The loyalist paramilitary periodicals are less easy to document in full. The UDA, originally beset by vicious internal vendettas, achieved relative stability under Andy Tyrie's leadership (1973-1988). This was reflected in its papers. A crude cyclostyled *UDA News* appeared in October 1971, but this was superseded in March 1972 by an *Official UDA News*, advertised as the first authorised paper of the movement, under the direct control of its officials. While the earlier paper had toyed with the symbolism of ancient Gaelic culture, the 'official' replacement was more orthodox in its sectarianism. In August 1973 a new UDA paper, the *Ulster Loyalist*, of which Sam Duddy, previously a press officer for the UDA, was later cited as editor, announced that the organisation had a completely new organisational structure in which the supreme commander (Andy Tyrie) would control all aspects of the organisation.[104] The *Ulster Loyalist* was available to back the 1974 strike against Brian Faulkner's power-sharing executive, or 'appointed government' as the paper called it.[105] On 18 March the smaller, but even more aggressive UVF, now legalised by Rees, produced its *Combat*, edited by Billy Mitchell, or 'Richard Cameron'. Like the earlier *UDA News*, *Combat*, in the period of loyalist disillusionment with the British Government over power-sharing, flirted with Gaelic culture. 'Cameron', apparently known as 'a head case', was an eccentric supporter of the National Front, virulent anti-Catholicism, Northern Ireland Labour Party (NILP) labourism and practical terrorism.[106] The *Ulster Loyalist* now temporarily dropped its interest in Gaelic identity and denied that Northern Protestants were Irish.[107] In the next two years the *Ulster Loyalist* and *Combat* reflected the bitter strife of their respective organisations. The UDA denounced the UVF's meetings with OIRA, partly inspired by the UVF imprisoned hero, Gusty Spence. *Combat*, or 'Billy's Fortnightly Liar', attacked the 1974 UDA mission to Gaddafi's Libya, its racketeering, and its 'romper room' assassinations with torture. In reply an *Ulster Loyalist* poet summed up the UVF in a verse:

So run and hide, you yellow swine
You can't escape this wrath of mine
I'll watch you squirm, and plead and dance
For you there is no second chance.

The UDA's *Ulster Loyalist* left the liquidation of its rival, the UVF *Combat* editor Billy Mitchell, to disillusioned UVF members. This was despite a death threat from the UVF to Duddy, the *Ulster Loyalist* editor, and the belief that Mitchell had 'grassed' to the security forces about the UDA.[108] Mitchell, who had originally worked for Paisley as a Free Presbyterian Sunday School teacher, became a notorious gunman, eventually sentenced to life imprisonment for the murder of two UDA members. He continued to write (as 'Richard Cameron') from his prison cell for *Combat* into the 1980s.[109] Both groups claimed that their rival was infiltrated by communists, but the few left-wingers in the two organisations were soon neutralised. By 1987 the UDA and UVF held joint ceremonies.[110]

In October 1975 Rees again proscribed the UVF and a series of UVF arrests and convictions followed. A senior UVF officer admitted in *Combat* in 1977 that there was very little current UVF support.[111] The organisation continued its assassinations in the 1980s, while *Combat*, for a time, grew glossier. Interest in Irish culture continued[112] *pari passu* with the killing of Catholics. More significant was the development of the UDA's political initiatives.

In 1978, the *Ulster Loyalist* was replaced by *Ulster*, of which 'Big Jim' Donaghy followed Duddy as editor. The paper, now a glossy monthly, became a vehicle of the historical opinions of Dr Ian Adamson. Some of his ideas, discussed in the next chapter, formed a basis for the 'Independent Ulster' proposals of the UDA's offshoot, the New Ulster Political Research Group (NUPRG) which advocated a non-sectarian Ulster loyalty. In 1987 the UDA's pamphlet *Common Sense* went as far as to suggest a variant of the power-sharing which the movement had taken so much pride in destroying in 1974. *Ulster* in the late 1980s exhibited changes akin to those of *An Phoblacht*. There were, for example, some articles on women's issues and the rejection of the crude religious bigotry of Protestants in the past. The columns advertising UFF killings were, like *An Phoblacht's* 'war news', in stark contrast to this modernism and made Catholics unwilling to take it seriously. This fact was underlined by the blowing up of John McMichael, architect of much UDA new thinking, in December 1987. PIRA's Belfast Brigade claimed to have executed McMichael as the Commander of the

UFF who had organised many sectarian attacks, personally shot three Catholics and been responsible for burning many Catholics out of their homes. It implied that McMichael's role as politician opposing sectarianism was a cover for his terrorist activities.[113] To the UDA's *Ulster*, with the paper and organisation as a whole under new management after the ousting of Tyrie in March 1988, McMichael became a martyred hero in song and story, like Bobby Sands with the Provisionals. It was suggested that he had been 'fingered' to the Provisionals by a traitorous UDA man who feared his investigation of racketeering.[114] After August 1992 the banned UDA adopted the role of the IRA with the Ulster Democratic Party acting as Sinn Féin. The latter had emerged from the ashes of McMichael's unsuccessful Ulster Loyalist Democratic Party, through the agency of Raymond Smallwood. Its policy was McMichael's *Common Sense*.[115] The Ulster Information Service, headed by David Adams of Lisburn, compiled and edited the *Loyalist*, ostensibly from the old Gawn Street headquarters. John McMichael's son Gary was also active in the party which now emphasised honest government and social and economic issues. Other UDA papers like the *Warrior* and *Freedom Fighter* emerged at this time. These papers continued the policies of *Ulster*. 'An Ulsterwoman's View' condemned the patriarchal attitudes of traditional loyalist parties and asserted that the UDP was different.[116] When the horrendous conflict in Bosnia relegated Northern Irish issues to newspaper back pages, it was used by the UDA to demonstrate that Protestants in border regions like South Armagh had long been victims of 'ethnic cleansing'. Needless to say, the Provisionals saw ethnic cleansing as the elimination of unpolitical Catholics by loyalist death squads.[117] Cuchulain, the hero of the Irish sagas, used to symbolise the 1916 Rising in Dublin and regularly depicted in Provisional journals, was portrayed by loyalists as a defender against attempted Irish ethnic cleansing in Ulster.[118] Paisley less obscurely attributed the decline in the Protestant population of the Irish Republic to insidious ethnic cleansing.[119] Meanwhile killings of Catholics continued and the *Loyalist* boasted of the 'ferocious assault' on the republican movement that had sent PIRA reeling back.[120]

Conclusion

Newspapers published by loyalist and republican militants are central to the conflict, enabling propaganda to be disseminated despite censorship of the electronic media. According to a spokesman for *Republican News* in 1978, the newspaper was the 'public face of Republicanism' and 'a most important vehicle. It is an opportunity to put our views across, to answer criticisms from either local groups or from the Brits.'[121] When Sinn Féin went political the value of the papers was greatly increased. The loyalist editors would have agreed with the *Republican News* assessment. There are certain divergences of purpose: Paisley, for example, tends to preach to hardened anti-Catholics, while the republican papers, deprived of many other publicity outlets, not only seek increased support in the Catholic community but endeavour to reach world liberal opinion. The UDA's *Ulster* and the UVF *Combat* oscillated between these positions, sometimes discarding and sometimes accentuating sectarian animosities. All these papers have experienced some difficulties with the security forces, but the Provisionals have suffered the most. There are many examples of convergence across the sectarian barriers. Apart from Paisley's prints, there has been an attempt on both sides to modernise, but this dovetails badly with the 'war news' columns and the suggestive descriptions and photographs of enemies which set them up for the hard men. Considerable scepticism must greet apparently constructive policies and suggestions when the links with violence are always apparent. Yet violence often seems essential to obtain a hearing for strongly supported political views. While this appears true the periodicals of the Ulster Troubles will remain as permanent institutions.

Notes

1.   Taber, Robert (1970), *The War of the Flea: A Study of Guerrilla Warfare, Theory and Practice*, London: Granada Paladin, 31. This was a popular work with the Provisionals whose RN, 13 July 1974, rated it 'excellent'. The book was long sold in the Sinn Féin bookshop on the Falls Road. *The Volunteer* (V), a Provisional journal, 1972, 50 and 52, deemed Taber 'compulsory reading', and maintained that 'the sole purpose of the Revolution was to arouse international public opinion and focus attention on the situation in Ireland.'

2.   Davis, R. (1977), The Advocacy of Passive Resistance in Ireland, 1916-1922', *Anglo-Irish Studies*, III: Chalfont St Giles: Alpha Academic, 35-55.

3.   Gray, John (1989), Linen Hall Librarian, introduction to *Northern Ireland Political Literature on Microfiche: Catalogue and Indexes: Phase 1—Periodicals 1966—1987*, Belfast: Linen Hall Library, i-ii.

4.   AP, 8 March 1990.

5.   The *News Letter*, after being owned for 250 years by the strongly unionist Henderson family, was saved by the Monopolies Commission

from takeover by the Thomson group which already controlled the *Belfast Telegraph*. The *News Letter* is now owned by a consortium of unionist businessmen. Editorial opinion is now less strident in its unionism than immediately after the Anglo-Irish Agreement of 1985, but sales are continually falling as the paper fails to compete with the English dailies.

6.   Oram, Hugh (1983), *The Newspaper Book: A History of Newspapers in Ireland*, 1649-1983, Dublin: MO Books, 87.

7.   I am indebted to Dr Eamon Phoenix, former Lecturer in History at St Mary's College, Belfast, for much of the information in this and the preceding footnote. See also RN, 23 August 1975 and 29 November 1975 for a similar complaint that the *Derry Journal* is the mouthpiece of Bishop Edward Daly. Bishop Daly himself considered the paper a good repository for his views. Interview with present writer 16 September 1982.

8.   See Bromley, Michael (1989), 'War of Words: The *Belfast Telegraph* and Loyalist Populism' in Alexander, Yonah and O'Day, Alan, *Ireland's Terrorist Trauma: Interdisciplinary Perspectives*, Hemel Hempstead: Harvester Wheatsheaf, 213-233.

9.   The *Republican News*, 15 June 1974, listed the papers accepted as republican by the Provisional movement: *The Northern Star* (200 years ago), *The Republic* (early 20th century), *An Siol* (1932-36), *War News* (1929-43), *An t-Oglach* (1940-44), *Republican News*, *Resurgent Ulster* (1951-55), *Gar Uladh* (1955-6), *Tir Gradh* (1963-5). Names were continually recycled.

10. Founded 1948, see AP, 4 February 1988.

11. See in general Bell, Robert (1985), 'Directory of N. Ireland Political Periodicals', *Fortnight*, Belfast, No. 229, 18 November,11-17.

12. Moloney, Ed and Pollack, Andy (1986), *Paisley*, Dublin: Poolbeg, 56. His church secretary, Bob Cleland, a printer, assisted.

13. RN, 24 January 1976. See also 8 February and 9 October 1976 for PD split, and 11 December 1976 for favourable review of Michael Farrell's *The Orange State*.

14. Started by the veteran republican Jimmy Steele, who died later in 1970, *Republican News* was then edited by Proinsias Mac Airt (1970-72), Leo Martin assisted by Henry Kane (1973-74) and Sean McCaughey (1974-75), before the coup by younger men in 1975 which installed Danny Morrison, recently released from internment, as editor. See Bishop and Mallie, *The Provisional IRA*, 145 and 285 and AP, 4 February 1988.

15. For list, see *Andersonstown News* (AN), 7 June 1975, which claimed that the *Volunteer*, in early 1970, was the first Provisional paper after the split. *An Phoblacht*, April 1972, recognised the *Tattler* and *Volunteer* as Provisional papers and in August 1972 welcomed the appearance of NORAID's *Irish People* as an auxiliary in the USA.

16. *Tattler*, No. 4, Vol. 2 [1972] for knee capping.

17. Seán O Brádaigh was succeeded in summer 1972 by Coleman Moynihan and in November by Eamonn Mac Thomáis (a Dublin historian). During the latter's imprisonment (July 1973-July 1974) the Dublin journalist Deasun Breathnach was editor. Mac Thomáis was

soon rearrested and Gerry Danaher (1974-75), Gerry O'Hare (1975-77) and Deasun Breathnach (1977-79) took over. See AP, 4 February 1988 and 1 February 1990.

18. See *Republican News* attack on *An Phoblacht* and latter's reply, *Republican News*, 3 and 31 July 1976. In general, the Northern 'hawks' considered the southern 'doves' too conciliatory towards the unionists.

19. *Belfast Telegraph* (BT), 28 April 1990.

20. AP, 4 February 1988 and 19 April 1990. According to *Ulster* (U) of the UDA, January 1987, there were rumours that O'Hare disagreed with Sinn Féin president, Gerry Adams. Jim Donaghy (Dunbar), the rival editor of *Ulster* (December 1985/January 1986), claimed that O'Hare, a leading member of Cumann na nBan, and now living in Dun Laoghaire, was responsible for a 'decline in quality' and style in *An Phoblacht*. O'Hare originally came from a Protestant, indeed planter, background. As a Belfast housewife she had 'jumped bail when charged with attempted murder of a soldier', but on escaping to the Irish Republic took advantage of the reluctance of courts there in the 1971-78 period to extradite for political offences in Northern Ireland. See 'Extradition: The Facts behind the Controversy', BT, 26 April 1990.

21. Some other Provisional overseas papers were *Saoirse, New Zealand Irish Post*, (Information on Ireland, formerly New Zealand H-Block/Armagh Committee) (1982-) and *The Irish People*, Australian Aid for Ireland (1989-). For latter, see U, April 1989. Australian Provisionals in the 1970s had also produced *Irish Republican Information*. In early 1989 the Provisionals produced the monthly *Ireland: International News Briefing*, distributed free to foreign journalists and politicians. See AP, 12 January 1989. From 1974 to 1980 a weekly cyclostyled *Irish Republican Information Service* bulletin had been supplied by the Provisional Dublin headquarters. According to RN, 28 February 1976 it and *An Phoblacht* were sold in Ghana.

22. Directory, *Fortnight*, No. 229, 12. AP, 2 May 1985.

23. See Browne, Vincent, 'Shadow of a Gunman' and 'The Secret World of the SFWP [Sinn Féin the Workers' Party]', *Magill*, April and May 1982; U, July/August 1989 quoted a Provisional Sinn Féin pamphlet on the robberies, intimidation rackets and fraud still perpetrated by the Official IRA.

24. See for a full discussion, Davis, R. (1974), *Arthur Griffith and Non-Violent Sinn Féin*, Dublin: Anvil Books, xxi and 235. According to RN, January-February 1971, 'Mac Giolla [Official leader] and Co. have gone the same way as Griffiths [sic] and Co.'

25. UI, September 1971 and March 1972. See also, Patterson, (1989), *The Politics of Illusion: Republicanism and Socialism in Modern Ireland*, 142.

26. RN, 6 August 1977.

27. Brooke, Peter (1987), *Ulster Presbyterianism*, Dublin: Gill and Macmillan.

28. [Tone, T.W.] (1791), *An Argument on behalf of the Catholics of Ireland* was reproduced; Clifford, Brendan (1984), ed., *The Life and Times of Thomas Moore (Ireland's National Poet)*, London: Athol Books.

29. Darby, John (1983), *Dressed to Kill: Cartoonists and the Northern Ireland Conflict*, Belfast: Appletree, 99.

30. The *UDA News* was preceded by a *UDA Bulletin*. See Boulton, David (1973), *The UVF*, 152-154.

31. Jim Donaghy (Dunbar), editor of *Ulster*, died on 21 June 1987, U, July/August and September 1987. Donaghy began life as a plumber's helper in Short and Harland's, rising to a works convenor. An active loyalist in the Suffolk area of Belfast, where it was claimed that Protestants had been forced out of their homes by Catholics, he was a founder member of the UDA and before being appointed editor of *Ulster* gained experience on its editorial committee. Donaghy had been an Orange Lodge master. He was succeeded by Stephen Taylor as editor. Under Taylor, *Ulster* publicised its editor and circulation.

32. *Ulster Loyalist* (UL), 17 February 1975.

33. RN, 1 June 1974; Nelson, Sarah (1984), *Ulster's Uncertain Defenders: Protestant Political, Paramilitary and Community Groups and the Northern Ireland Conflict*, Belfast: Appletree, 185.

34. Creighton, W. Irvine and 'Richard Cameron' are credited with the editorship, UL, 5 and 12 December 1974. For Mitchell, UL, 2 March 1975 and *Combat*, 2 (2) 1975.

35. The complexities of Loyalism are demonstrated by McKeague's claim in 1973 that he was in gaol as a member of the Red Hand Association, not the Red Hand Commandos, which, it was claimed, he had founded. His paper, however, supported both the Red Hand Commandos and the UVF, though on another occasion he mentions a 'ceasefire' between the latter organisations. LN, 17 Nov. 1973 and 17 Aug. 1974.

36. White, Barry (1985), *John Hume: Statesman of the Troubles*, Belfast: Blackstaff, 207.

37. RN, 23 August 1975, found McKeague's approach more sophisticated.

38. RN, 5 June 1976. earlier the same paper had complained that the LN, and the PT had abandoned politics for anti-Catholic hatred and referred to the former as an 'obsene publication', 12 December and 13 November 1971 respectively. The *Republican News*, 21 September 1974, credited McKeague with the founding of the Red Hand Commandos, insinuating his homosexuality in its depiction of him as a 'pervert'.

39. *Andersonstown News* developed as an anti-internment sheet in 1971, but extended itself to community weekly circulating widely in North and West Belfast. The UDA's *Ulster*, June 1987, denounced a leading Belfast store, or Co-op, for stocking the *Andersonstown News* which published IRA death notices. The Provisional *Volunteer*, April 1973, claimed that the *Andersonstown News* had no connection with either Officials or Provisionals but was published by the Central Civil Resistance Committee. The latter was clearly under Provisional influence.

40. Smyth was assassinated 12 March 1976.

41. *Ulster Militant* (UM), 30 September 1972. Fr Wilson, in the same issue, was described as 'that liar and reprobate from Ballymurphy ... posing as

an ecumenist'. Though Wilson later complained to Smyth of a cartoon depicting him with a Thompson gun (No. 18, 1972), he portrayed Smyth as a potential force for reconciliation in *The Demonstration* [Belfast, 1982].

42. *Protestant Blu Print*, Vol. 1, No. 42, 9 May 1986 for rough cartoon ridiculing Official Unionists Reg Empsey, John Carson, Dorothy Dunlop and others.

43. Darby, *Dressed to Kill*, 99. For RAB see *The Volunteer*, No. 23, 1972.

44. Hofstadter, Richard (1966), *The Paranoid Style in American Politics*, London: Jonathan Cape, 21.

45. Most commentators accept this. See, for example, Bell, Geoffrey (1976), *The Protestants of Ulster*, on Republican newspapers, 'there is no mention in them of wishing to kill Protestant scum, no caricature of Protestants as dirty, smelly and idle.'

46. Kormski's 'Dog Collars' cartoon strip appeared in *Fortnight* from late 1982 to early 1986. It also appeared as a booklet, Kormski, *Dog Collars (1985)*, Belfast: *Fortnight*.

47. *Irish Times*, 20 February 1982, quoted in Curtis, Liz (1984), *Ireland the Propaganda War: The British Media and the 'Battle for Hearts and Minds'*, London: Pluto, 248. According to AP, 17 January 1981, Bob Moore, the editor of *Visor*, was incorrigible. *Visor's* first issue was 28 February 1974.

48. AN, 10 May 1975.

49. The *Unionist Clarion* produced its first issue in March 1976 and its third and last in June 1976. It was preceded by the *Unionist Review* which published occasional issues between 1971 and 1973. Later *Unionist '82* produced three issues and new *Unionist Review* issues in 1983 and 1984.

50. AP, 19 January 1984. *Sunday News*, 13 December 1981.

51. White, Barry, *John Hume*, 276.

52. *Social Democrat*, April 1977.

53. In local council elections, Alliance dropped from 14.4 per cent in 1977 to 7.1 in 1985 and 6.8 in 1989.

54. *Alliance* (A), March and October 1973 (O. Napier and W.L. Warren) on integrated education.

55. *Peace by Peace*, 29 October and 17 December 1976, 8 April 1977. To the *Republican News*, 5 March 1977, Gandhi and Luther King condemned fringe violence but were opposed to the establishment. McKeown also edited the influential *Fortnight* for a period.

56. Deutsch, Richard, (1977), *Mairead Corrigan/Betty Williams*, New York: Baron's, 193.

57. Murphy, Dervla (1980), *A Place Apart*, Harmondsworth, Penguin, 272, extremists.

58. I am indebted to Dr Eamon Phoenix for this estimate.

59. *Andersonstown News*, 7 June 1975; for *Volunteer, Tattler*, 22 November 1971.

60. AP, 1 February 1990 and March 1970 and 24 August 1977; RN, 18 June 1977.

61. Curtis, *The Propaganda War*, 267 (raid 27 April 1978).

62. AP, 30 September 1978.
63. Bromley, 'War of words', 226. By 1989 it had apparently reached 150,000. See *The International Year Book and Statesman's Who's Who* (1989), E. Grinstead: Reed Information Services, for the circulation of daily papers. In the Irish Republic, the prestigious *Irish Times* distributed 88,739 copies compared to the best selling *Irish Independent* with 151,150.
64. Eamon Phoenix points out that the *Irish News* has declined from 70,000 sales in the 1970s to 40,00 in the 1990s. He suggests that the *News Letter* has done even worse, being in fact reduced to only 34,000 actual sales, with the balance made up of a free advertising sheet. For an alternative view, see Rolston, Bill (1991), ed., *The Media and Northern Ireland: Covering the Troubles*, London: Macmillan.
65. Burton, Frank (1978), *The Politics of Legitimacy: Struggles in a Belfast Community*, London: Routledge and Kegan Paul, 85. 'Outside perhaps those third or so (c. 1972-3) who are staunchly and consistently Provisional there is essentially a see-saw relationship between the IRA and the community.'
66. Circulated in New York, Boston, Philadelphia, Chicago and San Francisco, see Bishop and Mallie, *The Provisional IRA*, 297. Bishop and Mallie refer incorrectly to the *Irish Weekly*.
67. O'Rourke in AP, 4 February 1988 and 28 January 1990.
68. RN, 15 December 1973.
69. U, February 1989.
70. *Combat*, 18 March 1974 and December 1975.
71. See for example, U, Christmas 1984, 7, 'U.F.F. Assassinate I.R.A. Intelligence Officer', with photo of partly shrouded body.
72. Between 1975 and 1977 this group killed and mutilated 19 Catholics in North and West Belfast.
73. PT, 8 November 1969, 22 December 1973.
74. See Molone, Ed, in IT, 17 April 1982. BT, 14 April 1982. U, October/November 1989.
75. U, October/November and [December] 1989. In the latter issue it was complained that RUC lackeys, directed by Cambridge Deputy Chief Constable John Stevens, who was conducting an investigation into collusion between Protestant paramilitaries and the security forces, had led to the disappearance of many articles and greetings as the result of raids on the office and homes of Ulster workers.
76. IT, 22 February 1990.
77. *Warrior*, Vol. 1, No. 1, March 1993.
78. Bishop and Mallie, 186.
79. Rees, Merlyn (1985), *Northern Ireland: A Personal Perspective*, 49.
80. Morrison, Danny [1979], 'Censorship at Source: The raids on 'Republican News', Campaign for Free Speech in Ireland, *The British Media and Ireland*, London, 45-6.
81. See also Curtis, *Ireland: the Propaganda War*, 266-7.
82. In Collins, Martin (1985), ed., *Ireland after Britain*, London: Pluto, 89.
83. AP, 8 September 1979 and 11 January 1990.

84. AP, 1 February 1990 and RN, 23 August 1974. Morrison was arrested on 8 January 1990 and charged two days later with IRA memberships and conspiracy to murder.
85. Bishop and Mallie, *The Provisional IRA*, 331.
86. Quoted in Curtis, *The Propaganda War*, 266.
87. Boulton, D., *The UVF, 1966-73*, 31, 34, 38, 41, 54, 58 and 63. Moloney and Pollack, *Paisley*, 124-5. Doherty after two years of gaol on explosives charges established a printing business in South Africa.
88. *Protestant Blu Print*, 16 October 1987 (The article was labelled as unsuitable for children and Ligouri's 'filth' cited in the original Latin); PT, 3 December 1966. On Cherith, see Moloney and Pollack, *Paisley*, 421.
89. NPT, 10 March 1990 (Monk), May 1993 (Greeley) and June 1992 (Richard Snipe's study of chastity, Johns Hopkins.)
90. *Ulster*, Special issue, n.d., [October 1985].
91. Moloney and Pollack, *Paisley*, 295.
92. For condom culture and abortion, see *Protestant Blu Print*, Vol., 3, 12 February 1988 and 29 January 1988; On education see Moloney and Pollack, *Paisley*, 510-14 and PT, 13 June 1970, 26 February 1977 and 15 April 1978; on socialism, see PT, 23 September 1972, 27 October 1973 and 15 April 1978; on Southern Africa, see PT, 3 December 1966 and 11 November 1967. For further discussion on links across the sectarian divide see Davis, R. (1989 and 1986), 'Irish Republicanism v. Roman Catholicism: The Perennial Debate in the Ulster Troubles', Alexander, Yonah and O'Day, Alan eds, *Ireland's Terrorist Trauma: Interdisciplinary Perspectives*, 34-74. 'The Manufacture of Propagandist History by Northern Ireland Loyalists and Republicans', and 'Kitson versus Marigela: The debate over Northern Ireland Terrorism', in Alexander, Yonah and O'Day, Alan eds, *Ireland's Terrorist Dilemma*, Dordrecht (Neth.): Martinus Nijhoff, 145-177 and 179-209. See NPT, 24 March 1990, for Paisley's insistence on national sovereignty in the European Parliament.
93. NPT, April 1992 and January 1993.
94. NPT, July/August 1992.
95. Bishop and Mallie, *The Provisional IRA*, 145.
96. Bishop and Mallie, 285.
97. See RN, October-November 1970 (Vietnam) and January-February 1971 (Marxism).
98. In Collins, Martin, ed., *Ireland after Britain*, 89.
99. AP, 28 January 1988.
100. AP, 4 February 1988.
101. In Collins, ed., *Ireland after Britain*, 113-18. O'Hare had four children and two grandchildren herself.
102. Abortion on demand was endorsed by the Sinn Féin Ard Fheis in 1985 but reversed the following year, see Bishop and Mallie, *The Provisional IRA*, 443-4. The movement, however, supported contraception.
103. Bishop and Mallie, 355.
104. *Ulster Loyalist* [UL], [25 August] 1973.
105. UL, 5 May 1974.

106. 'Richard Cameron' appears to be the mysterious 'Richard' described by Nelson, Sarah, *Ulster's Uncertain Defenders*, 172, 175-6. 'Richard Cameron', the name of a Scottish covenanter who anticipated William of Orange in opposing James II, may well have been a nickname. See Moloney and Pollack, *Paisley*, 428. 'Head case' could also mean a target for assassination.
107. *Combat*, 25 April 1974 (1,6) and UL, 14 November 1974.
108. UL, 25 May 1975.
109. Moloney and Pollack, *Paisley*, 123, 140-1, 225, 369. The *Loyalist* (UDA), September 1992, advertised Cameron, Richard [1992], *Self-Determination? The Question Ulster must answer*, London: BCM Ameron.
110. U, December/January 1989.
111. *Combat*, Vol. 4, 4, 1977.
112. See for example, *Combat*, 4, 35, 1980.
113. AP, 31 December 1987.
114. See 'Davy Payne—The Facts', U, November 1988, p12-14.
115. *Loyalist*, May 1993.
116. *Loyalist*, September 1992.
117. *Loyalist*, February 1993. AP, 16 September 1993, quotes Anderson.
118. *Freedom Fighter*, Vol. 1, No. 1, June 1992.
119. NPT, May 1993.
120. *Loyalist*, May 1992.
121. AP, 30 September 1978, quotes interview in *Socialist Challenge*.

3 The uses of history

Anatomy of 'two nations'

One of the first tasks facing the paramilitary journals was always the historical question of whether Ireland is one nation or two. To many radicals, this issue is already an archaism in a world increasingly dominated by transnational capitalism. They prefer to substitute an analysis of 'divided class'[1] for an outdated propagandist device perennialy adopted to split the workers. The ramifications of this position will be considered in chapter seven; here it will be useful to start with some popular notions and their exploitation in the 'second Irish revolution' debate.

The idea of 'two nations' occupying the same territory has a long provenance throughout the world. Lewis Namier discerned numerous 'Ulsters' in Eastern Europe. In 1792, Edmund Burke, himself the offspring of a mixed marriage, complained that the Protestant 'garrison' of Ireland and the Catholic natives behaved, not as religious factions, but as 'two adverse nations'. Lord Durham's 1839 report on the French and English in Canada spoke of 'two nations warring in the bosom of a single state'.[2] Soon afterwards Disraeli's *Sybil* portrayed the English rich and poor as two antagonistic nations. Neither Burke, Durham nor Disraeli regarded division as permanent or desirable. Burke sought the enfranchisement of Catholics; Durham hoped that English culture would soon swamp the French; Disraeli aspired to a paternalist

78

raising of the poor. The latter, moreover, was quoted against his protégé Lord Randolph Churchill, who gave renewed momentum to the Irish 'two nation' division by his famous letter suggesting the 'Orange card' to defeat Gladstone's Home Rule bill in 1886.

The 'Orange card' was of course not intended to partition Ireland, but to keep all Ireland an integral part of the United Kingdom, a pin to burst the nationalist balloon. Right up to the establishment of the partitioned Six County parliament in 1921, a settlement denounced by the Ulster Protestants' southern Irish leader, Edward Carson, the suggestion of separate nationhood was avoided. After all, the object was adhesion to the British Empire not the discovery of 'two nations' in Ireland. Carson, who had played Gaelic games at the University of Dublin, regarded himself as an Irishman. He was in reality a great deal less intransigent than the famous Paisley-adopted harranguing photograph, with fist raised and jaw pointed, suggests.[3] Even by the 1960s, as M.W. Heslinga, whose acceptance of two basically religious nations is popular with loyalists, notes, Ulster Protestants rarely claimed national status.[4] During the first Irish Revolution, Griffith and other Sinn Féiners discussed the 'two nations' theory,[5] but the physical existence of the Stormont regime made 'two nations' a unionist dogma.

Protestant heritage or secular republicanism?

In his Ford Lectures, F.S.L. Lyons dissolved the 'two nations' into four cultures—the dominant Anglo-American, the Anglo-Irish, the Irish-Catholic and the Ulster Protestant—thus widening perspectives.[6] Our concern lies less with historical reality than with the historical imagination of second revolution propagandists. The duel between extremes can be likened to that in the Roman arena between the hoplite and the reticularis, as two different levels of argument confronted each other. On the republican side what was presented was ostensibly a secular nationalism. Against it was ranged not so much a rival nationalism as the ideal of a religious heritage. But can such generalisations be sustained? It is true, as the next chapter will show, that relations between republicanism and Catholicism were intimate, if antagonistic. Nevertheless it is undeniable that the republican tradition would be virtually non-existent if its Protestant progenitors were removed. When Padraic Pearse in his pamphlets before the 1916 Rising produced his 'apostolic tradition' of Theobald Wolfe Tone, Thomas Davis, John Mitchel, James Fintan Lalor, and Charles Stewart Parnell, he was not torturing his memory to discover, apart from Lalor, 'token

Prods' to give his philosophy a non-sectarian veneer. Padriag O'Snodaigh in *An Phoblacht* rebuked historian A.T.Q. Stewart for 'ignorant bigotry' when the latter suggested that some modern Protestant nationalists 'thought of themselves as honorary Catholics'.[7] The patriots cited seemed to epitomise in their lives and works Ireland's claim to nationhood. Tone, a deist contemptuous of the institutional papacy, Davis, an opponent of the Catholic Church's desire for educational separation, Mitchel, a Unitarian critical of the Catholic priesthood's role in 1848, and Parnell, whose final battle against priests and people baying for the defeat of an adulterer evoked memories of Cuchulain, the hero of the Irish sagas, were not crypto-Catholics. Ironically, they represented in their actions the very demand that Ulster Protestants make on the present-day Irish Republic: reduction of Vatican influence, separation of Church and State, legalised divorce, integrated education.

On the other side, can it be seriously maintained that, despite the Ulster Protestants' love for the symbolism of the union flag and the monarchy, heroic participation in Britain's wars, and glorification of their British character, their real cause is religious? David Miller's essay on the conditional nature of the Ulster Protestants' British loyalism contrasted it with the covenanting, or banding, tradition of Presbyterian democracy.[8] Ian Paisley put the issue succinctly when he declared that he would be loyal to the Queen, so long as she remained a Protestant.[9] Readers of his *Protestant Telegraph* soon discovered disquietude over religious dealings by the monarch and more open annoyance with the religious, or non-religious, activities of her husband.[10] When he himself admitted in 1971 that religion was his chief objection to a united Ireland, Paisley endorsed the argument suggested by Church of Ireland Canon J.O. Hannay earlier in the century. Indeed, when he talked of the conversion of all Ireland to Protestant fundamentalism, Paisley implicitly shed his unionism and became a religious nationalist who, in the Ireland of his dreams, would seek to preserve its ethos uncontaminated by English permissiveness. Though Paisley, despite his impressive popular vote, cannot speak for all Ulster loyalists in this regard, the idea of a 'Protestant heritage', however ill-defined, is probably common to most. The Tara paramilitary of the notorious Kincora child-molester, William McGrath, and his now disbanded Loyal Orange Lodge 1303, believed in an all-Ireland Protestant heritage, requiring the banning of the Roman Catholic Church. This is but an extreme version of an attitude shared by a number of Northern Ireland Protestants.[11]

At first sight the Northern Irish separate Catholic school system, confronting the state schools used by Protestants, belies the notion that the Irish republican heritage is basically secular. Political ideals filter through schools religious in orientation. Two points should, however, be made. First, the 'state' school system in Northern Ireland was traditionally as strongly Protestant as its counterpart was Catholic. Both must compete against F.S.L. Lyons' dominant Anglo-American culture.[12] Second, the important factor is not the religious formation provided by Catholic schools in Northern Ireland, but the type of political heritage transmitted. In the United States, for example, attendance at parochial schools hardly determines an individual's love of baseball, decision to join the navy, or membership of the Republican Party. In Northern Ireland, sport, national identification, and party preference depend upon group loyalties associated with religious divisions. It can happen that these group loyalties, though partly transmitted through schools based on religious ideals, may nevertheless be in considerable conflict with those ideals.

Chapter five discusses the problems for secular nationalism of a divided school system where both 'traditions' must compete against the dominant Anglo-American culture. Here we shall examine loyalist perception of the secular republican tradition. This will include those aspects of the 'Protestant heritage' which have evoked debate. These range from St Patrick, through the Reformation to the Battle of the Boyne, and finally merge in opposition to the secular nationalist or republican tradition. But that is not the end of the story. Even before the suspension of Stormont in 1972 and the attempt at power sharing in 1973-4, there was increasing awareness by paramilitary extremists that Protestant and British interests were not identical. They had, therefore, to secure an identity of their own as 'Ulstermen'. But where were they to draw water to nurture this sapling? The only answer was to divert their share of the nationalist stream of history. Eventually this diversion was to end in the channels of straight Gaelic appropriation, and the pre-Gaelic tributary, identified as Cruthin, or Pict.

The United Irish and modern loyalists

First consider the orthodox republican tradition, defined originally by Tone and the United Irishmen in the 1790s. Originally, the United Irishmen were a Protestant movement, influenced by the French Revolution and heavily dependent on the radical

Presbyterians of Antrim and Down. It aimed at democratising the Protestant ascendancy in the Irish parliament and working for the complete emancipation of Catholics, still hampered by vestiges of the early eighteenth-century penal laws. The 1798 rebellion, despite risings in Antrim and Down, was more effective amongst the Catholic peasantry of Wicklow and Wexford who, before their ultimate defeat, killed a number of Protestants at Wexford Bridge and Scullabogue. This, after the Act of Union in 1800, was to be a propagandist staple of the new 'unionists'. Tone, whose task was to obtain French aid, which arrived too little and too late, played small part himself. He was captured and anticipated the executioner by slitting his own throat. This 'Roman' death was to create controversy akin to that of hunger strikes later. Was it suicide? Were gaolers fearing a reprieve responsible? Was Tone as a non-Catholic exempt from condemnation for taking his own life? Paisley's *Protestant Telegraph* did not think so, denouncing Tone's 'cowardly' and 'ill-timed' death.[13]

During the current Ulster troubles republicans have naturally emphasised the Northern Protestant United Irishmen. Tone, a southern Irish Protestant, with a Catholic mother, was always number one in the pantheon. His *Autobiography* is accepted even by the disillusioned novelist, Sean O'Faolain,[14] as defining the essence of republicanism. Arthur Griffith and William Smith O'Brien[15] were exceptional Irish revolutionaries, somewhat sceptical of a hero whom revisionist historians have shown to be much less wavering in his total opposition to Britain than admirers have insisted.[16] The doyen of northern republicanism was undoubtedly Henry Joy McCracken, a Presbyterian cotton manufacturer managing a mill in the Falls Road who commanded the United Irishmen in Antrim, and was hanged after defeat. Other Presbyterians were William Drennan, who withdrew from the movement after his sedition trial in 1794 but later played an important part in the development of Belfast, William Orr, a Presbyterian elder and Antrim farmer hanged in 1797 for administering an illegal oath, the Rev. Dr William S. Dickson, Presbyterian minister of Portaferry, adjutant-general of the Down United Irishmen but arrested on the eve of the revolt, the Rev. James Porter of Grey Abbey, hanged though an advocate of non-violence, Henry Munro, a linen merchant, hanged for commanding the United Irishmen at the Battle of Ballynahinch, and the luckier Samuel Neilson, linen merchant and editor of the *Northern Star*, who escaped death by plea bargaining.

With such an array of Presbyterian republicans to recall, the *Republican News* soon after its inception in 1970 ran a series of articles on Protestant patriots. The message was simple. Ours is clearly a non-sectarian cause, numbering even Presbyterian ministers amongst its heroic and revered martyrs. Let this generation of Ulster Protestants emulate them. Nationalists, moreover, needed the Protestant contribution of 'honesty, frankness and hard work' represented by Orr, Porter, and the heroic Betsy Gray, cruelly killed after inspiring the rebels at the battle of Ballynahinch. The presentation was naive. No real attempt was made to penetrate the outward actions of these people. No effective reply was made to Bob Cooper of Alliance who condemned Provisional violence as false to the ideals of Tone, McCracken and Hope.[17] Nevertheless, citation of Protestant republicans was good propaganda. To Paisley, who was outspoken in his insistence that most modern ecumenical Protestant Churches were leading their flocks to perdition, the citation of such names was unimpressive; they were simply turncoats and `Lundies'. 'There has been a long line of Protestant traitors from Phelim O'Neill, through Wolfe Tone, Robert Emmet, Parnell and the Gilmore brothers,[18] to Sir Roger Casement.' These were, Paisley claimed, usually idealistic and humanistic socialists or Unitarians and only nominally Protestant.[19] But the Protestant paramilitary journals sometimes took a different line in their post-1974 reaction against Britain and the 'fur coat' unionists. They accepted the Protestant United Irishmen as having some justice on their side against Britain, while mistaken in their tactics.

Henry Joy McCracken's aphorism 'the rich always betray the poor' was quoted frequently not only by republicans but also by McKeague's *Loyalist News*.[20] The latter used it in his anti-Paisley vendetta. Paisley, said McKeague soon after the suspension of Stormont, 'can now be counted among the Quisling throng'. The Provisional *Republican News* was delighted at this hint of working-class unity, suggesting that as McCracken was a Presbyterian and 'a very religious man', he was 'one person both nationalists and unionist workers can be very proud of'. But the *Protestant Telegraph* found 'his name stinking in the nostrils of every true Presbyterian as being a traitor and a renegade.'[21] The UVF *Combat* also read its history differently. A contributing East Antrim UVF officer was reared in a staunch Orange area of Sixmilewater where the United Irishmen had once been strong. To him McCracken, Dickson, Porter, Orr, Neilson, James Hope and the Rev. Sinclair Kelburn who preached with musket beside him, were not disloyal to the crown but to 'the English parasites and their Anglo-Irish henchmen', the forerunners of Heath, Wilson and Faulkner.

Combat likened loyalists in 1974 to the United Irishmen in 1798, opposing treachery, corruption and the brutal treatment and internment of Ulster patriots. Modern loyalists would not make the mistake of alliance with Catholics, but 'stand alone and fight our own battles'.[22] Another article claimed that Protestant loyalists had more in common with the United Irishmen than modern republicans in that, apart from Wolfe Tone, few of the United men were separatists. Like Craig's Vanguard they saw separatism as a last resort. The writer claimed that United Irish leaders Arthur O'Connor and Samuel Neilson in fact welcomed the Union. Drennan, Archibald Hamilton Rowan, T.A. Emmet and Thomas MacNeven were against separation. Their object was 'the promotion of democracy, liberty and property'. McKeague's *Loyalist News*, sympathetic to the UVF, criticised modern republicans as false to the ideals of Tone and McCracken. It also used the Protestant leadership of early republicanism to demonstrate the superiority of Protestantism over Catholicism.[23]

Though still antagonistic to republicanism, this was new thinking indeed by the UVF and marks a sharp break from the Paisley position. The UDA, the largest Protestant paramilitary force, was not then much interested in the United Irishmen but used Irish culture later for its own purposes. However, Sammy Smyth, a UDA founder member, rejoiced that Presbyterian United Irishmen had done the main fighting against the English. This debate demonstrates the ease with which history can be manipulated through antithetical interpretation. Both PIRA and the UVF were partly right in their analysis. The Provisionals correctly asserted the basic liberalism of the United Irish Presbyterians in the 1790s, but there was also truth in the suggestion of the *Combat* columnists that some were less than wholehearted in their approach to the Catholic majority. The mind of the latter, said Dr William Drennan, was 'churlish soil'[24] requiring Protestant training. The Provisionals, however, argued reasonably that, although McCracken was proud to be an Ulsterman, he fought in the name of Ireland.[25]

There remained Wolfe Tone for whom none of the loyalists, except McKeague, felt much admiration. Tone provided the lynch-pin of the republican system. In analysing Tone, the loyalists claimed, first, that he and his friend Thomas Russell (executed in 1803) were exceptions to the rule in their separatism. *Combat* argued that the policy of the constitutionalist Henry Grattan was far superior to Tone's as Grattan and the Irish Volunteers had fought bloodlessly for Irish independence, while Tone's sanguinary war was the death-knell of Ireland's freedom. Tone was 'nothing more than a disgruntled and unpatriotic revolutionary'.[26] Criticism of bloodshed was ironical, given the UVF record of Catholic assassination. The UDA was also contemptuous. Tone, declared *Ulster*,[27] 'has been held up as a famous person without too many people knowing his motives and objectives'. It accused him of having little feeling for the common people. Conversely, the Provisionals and Officials (OIRA) used Tone's appeal from the men of property to 'that highly respectable class, the men of no property' to prove Tone a socialist. Here the loyalists were closer to those analysts who argue that Tone was simply disillusioned with the gentry whom he regarded as the natural leaders of society.[28] The loyalists of both UDA and UVF were partly correct in their general argument that the United Irishmen had no real interest in Irish culture and accepted the Union. There are some exceptions such as Russell and the Gaelic revivalist efforts in Belfast and Dublin in the early years of the United Irish movement.[29]

Though they agreed with Paisley's *Protestant Telegraph* in totally repudiating Tone, the two paramilitary bodies did so for opposite reasons. Paisley's technique for dealing with Irish nationalism in all its manifestations was the blanket assertion that it was simply an instrument of the ubiquitous Vatican conspiracy. Accordingly, he produced, out of context, a quotation in which Tone, depicted as leader of the United Irishmen in their butcheries, had 'described himself as a "red-hot Catholic"'.[30] In fact, Tone was 'red-hot' only in his opposition to religious monopoly. His *Autobiography* shows that Tone shared some of Paisley's own views on Catholicism when he sneered at priests, bishops, the 'trumpery' of the Mass, and the exiled Pope Pius VI. The Free Presbyterian would surely have agreed with the United Irishman in regretting the loss of 'an opportunity to destroy for ever the papal tyranny'.[31] Paisley's lack of finesse here missed a very good debating point which would have embarrassed republicans, usually most reluctant to mention Tone's attitude to Catholicism. The point, however, was taken by the more flexible UDA journal, *Ulster*, that if Tone did not like the English, he did not care for the Roman Catholic Church either.[32] In 1971 loyalists attempted to blow up Tone's statue in St Stephen's Green, Dublin. The *Protestant Telegraph* had advertised the unveiling.[33]

This debate on Tone and the United Irishmen demonstrates an energetic effort to claim the same men for opposing 'heritages'. The existence of such antithetical interpretation indicates that the theoretical gulf between the 'two nations' is communicable. A relatively balanced debate over the motives or real intentions of the insurgents is far removed from the Paisleyite attempts, through derogatory cartoons and verbal caricature, to portray Irish Catholics as a sub-human species. To this viewpoint, Presbyterian rebel clergy of the 1790s and ecumenical Protestant parsons of the 1970s posed the same threat to the mythology of total division. Dr Ian Adamson, intellectual mentor of the UDA, celebrated the United Irishmen as the true members of the ancient Cruthnic people, whom he presented as the ancestors of Ulster Protestants.[34]

The republican 'apostolic succession' moved from the United Irishmen to the Young Irelanders, whose leadership contained many Protestants such as Davis, Mitchel, and Smith O'Brien. Unlike the Presbyterian rebels, or 'blackmouths' whose lips were stained with berries eaten in hiding during the United Irish period,[35] these later Protestants had little appeal to any section of loyalist opinion in the 1970s. Although John Mitchel's father was a Presbyterian minister, the elder Mitchel belonged to Henry Montgomery's liberal wing which in 1829 deserted the Presbyterian synod dominated by Dr Paisley's hero, the anti-Catholic Henry Cooke. Apart from noting that Pearse had derived his ideas on violence from Mitchel, *Ulster*, representing the UDA whose knowledge of violence was a great deal more practical than that of Pearse or Mitchel, originally had little further to add.[36]

From Davis to Easter Week: secular apostles or clerical Marxists?

The most eminent of the Young Irelanders, Thomas Davis, who according to republicans of the 1970s, following Pearse, deepened and spiritualised the patriotism of the United Irishmen, did not appeal to loyalists either. Their apparent insistence on one of his chief objectives, integrated education, made no difference. To Paisley he was simply 'the rebel', a tag applied to the *Protestant Telegraph's* citation of RTE's regular Thomas Davis Lectures.[37] *Ulster* again came closer than the Paisley journal to the real issue by demonstrating that Pearse was impressed by Davis's ideas on reviving Irish culture, which the UDA journal categorised as 'romantic in the extreme'.[38] Davis, though not himself fluent in Gaelic, nor sufficiently conversant with the ancient Irish sagas to use their imagery in his patriotic poetry, does mark the beginning of a self-conscious binding of Irish republicanism to a cultural revival. In this sense he spiritualised and deepened Tone's message,[39] and produced the basic ingredients for what was to become the political culture of Northern Irish Catholicism.

But what of Davis the educator who believed that without integrated education, there could in fact be no Irish nation? It is ironical that the Northern Ireland divided school system has a Catholic sector providing a cultural mix largely based on the ideas of such a Protestant. An even greater irony was to appear when, as will be described later, loyalists themselves attempted to emulate Davis's methods by asserting their right to Gaelic, and even pre-Gaelic culture.

Republicanism after the Young Irelanders was a powerful, if not a totally coherent, creed. The Fenians of the 1860s, who contained fewer Protestants of note,[40] saw themselves as the successors of the Young Irelanders; Pearse and the men of 1916 were in their turn linked through the IRB with Fenianism. The decline in the number of nationalist Protestants made it easier for subsequent loyalists to accept the Paisleyite rejection of Irish republicanism as a weapon of the Vatican. Thus the *Protestant Telegraph*, which partly owed its inception in 1966 to the celebration of the fiftieth anniversary of the Easter Week Rising by the Northern Irish nationalist community, used the age-old devices. Pope Benedict XV[41] was alleged to have blessed the Rising. Sammy Smyth's *Ulster Militant* agreed on the blessing and added that the Rising's socialist leader, James Connolly, was a priest. The Irish tricolour was not, as republicans maintained, the visual symbol of Thomas Davis's ideal that 'Orange and Green will carry the Day', linked by the white band of friendship, but rather the pope's colours.[42] Loyalist propaganda, like the conservative Ancient Order of Hibernians, paints the orange band yellow. Protestant loyalists, moreover, had their answer to the executed martyrs of Easter Week in the terrible casualties inflicted on the undaunted Ulster Division at the Battle of the Somme. Continued celebration of the Somme on Orange banners and by loyalist paramilitaries does not necessarily imply undeviating devotion to England; Gallipoli, remembered in the Antipodes with the same zest as the Somme in Ulster, is considered to mark the attainment of nationhood by Australia and New Zealand rather than increased subordination to the mother country. Republicans see the Somme as an argument for 'Brits out' as they believe it demonstrates that loyalists can fight only under British direction.[43]

On the republican side, 1916 provided the watershed. The pamphlets of Pearse and the 1916 Proclamation encapsulated the political philosophy of the United Irishmen, the Young Irelanders, and the Fenians, while the executions sealed them in blood. The only direct influence of an Ulster Presbyterian at this time can be found in the essay, 'If the Germans conquered England', published anonymously in the insurgents' single issue *Irish War News*. This article by the early Sinn Féiner Robert Lynd was equally popular with British officers as it demonstrated the soul-destroying character of an alien though efficient government like Germany's. Revived by the Provisionals as applicable to Ulster in the 1970s, Lynd's essay effectively demonstrates the convergence of nationalism and counter-nationalist patriotism.[44] The Provisionals depended on the 1916 Rising for their 'mandate'. As already indicated, their very name attracted support by association with Pearse's 'provisional' government of Easter Week.[45] When informed in the 1970s and 1980s that they had no mandate from the people to take life, Provisionals pointed to the fact that Pearse had no mandate either, but was nevertheless endorsed by posterity, in his case only two and a half years later at the 1918 general election. On the other side, organisations like the modern UVF and the UDA, whose efforts at the polls have been ineffectual, are concerned to claim continuity with the old UVF of 1914, mainly absorbed into the Ulster Division of the Somme. This continuity was scornfully rejected by the British Army magazine, *Visor*.[46]

After the 1916 Rising the republican tradition was identified with the IRA which fought the guerrilla war against Britain, 1919-21. Paisley claimed that Michael Collins, organiser of ruthless urban operations, was a Catholic priest working under the direction of the Vatican. Similar beliefs in the 1920s inspired loyalist attacks on Catholics known as the 'pogrom'[47] and the Altnaveigh massacre of Protestants.[48]

Northern republicans could not but reject the Treaty signed by Collins and Griffith in December 1921, which, as it turned out, accepted partition and the consequent unfinished business. The vicissitudes of the post-civil war IRA have been chronicled by J. Bower Bell and T.P. Coogan, the former to the annoyance of the *Protestant Telegraph*, the latter to the irritation of *An Phoblacht*.[49] The Provisionals continued the quest for apostolic succession from the first and second pre-treaty Dails by securing the adhesion of Thomas Maguire. As the last survivor of the second Dail, elected in 1920, Maguire was appointed to the PIRA army council in 1970.[50] Thus a Bourbon sense of legitimacy compensated for the votes won in Catholic areas by the SDLP.

This survey of some aspects of the Irish republican tradition provoking loyalist interest or hostility shows, first, that the intellectual tradition was, despite the clumsy diversionary tactics of the *Protestant Telegraph*, basically secular, or at least non-denominational. Separation of Church and State was included in the Provisionals' Eire Nua programme.[51] The Proclamation of 1916 did invoke God, but hardly in any sectarian sense, and promised to cherish 'all the children of the nation equally'. Second, the insistence that divisions were the work of the British government provided substance for the Provisional 'Brits out first' philosophy, more clear-cut than the Tone and Davis belief in Irish unity as a prerequisite for independence. Third, by setting their nationalist philosophy in the form of an historical imperative, republicans could continue the struggle in the teeth of majority opinion in their own community, while asserting a moral superiority over that community, conditioned as it was to accept force as the fulcrum of nationalist development.

Historians confront Provisionals

In this context the bitter hostility of the Provisionals to the revisionist historians of the 1970s, 1980s and 1990s is understandable. 'History books are to be re-written 1984-style.'[52] The chief enemy was Dr Conor Cruise O'Brien, 'the Nepot of Howth' whose excellent study of Parnell's party was written before a controversial career in the United Nations, Ghana, and Dail Eireann. O'Brien was a member of the Cosgrave government of 1973-77, vital years of the Ulster troubles. As minister controlling communications O'Brien put historical revisionism into practice by reinforcing earlier legislation banning advocates of violence from Radio Telefis Eireann.

Developing from a relatively orthodox Irish patriotic position, O'Brien became increasingly convinced that the Ulster unionists, too often ignored in the polemic of those like Tone who saw only British divide and rule at work, were actually the determining factor in the Irish equation. O'Brien lost his Dail seat and resigned the compensatory Senate position after appointment as editor of the London *Observer*. His popularity with loyalists then rose in proportion to its decline amongst nationalists. Republican journals were full of cartoons, wisecracks and straight invective against the errant doctor who quipped that, after being beaten up by an Orange crowd in 1970, he had been offered another thrashing by Belfast nationalists: 'an oecumenism of vindictiveness'.[53]

The revisionist case was the work of many historians who, since World War II, had been steadily nibbling away at some of the foundations of the republican tradition. In 1939 Frank McDermott reinterpreted Wolfe Tone as a reluctant revolutionary; forty-three years later Tom Dunne described Tone as a Whig protectionist who belonged to the colonisers rather than the colonised. In 1945 Professor Dennis Gwynn found Thomas Davis an aggressive Protestant at fault in his disputes with the long-suffering O'Connell; Alf MacLochlainn subsequently argued that Davis was a racist. In the 1950s and 1960s Drs O'Brien and F.S.L. Lyons destroyed the republican view of Parnell as a separatist at heart. Suggestions were made that John Mitchel was a fascist. Gradually, the new scientific historians, who dropped capitalisation to indicate their objectivity, approached the republican holy of holies, the Easter Week Rising. Fr F.X. Martin demonstrated that republicans opposed to the Rising had an excellent case and that Pearse and his colleagues had used morally dubious tactics to dispose of their objections. In a *Studies* article in 1972 Fr Francis Shaw attacked the whole canon of Irish history, arguing that the ideas of men like Tone and Pearse were quite unacceptable. Modern writers insisted that the black diaries of Sir Roger Casement, executed for his efforts to obtain German help for the Rising, were genuine and he was in fact a promiscuous homosexual. More embarrassing for conservative republicans, Pearse himself was found to have homosexual inclinations.[54] The Officials now objected to his 'canonisation'.[55] Some of this was of course mere range-finding for more serious criticism. Historians now asked whether the 1916 Rising was necessary, whether sufficient attention had been given to the problem of Ulster, and whether the Irish people had ever really sanctioned violence or even republicanism itself. Roy Foster's *Modern Ireland* of 1987 encapsulated two decades of revisionism,[56] sometimes itself a reaction to the endless strife in Northern Ireland. Complaining in 1974 that only Professor David Greene and the Christian Brothers were on their side,[57] republicans could not allow such suggestions, totally destructive of their historical case, to go unanswered. *Republican News* and *An Phoblacht* were assiduous in their savage reviews of books and television documentaries critical of the argument that only by forcing out the British could Ireland ever hope to be pacified or united.

By the 1990s the battle against 'revisionism', 'the historiography of the counter-revolution', warmed up. It became less the reliance of terrorists on exploded myths in old pietistically nationalist histories than a serious debate with high-powered scholars on both sides. True, the Provisionals tended to admire older writers such as Cecil Woodham-Smith on the famine and Desmond Greaves on

Connolly and Tone.[58] But a number of academically trained historians and social scientists were coming to the conclusion that Irish revisionism had gone beyond the normal destruction of myths and fallacies and that, far from being scientific and unprejudiced, it had a strong anti-nationalist agenda of its own. The reviewers in *An Phoblacht* naturally supported the post-revisionists, praising Padraig O'Snodaigh, Brian Murphy, author of a book on Pearse, Declan Kibberd, Brendan Bradshaw, Seamus Deane, Kevin Whelan and others. Post-revisionist dissection of writers such as Fr F.X. Martin, Fr Francis Shaw, Roy Foster, F.S.L. Lyons, Patrick O'Farrell, John A. Murphy and Oliver MacDonagh evoked enthusiasm.[59] Independent historians were not necessarily demonised as totally bad. Joseph Lee, for example, was praised for his emphasis on the Irish language and dissection of the South, but blamed for his shallow treatment of the North.[60] Publishers such as Brandon, Mercier and Geography Publications received congratulations.[61]

Numerous issues were involved: British governmental responsibility for the famine, the veneration of Daniel O'Connell and the denigration of eminent republicans like Tone. The basic question, however, was as always secular versus Catholic nationalism. Were the noble, non-sectarian ideas of Irish nationalism simply the ideal of a few intellectuals who failed to convert a public motivated by Catholic factionalism, racism or local particularism? The latter interpretation, republicans felt, led directly to the 'two nations' theory, which, justifying the division of Ireland, appeared to motivate the revisionists.[62] Post-revisionists often appeared in league with the new feminist historians, seeking new paradigms for Irish history.[63] *An Phoblacht* duly provided favourable publicity for the latter.

Occasionally, loyalist periodicals made use of modern research to answer the Provisionals,[64] but the *Protestant Telegraph* Vatican conspiracy theory had no point of contact with the results of serious scholarship. Historians such as Conor Cruise O'Brien, and sometimes A.T.Q. Stewart, were naturally popular with loyalists. On the other side, as republican theory moved further from the original 'green' nationalism of the past towards greater emphasis on socialism versus multinational dominance, dependence on history increased rather than diminished. Republican forerunners like Connolly, himself reinterpreted, helped to bridge the gap between early nationalism and the new. Moreover, the Provisionals are aware that what gives their movement its long-lived tenacity, while other socialistic urban guerrilla movements come and go, is its firm base in the historical education and tradition of its community.

The Protestant heritage: back to St Patrick

What of the loyalist as opposed to the republican tradition? In tracing the latter's development we have found the Free Presbyterians dogging its footsteps with accusations of Roman influence, as they did physically to the People's Democracy (PD) marchers on their way to Derry in 1969. What then is the 'Protestant' version of Irish history to offset the republican? Protestants are as concerned as republicans to ground their philosophy firmly in the past. Christianity, in all its forms, is after all an historical religion, basing its theology on events in this world. The 'Protestant tradition' would appear to derive from the Reformation of the sixteenth century, but Dr Paisley claims that there were Free Presbyterians before that.[65] He means presumably that there existed 'born-again' Christians before Martin Luther.

The issue is best illustrated by the Irish Protestant attitude to St Patrick. Not only Free Presbyterians, but even members of the Church of Ireland have insisted that Patrick (a saint by usage not formal canonisation) was indeed a Protestant. He never, they maintain, received an official commission from the papacy for Irish evangelisation, though they admit that he studied in Catholic institutions on the Continent. In 1968, prior to the civil rights marches, the *Protestant Telegraph* published a characteristic article on St Patrick, denying that the Roman Catholic Church had any claim to him.[66] There was, it maintained, no evidence in Patrick's Confession or elsewhere that he practised aural confession, advocated clerical celibacy, believed in purgatory, or glorified the Mass. It was true that in the fifth century some of these practices and beliefs had not been defined with their subsequent precision. However, the argument went further, citing chroniclers like Baronius who declared all Irish bishops of the time schismatics separated from Rome. The article also insisted that Ireland was genuinely Christian from the days of St Patrick to the twelfth century when Henry II conquered Ireland, not only for himself, but for the Roman church. 'And popery was forced upon an unwilling people at the point of a bayonet.' This necessitated a long struggle, but 'Patrick's vision of Ireland, both North and South, is now a reality. May we in the Protestant North seek to complete the vision by evangelising the rest of the island before Popery envelopes us too'. The 'vision' seems to imply a mustard seed of pure

Protestantism growing to unfold the whole island, as in the Tara/Loyal Orange Lodge 1303 theory.

The emergence of the Provisional IRA was still two years away. Yet the *Protestant Telegraph's* article described a clear ideal for a united Ireland, albeit on Free Presbyterian terms. Paisley's 1971 admission that only religious difficulties stood in the way of unity should be seen in this perspective. Its implications were every bit as revolutionary as those of the subsequent republicans, whose militancy was to some extent a by-product of the Paisleyites' attempt in 1968-69 to realise by forceful means their own vision of the future. But this was not all. By invoking the conquest of a contented 'Protestant' Ireland—presumably St Malachy and the Celtic reformers were Free Presbyterians in Paisley's book—Paisley mirrored the '700-years-tyranny' of traditional nationalists: Anglo-Norman invaders confronted stolid, religious Celts. Even this did not end the convergence. If Paisley denounced the imperialism of the papacy which used Henry II to destroy traditional Irish liberties, the Provisionals did likewise in their journals. In replies to Catholic bishops and clergy who had decried their violence, Provisional journals referred repeatedly to the Irish hierarchy's long history of collaboration with Britain in the denial of Irish popular liberties. They had no hesitation in dating it back to the Bull *Laudabiliter*, granted by the Englishman, Nicholas Breakespeare. As Pope Adrian IV, Breakespeare conveniently handed over, for needless ecclesiastical reform, Ireland to the English king.[67] Nowhere else did the mirror-image reflect so brightly.

The ecumenist challenge: Bishop Hanson

Later in 1968 a Nottingham University professor of Irish extraction published a scholarly and judicious *Saint Patrick: His Origins and Career*.[68] It accepted Patrick's 'truly evangelical understanding of the Christian faith', admonishing those wishing to use him for their own purposes. Patrick was neither a modern Roman Catholic bishop nor a Protestant evangelist, merely a fifth-century bishop: 'He does not have occasion to mention the eucharist and the papacy', but would probably have accepted the idea of the real presence in the sacrament and acknowledged the pope.

No analysis could have been further removed from the emotional fundamentalism of the Free Presbyterians and their Northern Irish fellow travellers. By a quirk of fortune, two years later the author, Professor R.P.C. Hanson, was appointed by the Church of Ireland bench of bishops to the diocese of Clogher and became an outspoken opponent of Paisleyism. He denounced the Orange Order as unchristian, lamented the bullying tradition of Ulster Protestantism, and insisted that the duty of parish clergy was not to 'make the people happy at any cost but to lead them to the truth'. Free Presbyterians demonstrated against Hanson, who, accused of lacking political finesse, returned to academic life in 1972. His episcopal successor was a conservative.[69] As a bishop attacking the 'Protestant tradition' Hanson mirrored Bishop Edward Daly's rejection of the 'Republican tradition' of 1916. Hanson's experience illustrates the paradox, well known to sociologists, of using religion as the basis for tribal identity, while rejecting its inconvenient doctrines.

In his earlier writings Professor Hanson had already struck at the heart of Biblical fundamentalism when demonstrating that 'the Bible does not preach itself. If you place a Bible in the market-place it does not expound itself; it does not behave like a gramophone.' Moreover, the Bible could not be separated from the tradition of the church. 'Tradition is, in short, the deposit left by the Church in interpreting the Bible.'[70]

Biblical criticism raises the essential question of 'Protestant tradition' grounded in the Reformation. Bishop Hanson, representing the ecumenical movement of the 1960s, exhibits a form of Christianity closer to Roman Catholicism than Free Presbyterianism in its recognition of church tradition rather than the Bible enthroned in its apparent meaning. The problem is not solved by declaring Hanson the pope's right-hand man for the subversion of British Protestantism.[71] The exact nature of the 'Protestant tradition' must be defined. Is there indeed a basic common denominator Protestantism which Paisley can claim, rightly or wrongly, to represent, or is this concept in itself based on confusion? The *Protestant Telegraph* not only attacked its editor's ecumenical opponent, the Methodist cleric Lord Donald Soper, for claiming that Dr Paisley was not a traditional Protestant at all[72] but denounced the former Archbishop of Canterbury, Geoffrey Fisher, for his desire to drop the word 'Protestant' completely.[73] These statements, inconsistent with each other, nevertheless indicated a trend towards the dissolution of Protestant certainties outside Ulster.

Fundamentalism or consensus Protestantism?

What then was the Paisleyite conception of the 'Protestant heritage' and how was it located in the sixteenth century and subsequent history? Although the *Protestant Telegraph* and Paisley himself never seem to have spelled this out in detail, a very clear distinction appears between the ultimate doctrine of Bible Protestantism and their contrived Protestant consensus. First, Bible Protestantism: 'No one can be saved unless he is born again by the power of God's Holy Spirit. (John 3: 3-7) .... You can be orthodox upon every doctrine, and be lost forever.' If the original text could be subject to different interpretations, the Free Presbyterian gloss could not. This is what the sociologist of religious sects, Bryan Wilson, has described as a 'heart experience', which 'must occur at a given time' and is 'essential to salvation'.[74] Such a doctrine has a very long tradition behind it, but in no sense provides a consensus for the Churches which have conventionally accepted the label 'Protestant', with, as in the case of High Church Anglicans, some opposition. The implications of the born-again doctrine must be faced. There are no gradations. As pointed out by R.A. Torrey in the extract cited above, orthodox belief is no help. Weekly attendance at the Martyrs Memorial would prove no more effective than Sunday golf in Ormeau Park or eight o'clock Mass at St Matthew's Church, Newtownards Road, were the vital experience of spiritual rebirth lacking. Thus to talk of a 'common Protestantism' should make no sense to a Free Presbyterian. Nor was there any logical reason for denouncing Rome rather than any other Church that believed, say, in intellectual conversion, the maintenance of a religious inheritance, a purified personal life, or the ultimate salvation of all sinners. For Paisley to stride about with his Biblical bludgeon seeking ecumenists and Romanists to devour was only logical if regarded as a crusade for his own Church; it was irrelevant as a defence of a 'Protestant consensus'.

Yet Paisley's political activities required the ultimate advocacy of such Protestantism, despite the fact that he would merely be saving the pseudo-Protestant damned from the Catholic damned. John Calvin had faced this problem in sixteenth-century Geneva, arguing that the elect had the right to force the reprobate to preserve outward decencies. Dr Paisley, however, was less willing to make this explicit. An elaborate Protestant consensus position was put forward in the *Protestant Telegraph*, though the spectacular diversionary attacks on the harlotries of Rome and the iniquities of ecumenists (surely a logical and natural union of the reprobate?) distracted attention from it. Greatest emphasis was placed on the notion of civil and religious liberty, Paisley asserting that Catholics, far from having anything to fear from political Protestantism, should support it.[75] The Protestant heritage was summed up in one illuminating article.[76] On four levels Protestant freedom asserted itself against Roman Catholic thraldom. First, the soul of a Protestant was free to meet its maker without intermediary. Second, the home of the Protestant was inviolate against the intervention of a priestly class. Third, the Protestant was untrammelled at the ballot-box by ecclesiastical supervisors. In addition, Church and State were completely separated.

This list was indeed an effective assertion of what a Protestant probably believed his or her tradition to imply. It was supported by allegations of Roman Catholic denial of these propositions in the Irish Republic or further afield. The 'sin box' confessional, repeatedly pilloried in article and cartoon as a means to political terrorism and clerical debauchery,[77] underlined the first Protestant assertion. Birth control (*Humanae Vitae*) and restrictive mixed marriage regulations (*Ne Temere*) were prime indications of the second. The Irish censorship board immediately might evoke number three. Finally, the Mother and Child Health scheme of Dr Noel Browne, which failed in 1951 because of hierarchical opposition, was on the tip of every Northern Protestant tongue, to indicate the fourth category.

So far so good. In all these matters the Northern Irish Protestant heart could be said to beat in tune with that of Dr Paisley, whose *Protestant Telegraph* was certainly foremost in asserting the dangers to be feared from the Vatican. But was it really so simple? Did the four propositions mark a clear distinction between the ethos of the Falls Road and that of the Shankill? Were they inherent in Bible Protestantism as the true descendant of the real Reformers of the sixteenth century? The first and second questions can easily be dealt with. The confessional, according to strict Roman Catholic doctrine, does not demonstrate a sharp divergence from the Protestant Churches. The individual Catholic also communicates directly with God; the priest does not ultimately forgive sins, but registers the fact of contrition.[78] This issue was raised by republicans in their conflict with the hierarchy. Here it should be noted that loyalists, believing the confessional unscriptural, have always insisted that Catholic members of the IRA be excommunicated, in other words compelling confessors to exclude physical-force republicans from the Catholic sacraments, of which many loyalists disapprove.[79]

Similar considerations apply to the home, the book, and the ballot-box. The Catholic hierarchy wishes the law in the Irish Republic to maintain Catholic moral teaching on divorce, abortion and contraception; Dr Paisley's Free Presbyterians want the law in

Ulster to prohibit homosexual practices between consenting adults. They are almost equally hostile to abortion.[80] The Irish Republic has banned Steinbeck;[81] Paisley's supporters work for the exclusion of Steinbeck from Northern Irish schools. In the Irish Republic Catholic clerics pressure government ministers on Catholic moral teaching; in Northern Ireland Protestant clerics lead political parties, stand for, and sit in parliament as well as pressuring government ministers on their churches' moral teaching. These incongruities have long been pointed out. The 'blackmouth' Presbyterian, the Rev. J.B. Armour, celebrated in both Provisional and UVF literature, demonstrated during the first Irish Revolution that Ulster Protestants were addicted to authority, not private judgement.[82] Dr Paisley's loyalist critics portray him as a rival pope, or even a rival God. For example, the UDA's *Ulster* depicted a cynical pope in dialogue with an equally cynical Paisley who declared: 'For goodness sake can you not see / That God is Ian Paisel-ey'. According to McKeague's journal, Ian Paisley 'calls for unity within the Protestants ranks, but forgets to tell the people on my terms only.'[83] In personal style Dr Paisley is nothing if not authoritarian. There is, however, a more important issue, less frequently emphasised. Paisley's claim that he stands unequivocally for the separation of Church and State must be taken alongside his insistence that, unlike modern trendy Presbyterians, he unequivocally adheres to the *Westminster Confession of Faith,* 1647.[84] These are incompatible as the *Confession* enjoins the civil magistrate to 'maintain piety', suppress 'heresies and blasphemies', and even 'call synods'. The campaign of Paisley's friend Dr Bob Jones and others to ensure, contrary to decisions by the United States Supreme Court, that a non-ecumenical translation of the Bible be read in public schools,[85] must be seen in this connection.

Thus the chief aspects of a consensus Protestantism as portrayed in the *Protestant Telegraph* are neither particularly good indicators of the divide between Northern Irish Protestants and Catholics, nor particularly suitable for asserting the leadership of Free Presbyterianism. In another article,[86] P.E. Donovan came closer to the religious reality by asserting the essence of Protestantism to lie in the supremacy of the Bible, private judgement and salvation by faith alone. But here again there were difficulties. On the Bible, ecumenists like Bishop Hanson insisted not only that it was indissolubly linked with Church tradition but that old translations were faulty and divisive. The production of new translations acceptable to Roman Catholics and many other Churches was clearly an important breakthrough. Free Presbyterians who insisted on the *Authorised Version* of 1611, rejecting the more modern translations as Bibles of Antichrist,[87] were surely removing themselves even further from leadership of an increasingly hypothetical 'Protestant consensus'. The same may be said for their understanding of 'private judgement'. The *Protestant Telegraph* definition was hardly that of most Protestant churchmen, though certainly rooted in the early Reformation. According to Donovan, it was not private opinion. The individual must accept Christ's teaching from the 'Book'. But what 'Book'? Was the *Authorised Version* 'indefensibly bad'[88] and incapable of expounding itself? The argument was circular. Republicans and loyalists were equally hostile to the respective scholars undermining their traditions.

The Reformation: freedom of conscience or muscular Christianity?

On Donovan's third point, the issue reverts to Luther and the early Reformation. Justification by faith alone appears in popular theology as a radical departure from the Roman Catholic system. Luther had apparently broken with the pope on this issue, refusing to accept any intermediary between his view of the Bible and God. The Bible said 'the just shall live by faith' (*Romans* 1, 17),[89] without any mention of works or Masses. Thus the essential revolution was accomplished. But the theological issues are less simple than people in the pews of churches deriving from Luther are encouraged to imagine. It is not necessary to give a detailed examination of how much Luther owed to the medieval church, or the efforts of the Council of Trent to reach a compromise on the various knotty theological issues raised by the Reformers. Suffice it to say that a number of authorities who are not themselves Roman Catholics believe that the doctrinal decisions of the Council of Trent were a victory for common sense.[90] This is not to deny the bitter hatreds aroused by the sixteenth-century wars of religion which led to scurrilous language and atrocities like the Massacre of St Bartholomew in France, which Paisley compared to the Irish 1641 Rising.[91] If the sixteenth century has a particular message for Northern Ireland it is surely the discrepancy between the passionate intensity of the physical force struggle and the fine philosophical distinctions ostensibly at issue. Community identity, sociologists tell us, is achieved by submission to a leader, not to theoretical principles.

Leaving aside theological minutiae, did Luther really represent a movement towards greater freedom on which a consensus Protestant position could be based? The radical priest, Fr Desmond

Wilson, suggested in 1982 that neither Luther nor Calvin could be regarded as agents of liberty. As for the *Protestant Telegraph*, it agreed with Donovan that Luther freed men from the pope but subjected them to God and the Bible. Was he a liberator of human mind and conscience? 'Yes, he was—but only over against the "other masters".'[92] The Orange Grand Master, Martin Smyth, accepted that private judgement does not allow any man either to believe or do what he wants irrespective of all other considerations.[93] This was hardly what the average Protestant means by freedom. But Martin Luther, like the two other great Reformers, John Calvin and Huldrych Zwingli, 'developed forms of organisation which closely identified Church and State and shut the door to religious and social dissidence'.[94] Though some of the relatively minor figures of the Reformation, like Sebastian Castellio, advocated a more modern type of tolerance, it can hardly be claimed that freedom of worship or speech derived from the early Protestants, named after the protest at the German Diet of Spires in 1529. The princely protesters involved certainly declared passionately for the individual's direct responsibility to God. But their main objective was to allow prince-bishops, converted to Lutheranism, hereditary rights over their ecclesiastical principalities. The morality of such acquisitions was doubtful. They rejected, moreover, any toleration of Anabaptists or Zwinglian Reformers. The editor of the *Orange Standard*, Church of Ireland Canon S.E. Long, admitted the compulsory worship of the Reformation period but still insisted on a tradition of human equality, citing Thomas Jefferson, a child of the eighteenth-century rationalist Enlightenment rather than the Reformation. To Long, like Martin Smyth, liberty means doing what one ought, not what one wants.[95]

In asserting the principle of Protestant consensus liberty, some of the Ulster loyalist heroes are revealing. The *Protestant Telegraph* was particularly impressed by the passionate, dynamic, red-haired William Farel, a whirlwind of anti-popery, who travelled from village to village in Switzerland. His tactics were to interrupt the Mass, take over the pulpit, thunder out a sermon, and quickly convert the area to the Reformed faith.[96] This was not simply the power of the Word for, as Kamen points out, 'the ruthless methods of the Protestant soldiery' had a part to play.[97] A mixture of verbal and physical force also characterised the advance of Lutheranism. As a precedent for Ulster in the 1960s and 1970s it was not reassuring; it evoked the tactics adopted by loyalists against

NICRA and PD marches in 1968-9, not to mention the British Army in Catholic ghettoes.

Calvinism and politics: an ambivalent legacy

Farel eventually called his more scholarly French compatriot, John Calvin, into Geneva to consolidate his gains. Calvin was another hero of Ulster loyalists in the 1970s. Even the UVF *Combat*, which did not always agree with Paisley, had for a time a columnist, 'Calvin', who preached the predestination of the original, emphasising the total depravity of mankind. Inevitably, the *Westminster Confession* was recommended as the pure expression of this doctrine. The writer opposed 'authentic Protestants' to Arminians who believed that Christ's sacrifice was intended to make salvation available to all. 'Calvin' inadvertently exposed the weakness of Paisley's consensus advocacy of secular government by insisting that there was no need for the absolute separation of Church and State.[98] More surprising was a piece of unconscious ecumenism by 'Calvin' who stated very succinctly an educational philosophy identical to that of the Roman Catholic Church. The impossibility of state school neutrality, the priority of parental rights, and the necessity for moulding character were all raised.[99] In the same journal, Hugh Smyth asserted that the Ulster-Scot tradition was basically Protestant and Calvinist.[100]

Such identification, important when the Church of Ireland is classified as Calvinist,[101] can be double-edged. The socialist James Connolly made shrewd nationalist propaganda when he quoted the Irish rationalist and unionist historian W.E.H. Lecky against the invariable despotism of Anglicanism and the Scottish Presbyterian tyranny buttressed by 'inexorable barbarity' and 'religious terrorism'.[102] F.S.L. Lyons, however, has called attention to that 'kindliness' and 'liberality' in the private lives of North-East Ulster Calvinists which was offset by a history of frontier insecurity.[103]

The other great Calvinist reformer was John Knox, according to Lecky 'this great apostle of murder'.[104] Knox, who broke with his master on non-resistance to ruling powers, was probably more popular with Ulster loyalists who sometimes depicted him on Orange banners. The UDA *Ulster Loyalist* demonstrated that Knox, unlike other Reformers of his time, did not merely criticise Romanist errors, but struck at the very base of the system by declaring the pope Antichrist. Paisley, a master of such rhetoric, was nevertheless criticised for presiding over a congregation that had never manned a road block or guarded life and property at night.[105] Practice notwithstanding, Paisley included an article on Knox in one of the first issues of the *Protestant Telegraph*.[106] He later compared modern ecumenists unfavourably with Knox. Paisley believed, for example, that the publication of the Presbyterian 'blackmouth' Professor John Barkley by the United States John Knox Press was 'the last straw'.[107] Of greater significance was the *Protestant Telegraph's* inclusion of an article discussing the famous confrontation, given in dialogue by Knox's autobiography, between himself and Mary Queen of Scots. The former, despite Calvin's strictures, promised resistance by 'power' if his sovereign refused to maintain the true kirk.[108] Such was the conditional nature of the Free Presbyterian loyalty; Paisley said much the same to the descendant of Mary Queen of Scots, Elizabeth II, especially when the latter engaged in unacceptable papal visits. Indeed, the *Protestant Telegraph* more than hinted at resistance when commenting in a later article that 'the Stuarts were abominable kings. The virus of that temptress and adulteress Mary, Queen of Scots, coursed through their veins.'[109] The article, however, omitted to mention that both William III and Elizabeth II sat on the throne by virtue of 'the virus of that temptress'. This was only a minor problem. The whole issue of resistance to government teems with confusion in Calvinist and Paisleyite thinking. The *Westminster Confession*, even in the form printed for distribution by Free Presbyterians, shows clearly that the Presbyterian members of the Long Parliament, after Charles I's defeat in the English Civil War, were determined to maintain a strong State which could not be undermined by factious clerics. Hence the stipulation that 'infidelity, or indifference to religion, doth not make void the magistrate's just and legal authority'.[110] Nevertheless, Paisley's hero Cromwell had no hesitation in turning out the Presbyterian majority whose Erastianism in the *Westminster Confession* made little appeal to the sectaries of the New Model Army. Paisley, using Carlyle to justify Cromwell's sack of Drogheda,[111] an event celebrated on the banner of at least one Orange Lodge, neglected the tension between Cromwell and the *WCF*. Cromwell, recognised as 'a man of God', met the requirements for salvation as demanded by the Free Presbyterians.[112]

Seventeenth-century plantations: towards Derry and the Boyne

This is to move too quickly ahead of chronology. The transference of the Reformation to Ireland aroused relatively little interest amongst the loyalists. The Ulster plantations of the early seventeenth century were the essence of the controversy. Here was the key to the 'two nations' question.[113] On the republican side it was generally maintained that an alien element had entered the country at that time, and, as history progressed, these aliens had the choice of identifying with the majority or departing when the majority ultimately came into its own as an independent nation. In the mid-nineteenth century, Thomas Davis took up the ideas of Wolfe Tone for a union of peoples of different origins into a new and enriched Irish nation,

> As filled by many a rivulet
> The stately Shannon flows.

Arthur Griffith wrote later that the declaration in favour of Irish unity by the mainly Protestant Irish Volunteers in 1782 annihilated earlier differences and created one nation. Amalgamation was still the official policy of the republican movement during the first Irish Revolution. It was often associated with the concept of the basically good and nationalistic Orangeman. Nevertheless, there were occasional suggestions that the Calvinists of the north-east had as little place in the Irish nation as the English sahibs in India, and would ultimately have to leave.[114] During the Ulster troubles this attitude appears to linger on behind the bland assumption of some republicans that there will be no problem in Northern Ireland after the British departure. 'Freeman' (identified as the southern Irish author, Desmond Fennell) in *An Phoblacht* hinted that two cultural nations, giving allegiance to Ireland and Ulster, might remain for some time before merging in a new Irish nation. This was dangerous ground. On the other side, Michael Dolley, a Queen's University, Belfast, historian sympathetic to the Provisionals, was accused of telling the planters to conform or get out.[115]

The original loyalist argument agreed entirely with that of republicans or nationalists, except for the final outcomes. Yes, said the loyalists, we were invaders and intend to remain apart. As the *Protestant Telegraph* put it, if Ulster loyalists were driven out after so long an occupation, then the United States would have to be given back to the North American Indians, colonised at about the same time. This attitude was to make many loyalists extremely sympathetic towards colonial and settler regimes such as those of South Africa and Rhodesia (Zimbabwe). Dolley was answered by the insistence that the seventeenth-century planters were returning to the home of their ancestors. As for the 'Freeman' position, unionists, originally sure of their British identity, had given a resounding 'no' when asked to become a rivulet feeding the greater

Irish Shannon. However, by 1974 when many loyalists, especially in the paramilitaries, felt that they had been sold out by the British they began to see merits in Davis's racial merger. The contrast with Paisley's *Protestant Telegraph,* which continued to interpret post-plantation seventeenth-century events in terms of total racial-religious divergence, is sometimes marked.

In the loyalist historical tradition the 1641 rebellion of native Irish against planters and the resultant atrocities is followed by the Protestant Cromwellian repression, the final epiphanies of the Protestant defence of (London)derry against Catholic James II and the latter's ultimate defeat by William III at the Boyne on 1 (subsequently 12) July 1690. The DUP deputy leader, Peter Robinson, has appropriately written an account of the siege of Londonderry which dwells on atrocities against Protestants earlier in the seventeenth century.[116] Against these, nationalists have set the heroism of the Jacobite commander, Patrick Sarsfield, the siege of Limerick, and the broken treaty of that city, which was followed by the anti-Catholic penal laws of the late seventeenth and early eighteenth centuries. These nationalist symbols have never become the focus of a cult quite as extensive as that of their loyalist counterparts, but the banners displayed by modern demonstrations of the Ancient Order of Hibernians balance the seventeenth-century history of their Orange counterparts. The Young Irelander, John Mitchel, considered the period particularly important: the Irish parliament of 1692 ensured that 'the division into two nations became definite' by excluding Catholics from membership.[117] Here the 'two nations' are perceived as political, not racial or cultural.

Propagandist history often lingers without visible means of support. Scientific historians may demonstrate that the papist atrocities of 1641 were deliberately exaggerated to justify the seizure of Irish land by the English Long Parliament, but this will scarcely affect the loyalist rabblerouser's anticipation of forthcoming massacres. Ironically, the *Loyalist News* of the post-1975 McKeague was the most balanced: 'Faults on both sides swayed back and forth, Protestant Ireland or Roman Catholic Ireland. The native Irish find it hard to forget Cromwell and the Plantation. Ulstermen find it hard to forget 1641 and 1798'. When discussing the siege of Londonderry, Paisley's paper made considerable use of the description from T.B. Macaulay's *History of England,* which John Mitchel had formerly denounced as a bitter attack on the Celtic people.[118] Paisley could revel in the contrast between the 'aboriginal peasantry' harangued by their priests, and the upstanding Protestant settler defenders of the city.[119] As has already been shown, Paisley projected this racial-religious cleavage into the controversies of the 1970s.

Protestants and the Gaelic tradition

In 1974 the UVF *Combat* published an appreciative article based on a pamphlet, *The Hidden Ulster*, by Padriag O'Snodaigh, with a forward by a retired Church of Ireland cleric, the Rev. Cosslet Quinn.[120] Here it was shown that the cultural gap between seventeenth-century planter and the native Irish was much less than had been supposed, linguistic and cultural affinities easily bridging the narrow seas between Scotland and Ulster. As for the siege of Derry-Londonderry, analysis of the famous song *Lillibulero*, which is reputed to have whistled James II out of three kingdoms, demonstrates the title to be, not meaningless gibberish, but perfectly good Irish: 'An Lile ba Leir Dho, Ba Linn an La.' ('The Lily was triumphant, it won the day.') The celebrated Apprentice Boys who closed Derry against James II, and whose commemoration in 1969 helped to spark off the second Irish revolution, may have been Irish-speaking. O'Snodaigh demonstrated that early nineteenth-century Catholic clerics were more dubious about Gaelic than their Presbyterian counterparts. The Orange leader, R.R. Kane, signed his lodge minutes in Irish. As late as 1992 a UDA paper cited 'Ba Linn An La, The Day Was Ours' to prove that the Irish Gael had never conquered Ulster.[121]

Cosslet Quinn, a Protestant traitor according to Paisley's paper,[122] showed, moreover, that there was a common Irish-Scottish Gaelic culture shared by the Catholic and other Churches. The Church of Ireland had produced the first Gaelic Bible, while the Scottish Presbyterians had translated major works by Calvin and Knox into Gaelic. Of course, these translations were to facilitate conversion, not to perpetuate the cultures themselves. Indeed, the failure of the Reformation in Ireland was partly due to the inability of English churchmen to provide immediately a Gaelic translation of their new prayer book. *Combat*, quoted with interest by the Provisionals,[123] demonstrated that the identification of Gaelic culture with Roman Catholicism should be abandoned, and that loyalists, who could remain unionists like the Scots, should regain their heritage 'in folklore, in music, in literature, in song and in the Gaelic language'. It was not so much that papists had stolen Protestant culture, but that Protestants had foolishly given it away to Roman Catholics. The unionist British and Irish Communist Organisation (BICO), which endeavoured to influence Protestant paramilitaries, published a pamphlet in reply to O'Snodaigh.[124] But the eminent historian Oliver MacDonagh accepted that 'the quest for Gaelic culture was largely Protestant in origin'. Even the Battle of the Boyne, the most holy of all loyalist commemorations, now came under review. Republicans and nationalists sometimes argued that celebration was misplaced as William III was leader of a European coalition against Louis XIV, the patron of James II. The coalition contained a number of Catholic powers including the pope, who was said to have marked his ally's victory with a *Te Deum* in Rome. Loyalists usually ignored such talk. In 1974, for example, the UDA *Ulster Loyalist* published an article on the battle which adopted the usual depiction of William III as an enemy of Rome. The following year, however, the same journal changed tack. Tongue in cheek, it suggested that the 12 July celebration was not sectarian as 'William of Orange's victory was particularly welcome to the Pope, among other Europeans. Its traditional commemoration nowadays had rather the character of an Independence Day celebration.' The unionist historian, Dr Hugh Shearman, agreed.[125] Paisley, again quoting Macaulay, showed that the pope in question, Alexander VII, was closer to Louis XIV than his predecessor, Innocent XI.[126] A *Te Deum* was certainly sung in Catholic Vienna, but probably not Rome.

The UDA and Ulster separatism: Adamson's Cruthin

As for other post-1974 loyalists, the UDA through its New Ulster Political Research Group (NUPRG) aimed at the establishment of an independent Ulster. This, it hoped, would reconcile both Protestants and Catholics to a common Ulster identity, opposed both to British and Irish cultural imperialism. The philosopher of this group was a medical doctor and prolific publicist, Ian Adamson, who appears to have sold his ideas to the UDA commander, Andy Tyrie, and some other leaders. Adamson epitomised his message in a 1982 volume, *The Identity of Ulster*, after previous publications such as *The Cruthin*, 1974, *Bangor, Light of the World*, 1979, and a number of articles in the UDA's *Ulster*, sometimes under the name 'Sam Sloan'. Adamson developed the not entirely original idea of seventeenth-century Ulster planters as a returning, rather than an alien, force. Even Paisley and the OUP leader Molyneux seem to have accepted this. But Adamson went a step further, arguing that the Ulster Protestant community was represented by the pre-Milesian Cruthin, or Picts, who as the original inhabitants were driven to

Scotland or absorbed into the invading Gaelic culture which accepted many Cruthnic forms. The Cruthin, unlike the Gaels, were not Indo-European[127] but contributed to the cultural mix, making Irish an exceptional language. The Cruthnic apogee was reached, according to Adamson, in the foundation of the Bangor monastery in north Down in 555. This produced in Columbanus the Pict the greatest of all Irish missionaries. In 637 the Picts were finally reduced to vassalage by the Gaelic O'Neills. In the seventeenth century many of the settlers from Scotland had Pictish ancestry; therefore it could be said that they were coming home. What did all this mean politically?

In the 'Sam Sloan' articles in the UDA's *Ulster*, Adamson's theory is a great deal more explicit than in *The Identity of Ulster*. His message was clear: 'We affirm that Ulster is a Pictish not a Gaelic nation'. Even Cuchulain, the inspiration of Padriac Pearse the leader of the 1916 Rising, is annexed as a Pict who defended Ulster against the invading Gaels. Adamson was preceded by the first issues of the *UDA News* in 1971 which used Cuchulain and his famous hound as its emblem: Cuchulain 'particularly symbolises Ulster today.... He was Ulster's one and only hero and he defended Ulster against the rest of the provinces of Ireland. They killed him in the end but only by treachery, deceit and subversion'. This was not the first time that Cuchulain had been put to loyalist use. Andy Tyrie, the UDA Commander, had a 'tinny bas-relief' of Cuchulain on the wall of his office and was able to expound the Adamson theory.[128]

Adamson developed the argument by claiming that the six counties of Ulster were not an unnatural unit seized in 1920 by opportunist unionists working through a complaisant British government but a reasonable compromise between the varying frontiers of Cruthnic or Pictish power.[129] The ultimate call was emotional: 'you are the children of the Cruthin, the sons and daughters of the Picts. This is OUR land, YOUR culture, YOUR heritage—You are indeed the people. You are older than the Gaels, older than the Welsh, older even than the English. You have a [right] to belong here, no less than the trees. You have a right to be HEARD here. You have a right to be FREE!'[130] Unlike Paisley, Adamson accepted the United Irishmen, including the 'noble' Henry Joy McCracken, as Cruthin.[131]

Like the Provisionals, the UDA historians had to contend with academics. At first response from specialists was fairly muted, but in September 1993 H.J. Morgan attacked the propagandist use of Cuchulain (properly Cú Chulainn) by both republicans and loyalists. Adamson was dismissed as a 'pseudo-historian'. Cuchulain was not a Cruthin, nor were the Cruthin Picts. The Cruthin were not driven out and the seventeenth-century settlers in Ulster were not returning Cruthin but mainly lowland Scots and English. So the debate continues.[132] Dr Anthony Buckley, the eminent sociologist of Northern Ireland religion, however, maintains that Adamson's 'thesis is neither new nor intellectually disreputable', being based on the views of the scholar T.F. O'Rahilly. Adamson, according to Buckley, secularised the religious notions of a Protestant elect, associated with British Israelism. The religious ideal has little appeal to working-class Protestants who accept the general, if illogical, 'Protestant consensus' analysed above. This certainly helps to explain why Adamson's theory is popular with the UDA and some Official Unionists, though not with Paisley who insists on the non-secularised religious tradition.[133]

Regardless of the argument's academic merit, winning support for its corollary, the independence of Ulster, was difficult. The Catholic community was generally unwilling to become Ulster Picts with the UDA and preferred to see themselves as Gaels in a united Ireland. Indeed, once the amalgamation of cultures was admitted in Ulster, why not accept Irish identity? Some southern Provisional allies seem privately to have been interested.[134] The unionists themselves were not very impressed. Those working for greater integration with Britain rejected the suggestion without consideration, and even on the devolutionist wing Paisley was hostile. When the bicycling traveller, Dervla Murphy, published the best-selling *A Place Apart*, accepting the relevance to Ulster of the NUPRG ideas, the book was acclaimed by the UDA[135] but denounced by the *Protestant Telegraph*, not only for misrepresenting Dr Paisley, but for attributing papistical superstition to Protestant working-class ghettoes. An independent Ulster, 'Protestant Sinn Féin', was rejected on the intransigent ground that 'while popery exists in Ireland, there will continue to be trouble.'[136] NUPRG's *Beyond the Religious Divide* was followed up in 1987 by *Common Sense*. This latter policy, though containing the daring idea of power sharing, likewise failed to emulate Paisley's DUP in commanding a sizeable portion of loyalist votes. Unlike Provisional Sinn Féin, the UDA's 'blood-stained history' has limited its constitutional appeal.[137] John McMichael, the chief architect of the New Ulster policy, proved no vote spinner, but his leadership of the UFF led to assassination, less than a year after the publication of *Common Sense*.

Nineteenth-century Protestant clericalism: Paisley versus UDA and UVF

The discussion of the seventeenth-century plantations has thus ranged far beyond that period and carried the reader rapidly from pre-history to the present day. Such is the diffuse nature of the historical argumentation in unionist and republican self-justification. The nineteenth century, which saw the development of the Orange Order and the tradition of riot-provoking sermons in Belfast by preachers like 'Roaring' Hugh Hanna, provided numerous incidents for local folk-lore. Paisley identified chiefly with churchmen like Hanna[138] and the conservative Presbyterian Henry Cooke[139] who did much to unite Presbyterians and Anglicans against Roman Catholicism. All loyalists were inspired by the resistance to Home Rule in the late nineteenth and early twentieth centuries. Paisley, temporarily dropping the Cooke image, went on the 'Carson Trail'. On another occasion he assisted in bringing the *Clyde Valley*, the original UVF gun-running ship, back to Ulster. According to McKeague, Paisley failed to account for the money raised when the project was literally scrapped.[140]

The 'Protestant heritage' thus confronts the theoretically secular republican ideal. But Paisley's attempt at a Protestant consensus was challenged in the 1970s by a more secular ideal of a cultural Ulster identity. Sometimes there was convergence, though the paramilitary journals increasingly distanced themselves from clerical tutelage. The surprising result was that, though an anachronism in its continued emphasis on racial and cultural divergence in an increasingly cosmopolitan world, the New Ulster idea was a refreshing break with Paisley's naked anti-popery. UVF men who learned Gaelic in gaol and sported the Irish speaker's *fainne* badge could lament that earlier in life they had been cut off from their rightful heritage of Irish history and culture. John McKeague, a peddler of extreme anti-popery, seems to have gone through a type of conversion to a broader view of Ulster identity before being laid low by an assassin's bullet. Tara and the Loyal Orange Lodge 1303, which emblazoned Irish mottos on its banners and looked for a Protestant to teach its members Irish, were, however, ludicrously illiberal and anti-ecumenical in their aim of destroying Catholicism throughout Ireland.[141] By 1993 an official of the Young Unionists at Queen's University was involved in starting an Irish language class: 'There is essentially a great interest in the Irish language among non-nationalists.'[142] To adapt Dr Johnson's comment on the woman preacher, the surprise was not the loyalist numbers involved, but that any should participate in Irish culture at such a period. Whatever the precise motives or nature of participators, an alternative to the 'Protestant heritage' was developing.

Prot-stats and Prot-ecums

Analysis of the 'Protestant heritage' as it ransacks history demonstrated many discrepancies. Only verbal sleight of hand could enable Free Presbyterians to pose as defenders of a Protestant consensus. The 'popery barefaced' which consisted of seeking salvation 'by doing no harm, paying every man his own, saying your prayers and going to church and sacrament' probably epitomised the religion of most Protestants.[143] Furthermore, the history of the Reformation is too complex to admit of an easy identification with principles like 'private judgement' and 'the separation of Church and State'. The aim of removing popery from Ireland is irreconcilable with peaceful religious co-existence. Indeed, the Paisleyite view of history leads to an exceptionally muscular Christianity. The secularised version of the Ulster heritage makes a Protestant consensus even more elusive. Clarity of thought might be increased by dropping the use of the word 'Protestant' in this connection and using a neologism such as 'Pro-statist' or 'Prot-stat', implying a vigorous political anti-Catholicism, sometimes secularised into an apparent anti-republicanism which often assassinates Catholics at random. Ecumenical Churches, prepared to live and let live, could then be described by their individual names or generally as 'Prot-ecums'. A Methodist, for example, only becomes a 'Prot-stat' when he or she holds strong views on the need to resist the encroachments of Catholicism by political or forceful means. The 'Protestant consensus' view, easily manipulated by Free Presbyterians for their own specific ends, could be quietly phased from popular thought, an operation easier to conceive than translate into reality.

Prot-stats and mirrored republicans

Generally, the still predominant religious 'Prot-statism' mirrors secular republicanism. Both viewpoints are blurred in the details of their rationalisations, and extremely vulnerable to the erosion of revisionists. Their dependence on historicism increases this vulnerability. Antagonistic history results from abandoning the democratic, problem solving, social engineering attitude in favour of absolutist solutions. Force lies at the heart of each credo. Thus we revert again to the old symbiosis. Religion, however, operated differently, or appeared to do so, on the opposing viewpoints. To balance the argument, a full discussion of the relations between republicanism and the Catholic Church is now required.

Notes

1. See Morgan, Austen and Purdie, Bob (1980), *Ireland: Divided Nation Divided Class*, London: Ink Links. For an earlier version of this chapter, see Davis, R. (1986), 'The Manufacture of Propagandist History by Northern Ireland Loyalists and Republicans', *Ireland's Terrorist Dilemma*, 145-177.
2. Namier, L. (1963), *Vanished Supremacies: Essays on European History, 1812-1918*, New York: Hayer, 166-7. Durham, Lord (1905), *The Report of the Earl of Durham, Her Majesty's High Commissioner and Governor-General of British North America*, London: Methuen, 8. Burke, Edmund (1872), *Burke's Works*, 111, London: Bell and Daldry, 320 (Letter to H. Langrishe, 1792).
3. Stewart, A.T.Q. (1967), *The Ulster Crisis*, London: Faber, 166-7, 179. Paisley superimposed himself on the photograph in the 1981 Carson Trail. See Wilson, Sam (1981), *The Carson Trail*, Belfast: Crown, 64.
4. Heslinga, M.W. (1971), *The Irish Border as a Cultural Divide*, Netherlands: Van Gorcum, 62. See also PT, 15 December 1972. (Review of Tony Gray).
5. Davis, Richard (1980), 'Ulster Protestants and the Sinn Féin Press, 1914-22', in *Eire-Ireland*, St Paul, winter, 60-85.
6. Lyons, F.S.L. (1982), *Culture and Anarchy in Ireland, 1890-1939*, Oxford: OUP.
7. AP, 20 May 1993. O Snodaigh reviews.
8. Miller, D.W. (1978), *Queen's Rebels: Ulster Loyalism in Historical Perspective*, Dublin: Gill and Macmillan.
9. PT, 2 October 1978. Paisley promised unswerving support for the union while the Queen remained a Protestant. Martin Smyth, Orange Grand Master, also asserted that loyalty depended on the Queen's Protestantism, see *The Christian Irishman*, Belfast (Presbyterian), July-August 1982, 12.
10. PT, 17 February 1968: (criticism of Queen's visit to pope); 27 July 1968 (attack on Duke of Edinburgh for Sunday sport, declaration of man's independence of God, support for EEC and involvement with Prince Bernhardt's international financiers); 10 April 1971 (criticism of Duke's Australian suggestion that Partition was the cause of the Irish problem). See also NPT, January 1993, for complaints that Prince Philip was reverting to Greek Orthodoxy while Princess Diana was taking Roman Catholic religious instruction.
11. PT, 2 March 1968. For McGrath, see Foot, Paul, *Who Framed Colin Wallace?* ('Kincora'), 115-146 and Curtis, Liz (1984), *Ireland: The Propaganda War: The Media and the 'Battle for Hearts and Minds'*, 238.

12. Lyons, F.S.L. (1979), *The Burden of Our History*, W.B. Rankin Memorial Lecture, Belfast: Queen's University, 16.

13. PT, 2 September 1961. For anti-Tone Catholic view, see McCabe (1939), *Wolfe Tone and the United Irishmen: For or Against Christ?* London: Heath Cranton, 188 and 250. By contrast RN March 1971, was content to refer simply to Tone's death in gaol. PT, 2 September 1967, for evocation of massacre of Protestants at Scullabogue. See also LN, 27 October 1974, and 15 March 1975, for Scullabogue and Wexford Bridge.

14. O'Faolain, Sean, ed. (1937), *Autobiography of Theobald of Wolfe Tone*, London: Nelson, xix: 'His personality the man himself, is a definition of Irish Republicanism. It is the only sensible definition that exists.' Elliott, Marianne (1989), *Wolfe Tone: Prophet of Irish Independence*, New Haven: Yale University Press, 419, accepts that 'Tone's autobiography will continue to be the centrepiece of popular Irish nationalism.'

15. Smith O'Brien, leader of the Irish Rebellion of 1848, considered the proceedings of the United Irishmen 'most disastrous' to their country's interests. *Dublin Evening Mail*, 21 February 1861. For Griffith, see Davis, *Arthur Griffith and Non-Violent Sinn Féin*, 120.

16. See Jimmy Drumm's Bodenstown denunciations of politicians and 'pseudo-intellectuals' who 'take Tone out of his context to say he would not agree with our methods'. RN, 18 June 1977. MacDermott, Frank (1939), *Theobald Wolfe Tone*, London: Macmillan, was an early neo-unionist work.

17. AP, September 1971; A, October 1975.

18. Charlie and George Gilmore from the 1920s to the 1960s represented the left-wing of the IRA. Sir Roger Casement was originally a British diplomat who was hanged in 1916 for attempting to raise an army for Irish independence amongst Irish prisoners of war in Germany.

19. PT, 27 February 1971. In Paisley, Ian (1972), *United Ireland: Never!* Belfast: Puritan, (11) he suggests that 'some deluded Unitarian Presbyterians were caught in the trap.'

20. LN, Belfast, 15 April 1972, quoted in RN, 23 April 1972.

21. PT, 4 November 1972.

22. C, 1 April 1974.

23. C, February 1976 and 8 April 1974. LN, 26 October 1974, and 29 September 1973.

24. Quoted in O'Brien, C.C. (1972), *States of Ireland*, London, Hutchinson, 39. For Sammy Smyth, UM, July 1972.

25. RN, 30 April 1975.

26. C (1, 11) 1974. McKeague's LN, 24 January 1976 complained of Tone's instability.

27. U, January 1979.

28. Morgan and Purdie, *Ireland*, 76-77. Elliott, *Wolfe Tone*, 418-19, also shows Tone as an equivocal democrat: 'he was part of an élite and had a very Protestant perception of the Irish masses.' According to Neil Forde in *An Phoblacht*, Elliott 'literally recolonised the middle and late 18th Century period and its politics.' Preferable was Smyth, Jim (1993)

The Men of No Property, Dublin: Gill and Macmillan, which saw the period in its own, not 20th century terms, AP, 11 March 1993.

29. I am indebted to Nancy Curtin for this point.

30. PT, 15 May 1971. For 1791 context of 'red-hot', see MacDermott, *Tone*, 67.

31. See O'Faolain, ed., *Autobiography of Theobald Wolfe Tone*, 52, 56, 60, 216, 255, 258. McCabe, Leo, *Wolfe Tone and the United Irishman: For or Against Christ?* was written to defend the bishops against Tone.

32. U, January 1979.

33. PT, 15 May 1971.

34. Adamson, I., *Cruthin: The Ancient Kindred*, Newtownards: Nosmada, 85-7.

35. 'Blackmouth' is sometimes used in a conservative sense.

36. U, January 1979.

37. PT, 1 May 1971.

38. U, January 1979.

39. RN, Easter 1972 (2.28).

40. T.C. Luby, prominent on the *Irish People*, was a Protestant. According to Marx, 'Luby, etc of the *Irish People* were educated men who treated religion as a bagatelle.' Marx to Engels 10 December 1969, *Marx, Engels and the Irish Question*, 399.

41. PT, 31 May 1969.

42. PT, 15 August 1970. Yellow was the pope's colour or the emblem of murder. The contention does have some truth for the AOH who appear to prefer yellow to orange. UM, 3 and 4 (1972).

43. Gerry Adams believed that loyalists were consistently out fought by the IRA, AP, 10 February 1979. SP, December 1976, claimed that loyalist bluff against Britain had never been called and that their current actions depended on British support.

44. AP, 1 February 1977 and Davis, Richard (1982), 'Robert Lynd: A Man for all Seasons', *Pace*, Belfast, Vol. 41, No. 2, Summer/Autumn, 20-22.

45. MacStiofain, *Memoirs of a Revolutionary*, 138 and 142.

46. PT, 28 December 1968, (links it with Bible Protestantism), 12 July 1976. C, July 1974. UL 31 January 1974. The British forces journal, *Visor*, 27 June 1974 rejects this identification: 'There is no connection between the original UVF and the bunch of gangsters and psychopaths who nowadays use the same name.' See also Curtis, *Ireland: The Propaganda War*, 232.

47. Between July 1920 and July 1922 453 people had been killed in Belfast (37 Crown forces, 257 Catholics, 157 Protestants and two doubtfuls). See Farrell, *Northern Ireland: The Orange State*, 62.

48. At Altnaveigh near Newry, 18 June 1922, six Protestants were killed by Catholics. See PT, 19 October 1968; OUDAN, (2,9) 1973.

49. PT, 2 January 1981; AP, 16 November 1977.

50. RN, November -December 1970.

51. RN, 30 October 1971.

52. RN, 1 June 1974.

53. O'Brien, C.C. (1980), *Neighbours: The Ewart-Biggs Memorial Lectures 1978-1979*, London: Faber, 25.

54. Gwynn, D. (1948), *O'Connell, Davis and the Colleges Bill*, Cork: Cork University Press; MacLochlainn, A. (1973), 'Thomas Davis and Irish Radicalism', *Irish Times*, 20 November 1973; O'Brien, C.C. (1957), *Parnell and his Party, 1880-90*, Oxford: Clarendon Press; Lyons, F.S.L., (1960), *The Fall of Parnell, 1890-91*, London: Routledge and Kegan Paul; Martin, F.X. (1968), 'The 1916 Rising—coup d'etat or a bloody protest?, *Studia Hibernia*, no. 8; Shaw, Fr Francis (1972), 'The Canon of Irish History—a Challenge', *Studies*, Summer 1972; Inglis, Brian (1973), *Roger Casement*, London: Hodder and Stoughton) (criticized by RN, 9 June 1973.); Edwards, R. Dudley (1977), *Patrick Pearse: The Triumph of Failure*, London: Faber, 127 (for Pearse's homosexuality); Dunne, Tom (1982), *Theobald Wolfe Tone: The Colonial Outsider: An Analysis of his Political Philosophy*, Cork: Tower Books, 53.

55. UI, November-December 1979.

56. For a two page review of Foster's *Modern Ireland, 1600-1972*, as 'the most towering accomplishment' of revisionism, see AP, 6 April 1988. For other criticism of Foster see Brian Murphy, quoted in AP, 3 September 1992, and Brendan Bradshaw, AP, 29 August 1991.

57. RN, 1 June 1974.

58. AP, 30 May 1991 (Woodham-Smith); AP, 31 October 1991 (Greaves, C.D. (1963) *Theobald Wolfe Tone and the Irish Nation*, Fulcrum Press)

59. AP, 25 April 1991 (Whelan); AP, 23 November 1989 (Kibberd), Desmond Greaves Summer School; AP, 3 September 1992 (Foster, Lyons, O'Farrell, MacDonagh, criticised, Deane an anti-revisionist.)

60. AP, 22 March 1990.

61. Jack Madden in AP, 9 January 1991.

62. See Padraig O Snodaigh (1991), *Two Godfathers of Revisionism*, Fulcrum Press (Frs F.X. Martin and Francis Shaw), reviewed in *An Phoblacht*, 9 April 1992; Desmond Greaves Summer School, Dr Brian Murphy's attack on Roy Foster accusing him of being sectarian and racialist and a two nations advocate, AP, 3 September 1992;

63. See for example, AP, 28 May 1992, report of Gender and Colonialism conference at University College Galway, especially Liz Curtis on challenge to revisionists. Feminists were critical of historians such as Foster and Lyons, see Margaret Ward (1991), *The Missing Sex: putting women into Irish History*, Dublin: Attic Press, 5 and 7-10. See also, Pauline Bennett in AP, 21 November 1991.

64. Especially the works of Ian Adamson.

65. Paisley, I.R.K. (1976), *Paisley: the Man and His Message*, Belfast: Martyrs Memorial, 159. The dying thief crucified with Jesus was claimed as a Free Presbyterian.

66. PT, 2 March 1968.

67. AP, 9 May and 18 July 1975.

68. Hanson, R.P.C.(1968), *St Patrick, his origins and career*, New York: OUP, 203.

69. Hanson, though a Dubliner, was then professor of theology at Nottingham University. A strong opponent of clergy in politics, he talks of the 'Babylonish captivity to political ideologies'. See (1980), 'It is a Religious Issue', *Encounter*, Vol. XV, No. 4, April 19, October, 19. For

lack of finesse, Gallagher and Worrall, 57 and 75. Opposition to clergy in politics, Hanson, Richard (1973), 'Politics and the Pulpit', *Community Forum*, Belfast, Vol. 3, No. 3, 14-18. Duty of clergy, Hanson's (1972) review of Akenson, D.H., *The Irish Education Experiment*, *Irish Theological Quarterly*, Vol. 39, No. 2., April, 201-2. Hanson's demand for ministers of religion to eschew parliament and the Orange Order were endorsed by the future Cardinal Cahal Daly, see Daly, Cahal B. (1979), *Peace: The Work of Justice: Addresses on the Northern Tragedy*, 1973-79, Dublin: Veritas, 19.

70. Hanson, R. (1963), *The Bible as a Norm of Faith*, Durham University, 10 and 12.

71. PT, 4 November 1972.

72. PT, 14 December 1968.

73. PT, 11 May 1974.

74. Torrey, R.A. in PT, 12 May 1973. Wilson, Bryan (1970), *Religious Sects: A Sociological Study*, London: Weidenfeld and Nicholson, 38. Paisley, I.R.K. (1982), *No Pope Here*, Belfast: Martyr Memorial Publications, 79.

75. PT, 9 February 1974 (guarantee liberty). See also Nelson, Sarah (1984), *Ulster's Uncertain Defenders: Protestant Political, Paramilitary and Community Groups and the Northern Ireland Conflict*, 71 on Calvinist opposition to freedom.

76. PT, 3 June 1974.

77. See PT. 3 December 1966. on the confessionals which are 'in reality sin-boxes leading to greater villainies between confessors and penitents'.

78. See Fr Art O'Neill, RN, 6 April 1974 and the Liberal Presbyterian Barkley, Professor J.M. (n.d.), *The Roman Church: A Handbook for Parents and Teachers*, Belfast: Presbyterian Church in Ireland, 7-8. Barkley argues that Protestants do not object to voluntary confession.

79. PT, 12 May 1973, criticised the Church of Ireland for almost accepting the 'Real Presence' in the sacraments like the Catholics.

80. In 1990, in a Commons debate on reducing the time limit for legal abortion, Paisley praised his colleagues of the SDLP for their support. He did, however, argue that Protestants placed a higher value on the life of the mother and that matters like rape, incest and serious handicap might qualify the principle of sanctity of life. See NPT, 5 May and July/August 1990. The Miss X case in the Irish Republic in 1992, when the Irish Supreme Court (5 March) decided that fear of suicide after rape justified abortion, and a referendum on 28 November 1992 which endorsed the High Court and extended opportunities for abortion travel and information, narrowed any perceivable gap between Paisley and Irish constitutional law. Provisional Sinn Féin has been ambivalent on abortion, refusing at its Ard Fheis of 1993 to further liberalise its policy. Jim Gibney claimed that the existing policy was a compromise between the conservative position and women's demands. AP, 25 February 1993.

81. See Adams, Michael (1968), *Censorship: the Irish Experience*, Dublin: Scepter, 250 for banning of Steinbeck. PT, 12 August 1978, claimed that Steinbeck's *Mice and Men* had blasphemous sentences.

82. See Davis, R. (1980), 'Ulster Protestants and the Sinn Féin Press, 1914-22', *Eire-Ireland*, St Paul, Winter, 60-85; C, 12 April 1974 and RN, 24 November 1973.
83. U, February 1980; LN, 9 January 1971.
84. See for example Paisley's Stormont speech, PT, 1 August 1970, and the Free Presbyterian edition of the WCF.
85. PT, 4 February 1967.
86. Donovan, Rev. P. E. (1975), 'Why I am a Protestant', PT, 23 August 1975.
87. PT, 17 February 1973.
88. Bishop Hanson quoted by PT, 13 March 1971.
89. See Paisley, I.R.K. (n.d.), *Three Great Reformers*, Belfast: Puritan, 2.
90. Sykes, Norman (1959), *The Crisis of the Reformation*, London: Geoffrey Bles, 103. 'A sounder theological definition than that of the German and Swiss Reformers'. Most Protestant scholars admit 'the service rendered to truth and common sense by the Council of Trent when it repudiated the more emphatic expressions of that quasi-Pauline determinism to which the great Reformers were addicted'.
91. Paisley, Ian (1972), *United Ireland: Never!*, (9) for 1641. McKeague, John, LN, 17 October 1970 to 5 December 1970, published a series of articles on the massacre of St Bartholomew.
92. PT, 25 October 1969.
93. *Orange Standard* (OS), Belfast, February 1975.
94. Kamen, H. (1967), *The Rise of Toleration*, London: Weidenfeld and Nicholson, 56.
95. OS, October 1973.
96. PT, 13 March 1971.
97. Kamen, *The Rise of Toleration*, 47.
98. C, (1:12, 23-4, 31) 1974.
99. C, (1:11, 17-19) 1974.
100. C, June 1975.
101. MacNeill, J.T. (1962), *The History and Character of Calvinism*, New York: OUP, 321-2.
102. Connolly, James (n.d.), *Labour in Ireland*, Dublin, 156-8.
103. Lyons, F.S.L., *The Burden of our History*, 19.
104. Quoted Kamen, *The Rise of Toleration*, 54, from Lecky, W.E. (1910), *History of the Rise and Influence of Rationalism in Europe*, London: Longman, Vol. 2, 44. Ridley, Jasper (1968), *John Knox*, Oxford: Clarendon, 448, fully endorses this view.
105. UL, 6 April 1975.
106. PT, June 1975.
107. PT, June 1967.
108. Article by McGie, Thomas, PT, 6 January 1973.
109. PT, July 1978 and Paisley, *Three Great Reformers*, 46, which compares Rome's tactics in the days of Knox to modern attempts at 'papalising our Royal House of Windsor'.
110. *Westminster Confession of Faith* (1978), Glasgow: Free Presbyterian Publications, 19 (XXIII, IV).
111. PT, 17 September 1977. For republican use of the Sack of Drogheda as anti-British propaganda see AN, 14 December 1974.

112. PT, 17 April 1976.
113. Some historians, such as Stewart, A.T.Q. (1977) *The Narrow Ground: Aspects of Ulster, 1609-1969*, London: Faber, 41, do not accept the absolute division of this time. ('There never was any true confrontation of archetypal Planter and Gael'). See also Buchanan, R.H. (1982), 'The Planter and the Gael: cultural dimensions of the Northern Ireland Problem', in Boal, F.W. and Douglas, J.N.H. (1982), *Integration and Division: Geographical Perspectives on the Northern Ireland Problem*, London: Academic Press, 67 and 69.
114. Davis, R. (1974 and 1977), *Arthur Griffith and Non-Violent Sinn Féin*, 56 and 'India in Irish Revolutionary Propaganda, 1905-22', *Journal of the Asiatic Society of Bangladesh*, Vol. XXII, No. 1, April 1977, 66-89.
115. AP, August 1972 claims that the republican movement has always accepted the Orangemen as Irish not British. Desmond Fennell (Freeman) insisted (AP, 11 July 1975) that there were not two nations in Ireland, but two allegiances: the British allegiance did not make a nation but part of a foreign community lodged in Ireland. He later (AP, 5 September 1975) qualified this by saying that Provisionals did not demand abandonment of British nationality or departure from Ireland, but anticipated that the two nations would merge into a common Ulster and Irish citizenship, constituting a new Irish nation. RN, 4-6 September 1971, compared the pro-British Ulstermen with Algerian colons who must decide between England and Ireland. The historian Michael Dolley was reported by PT, 18 November 1972, as saying that planters could take it or leave it.
116. Robinson, Peter (1988), *Their Cry was "No Surrender": An Account of the Siege of Londonderry, 1688-1689*, Belfast: Crown Publications. Paisley wrote the foreword.
117. Mitchel, John (n.d.), *Ireland from the seige of Limerick*, London: Washbourne, 18.
118. LN, 29 August 1975 and Davis, *Arthur Griffith*, 109. Nelson, S., *Ulster's Uncertain Defenders*, 33 on the 1641 myth.
119. PT, 3 September 1977.
120. C, 25 April 1974.
121. *Freedom Fighter*, Vol. 1, No. 1, June 1992.
122. PT, 3 February 1973.
123. AP, 5 May 1974, talked of important bridges. RN, 25 May 1974, quoted the article in full.
124. See BICO (1974), 'Hidden Ulster' Explored: A Reply to P. O'Snodaigh; MacDonagh, Oliver (1983), *States of Mind: A Study of Anglo-Irish Conflict, 1780-1980*, London: Allen and Unwin, 105.
125. UL, 21 November 1974 and 2 March 1975. See also Shearman, Hugh (1972), *27 Myths about Ulster*, Belfast: Ulster Unionist pamphlet, 5.
126. PT, 3 April 1976.
127. *Cruthin*, 115.
128. Sam Sloan in U, August and September 1978. For Tyrie and Cuchulain, see Belfrage, Sally (1987), *Living with War: A Belfast Year*, New York: Elisabeth Sifton Books, 112.

129. UDAN, 19 October 1971 and Shearman, Hugh (1942), *Not An Inch*, London: Faber, 5.
130. U, October 1978.
131. *Cruthin*, 86-7. Hanson, R.P.C. (1983), *The Life and Writings of St Patrick*, New York: Seabury Press, 55.
132. Morgan, H.J. (1993), 'Deceptions of Demons', *Fortnight*, September 1993, No. 320, 34-6. For a reply to Morgan, claiming that neither Adamson nor Morgan can prove their contentions, see W.A. Hanna, *Fortnight*, January 1994, No. 324, pp. 34-5.
133. Buckley, Anthony (1989), '"We're Trying to Find our Identity": Uses of History among Ulster Protestants', in E. Tonkin, M. McDonald and M. Chapman, eds, *History and Ethnicity*, London: Routledge, 192-5.
134. According to Holland, (1981) *Too Long a Sacrifice: Life and Death in Northern Ireland since 1969*, New York: Dodd Mead, 118, PIRA rejected NUPGR but 'privately they played with the idea of Ulster independence'.
135. U, Christmas 1979, published Dervla Murphy's 'A return' praising the UDA's *Beyond the Religious Divide* (29 March 1979.).
136. PT, 29 April 1978.
137. U, March 1979.
138. PT, 15 May 1971 on Hanna's great rally in 1862.
139. PT, 8 October 1966, Paisley on 'that Great Irish Presbyterian leader'.
140. PT, 28 December 1968, Paisley welcomes the return. For McKeague, see *Loyalist News*, 6 February 1971.
141. OS, September 1975 and April 1982. The republican AN, 3 January 1973, commended the development.
142. NPT, May 1993.
143. PT, 12 July 1974.

4 Republicanism and Catholicism

Republicanism: puppet or adversary of Rome?

Loyalists, as demonstrated in the last chapter, have traditionally insisted that it is pure hypocrisy to claim republicanism as a secular doctrine. The Roman Catholic Church, they believe, dominates Irish politics and social life. As the chief argument against a united Ireland, Romanist aggression is essential to their philosophy. Republicans must demonstrate both their immunity from clerical pressure and, if they are to retain support in the Catholic communities, the compatibility of their actions with true religion. The debate is a good example of patterned opposition. Both republicans and loyalists began the 1970s with prepared scripts. Republicans cited a history of resistance to clerical condemnation dating back to the twelfth century. The loyalist counter-script also traced Roman aggression to twelfth-century Ireland.

By World War I and the first Irish Revolution anti-Catholic writers such as M.J.F. McCarthy, and J.A. Kensit lumped all current evils—Prussianism, Bolshevism, Sinn Féinism—into one colossal Vatican conspiracy, 'the Celibate internationale', against the British Empire. In applying their scripts to the Northern Irish events of the 1970s, there was antithetical understanding between republicans and loyalists.[1] The former listed honourable exceptions to traditional Catholic hierarchical opposition to Irish nationalism; the loyalists cited the same names, but insisted that they represented the true policy of the church. When republicans produced catalogues of unpatriotic clergy, loyalists complained that these men rejected republican methods, not ideals. From the 1970s, republicans denounced clerics who condemned their activities as exceeding their spiritual powers, while loyalists complained that Catholic churchmen refused to apply their legitimate religious sanctions. Great issues were involved, confession, excommunication, last rites, Church reform, and the existence of revolutionary clergy.

The anti-national tradition of Irish bishops

In early 1971, less than a year after the Provisionals had established their press, the tradition of republican resistance to clerical denunciation was invoked, and the list of exceptions sketched.[2] During the next decade numerous articles delineated a detailed picture. Irish bishops, declared the republicans, gravitated naturally towards British interests. The English Pope Adrian IV's Bull *Laudabiliter*, granting Ireland to Henry II,[3] demonstrated an early liaison between the English monarchy and the Holy See. On the other side, however, the Orange Grand Master, Martin Smyth, like Paisley, used *Laudabiliter* to denounce Rome's initial interference in Irish affairs.[4] Opponents as usual were at cross-purposes. Republicans, moreover, insisted that Rome altered its policy to suit circumstances. In 1600, for example, when England had rejected Catholicism and made it illegal, Pope Clement VIII granted a plenary indulgence to the liberators of Ireland.[5] Republicans endorsed the embattled bishops of the eighteenth-century penal era, but denounced the British government's 1795 establishment of the Maynooth seminary as a blatant liaison between Church and occupying power.[6] The Official Sinn Féin journal, the *United Irishman*, which tried to ignore the Catholic Church except on education, pointed out that bishops had condemned both the 1798 rebellion and that of Robert Emmet in 1803.[7] Fr John Murphy, who emerged as one of the leaders of the Wexford rebellion of 1798, was a good priest according to the Provisionals,[8] but a typical political cleric to loyalists.

In the nineteenth century clear polarisation between nationalism and the official Catholic hierarchy seemed evident. The Young Irelanders were stigmatised as 'infidels' by numerous clerics and the church condemned their 1848 rebellion. The rise of Fenianism in the 1860s posed particular problems for the Catholic Church, experiencing a 'devotional revolution' and 'Romanisation' under the determined Cardinal Paul Cullen, which he became in 1866. The Provisionals followed a well-worn nationalist tradition in condemning Cullen as 'largely to blame for the peculiar type of snobbery and intolerance of priests which, unfortunately, has survived to our own day.'[9] Cullen's alleged protégé, Bishop David Moriarty, was duly remembered for his famous statement that 'Hell was not hot enough nor eternity long enough' to punish the Fenians.

Cullen versus the Fenians

Though the debate of the 1970s and 1980s cited the struggle between Cullen and the Fenians as a typical phase of a longer tradition of hostility, it was a particularly important precedent. The short-lived Fenian journal, the *Irish People*, in 1863-5 operated under the shadow of Dublin Castle, much as the *Republican News* and *An Phoblacht* were to function under the aegis of British Army patrols and helicopters. It conducted a debate with Cullen analagous to the dispute between the Provisionals and the Northern Irish bishops in the 1970s, 80s and 90s.[10] The Fenians had delegated their defence to Charles J. Kickham, a devout Catholic, who sought to demonstrate that Catholic clergy were exceeding their functions in condemning a movement, compelled by repression to act secretly, but designed to enable the Irish nation to exercise its God-given right to self-government. Cullen was not impressed. He tried to implement a long-ignored papal rescript of 1844 by ordering his priests to abstain from politics and instructing confessors to refuse absolution to penitents who had taken the Fenian oath. In 1870 he secured a papal rescript condemning the Fenians by name. The movement, however, continued, even after the dismal failure of the 1867 Rising. Not all Catholic clergy obeyed Cullen in questioning penitents on the Fenian oath: there were religious orders and bishops outside his control. The precedent of finding patriotic confessors to absolve republicans was thus established at a time when the physical force preached was in many cases theoretical. Cullen was nevertheless condemned and disparaged by his opponents. They accused him of being an agent of Britain and enriching his family in Carlow.[11] The propaganda was true in the sense that Cullen, who had no love of the British, certainly did what he could to pressure the government into putting down Fenianism. Cullen, however, considered himself a prince of the Universal Church rather than an Irish patriot.[12] Republicans in all ages have refused to understand or accept this attitude. To them, churchmen must be either advocates of an independent Ireland or traitors bought by the British. As Donal McCartney, in an article published shortly before the beginning of the second Irish Revolution, argued of the Fenians, Cullen merely employed 'the sort of clever but distorted argument against them which they had used against him'.[13] This type of misunderstanding was to occur frequently in the 1970s and 1980s.

McCartney's article, 'The Church and the Fenians', and R.V. Comerford's *Charles J. Kickham*, set 'The Church and Provisionals' in perspective. They show, first, that Kickham in his polemic used strong language but avoided theological questions, insisting on the separation of religion and politics, a proposition condemned by Pius IX's *Syllabus of Errors* in 1864. Kickham, however, argued that by the 1860s the Irish had shed the old dependence on the clergy necessitated by 'fiendish' British tyranny. Better-educated Irish could judge for themselves 'in all worldly concerns'. This was not far from the so-called Protestant principle of 'private judgement' which can be abstracted only with difficulty from the realities of the Reformation period. A second important precedent for the first and second Irish revolution was the comment of the *Irish People*, shortly before its suppression in 1865, that 'the people are now so used to denunciation there is no room to fear they will be frightened of it when time has come for the final struggle.'[14] This optimistic editorial was partly correct. Bishops were slower to condemn thereafter, but they eventually came out against Parnell. Only seven actually denounced the 1916 Rising, while twenty-two remained silent. A third precedent was the Fenian insistence that Vatican condemnation was based on errors fostered by British diplomacy; this proved of value when the pope came in person to Ireland in 1979. Finally, the Fenians played an essential role in insisting that the onus was on the Church, not the individual penitent, to prove that patriotic activities were immoral. Comerford may not have overstated the case when he awarded Kickham's defence 'a permanent place in Irish republican tradition and in Irish historiography'. Even more significantly, the president of Maynooth, writing of the Church and the Fenians, concluded that clerics, even after the *nominatim* condemnation of Fenianism by the Vatican in 1870, remained much divided on the issue. As Cardinal Tomás O'Fiaich, this ecclesiastical historian was to play a leading role in a similar contest in Northern Ireland.[15]

National and anti-national clergy after 1916

Not all the arguments of republicans in the 1970s were based on a
clear understanding of the Fenian debate as summarised above, but
much of their spirit filtered down through other insurgents.
Cullen's great enemy in the Irish hierarchy, Archbishop John
MacHale of Tuam, was excepted from this tradition of anti-
national prelates. So too was Archbishop Croke of Cashel, though
originally recommended for the episcopate by Cullen and, despite
much ambiguity, in agreement with the latter of the need to defeat
Fenianism at the polls. Dr O'Fiaich incorporated these clerics in his
argument. In the aftermath of the Easter Week Rising Bishop
Thomas O'Dwyer of Limerick and Archbishop Daniel Mannix of
Melbourne became republican heroes. On a lesser level, Fr Michael
O'Flanagan, president of Sinn Féin for a period and disciplined by
his superiors, was a model cleric to the Provisionals.[16] During the
first Irish Revolution Bishop Fogarty of Killaloe had associated
himself with Sinn Féin, on the non-violent side. After partition
Cardinal McRory, denounced by loyalists for denying that
Protestants were true Christians and asserting that there would be
no Protestants after fifty years of a united Ireland,[17] was regarded
as basically patriotic in his sympathies. A somewhat surprising
inclusion in the canon of good clerics was the Englishman, Cardinal
Manning, whose letter to Gladstone (24 February 1865) was
quoted: 'I am convinced that we hold Ireland by force, not only
against the will of the majority, but in defiance of all rights, natural
and supernatural'.[18]

On the other hand there were many prelates accused of following
the pro-British tradition. Bishop Daniel Cohalan of Cork was
singled out as the one authority in the first Irish Revolution who
had actually excommunicated IRA men in his diocese.[19] During the
Irish Civil War many republicans opposed to the new Free State
government were excommunicated. This was a double-edged
precedent as it indicated that the hierarchy, whatever its actions
during a revolutionary struggle, would, as Connolly predicted,
very soon rally behind the ultimate victor. On the other hand it
appeared a particularly vicious instance of perennial clerical anti-
republicanism. A final example of the anti-national tradition before
the Ulster Troubles was revealed in 1982 when the newly released
cabinet papers of 1951 showed that Archbishop McQuaid of Dublin
had asked the British ambassador to prevent the release of IRA men
gaoled in England.[20] Though not realised by republicans, this was

analogous to Cullen's letter to Gladstone asking for the suppression of the Fenian *Irish People*.[21]

Irish republicans could thus make out a fairly effective historical case against the Irish bishops. This was partly for home consumption, to enable young Catholics to join the IRA without jeopardising their immortal souls. But there was another side. Republicans needed to refute the Rome Rule argument so dear to loyalists. In the first Irish Revolution the *Irish Bulletin*, directed at foreign opinion, laid great stress on the unpatriotic character of the Irish hierarchy. Traditional Irish nationalist non-sectarianism was depicted as inevitably condemned by bishops.[22] Similarly, the Provisional press of the 1970s and 1980s was extensively disseminated in the USA and other countries. Donal McCartney claimed, ironically, that the outspoken Fenian dialogue with the Catholic bishops rendered sectarianism 'largely irrelevant'. It was not quite eradicated in 1865, 1921, or 1975. Opponents ridiculed the notion of non-sectarian republicanism; even less prejudiced outsiders were sceptical of distinctions between religion and politics. Sometimes the Provisionals, moreover, appeared to protest too much. If really free from clerical influence why reject it so vehemently? The tradition of counteracting clerical denunciation required refurbishing in every generation.

Catholic bishops and Ulster Troubles: politics and personalities

The Catholic bishops themselves had no easy task. In the initial stages of the Ulster Troubles, the *Protestant Telegraph* gloated that republicans rejected the clergy in political celebrations such as the fiftieth anniversary of Easter Week in 1966 and the Connolly commemoration of 1968. Paisley's paper attributed this rejection to the advance of socialism in the ecumenical age; no longer could the Roman Catholic Church claim to be a bulwark against communism.[23]

In Northern Ireland, though six dioceses touched on the area, only two sees were restricted entirely to the six counties. Three bishops had the main responsibility for the embattled nationalist population: the primate, the bishop of Down and Connor, and the bishop of Derry. In 1968 the cardinal archbishop of Armagh and primate of All Ireland was William Conway, a prelate of the old school appointed in 1963 after the normal career of pastoral and academic life. Conway was born in 1913 in a street between the Protestant Shankill and the Catholic Falls. He had played no notable part in the Second Vatican Council and might have found adjustment to the new reforms sufficiently difficult without any political disturbances. His cautious ecumenical advances, however, appealed to Prot-ecums.[24] The 'cruel see' of Down and Connor was held by a very much more controversial figure. William Philbin was born in 1907 in Mayo, educated at Maynooth where he eventually became a professor of theology, and appointed bishop of Clonfert and Galway in 1953. There Philbin demanded a reduction in the political influence of the 5 per cent Protestant minority and insisted that the Republic was a Catholic state. He was translated to Down in 1962. A theological conservative, he protested at Vatican II against a more liberal interpretation of revelation. Working closely with Monsignor Patrick Mullally and Canon Padraig Murphy (according to Labour prime minister James Callaghan 'a wonderful leader of his flock who constantly strove for peace'), Dr Philbin built schools and reorganised Church property. He has been accused of encouraging the building of the notorious Divis Flats at the City end of the Falls Road to populate the mensal parish from which he derived most of his revenue. Republicans complained that he worked closely with the unionists, especially during the O'Neill regime. He has been classified as the only Catholic bishop to give 100 per cent support to the security forces.[25] In 1970 he and Conway appointed a Catholic chaplain to Stormont. To some an ecumenical gesture of reconciliation, to republicans it was a blatant sellout of nationalist principles. Inevitably, the *Protestant Telegraph* was equally irate: 'a Priest of Baal cannot be at the same time a Minister of God'. It demanded protest from all Protestants and subsequently denounced Dr Philbin for part-authorship of a draft on ecumenism.[26] Thus a mirrored antithetical interpretation emanated from opposing extremists. To Philbin republicans attributed offences similar to those of Cullen: personal or family enrichment, association with the British government—especially dinner with the Queen and attendance at a royal garden party—and valuing stained glass windows above Catholic lives.[27]

Two other prominent bishops were men of different styles. Bishop Cahal Daly was born in 1917 and served a lengthy apprenticeship as professor of scholastic philosophy, not in a Catholic seminary, but at the non-denominational Queen's University of Belfast. Before succeeding Philbin in Down in 1982 and O'Fiaich in Armagh eight years later, he was appointed bishop of Ardagh and Clonmacnois, a diocese outside the six counties. Daly's background soon established him as a spokesman on Northern Ireland. In 1973 he published *Violence in Ireland and the Christian Conscience*.[28] The bishop denied the Provisionals' legitimacy as successors of the first Irish Revolution IRA, arguing that the latter were supported by the Sinn Féin victory at the 1918 general election. His acceptance of the 1916 Rising, however, was controversial. In 1974, Dr Cahal Daly was joined in the northern episcopate by a namesake, Dr Edward Daly. The latter's background was less academic but he had considerable media experience. Daly was appointed in the wake of Derry's 'Bloody Sunday' where he gained TV publicity and later gave evidence to the Widgery Tribunal on the nightmare shooting of thirteen in ten minutes. Daly, born in Fermanagh in 1933, the son of a grocer and undertaker, was educated at the Irish College in Rome, but was 'shattered' when appointed, as a mere curate, bishop of Derry. His Bloody Sunday experience 'highlighted the obscenity of killing' and made him abhor all violence. Dr Edward Daly's outspoken condemnations of violence enraged Provisionals; he figured almost as prominently in loyalist demonology. However, after Dr Cahal Daly's appointment to Down in 1982, he drew most Provisional fire. According to *An Phoblacht*, the new bishop was 'more intellectually sophisticated but every bit as reactionary' as Philbin. His father, it was claimed, had supported the Black and Tans.[29] According to Gerard McElroy, neither of the Dalys had any clearly defined political model.[30]

Cardinal Tomás O'Fiaich was born in 1923 in the strongly republican town of Crossmaglen on the south Armagh border. He succeeded Cardinal Conway in Armagh on the latter's death in 1977. The appointment gave rise to the Ian Paisley aphorism that you can take a man out of Crossmaglen, but you can't take Crossmaglen out of a man. Many loyalists were apprehensive of a new primate originating from what they regarded as Provisional-dominated 'bandit country'. Did he not sign his name in Irish and please republicans by his views on language?[31] Even ecumenists lamented the loss of the less doctrinaire Conway. In fact, Cardinal O'Fiaich soon incurred the wrath of republicans who discovered that the prelate had been a ruthless disciplinarian as president of Maynooth. Meanwhile Dr O'Fiaich's tentative offer to engage in dialogue with Dr Paisley evoked a ferocious sermon at the Martyrs Memorial which asserted the Free Presbyterian moderator's readiness for public debate, but no dialogue, with Antichrist's representative.[32]

The bishops of Clogher, Dromore and Kilmore, whose dioceses contained part of the six counties, were less frequently drawn into the revolutionary debate. Dr Duffy of Clogher, however, was anti-partitionist.[33] Occasionally other southern bishops who, like Dr Cahal Daly, when in Ardagh, had no direct responsibility for the north-east, participated. Generally, the primate, the bishop of Derry, and the bishop of Down and Connor, plus their personal clerical lieutenants, were the embattled prelates. Drs Eric Gallagher and Stanley Worrall, eminent Methodist ecumenists, epitomised the hierarchy's problem of antithetical interpretation when describing the republican view that Cardinal Conway was a government agent as a 'mirror image' of the loyalist belief that he was a crypto-Provisional.[34]

The early troubles: the peacemakers' dilemma

In the first years of the Troubles, before the republican propaganda war gained momentum, Cardinal Conway, a warm supporter of the early civil rights movement,[35] tried to moderate passions. After Paisleyites and Civil Righters had clashed at Armagh in November 1968, Conway and the Church of Ireland primate issued an unprecedented joint appeal for restraint. Nevertheless, at the Methodist conference in June 1969 the cardinal was rebuked for his silence. When he did speak out on the conditions in Derry which led to the explosion in August 1969, Conway received a characteristic blast from the *Protestant Telegraph*: 'instead of making an appeal for peace, [he] is actually revealing the plan of campaign.... He cants with the hypocrisy dripping from his polluted lips about the manifest injustices of forty years ... his corpulent belly, his extravagant (albeit effeminate) dress and luxurious surroundings, give the lie to this indictment of the Protestants of Ulster.' Bishop Philbin, later criticised by republicans for persuading Catholics to remove their barricades in Belfast, was denounced, before the emergence of the Provisionals, by Paisley's journal for whitewashing Roman Catholic murders; 'Well may the Pope be indicted as a man of blood and the Papacy as a system of murder'.[36]

Roman Catholic bishops were in a quandary in the Northern Ireland of the 1970s and 1980s. If their duty lay in neither uncritically defending the union nor devoting all energies to a united Ireland, what could they do? They had, first, as the Provisionals recognised in their fairer moments, to condemn outrages on both sides. Second, they had to maintain communications with both the British government and the nationalist community. Conway was pressured by unionists to accept *de jure* the northern regime by publicly attending government functions. But this would have neutralised his influence in Catholic areas and he had to act very cautiously, talking quietly to the authorities when necessary. Cardinal Cullen had faced a similar dilemma. From another perspective, the Roman Catholic Church had an opportunity to demonstrate its superiority over the rival force of secular nationalism. Neither side, however, wanted to provoke mutually destructive confrontation.

Ecumenism was a new element in the history of Irish nationalist activity. At the very beginning of the Troubles the precedent had been set for joint Church appeals for peace. With Conway's support, such declarations and services of intercession continued. The Churches most involved were the Roman Catholic, the Church of Ireland, the Presbyterian, and the Methodist, or at least some members of them. A number of clergy in the latter three Churches took the Free Presbyterian position. These conservatives belaboured many joint initiatives as a sell-out to Rome. As late as 1985 the theologically conservative Presbyterian minister of Limavady, David Armstrong, was hounded, at Paisleyite instigation, from his parish. He had invited the local Catholic priest to say 'Happy Christmas' to his congregation. When ecumenism did occur it was often directed, in joint Church statements, against the Provisionals. The latter, opposed to the 'two nations' theory, bracketed Cardinal Conway with the Church of Ireland Archbishop Simms in their counter-denunciations,[37] and were prepared to negotiate through ecumenical Protestants, as at Feakle in late 1974. There was no simple Catholic versus Protestant dichotomy, but a more fluid division, cutting across individual Churches, between Roman Catholics (radical and conservative), 'Prot-ecums', and 'Prot-stats'.

In 1968-70, therefore, Cardinal Conway and the other Roman Catholic bishops endeavoured to steer cautiously between outright support for the government and encouragement of revolt by the Catholic community. Conway insisted[38] on the need for reforms to be implemented, but was prepared to attend meetings at Stormont. He also distanced himself from Fr Denis Faul's demand for English and Scottish judges to replace biased Northern Irish counterparts.[39] In April 1970 the Cardinal appealed to his community for 'dignified silence' in the face of provocation.[40] The policies of Bishop Philbin and Bishop Farren of Derry were similar. Certainly, such admonitions were unlikely to assist the revolution; Conway was later accused, like his predecessor Cullen, of assisting Stormont in return for total control of Catholic education. On the other hand, when Conway praised the people of the Bogside in 1969, a *Protestant Telegraph* correspondent in Australia accused the cardinal of ignoring the 'diabolical petrol bomb throwing'.[41] Even Conway's dissociation from Faul did not appease the Paisley paper, which complained that Conway had asserted that the remarks on the judiciary were 'unauthorised and unfortunate' but not a lie.[42] Not surprisingly the *Protestant Telegraph*, reporting that 'Mr Philbin' had been booed off the Falls Road,[43] failed to draw the conclusion that, as the Catholic authorities could no longer count on the uncritical support of their flocks, Prot-stats had little to worry about.

Provisionals challenge the hierarchy

By 1971 the emergence of the Provisionals as an urban guerrilla army inaugurated insurgency proper. Meanwhile, Conway, who claimed on UTV to have already condemned violence twenty-three times,[44] broke a fifty-year precedent by conducting, at his own request, private discussions with the prime minister. He also met the home secretary, James Callaghan, when the latter visited Northern Ireland later in the year. Such interviews could not stop the escalation of violence which led to internment on 9 August. This turning-point embarrassed the cardinal and his bishops who had virtually acknowledged the existing regime as all Prot-stats and many Prot-ecums wished. When internment was mooted earlier in the year, the *Republican News* complained that only Bishop Philbin had refused to protest. Cardinal Conway appeared to condemn internment on 14 August and criticised the brutal treatment of innocent people by the security forces. Though a radical priest complained that the protest was not against internment as such, Prot-stats were furious.[45]

But the Provisionals were even more irate about what followed. On 12 September, the cardinal and six bishops issued a statement condemning the IRA for disgracing noble causes. It contained the famous rhetorical question, how could a million Protestants be bombed into a united Ireland? The Provisionals' Irish Republican Press Bureau issued an immediate retort, accusing the bishops of double standards. There had been no condemnation, it claimed, when 500,000 Catholics were forced to live under a regime condemned by 80 per cent of the country's population. The American Fr Sean McManus, recently fined for disorderly conduct at Enniskillen, was quoted on the illegal and violent origin of the six county regime. Moreover, the Provisionals insisted that they were not forcing Protestants but fighting the British Army. The Provisionals invited the bishops to provide defence against 'marauding British troops, partisan police forces and extreme unionist mobs'.[46] The 'bombing of a million Protestants' was long remembered; as late as 1976 the *Republican News*[47] attributed to Conway 'one of the most unfortunate phrases' by a recent political figure. It claimed that the 1971 census, which showed 625,000 Catholics to 865,000 Protestants, demonstrated the phrase's inaccuracy.

The bishops' statement of September 1971 appears even-handed. It criticised the brutality of internment and asked Protestants to heed the very strong adverse reaction in the Catholic community. Moreover, it anticipated the power-sharing experiment by suggesting a reform of parliament to allow something other than the strictest majoritarian democracy. Interrogation in depth by torture was condemned as un-British by Conway and other bishops in October and November. Even the Provisionals were constrained to admit that their *bête noir*, Bishop Philbin, had spoken out against the British Army's interference with the funeral of a PIRA lieutenant, Terence MacDermott, and had demanded the investigation of CS gas in the precincts of St Agnes Hall.[48] Earlier in the year, the bishop had refused to open his suitcase when challenged by the Army.[49]

Hopes of rapprochement were dashed in late October by another condemnation of the Provisionals, this time by the whole Irish episcopal conference of 30 September.[50] It aroused the fury of the *Republican News* which used language which would have horrified the more circumspect C.J. Kickham in 1865. The previous efforts of the 'episcopal vipers' had been bad enough but 'the back-stabbing edict issued this week by the Irish hierarchy's commissars must rank as the greatest act of premeditated treachery against an innocent people since Judas betrayed his Saviour with a kiss. That so-called men of God should issue such a damnable lie, on the very day that two young innocent women were being buried, defies understanding.'[51] Invective could scarcely be stronger. Once again, the conference statement had been balanced in the sense of attributing much of the current violence to internment. Revolutionaries, however, have no use for 'balance', but require total endorsement: *'Bas go Bua'* (Death or Victory).

The Church confronts internment and Bloody Sunday

In the wake of internment some of the Catholic clergy seemed prepared to endorse PIRA. 'Each week', rejoiced the *Republican News*, 'gives new evidence of more clergy throwing their full weight behind us'.[52] Though the hierarchy 'was as reactionary as ever', it was 'clearly becoming more and more isolated as every day brings news of the ordinary clergy rejecting the false doctrines of their superiors and rallying to the support of their people'.[53] It quoted Fr Murray of St Paul's, Falls Road, who could not distinguish between a murderer and a patriot, and Fr C. O'Donnell, former rector of the Holy Cross community, Ardoyne, who believed the people considered the IRA their only protectors.[54] On 25 October, sixty Armagh diocesan priests signed a protest against brutality at the Holywood Barracks. A month later eight priests identified with internees by refusing to pay fines for boycotting the census. Fr Faul was as usual particularly active in campaigning against torture.[55] With Fr Brian Brady of St Joseph's Training College and Fr McEvoy of the New University of Ulster, Faul was congratulated by the *Republican News* for his work on behalf of the internees and their families.[56] Sympathy from Catholic educationalists like Fr Brady may have defused ominous talk in Provisional ranks of abandoning segregated schools and enforcing strict separation of Church and State in a united Ireland.

Conway's even-handed policy was wrecked by internment. On 10 May , Fr Padraig Murphy claimed 50,000 signatures for peace. But after internment the nationalist community became so aroused that even the loyalty of priests to their ecclesiastical superiors was put at risk. Though the British and Stormont governments hoped that the Roman Catholic Church would be a moderating factor in the nationalist ghettoes, the authorities themselves had revived the traditional rejection of clerical leadership in times of great patriotic excitement. The republican rhetorical excesses against any Church criticism was based on a deep understanding of this tradition. Republicans, unlike the two governments, read the relevant history. Stormont and Westminster contrived to fall simultaneously into the loyalist trap by making Catholic clergy behave as the rebels the Prot-stats traditionally asserted them to be. Some years later, in changed circumstances, several of the militant priests were to reverse their direction. As Oliver MacDonagh has shown, Irish churchmen shared the dilemmas and evasions of their congregations.[57]

Ironically, the Catholic hierarchy was saved from further exploitation of its difficulties by another outrage, Bloody Sunday, 30 January 1972. As Cardinal Conway led the obsequies of the thirteen dead on the Catholic side, there could be no breach in the unanimity of the community's abhorrence for an act regarded as wilful slaughter. Even unionists, according to Gallagher and Worrall, with the usual exception of Dr Paisley, were sufficiently shocked to await an inquiry at the beginning of this cruel and brutal year.[58] The Catholic consensus soon disintegrated. Conway duly condemned the Official IRA's retaliatory bombing at Aldershot. The logic of their rival's action was accepted by the Provisionals. The cardinal described the men of violence in his community as but a microscopic minority. Accordingly, in an RTE interview on 2 April, after the fall of Stormont, he insisted that most northern Catholics were opposed to the IRA and demanded a ceasefire. Two days later about 100 Andersonstown women met to support Conway, but, on 16 April, 800 people, mainly men, also gathered in Andersonstown to support continuance of the Provisional campaign. The *Republican News* recited the traditional list of unpatriotic prelates. Its columnist, Seamus O'Kelly, warned the primate that 'no churchman, be he bishop, cardinal, or even the Pope himself, has a right to deny our claim to nationhood.' Conway was to be respected as a cardinal, but not as an advocate of 'Imperialism or British Dominionism'. Fr Sean McManus insisted that 'to be against the Provisionals is to be against Ireland'.[59] Conway, however, persisted in his assertion that only a hundredth of the Northern Irish population supported violence.[60] In August 1972 the cardinal was appalled by the Bloody Friday bombings. The Provisionals, insisting that adequate warnings had been given, maintained that Conway's silence on the twenty deliberate killings of innocent Catholics by the UDA was evidence of double standards.[61]

Catholic bishops versus loyalist paramilitaries

Such criticism was hardly justified. On 18 August Conway and other heads of leading Churches condemned the 'appalling assassinations', the vocabulary of disapproval becoming sorely depleted. In November the cardinal was more explicit, complaining of a second campaign of extermination directed against the Catholic population, sixty of whom had now been shot, while hundreds were forced out of their homes.[62] Even the *Republican News* admitted that Conway had at last spoken out against violence to the Catholic community. Nevertheless, both primate and Catholic bishops had been 'strangly silent on the whole question of the sufferings of the nationalist people'.[63] This was very far from the truth. Indeed, the difference between the cardinal and Fr Faul, author of numerous protests and pamphlets on the harassment of Catholics, was less than appeared at first sight. Conway certainly continued his denunciations of loyalist killings into the following year when they appeared to increase. On 9

November 1973 he used the very argument that the Provisionals had used against him by accusing the authorities of a 'muted' response to the problem.

Loyalists had good reason to divert accusations from themselves. The Rev. Roy Magee, a Prot-stat Presbyterian minister and president of the UDA auxiliary, the Loyalist Association of Workers, agreed with the Provisionals that the Roman Catholic Church was ambivalent on violence, but detected bias towards the IRA, not the loyalists. He denied that the Catholic Church was a true New Testament Church.[64] This mirrors Cardinal McRory's earlier rejection of Protestantism. The *UDA News* claimed that Conway had said that it was no murder to kill a British soldier; in a war situation the intention of the act was the vital factor.[65] It also emphasised the use of the confessional[66] to absolve murderers from dastardly crimes. Paisley's paper named an Australian, Fr W. Creede of Clonard Monastery, as willing to give absolution to Provisionals.[67] Paisley himself, despite an attack in parliament on 65 priests who had claimed that Army undercover men shot innocent Catholics to provoke IRA exposure, admitted loyalist assassinations. When stigmatising the Roman Church as 'drunk with martyrs' blood' in late 1972, he warned Protestants not to copy the enemy. Perhaps the most useful diversion at this time was the visit of the Archbishop of Dublin, Dr Dermot Ryan, and his predecessor, Dr McQuaid, to the Provisional chief of staff, Seán MacStiofain, then on hunger strike in a southern gaol. This was long remembered as proof that the Roman Catholic Church connived at terrorism, though, at the time, the *Protestant Telegraph* also condemned an ecumenical Church of Ireland cleric, the Rev. Joseph Parker, who tried to secure MacStiofian's release.[68]

In 1973 Cardinal Conway himself emphasised the Protestant assassination campaign in his most publicised public utterances and enthusiastically supported the government's plans for power sharing, partly anticipated by the Catholic bishops in 1971. Everyone who believed in democracy, said the Catholic primate in December 1973, should back the Sunningdale agreement.[69] Power sharing was the logical outcome of the cardinal's work for inter-Church co-operation after Vatican II. His stand meant effective support for the constitutionalist SDLP, the eternal rival of the Provisionals in Catholic areas. Naturally, Provisional propaganda was now geared to demonstrating that the Catholic hierarchy and SDLP were working together in collaboration with the British. As for the more immediate struggle between republicans and clerics, a front-line priest was Fr Aquinas, C.P., of Holy Cross Church, Ardoyne.

The contrasting tribulations of Fathers Aquinas and Wilson

Fr Aquinas, in August 1972, argued in his parish magazine that 85 per cent of his congregation opposed violence. This conceded a higher percentage of supporters for physical force than that suggested by his primate. In March 1973 Aquinas extended his attack on the Provisionals.[70] In an open letter he claimed to speak for the majority of his people who wanted protection by troops but were afraid to speak out in the face of Provisional intimidation. This struck at the roots of Provisional propaganda. Aquinas was answered by PIRA leaders such as Billy McKee and Martin Meehan who insisted that violence was used mainly in defence against Orange mobs burning Catholic homes.[71] Aquinas was also attacked by republican prisoners.[72] In May he was removed from his position as editor of the parish journal. The *Protestant Telegraph* complained that he was dismissed for opposing the Provisionals.[73] Three years later, Paisley's paper noted that Aquinas had been sent to Dublin for his own protection: 'I have got on a confidential telephone, I have informed the authorities that such and such a person had done such and such a deed.' Even this was not enough for the Free Presbyterian newspaper which accused Aquinas of failing, with 'Jesuistical dexterity', to offer full co-operation to the security forces or to condemn the ideals of the Provisionals. It also rejected an alleged admission that he had used material obtained from the confessional.

Without accepting the *Protestant Telegraph* rumour, Fr Aquinas's apparent support for established authority prejudiced him in the eyes of his congregation. Provisionals insisted that his use of the confidential telephone sent Catholics to RUC torture compounds. But Aquinas, who had worked with Protestants in England, Scotland and Australia, had previously spoken out against the Stormont regime, internment and torture. Like Bishop Cahal Daly, he distinguished between the Easter Week insurgents and the modern IRA. Aquinas cannot therefore be dismissed as a unionist sympathiser. His case has been used by Frank Burton to illustrate the tension in the Ardoyne between the Provisionals and the Catholic Church. About one-third of their community, says Burton, usually those who were only nominally religious, consistently supported the Provisionals, while the rest had a 'see-saw relationship' with them. The IRA and the Church were 'persistently at variance'.[74] According to a 1986 survey of Catholic clerical opinion in Northern Ireland, only 3.9 per cent of priests were prepared to vote for Sinn Féin, while a massive 87.9 per cent supported the SDLP.[75] Fr Faul concentrated on avoiding conflict. When he received information about a forthcoming Provisional action, Faul endeavoured to inform the authorities in such a way as to stop the action without causing any arrests.

1973 also saw a countervailing internal Catholic division on the left. The priest involved was Fr Desmond Wilson of Ballymurphy, 'the worst housing estate in the British Isles'.[76] Fr Wilson, an ecumenist before Vatican II, identified completely with the extreme poverty of many of his congregation. Wilson came to the conclusion, like many Latin American Catholic priests, that the official Church was doing little or nothing to relieve the real needs of its people. In January 1972, a few days before Bloody Sunday, Wilson created a furore by stating, contary to the efforts of Cardinal Conway and other bishops, that no one had the right to denounce violence unless they could offer something in its place.[77] He had also organised the 65 priests attacked by Paisley for condemning British Army undercover operations against Catholics. In August 1973 Fr Wilson was involved in a public dispute with Fr Mullally, representing Bishop Philbin, over the issue which, in a different context, led to Fr Aquinas's precipitate departure for Dublin. Wilson accused certain Catholic army chaplains of abusing their position by giving information to the authorities. Mullally did not justify such activities but claimed that Wilson should not have made public criticism without proof.

In 1975, after criticising British influence on the Vatican, another perennial republican complaint, Fr Wilson resigned his ministry and continued in Ballymurphy as a social worker. He was supported by a public meeting of 1,500 people and a petition signed by 2,000. The affair provoked widespread controversy. The former priest, Fr Terry O'Keefe, defending Wilson, claimed that the Down and Connor diocesan establishment 'exactly mirrors the pre-1968 State in Northern Ireland.' Wilson similarily compared Belfast church procedures with those of the Unionist Party before the current Troubles. He complained that in 1971 Ted Heath as prime minister had secured, via Philbin and London, a new Irish channel of communication with the Vatican, bypassing the traditional link between Conway and the Irish nuncio. These were weighty criticisms indeed. Nevertheless, in 1982 Bishop Cahal Daly, as Philbin's successor, lost no time in restoring Wilson's clerical faculties. Rehabilitation failed to diminish the vigour of Wilson's denunciation of British militarism and insistence on episcopal condemnation of institutional violence, ideas expanded in his *An End to Silence* of 1985. Wilson grew increasingly critical of Daly, and was not deterred by the latter's elevation to the Cardinalate. Reviewing Daly's *The Price of Peace* for *An Phoblacht* in 1991, Wilson dismissed it as a 'theologically and intellectually incompetent book'.[78] Wilson was joined in his attacks on Daly by Fr Joe MacVeigh.[79] Another thorn in the side of Cardinal Daly was Fr Pat Buckley; though suspended from his office as a Catholic priest, Buckley proved equally willing to confront publicly loyalists, republicans, and his own bishop.

Loyalists took advantage of such divisions, but rarely to suggest that the Catholic Church, demonstrating a variety of opinion, was no longer a threat to Prot-stats. The *Orange Standard* compared Buckley with the sixteenth-century Reformers.[80] The *Protestant Telegraph* compared Wilson with the 1916 leader James Connolly and contrasted the priest's adherence to socialism with Conway's repudiation of it. The *Orange Standard* noted the great support accorded to Wilson by his community. Again it failed to draw the conclusion that the Catholic Church had thus demonstrated it was not the monolith claimed in loyalist propaganda. However, McKeague's *Loyalist News* saw this initial revolt against the hierarchy as a good omen. McKeague, ironically a personal friend of Wilson, was posthumously praised in the latter's 1982 novel, *The Demonstration*, as a unifying force. Fr Wilson, as the Provisionals admitted, did not endorse their physical-force campaign. He appears, nevertheless, a self-conscious exponent of liberation theology.[81]

Power sharing and hunger strikes: two Bishops Daly embattled

The Church-nationalist dispute grew vituperative in 1974 when the power-sharing executive, upon which so many hopes were set, collapsed under the UWC strike. Conway did what he could in January to aid the executive by denouncing, as a mortal sin, the taking of life without the sanction of elected representatives. In this, said the *Republican News*, he surpassed himself. The Provisional reply rehearsed the familiar story of Church opposition to Irish nationalism, attacked the bishops for their apathy under the Stormont regime, and warned that there existed patriotic priests willing to provide spiritual consolation.[82] Nevertheless, the Provisionals had to endure what was virtually an episcopal 'spring offensive' led by the primate. From St Mel's cathedral in Longford across the border came the admonitory voice of Bishop Cahal Daly comparing contemporary Northern Ireland with Al Capone's Chicago, suggesting that republicans were irreligious, and offering to talk to the Provisionals at the risk of his own life.[83] This 'immoderate sophistry', said a *Republican News* columnist, was 'nothing more than a sycophantic sop to the forces of British Imperialist oppression with which the Irish Church has invariably sided against its own people.'[84]

The Provisionals could expect no better from Bishop Philbin, who in January asked Irish-Americans not to contribute to funds which brought increasing misery rather than protection to the Catholic minority in the six counties. Surely the new bishop of Derry, Edward Daly, who had experienced British imperialism at first hand on Bloody Sunday, would have something better to offer? On 19 April Dr Daly, less than a month after his consecration, did indeed produce a peace plan of three points, applicable in the first instance to Derry: a Provisional ceasefire, release of internees, and British Army withdrawal to barracks. There was no political honeymoon for the new prelate. The bishop, declared the *Republican News*, had entered the political arena on the side of the English. The trade-off suggested was a 'despicable attempt to help the English divide and conquer the Irish people'. It agreed only with the third point.[85] The *Protestant Telegraph* also ridiculed the peace plan which it wrongly believed 'will give the guerrillas a chuckle of delight' as the security forces would stop raiding and arresting while the internees were released. Thus it disagreed with the third point. Moreover, Dr Daly appeared in bad company as Dr 'Mick' Ramsey, the former archbishop of Canterbury whose service in Belfast was disrupted by Free Presbyterians, supported his plan.[86] The bishop of Derry found the onslaughts from both sides in his first weeks a recurrent challenge.

The Provisionals met their episcopal critics not only with abuse but rival authorities such as Bishop Thomas Drury of Corpus Christi, Texas, who, like Mannix in the first Irish Revolution, endorsed from a distance. Drury was 'heart-sick to know that some of our Irish bishops have become so calloused not even to ask for prayer for our prisoners'.[87] The republicans had an excellent issue at this time to counter the attraction of the power-sharing executive, with Catholics for the first time[88] in the state's history in ministerial positions. They emphasised the hunger strikes of the Price sisters, Marion and Dolours, and Michael Gaughan, all seeking repatriation to Ireland from their English prisons.

The Catholic Church was again in a difficult position. Cardinal Conway made private representations on behalf of the Price sisters, and Dr Edward Daly asked for their repatriation, pointing out that the British were not without guilt in their relations with Ireland. Both bishops publicly stated their hope that the girls, serving life sentences for bombing in England, would not be allowed to die. Dr Cahal Daly also believed that repatriation would be yielding to humanity rather than violence, though, to the Provisionals' annoyance, he added that the hunger strikers were 'misguided' and 'culpable'.[89] The Price fast did not end in tragedy as the sisters ceased their strike in June 1974 and were sent to Ireland in the spring of 1975. Even the Red Hand Commandos had supported repatriation. Both women were eventually released on grounds of ill-health. 'A public disgrace beyond all description', roared Paisley's paper.[90]

Not so lucky was Michael Gaughan who died after a 65-day hunger strike. His funeral opened a rift in the Roman Catholic Church. The priest who held a requiem Mass for him in London, Fr Michael Connolly, was subsequently suspended for anti-British remarks by his superior, Archbishop Dwyer of Birmingham. In November the same prelate refused to allow the body of James McDade, killed by the bomb he was laying in Coventry, to lie in his cathedral on the way back to Belfast for burial. The *Republican News* denounced this 'despicable' contradiction of all Catholic teachings. Catholic prelates in England and Ireland faced different pressures. The *Protestant Telegraph*, unwilling to give any credit, maintained that in the end Archbishop Dwyer did say Mass for McDade.[91] Fr Connolly joined its catalogue of priests proving the interchangeability of Romanism and revolution. Regardless of all condemnation, loyalists continued to insist that the Catholic Church always gave last rites and failed ultimately to excommunicate the IRA. When, however, Catholic Churches refused tricolour-draped IRA coffins, the Provisionals were outraged; when union flags were banned from Catholic RUC coffins the *Protestant Telegraph* attacked Bishop Philbin.[92]

The fall of the power-sharing executive to the loyalist workers in May 1974 did not end the antagonism between the Provisionals and the Catholic hierarchy. The *Republican News* in July claimed that the bishops were 'in full swing behind the British'.[93] It accused Philbin of following the UWC's demand for a condemnation of the IRA by a statement of 'utter fanaticism' in declaring the violence Satanic and perpetrated by 'devil people' in full revolt against God. Edward Daly, who denounced the purposeless violence that was destroying the depressed town of Strabane, was stigmatised as neutral only in name: he failed to take account of institutional violence by governments.[94] These ecclesiastics, in Provisional eyes, were on a par with the Church of Ireland bishop of Down and Dromore, Dr George Quin, who described the IRA as 'scum-like fiends'.[95] Many important politico-theological issues were vehemently debated at this time. The difference between the two Dr Dalys on the 1916 Rising—Edward against, Cahal for[96]—was openly ventilated. To Cahal Daly, Pearse's surrender in 1916 to save Irish lives was a lesson that the Provisionals had failed to accept.[97] Much was also made of the Catholic Church's desire to control its schools, an issue on which Cahal Daly was vocal.

Republicanism and the Catholic Church were now locked in stalemate. In 1977 the Provisionals contrasted prelates like Cardinal Conway, Edward Daly, Philbin, and Casey of Galway (later to resign in disgrace) with Des Wilson, Fr Sean McManus, Fr J. McDyer (renowned for the Glencolumbkille co-operative), Faul, Camilo Torres, and Dr Newman of Limerick, the only bishop to demand straight British withdrawal. Dr Newman was an outspoken opponent of state secularism. Cardinal Conway, who had fought bravely for a politically untenable *via media* in one of the most troubled primacies Ireland had ever experienced, died in April 1977. His condemnation of the assassination in 1976 of the British ambassador to the Irish Republic, Ewart-Biggs, received the usual cries of partiality from republican sources. Why had he not protested when the SAS murdered IRA volunteer Peter Cleary?[98] The debate was nothing if not repetitive.

New issues in the second half of the 1970s included the emergence of the Peace People and the prison protest against criminalisation. The Peace People raised the same question that had already been canvassed in so many forms: co-operation with and reform of the establishment or a 'zero sum' insistence on full revolutionary objectives. Father Desmond Wilson empathised with the Provisionals when he declared himself 'blazingly angry' at the Peace People's desire for a settlement which would leave society as it had always been.[99] Cardinal Conway, however, participated in peace marches, and Wilson himself later apologised for the severity of his words. The prison protest was longer-lived and led to the hunger strikes of 1981. Here again the bishops' effort to steer a middle road proved extremely difficult. When Dr Edward Daly visited the H-Blocks in 1978, describing them as a health hazard, but arguing that the miseries were self-inflicted, he was accused by the Provisionals of enemy propaganda at its most blatant.[100] When

Cardinal O'Fiaich was shocked by the H-Blocks several months later, the *Protestant Telegraph* used the self-inflicted argument on him. Edward Daly was then a front-runner for the northern Catholic bishops with Conway dead and Bishop Philbin facing more opposition from his flock. The latter was picketed after Mass at Twinbrook in November 1977 by demonstrators demanding his condemnation of the H-Blocks.[101]

Dr Edward Daly, with a less conservative image than Philbin, was also heavily involved in the hunger strike debate of 1981. More than O'Fiaich, he incurred the violent opposition of the Provisionals. Though Daly in 1980 supported political prisoners demanding their own clothes, in March 1981 he bluntly declared the hunger strikes morally unjustified.[102] He was accused by *An Phoblacht* of 'vicious attacks on the dying hunger strikers at critical periods',[103] and of 'hysterical euphoria' when the mother of a striker set the precedent by having her son treated.[104] In 1982 the battle continued with Bishop Daly calling on Catholics to give information to the security forces. The issue had been anticipated in 1865 by Charles Kickham in the *Irish People*.[105] The Provisionals challenged the bishop to do so himself. Daly promised to supply information received as a private citizen to the authorities.[106] Thus from his initial attempt to maintain a balance between the nationalism of the Catholic community and the requirements of order, Bishop Daly seemed closer to the latter. However, later in 1982 the cycle continued when his attack on plastic bullets incurred the wrath of unionists like the rising lawyer Robert McCartney. The problem was exacerbated by the fact that in 1974 Catholic power-sharing ministers were potentially involved in the maintenance of order, while in the early 1980s the possibility of this soon recurring seemed remote.

PIRA repudiates Fr Faul

The association of Fr Faul with Bishop Daly as an enemy of the hunger strike is particularly significant. Though Faul never endorsed Provisional violence, his criticism of the security forces was always comprehensive; witness his twenty reasons why Catholics should not support the RUC, originally published in the *Irish News*.[107] Yet Faul found that Christ's injunction, 'those who are not with us are against us', especially applicable in a revolutionary situation, and agreed with Bishop Daly that evidence be given to the authorities to avoid both violence and arrests.[108] The priest who had published so much on the brutalities suffered by prisoners and internees over the decade discovered that none of this was remembered by Provisionals, who placed him with Dr Daly and Cardinal O'Fiaich in the 'treacherous trio', and by some irate blanket men who rejected him as 'a conniving, treacherous man, not in the least shy about twisting the truth to achieve his own ends'.[109] The *Protestant Telegraph* would have been delighted at this confirmation of its assertion that Faul's complaints were worthless and that there could be no neutrals.[110] Ironically, the Irish secularist *Church and State* accused Faul and Murray of encouraging the hunger strikes.[111] Ultimately, however, Faul's opposition to the Provisional pressure on the relatives of dying hunger strikers helped to end the protest.

Faul was not the only supporter of republicanism to become disillusioned. Such cases had apparently occurred even in the first Irish Revolution, Bishop Fogarty being an example. Fr Sean McManus, a comfort to the Provisionals in their early days, eventually condemned them.[112] Few Catholic clergy, despite the lists regularly drawn up in the *Protestant Telegraph*, could be wholehearted revolutionaries, and at the same time true to their calling. Even the radical Fr Wilson, frequently quoted with approval in *An Phoblacht*, was unable to reconcile his vocation with membership of a political party.[113] Camilo Torres, quoted by both republicans and loyalists for opposite reasons, may have died as a guerrilla in Colombia, but he renounced his clerical office first. However, as *An Phoblacht* correctly pointed out, he did so to be more truly a priest.[114] The hunger strikes are a classic example of the divergence of religion from social revolution. To a social revolutionary many people must accept death and bereavement, willing or unwilling, for the ultimate secular welfare; to the religious the nurture and the passage of the individual soul is the highest good. Hence the continued insistence of Conway and the other bishops on the sacredness of life, which, the Provisionals rightly asserted, they linked with anti-abortion. In 1979 the bishops had powerful confirmation of their position when Pope John Paul II, acting on their advice, denounced violence on Irish soil.

The Pope on the spot

Though John Paul II did not, like his predecessor Pius IX, repudiate the Irish revolutionary organisation by name, he made his position reasonably clear. 'I proclaim … that violence is evil, that violence is unacceptable as a solution to problems, that violence is unworthy of man. Violence is a lie, for it goes against the truth of our faith, the truth of humanity.' This was merely to repeat what the bishops had been saying for many years, in both Irish revolutions and earlier. It certainly conflicted with the romantic view of violence expressed by Pearse's rhapsody on 'the red wine of the battlefield'.

The pope's next sentence, 'Violence destroys what it claims to defend: the dignity, the life, the freedom of human beings', was also rooted in Irish history. This was the objection of some first Irish Revolution Churchmen to the early IRA: the latter's hit-and-run tactics left the civilian population exposed to reprisals. The same point had been made in the second Revolution. Canon Padraig Murphy, for example, in a Sunday plea for peace on 20 May 1972, argued that violence was not only against God's law but encouraged revenge against innocent people.[115] There was the related problem of bystanders killed in cross-fire or bombs exploding at the wrong time. The Provisionals had anticipated such criticism in the first issues of *Republican News* when they quoted a famous passage from O'Casey's *Drums Under the Windows*, describing the 1916 Rising: The dying young man clutched at a lamp-post, 'a young lassie' lying prone with 'a purple patch of death' on the back of her white blouse, an old woman's blood seeping through the floor of her tenement: 'all the goodly company of the dead who died for Ireland. Jesu, have pity! You didn't want to die. I know, I know. You signed no proclamation; you invaded no building; you pulled no trigger; I know, I know. But Ireland needed you all the same. Many will die like that before Ireland can go free. They must put up with it.'[116]

'Jesu, have pity' and 'they must put with it' encapsulate the essential difference between Catholic theology and secular revolution which John Paul II, albeit indirectly, appears to have distinguished at Drogheda. In 1922, the future Catholic primate, Bishop O'Donnell, stated clearly the objection of many churchmen to guerrilla warfare as killing the soul as well as the body by leaving those in mortal sin no opportunity for repentance.[117] The 'young lassie' surprised when returning from her holiday would indeed be dependent on the pity of Jesus. The secular revolutionary, on the other hand can call, without compunction, for the innocent to deliver up their lives for the great society to come.

The pope at Drogheda when appealing 'on his knees' to the men and women of violence, raised another relevant issue: 'You may claim to seek justice. I, too, believe in justice and seek justice. But violence only delays the days of justice. Violence destroys the work of justice.' This seems a direct reference to the slogan, 'Peace with Justice' that the Provisionals had used against the Peace People, accused simply of working for the *status quo*. It also recalls Bishop Edward Daly's contemplation of the ruins of Strabane which he attributed to terrorism. In his short address the pope could only call generally for a 'return to Christ'.

The Drogheda address appealed, moreover, for people to leave organisations caught up with violence and ignore leaders preaching 'hatred, revenge, retaliation'. This again evoked traditional episcopal hostility to secret organisations whose demands were often incompatible with Catholic moral teaching and Church authority. Leaving aside innocent victims—the 'murdering of defenceless people', according to the pope—no violent revolutionary organisation, despite all disclaimers, can operate without 'retaliation' against informers or dangerous opponents. Similarly, power of 'revenge' is vital in ensuring the safety of supporters, while the fostering of 'hatred' is an essential part of a political propaganda campaign. The Provisionals made no secret of these activities, however strongly they denied intentional injury to civilians. The pope, however, both at Drogheda, where he denied that the State could set aside the moral law, and at a Dublin ecumenical meeting moved some distance towards answering the traditional republican complaint that Catholic authorities were one-sided in their condemnations of force. It was not difficult to read into these remarks a criticism of interrogatory torture, loyalist assassinations, and SAS stakeouts, plus an endorsement of the untiring investigations of Frs Faul and Murray. Indeed, Paisley attacked the pope for these remarks.[118]

A pope had at last spoken on Irish soil. No student of republican propaganda, however, expected Provisional submission to arguments already rejected from Irish prelates who had briefed the pontiff. As early as 1972 the *Republican News* had declared that not even the pope himself had the right to deny 'our claims to nationhood'.[119] Secret contacts with Provisionals were apparently made before the address, but after Drogheda *An Phoblacht* proudly asserted that 'no apology was due'.

'P. O'Neill', speaking officially for PIRA, insisted on force as the only means for removing the British presence. Church leaders, politicians and the establishment had patently failed to resolve the massive social and economic problems created by the British. Moreover, other colonial countries—Zimbabwe was approaching its crisis—had demonstrated the high chances of success based on popular support. Finally, 'we know also that upon victory the Church would have no difficulty in recognising us'. The maverick cleric, Fr Des Wilson, agreed with the latter point in a *Hibernia* article. Danny Morrison, editor of *An Phoblacht*, took up the defence in person. Despite Paisley's complaints, Morrison was not satisfied that the pope had shown balance by condemning the institutionalised violence of the British. He also questioned the media emphasis on the pope's condemnation of violence rather than his reassertion of Catholic moral standards. Were the 400,000 Irish women estimated to be on the pill about to give it up?[120]

The papal visit to Ireland therefore settled nothing. Carefully analysed, John-Paul's remarks helped to re-establish the basic issues, so often overshadowed by smokescreens of rationalisation. Perhaps, as two Catholic bishops argued, some young men were dissuaded from joining PIRA.[121] Inside clerical ranks the pope's visit made it more difficult for priests to take a republican line. In early 1980 Fr Edmund Hogan of Cork complained that a number of Catholic priests were supporting the Provisionals, contrary to the Church's stand on violence, and also lamented the Provisionals' response to Pope John Paul II. Fr Hogan was challenged in the *Furrow* by Fr Des Wilson.[122] The *Protestant Telegraph*[123] was glad to note an apparent confirmation that its links between popery and revolution were valid. Similarly, the UDA *Ulster* quoted Bishop Cahal Daly's complaint that four priests from America were in the IRA. The secularist *Church and State* saw a developing rapprochement between clericalism and Provisionalism.[124] In his study, well reviewed by *An Phobtacht*, however, McElroy argues that only three priests failed to condemn IRA violence openly.[125]

Religious authority versus revolutionary mandate

How was such extreme antithetical interpretation possible? For Prot-stats, who considered the Roman Catholic Church an authority structure, based on total submission to the pope, the pontiff's appearance in Ireland should have been decisive. The only loophole was ambiguity of utterance. Yet the Provisionals and those clergy who continued to support them seemed to be deliberately rejecting ambiguity as a defence. It has been argued above that there was a clear line between revolutionary and Catholic doctrine. Why then continued confusion? In fact, the Roman Catholic Church exhibited a far more uncertain authority than appears on the surface. This may be demonstrated by another look at the issues of the revolutionary mandate, the cluster of problems associated with confession, excommunication and last rites, and the principle of hunger striking.

'By what authority?' The question has frequently been posed by Bishop Edward Daly and others in the condemnation of a particular IRA action. The answer inevitably comes pat: the same authority as Pearse and Connolly in 1916. Republican journals have repeatedly demonstrated that the insurgents of Easter Week were attacked by the clergy of that period for lacking a mandate for insurrection. This, as has already been mentioned, was a clever argument. The Irish Republic based its authority on the Easter Week Rising, and those who rejected the rebellion as unjustified, be they cleric or lay, could not but appear unpatriotic Irishmen or even unionist fellow-travellers. By the 1970s, however, the revisionist history, already mentioned, was eroding the use of Pearse and Connolly as incantations to prove nationalist orthodoxy. In 1971 Fr Francis Shaw made 'Pearse a skittle'.[126] Others like Conor Cruise O'Brien, John Hume of the SDLP, and Ruth Dudley Edwards were accused of disparaging 1916.[127] Republicans had therefore to explain themselves more fully. What exactly was Pearse's mandate?

Clearly Pearse was not an elected representative,[128] the Irish parliamentary party still possessing the field. Fr Art O'Neill denied that any theologian required a revolutionary to be a legislator in the regime he endeavoured to supersede. To Fr O'Neill, Pearse's mandate was found in the 1916 proclamation. This evidently meant a 'mandate of history'[129] to which the Provisionals and supporters like Fr Sean McManus sometimes appealed. So vague a concept meant endorsement by the risings of the past, showing that British rule had never gained legitimacy, plus the support of a future popular consensus. Alternatively, the mandate might be justice, fidelity and nationality, another vague formula amounting to much the same thing. Loosely attached to the mandate of history was the retrospective ballot-box. Regardless of clerical or contemporary opinion on the legitimacy of 1916, surely the 73 Sinn Féin representatives elected in December 1918 provided sufficient retrospective validation? Though accepted by Churchmen like Bishop Cahal Daly, this is a double-edged weapon which could destroy the moral effect of the present-day Church. As Conor Cruise O'Brien said, 'practically, the acceptance of a retrospective mandate would result in chaos. Any citizen could break any law he or she chose with the defence that the law in question may be repealed at some time in the future.' Dara MacNeil's reply in *An Phoblacht*, that the rights of women and trade unions had been obtained by breaking existing law, did not solve the problem on which O'Brien himself had changed his ground.[130] Many loyalists face the same difficulty.

The position of churchmen was particularly difficult. As the republican Frank Gallagher complained in 1922, the bishops in 1918 campaigned strongly against Sinn Féin and even when that party had won the election still refused to accept the 'mandate' of the people implicit in Dail Eireann's declaration of war.[131] The astute Fr Des Wilson showed that contemporary republicans could appeal from Bishop Cahal Daly's current denunciation to the endorsement of churchmen in the future, assuming that ultimate victory was achieved. Hence the Provisional retort to the pope was based on historical realism. The fact that black terrorists in Rhodesia were then metamorphosing into responsible Zimbabwe statesmen reinforced the argument.[132] However, another difficulty, affecting both churchmen of the Cahal Daly school and republicans, was that historians endorsed Arthur Griffith's insistence in 1922 that the Irish people had not voted in 1918 for maintaining the republic of Easter Week.[133]

This sceptical position did not, however, prevent Provisionals appropriating to themselves the mandate of the Irish revolutionaries of 1918-21. Bishop Cahal Daly and some old IRA men declared that there was no connection. Similarly, *Visor* claimed that there was no resemblance between the original UVF and the thugs of the new UVF. Yet this was not easy to prove on either side. Were the guerrillas of the original IRA less ruthless? The Provisionals published a pamphlet, *The Good Old IRA*,[134] to prove they were not. Circumstances simply required new methods. The flying columns of 1920-21 were replaced by the tactics of the modern guerrilla. They argued that, according to Catholic theology, the new war was even more justified than the 1916 Rising. Then the country was prosperous, Home Rule was imminent and there was no prospect of insurrectionary success. By the 1970s, however, the Provisional war, after fifty years' deprivation of rights, was obviously just, had a good chance of success, and was based on the support of the people. According to Fr Wilson, in 1975 some Catholic clergy had accepted this argument. The primate, Cardinal O'Fiaich, created a diversion in 1984 by asserting that it was not morally wrong to join Sinn Féin because of its work on housing and community projects.[135] Shortly afterwards Cahal Daly denied that the votes obtained by Sinn Féin when it contested elections after 1981 proved support for the IRA's fight. In reply, *An Phoblacht* quoted Gerry Adams, then Provisional Sinn Féin president and abstentionist MP for West Belfast: 'I don't think the IRA need a vote to continue their campaign' as the British presence in the country was a sufficient mandate.[136] Bishops and Provisionals tacitly converged in their distinction between the Armalite and ballot-box.

In such quasi-theological arguments the Provisionals held their own. They claimed that only total pacifism, condemning alike state and revolutionary violence, was a valid argument against them. As Desmond Fennell told Dr Enda McDonagh of Maynooth, non-violence was feasible only under a leader like Gandhi, striving for positive change. The Catholic bishops, he asserted, had plainly failed to give any such direction in the early days of attacks on Catholic homes. Hence they were in no position to denounce the Provisionals who provided that defence.[137] As the loyalists were never tired of pointing out, sometimes citing controversial articles during the first Irish Revolution, Catholic theology did make provision for violence. Provisionals would have said amen to the *Protestant Telegraph*'s evocation of Suarez: 'When an oppressed people are left with no alternative but to resort to the use of force in pursuance of legitimate basic human rights, then they are entitled to do so.'[138]

Prot-stat ambiguities on violence

Paisley could not consistently exploit Catholic disagreement as he faced the same difficulties with Protestant paramilitaries. He too condemned sectarian murders very forcefully on occasion, but found the UDA and UVF extremely unresponsive and, like the republicans, apt to talk back to the clergy. On the other hand, if, as some believe, Paisley was once very close to the UVF, he emerges as a Prot-stat Camilo Torres.[139] While Catholic bishops were accused of not defending their communities, Paisley and his colleagues were accused of talk and inaction. The UDA from the start repudiated clerical advisers, associating them with the feeble 'fur coat' affluent unionist politicans, as the Provisionals identified their clerics with the collaborationist SDLP. Paisley frequently accused the Catholic bishops of hypocritically denouncing violence; the same accusation was made against him. Again, the giving of the last rites to IRA terrorists was a constant complaint of Prot-stats against the Roman Catholic Church, yet Paisley officiated at the funerals of UDA leaders like Tommy Heron.[140] The pope condemned retaliation; so too did the UVF *Combat* which distinguished it from legitimate resistance.[141] The UVF journal agreed entirely with the Provisional insistence on avoiding civilian casualties. It asserted that the Protestant tradition required the 'greatest charity and compassion to non-combatants.' This tradition was the loyalist 'mandate of history', but not accepted by those Prot-stats who claimed that there were no non-combatants.

Sacraments: Catholic and Protestant

If there was such convergence in confusion over violence between loyalist, republican and clergy, why were the related issues so divisive? Confession, excommunication and the last rites of the Catholic Church seemed to Prot-stats positive proof that clerical condemnations of violence were insincere. Here were powers which the bishops possessed to snuff out revolution like a candle flame if they so desired. The issue was a Morton's fork or Catch 22. If the Church did snuff out the IRA by its authority, Prot-stats would fight its total control of the priest-ridden papists and resist a united Ireland to the death. If on the other hand the IRA persisted it was proof that, as Paisley's sometime correspondent Avro Manhattan pointed out in 1971, Paul VI's master plan for the domination of Ireland was on the move.[142]

The confession-excommunication problem was not quite what it appeared to Prot-stats. In the days of Cardinal Cullen and the Fenians, revolutionaries had usually found loopholes to evade excommunication. Very few became atheists like the Fenian 'Pagan' O'Leary whose English warders, to Karl Marx's indignation, ultimately compelled him, by a diet of bread and water, to attend Mass.[143] A relevant example is that of Cardinal Cullen's interlocutor, Charles Kickham. On release from a long prison sentence Kickham returned to the movement and became president of the supreme council of the IRB. Archbishop Croke of Cashel, however, insisted that he could have no absolution unless he renounced the IRB. Kickham refused. According to his colleague, John Devoy, Kickham declared that he would trust to God's mercy and die without confession. Though Croke then apparently relented, the significant fact is surely Kickham's apparently 'Protestant' reliance on direct intercession with the deity.[144] Other revolutionaries seem to have resolved this problem in the same way. As Eamon de Valera said, he had such a strong belief in the justice of his cause that he refused to believe it was wrong.[145] A priest during the first Irish Revolution accepted the assurance of a member of Collins's assassination squad that he sincerely believed he was doing right.[146] Cardinal Conway was attacked by the *Ulster Militant* for upholding a similar position. In 1974, the Provisional sympathiser Fr Art O'Neill explained the doctrine.[147] The British, he argued, had an interest in keeping Irish Catholics as confused as possible on Church teachings relating to insurrection and contraception. Conscience, however, was supreme. In confessional, the priest must explain the teaching of the Church but the penitent must decide on its application to his or her behaviour. Thus killing is permissible in self-defence, the execution of a criminal, or a just war. 'The Church has always insisted that under no conditions whatever may a Catholic priest attempt to control events through the confessional.' Thus it might be considered improper to ask a penitent if he belonged to a proscribed body. In fact, the Provisionals argued that by the 1970s the Catholic clergy hesitated to excommunicate republicans as in the past, not only because the latter had the support of the community, but because such excommunication was impossible after Vatican II.[148] It was thus logical for Prot-stats, who rejected ecumenism, to demand Vatican I conduct from the Catholic Church. In fact, the question of excommunication had often been discussed by the hierarchy, but none of the Northern Ireland bishops believed it useful in their situation. Edward Daly partly evaded the issue by declaring that terrorists excommunicated themselves.[149]

The issue can now be seen in perspective. The sacraments or last rites of the Church could hardly be denied when the intention, or private judgement of the individual, was ultimately a matter between himself or herself and God. The same factors applied to hunger strikes. Loyalists could sneer at the argument that there might be no intention to commit suicide, but what became of private judgement in their criticism? There was further convergence when the Provisionals in controversy with opponents like Paisley and the socialist Noel Browne cited their ultimate model, Theobald Wolfe Tone. As an admirer of the French Revolution, Tone wanted to apply the ruthless civil constitution of the clergy, which reduced the priesthood to dependence on the State, in the independent Ireland of his dreams. Fr Wilson and the UDA's *Ulster* emphasised this. Desmond Fennell, writing for *An Phoblacht*, considered Tone's project out of date. Instead, he suggested a reorganisation of parish and diocesan boundaries and councils containing elected lay representatives. Clergy and bishops would be vetted by the representative body and political bishops disciplined.[150] While obviously made tongue in cheek, this proposal would have enabled the Irish Catholic Church to converge into a variant of the Presbyterian Kirk or the Church of Ireland.

The Anglo-Irish Agreement of November 1985 created some remarkable new alignments. The Catholic bishops, including Cardinal O'Fiaich, were generally supportive of the Accord as raising nationalist morale. The radical Fr Wilson, who believed the Agreement likely to lead to the demise of the Irish Catholic Church, joined loyalists, lay and clerical, and Provisionals in total opposition. The Provisionals' support for divorce in the Irish referendum of June 1986, and their partial endorsement of abortion in 1985, did not prevent Paisley's paper, strongly opposed to both divorce and abortion, from discovering papal approbation for the IRA in May 1986.[151]

Summary: Catholic and republican loyalists divide

In a debate apparently impervious to current realities, certain facts stand out. First, the controversy between the Provisionals and the official Catholic Church was fundamental and contained relatively little shadow-boxing. Ultimately, there was a line beyond which a churchman could not go in support of revolution. On the other hand the Catholic bishops maintained a consistent slightly right of centre position from the outbreak of the Troubles in 1968 until 1989. Cardinal O'Fiaich was minimally to the left of his colleagues.[152] The pope's visit in 1979 simply confirmed the stance maintained by the Irish bishops. The loyalist complaint that the Catholic Church connived at PIRA's actions is unjustified on the evidence for the bishops but partly true of a handful of lower clergy. The PIRA counter-charge of collusion with the established authorities is also true from the republican viewpoint. Second, a number of very important long-standing issues between Irish revolutionaries and the Catholic Church re-emerged with a post-Vatican II twist. Compared with the debate between Charles Kickham and Cardinal Cullen, the dispute between *An Phoblacht/Republican News* and Cardinals Conway, O'Fiaich and Daly was more wide-ranging and bitter. Despite the ostensible secularity of the Provisional credo, republicans were intensely concerned with parrying episcopal barbs.[153] An increasing strain was placed on the old, comfortable, but theologically unjustified, distinction between religion and politics. As always there was tacit inconsistency when urging this principle: churchmen were sternly admonished for unpatriotic politics, but welcomed heartily when their message was favourable. In the 1860s, as Comerford has shown, Kickham did not oppose priests in politics as such, but only when they criticised Fenianism.[154] To ask whether nationalism or religion is the stronger force in the Irish context is unprofitable: both occupy their own areas of the mind and clash in a mental no-man's-land. As Oliver MacDonagh says, priests and people shared the same ambiguity. Usually, the Prot-stats, despite the capital they made out of divisions in the Roman Catholic community, found themselves involved in mirrored disputes with their own paramilitaries, and sometimes their bishops. Moreover, the very vigour of the intra-Catholic dispute undermined their basic argument against a united Ireland, namely domination by a Catholic monolith. Cardinal O'Fiaich's conclusion for the 1860s, that the Church was divided on Fenianism, is equally applicable to the 1970s and 1980s. The most monolithic aspect of the Roman Catholic Church, separate education, will now be examined.

Notes

1. McCarthy, Michael J.F. [1922], *The British Monarchy and the See of Rome: the Tragedy of Ireland*, London: Protestant Truth Society, and Kensit, J.A. (1921), *Rome behind Sinn Féin?*, London: Protestant Truth Society. See also Davis, R. (1986), 'The Manufacture of Propagandist History by Northern Ireland Loyalists and Republicans', Alexander and O'Day, *Ireland's Terrorist Dilemma*, 145-177.
2. RN January-February 1971.
3. AP, 9 May and 18 July 1975. As early as 1821 even ignorant Catholics knew that the pope had encouraged Henry II to invade Ireland. Garvin, Tom (1981), *The Evolution of Irish Nationalist Politics*, Dublin: Gill and Macmillan, xiv. See also the *Nation* on Laudabiliter, 4 November 1843.
4. UI, 14 November 1974.
5. RN, 1 February 1975.
6. AP, October 1971, RN, 14 January 1974.
7. UI, January 1974.
8. RN, January-February 1971. Fr Murphy is also a popular subject for AOH banners. Furlong, Nicholas (1991), *Fr John Murphy of Boolavogue, 1753-1798*, Dublin: Geography Publications, shows that Murphy took to rebellion reluctantly against the orders of his bishop when confronted by atrocities perpetrated against his flock.
9. AP, 6 August 1974.
10. See McCartney, Donal (1968), 'The Church and the Fenians' in Harmon, M., ed., *Fenians and Fenianism*, Dublin: Scepter, 11-23. AP, 25 November 1982 (Kickham and clergy).
11. Davis, R. (1981) 'Catholic Education and Irish Nationalism: O'Connell to Community Schools', *ANZHES Journal*, Adelaide, 10, 1, Autumn 1981, 1-12.
12. Bowen, Desmond (1983), *Paul Cardinal Cullen and the Shaping of Modern Irish Catholicism*, Dublin: Gill and Macmillan, 279-80.
13. McCartney, 22.

14. 16 September 1965.
15. Comerford, R.V. (1979), *Charles J. Kickham: A Study in Irish Nationalism and Literature*, Co. Dublin: Wolfhound, 65. O Fiaich, Tomas (1968), 'The Clergy and Fenianism', *Irish Ecclesiastical Record*, Vol. CIX, No. 2, February 1968, 81-103.
16. RN January-February 1971; AP, 15 March 1974. The Provisionals do not appear to have emphasised O'Flanagan's original desire to leave Ulster to the unionists.
17. PT, 1 May 1971, 31 May 1969. For Croke's ambiguities, see MacDonagh, 100-101.
18. RN, 28 April 1974.
19. RN, 9 April 1972.
20. AP, 7 January 1982.
21. See Cullen to Gladstone, 12 March 1870, MacSuibhne, P. (1962), *Paul Cullen and his contemporaries*, Vol. V, Naas: Leinster Leader, 78-9.
22. Davis, R. (1980), 'Ulster Protestants and the Sinn Féin Press, 1914-22', *Eire-Ireland*, 1980, 47.
23. PT, August 1968.
24. Gallagher and Worrall, *Christians in Ulster*, 117.
25. Gerard McElroy (1991), *The Catholic Church and the Northern Ireland Crisis, 1968-86*, Dublin: Gill and Macmillan, 92.
26. PT, 2 January 1971 and 29 March 1975. For Philbin and southern Protestants see White, Jack (1975), *Minority Report: the Protestant Community in the Irish Republic*, Dublin: Gill and Macmillan, 112. According to Callaghan, James (1973), *A House Divided: The Dilemma of Northern Ireland*, 72, he talked Conway into appointing the chaplain.
27. Belfast Workers Research Unit (1980), *The Churches in Northern Ireland*, Belfast Bulletin No. 8, Spring 1980, 27-8 for a very critical account. RN, January-February 1971 and 30 October 1971, 11 May and 6 July 1974; PT, 29 March 1975, accused Philbin of helping to draft ecumenism proposals, while virtually excommunicating Catholic children at non-Catholic schools, and doing nothing to stop terrorism.
28. Daly, Cahal B. (1973), *Violence in Ireland and the Christian Conscience*, Dublin: Veritas, 40-1, criticised in AP, 31 May 1974.
29. Interview with Alf McCreary, Radio Ulster, 21 February 1982. Widgery Tribunal, (HL 101 and HC 220), 16. AP, 6 January 1983 and 21 July 1983 (against Cahal Daly).
30. McElroy, 62-3.
31. RN, 1 February 1975.
32. PT, February 1979.
33. McElroy, 62.
34. Gallagher and Worrall, 118.
35. McElroy, 19.
36. PT, 30 August 1969.
37. AP, 6 June 1972. Armstrong, David with Saunders, Hilary (1985), *A Road too Wide: The Price of Reconciliation in Northern Ireland*, Basingstoke: Marshalls.

38. 17 November 1969. Deutsch, R. and Magowan, V. (1974-5), *Northern Ireland, 1968-74: A Chronology of Events* (3 vols.), Belfast: Blackstaff (D and M).
39. Deutsch and Magowan, 17 January 1969. According to McElroy, 121-3, Faul was the first priest to criticise the judiciary and was criticised by Cardinal Conway. Faul then appeared to be isolated in the Church.
40. Deutsch and Magowan, 3 April 1970.
41. PT, 25 October 1969.
42. PT, 6 December 1969.
43. PT, 27 September 1969.
44. Gallagher and Worrall, 60.
45. RN, March 1971. According to Wilson, Fr Des (1985), *An End to Silence*, Cork: Mercier, 75, Conway protested against torture, but not internment as such.
46. AP, October 1971.
47. RN, 3 April 1976.
48. RN, 9 October 1971.
49. RN, March 1971.
50. Gallagher and Worrall, 63.
51. RN, 30 October 1971.
52. RN, 5 December 1971.
53. RN, 6 November 1971.
54. RN, 5 December 1971.
55. RN, 9 October 1971.
56. RN, 25 September 1971.
57. See MacDonagh, O., *States of Mind*, 101.
58. Gallagher and Worrall, 64.
59. RN, 9 April 1972.
60. Deutsch and Magowan, 24 May 1973 and 17 March 1974.
61. RN, August 1974.
62. Deutsch and Magowan, 14 November 1972.
63. RN, 1 December 1972.
64. Law (1,28) 1972. McRory's statement was quoted in IN, 18 December 1931. See Arthur, P., *Government and Politics in Northern Ireland*, Essex: Longman, 42.
65. UDAN, (18) 1972.
66. UDAN, (13) 1972.
67. PT, 7 October 1972.
68. PT, 15 December 1972. *Law*, (2, 40) 1972.
69. Deutsch and Magowan, 10 December 1973.
70. Deutsch and Magowan, 16 March 1973.
71. AP, 6 April 1973. For Aquinas's leaflet and reply, see Burton, *The Politics of Legitimacy*, 94-5. For 1976 issue, 97-103.
72. RN, 24 March 1973.
73. PT, 26 May 1973.
74. PT, 2 October 1976. Burton, 8, 93 and 103 for non-religious natures of Provisionals, 85 for 'see-saw relationship', and 94 for Aquinas on Connolly and Pearse. See also IN, 11 August 1972 for Aquinas

interview on opposition to Stormont. See V, No. 3, Vol. 2, 1976, for republican opinion.

75. McElroy, 75-6.
76. An academic quoted by Insight (1972), *Ulster*, 202.
77. Deutsch and Magowan, 4 January 1972.
78. AP, 4 July 1991. 'It would take another book to deal with the evasions, the half truths, the inaccuracies, the invalid analysis, the false logic of this book.' His main complaint was that Daly refused to condemn the British in Northern Ireland.
79. See AP, 5 March 1992, review of Wilson, Des and MacVeigh, Joe, *Undermining Peace: A Report on Official Church Responses to Citizens in Crisis*.
80. For details of the dispute between Wilson and Philbin see AN, 21 and 28 June 1975. The article causing the trouble was published in AN, 19 April 1975 and quoted from *Hibernia*. A meeting of 1500 supported Wilson and 2000 signed a petition in his favour. There was a booklet, *Open the Window, Let in the Light* published by Wilson's followers. For Terry O'Keefe, AN, 5 July 1975. OS, November 1985 for Buckley. See Wilson, *An End to Silence*, 80.
81. PT, 7 March 1970; OS, August 1975; for McKeague, LN, 1 July 1975; Wilson, Des [1982], *The Demonstration*, n.p.; AP, 9 May 1975. According to Nicky Tamin of AN, 5 July 1975, Provisionals thought Wilson an Official, while the latter were convinced that he supported the former, and the IRSP considered him a supple reactionary.
82. RN, 19 January 1974.
83. Deutsch and Magowan, 18 March and 20 March 1974.
84. RN, 18 May 1974.
85. RN, 4 May 1974 and 11 May 1974.
86. PT, 27 April 1974.
87. RN, 29 May 1974.
88. Dr G.B. Newe had been a token Catholic in Faulkner's cabinet of 1971.
89. RN, 2 February 1974.
90. LN, 22 June 1974 and PT, May 1981.
91. PT, 30 November 1974.
92. AP, 19 December 1975 and PT, 29 March 1975.
93. RN, 6 July 1974.
94. For Philbin (25 June 1974) and Daly (23 June 1974), RN, 6 July 1974 and Daly's failure on institutional violence RN, 24 August 1974.
95. AP, 9 August 1974.
96. AP, 21 March 1975 and RN, 12 April 1975.
97. Daly, Cahal (1979), *Peace the Work of Justice*, Dublin: Veritas, 97.
98. RN, 3 April 1976. Newman, J. (1977), *The State of Ireland*, Dublin: Four Courts Press, 66-7 (British withdrawal), 123 (1916). For Peter Cleary, see Kevin Kelley (1982), *The Longest War: Northern Ireland and the IRA*, Kerry: Brandon, 248. Cleary was shot four times.
99. RN, 15 January 1977. *Peace by Peace*, 25 March 1977 (Wilson) and 22 April 1977.
100. AP, 6 May 1978.
101. RN, 12 November 1977.

102. AP, 7 March 1981.
103. AP, 10 October 1981.
104. AP, 22 August 1981.
105. See Comerford, *Kickham*, 71.
106. *Fortnight*, 187, July-August 1982 (4 April 1982). In an interview 16 September 1982, Daly said that he believed that large numbers used the confidential telephones.
107. IN, 18 November 1975, quoted in PT, 11 March 1978.
108. AP, 19 November 1981.
109. AP, 10 October 1981.
110. PT, 18 September 1976.
111. *Church and State: A Forum of Irish Secularist opinion* (1981), Cork, Autumn, 1981, 4.
112. AP, 11 August 1979, 5 January 1980.
113. PT, 10 January 1976: Fr Michael Connolly—PR's Holy War, 2 October 1976: Fr Burns, Fell and McManus (sympathy too weak to express feeling for IRA), Fr Connolly, Fr McGriel (gun sacramental in Ireland), Fr Kane, Fr O'Duill (blessed IRA man), Archbishop Ryan (visited MacStiofain), Fr Faul, Fr Marcellus Gillespie, Fr Burns (Glasgow arms case), Fr Fell (imprisoned in Coventry). Wilson, *An End to Silence*, 48.
114. Provisionals emphasised Torres, 'the Catholic who is not revolutionary is living in mortal sin', but Torres did ask for laicisation before joining the guerrillas. See Gerassi, J. (1971), ed., *Revolutionary Priest: the Complete Writings and Messages of Camilo Torres*, London: Jonathan Cape, 28-9. For Torres, see RN, 31 January 1976 and 6 March 1976. 22 January 1977 (radical interpretation of *Populorum Progressio*), 24 September 1977; AP, 5 July 1974, 27 July 1977 (took off cassock to be more truly a priest), 14 December 1977, 29 April 1978, 23 February 1980, 30 May 1981; PT, 7 March 1970, 12 May 1973.
115. Deutsch and Magowan, 20 May 1972. For John Paul II at Drogheda, see John Paul II (1979), *The Pope Teaches - including Speeches made in Ireland*, September, 1979, London: Catholic Truth Society, 390-99, esp. 392.
116. O'Casey, Sean (1973), *Drums under the Windows*, London: Pan, 283. RN, March 1971 and 23 August 1975.
117. Davis (1977), 'The Advocacy of Passive Resistance in Ireland, 1916-1922', *Anglo-Irish Studies*, III, 48-9.
118. Gallagher and Worrall, 122. *The Pope Teaches*, 27 September 1979, 'Christian Unity', 402. He opposed 'all violence and assaults against the human person - from whatever quarter they come'.
119. RN, 9 April 1972.
120. AP, 6 October 1979.
121. Gallagher and Worrall, 123.
122. AP, 10 May 1980.
123. PT, May 1980.
124. U, February 1980; *Church and State*, Autumn, 1981, 1-8, 'The Catholic Church in the H-Block Campaign'.
125. McElroy, 144: Fr Joe McVeigh, Fr McEvoy and Fr Des Wilson. AP, 9 May 1991.

126. AP, 6 January 1979.
127. RN, 7 May 1977.
128. Before the Treaty, the only leader of an Irish rebellion in modern times currently an elected MP was William Smith O'Brien in 1848.
129. AP, 10 February 1982 and RN, 9 April 1972.
130. AP, 11 April 1991.
131. *Republic of Ireland*, Dublin, 27 April 1922. Nelson, Sarah, *Ulster's Uncertain Defenders*, 90.
132. AP, 19 April 1980. and 10 May 1980. Wilson, *An End to Silence*, 56.
133. See, for example, Farrell, M. (1971), *The Founding of Dail Eireann: Parliament and Nation Building*, Dublin.
134. Sinn Féin Publicity Department (1985), *The Good Old IRA: Tan War operations*, Dublin, 3: 'no struggle involves a clean fight.' Compare with Daly, Bishop Cahal, *Peace the Work of Justice*, 97: the current IRA methods were 'repudiated by the men of 1916 themselves, the methods of "inhumanity and rapine"'.
135. AP, 6 June 1972. Wilson, *An End to Silence*, 57. O Fiaich on RTE Radio, 15 January 1984.
136. AP, 9 February 1984. McElroy suggests (156-7) that the shifts of bishops like O Fiaich and Cahal Daly on the violence issue, and their failure to publish an agreed statement, weakened the Church's position.
137. AP, June 1972.
138. PT, 12 May 1973 and 15 February 1975. They evoked the 'Killing No Murder' article of Charles Diamond in the *Catholic Herald* and the theology of Marianus de Luca, both mentioned by Kensit, 22-3, in 1921. Francisco Suarez (1548-1615) was an eminent Spanish theologian.
139. See AP, 12 November 1992: 'The DUP—A Party Committed to Violence.'
140. UL, 29 September 1973.
141. C, (1, 33) 1974.
142. See Manhattan, Avro (1971), *Religious Terror in Ireland*, London: Paravision, 87-90. The book was 'a must' according to a writer in OUDAN (1,13) 1972 but to AN, 30 August 1975, it was 'a Goon Show script from beginning to end'.
143. Marx, K. and Engels, F. (1978), *Ireland and the Irish Question*, London: Lawrence and Wishart, 257.
144. Comerford, *Charles J. Kickham*, 158-60.
145. See speech at 1917 Sinn Féin Ard Fheis, *Gaelic American*, 17 November 1917.
146. See Robert Kee (1981), *Ireland: a Television History*, Revolution episode.
147. RN, 6 April 1974. For Conway, *Ulster Militant*, 1, (1972).
148. RN, 30 October 1971; AP, 16 August 1974; UM, 1 (1972); LN's attempt (16 August 1975) to distinguish between Protestant and Catholic conscience by assuming that the latter was 'the collective conscience of the Catholic clergy, which is dictated by the Pope', does not answer these arguments.
149. See McElroy, 144.

150. AP, 16 May 1975. Wilson, *An End to Silence*, 35 (Tone and church), *Ulster*, December 1985/January 1986 (Paul Loane).

151. Wilson and Accord, AN, 23 November 1985 and AP, 20 November 1986. Pro-divorce, AP, 19 June 1986; abortion, 7 November 1985. *Protestant Blu Print*, Vol. 1, 41, 2 May 1986 (Paisley). Paisley differed from the Catholic Church in accepting the remarriage of the innocent party in a divorce and also the use of contraception in marriage. See NPT, June 1990.

152. *End to Silence*, 36 and 75: Wilson considered O Fiaich's demand for the removal of abuses and their cause an improvement on Conway. AP, 14 March and 25 July 1985, while admitting that O Fiaich believed British withdrawal the answer to Ulster's problems, complained that he did not justify the Provisionals. Ironically, an apparently tactless O Fiaich statement blaming Protestants for ninety per cent of Northern Ireland bigotry (IT, 20 July 1985), was later echoed and accepted by a remarkable article in the UDA's *Ulster*, June 1986 ('Connall').

153. McElroy maintains (158-161) that after great bitterness towards the hierarchy in the 1970s, the Provisionals later adopted a more secular philosophy and their self-justification was 'increasingly based on specific historical, social and political perspectives of Ireland.' However, there was still considerable criticism of the bishops.

154. Comerford, *Charles J. Kickham*, 74.

5 Disintegrated education

Ulster's ambiguous education lesson

Integrated education looms over any discussion on Northern Ireland. The issue has created perennial controversy throughout the English-speaking world and beyond. Northern Ireland is the *reductio ad absurdum* for contestants on both sides of the international debate. Advocates of mixed, non-sectarian education cite the total polarisation and endemic violence of the Six Counties as a grisly warning to the United States, Canada, Australia and New Zealand of the dangers of increased public funding of parochial schools. Educational denominationalists reach diametrically opposed conclusions. Separate schools in other countries, they argue, have been accompanied by none of the division so apparent in Ulster. The Northern Irish problem, they maintain, is *sui generis*, unrelated to educational systems. Integrated education thus appears unnecessary, even in Ulster.

As in the general conflict between the Roman Catholic Church and Irish republicans, nationalists have naively expected bishops to give priority to Irish social requirements, rather than religious universalism; loyalists, equally erroneously, have assumed Vatican manipulation of Irish education for republican ends. Antithetical interpretation of identical facts is apparent. Provisionals and Paisleyites agree in supporting theoretical integration while opposing it in practice; the Official IRA/Sinn Féin, later the

Worker's Party but described here as the 'Officials', and the loyalist paramilitaries insisted on rigorous but impracticable educational integration.

Origins of Catholic separatism

The historical background, from Roman Catholic, un-ecumenical Protestant, and Irish nationalist viewpoints, is revealing. Catholic separationist philosophy can be traced to the middle of the nineteenth century. Before this period, the Church traditionally controlled education in Catholic countries but was subject to various degrees of inconvenience in Protestant states, or those, like Ireland, ruled by a Protestant power. The eighteenth-century penal laws prohibiting Catholic schools are a case in point. With the progress of religious tolerance in the nineteenth century, Catholic authorities attempted to control areas where full Church management of its children's education was denied; by judicious compromise, however, the Church effected agreement with non-Catholic powers. In early nineteenth-century Ireland, as republican propaganda continually complained, the Catholic bishops were particularly accommodating towards the British government, being willing, until stopped by laymen like Daniel O'Connell, to accept its veto over episcopal appointments. By the 1820s and 1830s, Catholic prelates, Archbishop William Crolly of Armagh, Archbishop Daniel Murray of Dublin, and James Doyle of Kildare and Leighlin ('JKL'), were, to the astonishment of subsequent generations, prepared to accept the idea of mixed education, with safeguards, as beneficial. JKL's apostrophe to the ideal of uniting creeds and classes in friendship has been quoted *ad nauseam*.[1] When the British government in 1831 inaugurated a mixed education system in Ireland, Catholic prelates co-operated. Archbishop Murray even agreed with his Church of Ireland counterpart, Archbishop Richard Whately, on a common book of scriptural readings. Unfortunately, as reiterated in countless debates on denominational education throughout the British Commonwealth,[2] Whately later admitted that both he and Murray had had proselytist intentions. Nevertheless, it was not the Catholics but the Presbyterians in the north who undermined the first attempt at 'integrated education'. Gradually, Catholics themselves became more intransigent. In 1842, Archbishop MacHale appealed abortively to Rome for a definitive condemnation of undenominational education. Three years later, backed by O'Connell, MacHale opposed Peel's new undenominational university colleges as dangerous to the faith.

The hierarchy was then divided. Following the appointment of the future Cardinal Cullen to the see of Armagh in 1850, advocates of compromise faded away. The Synod of Thurles, 1852, insisted on a clear-cut system of Catholic schools. Separate Catholic education at all levels was one of the main preoccupations of Cullen till his death in 1878. The 'National' system became denominational in practice with local clerics acting as school managers. In 1878 payment by results was introduced for intermediate education which secured private subsidised schools controlled by individual Churches. In 1908 the establishment of the National University of Ireland gave the Irish hierarchy virtual control of Catholic tertiary education.[3]

As John Whyte pointed out, the Irish debate led in 1847 to the first specific condemnation of an educational system by the Vatican. Under Pope Pius IX, church policy hardened. In the *Syllabus of Errors*, 1864, a complete statement of the Roman Catholic educational position was provided in propositions 45-48. Suggestions for State control of schools and the separation of religious and secular education were firmly repudiated. The education of Catholics and non-Catholics in the same schools was not expressly forbidden, but tolerated only in schools under Catholic control. The same principles were laid down in relevant canons such as 1374, which prohibited Catholics from attending non-Catholic schools, except in rare circumstances with the permission of the local bishop.[4] The propositions of the *Syllabus* were generally derived from disputes between the papacy and Catholic countries, not Britain or Ireland. A form of liberal Catholicism, described as 'Americanism', was rejected in the 1890s.

New formulations of the policy appeared at regular intervals. In 1929 Pius XI's encyclical, *Divini Illius Magistri* (The Christian Education of Youth), gave another clear summary of official church policy. Besides the now traditional insistence on separate schools for Catholics, it, albeit in general terms, condemned the modern child-centred education and co-education. This encyclical, promulgated in the early years of the Northern Ireland State, was the high peak of the Catholic separatist movement. Not only was state-controlled education rejected, but neutral instruction was deemed a logical impossibility. Thus if Lord Londonderry in his Education Act of 1924 had succeeded in establishing a purely secular system, the Catholic bishops would not have been appeased. In practice, however, when the Church possessed insufficient schools to cater for the whole age group, it preferred its children in a secular system rather than one including Protestant observances.

Today there are some examples of ecumenical co-operation in which the Roman Catholic Church has agreed on a common religious education syllabus with other Christian Churches, and sometimes other religions. In the nineteenth century such agreement appeared chimerical. Catholic apologists sometimes denied the accord, often cited by non-Catholics, between Archbishops Murray and Whately.

Vatican II introduced many ecumenical changes, but did not end Catholic educational separatism. Though more liberal towards children forced for lack of facilities into state schools, Vatican II re-affirmed what was then the orthodox argument: 'As for Catholic parents, the Council calls to mind their duty to entrust their children to Catholic schools, when and where this is possible, to support such schools to the extent of their ability, and to work along with them for the welfare of their children'. This statement places in context the apparent paradox of prelates like Bishop Philbin, Bishop of Down and Connor, an advocate of ecumenism and reconciliation on the one hand, and, in loyalist eyes, an ogre who denied the sacraments to parents of Catholic children in mixed schools.[5] Philbin might have justifiably retorted, as Paisley had done with the strongly anti-papal Presbyterian *Westminster Confession of Faith*, that he had not invented the Catholic education policy. Vatican II, however, opened a debate in which many eminent Catholics questioned the practical value of separate schools. Surveys, often inconsistent with each other, sometimes indicated that the subsequent religious practice of Catholic school graduates was not markedly higher than that of contemporaries who had experienced state education. Nevertheless, to some conservatives separate education, instead of being a pragmatic policy, to be reviewed in every generation, had developed into an inflexible doctrine. As Sir Oliver Napier, a Catholic former leader of the moderate unionist Alliance Party, argued, canon law can be and is changed, 'so do not let a canon stand in our way.'[6]

Conscientious bishops maintained the standard position on separate education. The Roman Catholic Church had world-wide interests in no way connected with the particular needs of Northern Ireland. Regardless of the violence, community polarisation, and sectarian hatred, Northern Ireland Catholic bishops used the same educational arguments as their colleagues in Los Angeles, Sydney, and Wellington, New Zealand. First and foremost came the contention that all education must be permeated by religion. This argument was much ventilated in the nineteenth century. The Ulster Presbyterian leader and Dr Ian Paisley's model, Henry

Cooke, used it in the 1830s. But 'permeation' is probably more impressive in a theology seminar than in a contemporary classroom where teachers battle against the ubiquitous TV screen. A second argument stresses diversity, a dubious benefit in Northern Ireland. Third comes the double taxation contention that Catholic taxpayers support both their own and the public schools. This argument becomes two-edged when loyalists maintain that they are required to pay for indoctrination in Catholicism, or worse.[7] Significantly, such arguments represent the World Church, rather than its Northern Irish segment. To expect Roman Catholic bishops to drop them is to misunderstand their function. An argument against Catholic education policies cannot ultimately be couched in terms of terrestrial advantage, and appears a counter-productive attempt to erode the religious allegiance of Catholic children. If, as one archbishop far from Northern Ireland maintained, 'Catholic schools are the hinges on which the doors of the Catholic Church swing', there is no room for manoeuvre.[8] Catholic authorities did not, however, accept that integrated education would improve communal attitudes and cited sources to the contrary.[9]

Prot-stats take the Bible to world schools

As already mentioned, it was nineteenth-century Presbyterians who took the initiative in breaking up the first Irish attempt at non-denominational education. Ironically, they assisted the Anglicans and Methodists in the early twentieth-century by repeating the effort when the Londonderry Education Act of 1924 was passed by the fledgling Northern Ireland parliament. Yet it has always been a Prot-stat criticism of Roman Catholicism that the latter refuses to allow educational integration. This paradox is easily explained. Believing that popery was a dangerous error that must be eliminated, nineteenth-century Prot-stats hoped to achieve this with a certain finesse. As Catholics were thought to be forbidden the Bible by their clergy, they could receive simple Bible readings 'without note or comment' in the 'undenominational' schools. The Bible was, of course, the *Authorised Version* of 1611, totally unacceptable to Catholics and now found to contain serious errors of translation. Catholics naturally refused such proselytist bait and enabled Prot-stats to maintain that they were rejecting undenominational education. The built-in assumption was always that Prot-stat Bible readings and Prot-stat prayers were 'neutral'. The situation was complicated by the Catholic refusal to accept the feasibility of neutral secularity. In nineteenth-century Ireland it proved easiest for all to tolerate a tacit subsidence into denominationalism.

In some far-off places, however, there appeared interesting and revealing twists to the familiar tangle. Brash colonial and American politicians representing different sects or none, tired of the endless strife between the Churches, technically equal in the new societies. They then passed secular education acts. Sometimes the Prot-stat Bible readings were smuggled in at the last moment, but other legislatures held firm. In the Australian Colony of Victoria there was an attempt to remove the name of God from the textbooks. New Zealand did not go quite so far, but its 1877 Education Act rejected both aid to separate independent schools and Bible readings and prayers in the state schools. In the United States the Supreme Court evolved a tradition of rejecting both denominational aid and public school religious observances. Few of the Churches were satisfied, but some, like the Baptists, developed a strong sense of Church-State separation. The Catholic Church condemned the secular systems as godless and continued to demand aid for the separate schools they were building. The Prot-stats also condemned the secular system, but demanded 'the Bible in schools', not aid for separate systems. Prot-stat churchmen, unlike Catholic, lacked interest in maintaining primary systems, but concentrated on a few élitist secondaries, usually self-financing through fees. The system in some places achieved a restless equilibrium for about a hundred years. Had Catholics and Prot-stats been able to unite, as in the Netherlands, they could have satisfied each other at the expense of a small minority of genuinely secularist politicans. In fact, the Catholics often found themselves in tacit alliance with secularists to prevent legislation forcing the Bible on those Catholic students, sometimes a considerable number, compelled to use the state system. After World War II, the situation changed. Inflation eroded the finances of the Prot-stat secondaries and the latter with surprising speed forgot their objections to the promulgation of error and joined the Roman Catholics in demanding state aid all round. Throughout the British Commonwealth governments rapidly capitulated. Even the United States has been moving away from educational secularism.

Such external precedents provide a yardstick for Northern Ireland. They demonstrate that advocacy of integrated education must always be probed for hidden objectives. What, it must be asked, is the precise motivation behind a group arguing for common education? Second, the current controversy in Northern Ireland resembles philosophically the nineteenth-century battle over the Bible in schools and denial of aid to Catholic schools rather than the united Church movements in several countries today. The fact that Dr Paisley's friend and ally, Dr Bob Jones, is, alongside Paisley himself, a strong advocate of the *Authorised Version* in American schools, effectively demonstrates the link. Northern Ireland never passed through the phase of total rejection of aid to private schools, but some of Paisley's rhetoric suggests that this, if not a practical proposition at present, represents an ideal. Straight secularists have not had any influence in Northern Ireland to date, but they might have to be invented before a solution to the education question becomes possible. McKeague's *Loyalist News* went part of the way by demanding that 'religious education should be kept out of the syllabus'. He later qualified the statement by suggesting, 'it should be kept to the minimum'. It was 'the minimum' that caused the trouble.[10]

As demonstrated, Catholic educational separatism gradually congealed after an early nineteenth-century fluidity, and the more ambiguous Protestant acceptance of state education was buttressed by Bible reading and prayers. Time has caught up with Bible-in-schools advocates in that many, like Paisley, reject the modern Biblical translations, acceptable to both Prot-ecums and Catholics. But what of the Irish republican tradition on education? The chief feature of the latter is its extremely rare invocation.

Early republican integrationism: the Davis legacy abandoned

Wolfe Tone, amongst other attacks on Catholic bishops, denounced their rejection of a general system of education: 'Damn them. Ignorant bigots.' Integrated education was implicit in Tone's oft-quoted phrase, 'to substitute the common name of Irishman in place of the denominations of Protestant, Catholic and Dissenter'. Thomas Davis, a Young Ireland leader in the 1840s, is, however, the true author of the Irish republican tradition of educational integration. His anticipation of a 'theological police' railing off each sect anticipated the Northern Ireland peace lines of recent times. Many churchmen, however, remain unconvinced of his view that mixed education is 'consistent with piety'.[11]

Such nineteenth-century opinion indicates a clearly articulated philosophy. Given the republican repudiation of O'Connell, an educational integrationist who reversed his opinion, and exaltation of Davis, these ideas might have emerged as an integral part of the nationalist tradition, especially when there was such an ingrained habit of resisting Catholic bishops and their condemnations. This, however, did not happen. Integrated education became the lost or hidden tradition of Irish republicanism. After Davis's death in September 1845 most of his friends eventually advocated separate Catholic schools. There were even some ambiguities in Davis's own secularism.[12] The Fenians, while resisting Cardinal Cullen's denunciations, deliberately approached the educational issue gently, despite Cullen's own linkage of anti-Fenianism and Church control of schools in his fear that teachers in undenominational National schools were often Fenians. Of the Fenian leaders only John Devoy appears to have analysed Cullen's educational preoccupation. A tacit nationalist understanding developed that the Catholic Church should not be challenged in its educational policies.

Such was the position before the beginning of the current Ulster Troubles. The Irish Republic has had no difficulty in repressing the fact that it revered Davis while basing its education on O'Connell who supported the Catholic bishops opposed to undenominational institutions. The non-Catholic Churches did not complain as their control over Protestant schools was maintained. Though there is currently some opposition, educational denominationalism has remained basically intact.[13]

The dual system of Northern Ireland

During the fifty years of unionist rule in Northern Ireland the debate over integrated education was not quite as dead as in the south. The Catholic Church kept the issue alive, threatening legal action against Prot-stat observances in the state schools. Though conciliated by larger grants, it pressed for further increases. By the 1970s many Catholic schools had accepted 'maintained' status and gave local authorities a one-third representation on their boards. Catholics thus obtained almost 100 per cent of all their costs from the government. Their position was markedly better than parochial schools in a still secularist USA. Even in countries like Canada, Australia and New Zealand, where aid to denominational schools has increased since initial grants in the 1960s and 1970s, it is still sometimes incomplete. Loyalist propaganda has used such facts to insist, first, that the Catholics suffer no discrimination in Northern Ireland,[14] and, second, that it is disgraceful for the State to provide for disloyal popery from the public purse.[15] The Catholic Church in Northern Ireland is thus able to include nearly 100 per cent of its school age population in its institutions, a situation very different from other English-speaking countries overseas where it is a minority Church.

Many Prot-stats also find the education system of Northern Ireland satisfactory. The state schools used to operate with an agreed syllabus for religious education, accepted that is by the Presbyterians, Anglicans and Methodists. According to A.J. Menendez in 1973, it had 'a strong orientation towards the Reformed theology expressed in the *Westminster Confession* and the Thirty-nine Articles' and would be 'totally inappropriate for a pluralist society which reflects diverse theological viewpoints'. The syllabus, moreover, aimed at 'personal commitment'.[16] When loyalists criticise Catholic educational separatism, they frequently meant a refusal to participate in this 'undenominational' system.

Loyalists, as demonstrated, have a long tradition of criticising Catholics for rejecting the educational integration which Protestants did not themselves always accept. In 1911 the perceptive, nationally-minded Church of Ireland parson and novelist, J.O. Hannay (George A. Birmingham) pointed out that non-Catholics could scarcely demand educational safeguards under a Home Rule Bill as their clergy were equally insistent on preventing democratic control. However, when the Catholic bishops opposed the British 1919 education bills so emphatically that the legislation had to be dropped, loyalists were outraged. Even Sir Edward Carson entered the fray, insisting in 1920 that the current education bill, which would provide for up to 30,000 neglected Belfast schoolchildren, was a thousand times more important than Home Rule. Most of the arguments, once ventilated by Young Ireland nationalists, were re-aired by unionists: the divisiveness of separate schools being condemned, while the advantages of non-sectarian school benches were upheld. According to the UDA's *Ulster*, Carson's integrationist dream was ruined by the Churches which in 1985 still hypocritically preached reconciliation. On the republican side, this Orange integration 'fetish' was repudiated as 'camouflage' for persecutors and exterminators. Demands for integrated education could be rejected as Catholic-bashing by Orangemen, or the clumsy naivety of a politician like Terence O'Neill. Nevertheless, in a survey actually completed before the outbreak of the Troubles, Richard Rose found that majorities of both Catholics and non-Catholics supported common schools in theory. Subsequent polls have indicated the same opinion so consistently as to raise doubts about their value in the light of the patent fact that there appears to be no practical fervour for integrated education in any part of the community.[17]

The integration debate renewed

Several outside observers, shocked by the post-1968 violence and communal hatred, attributed the problem to the system of 'educational apartheid'. Some, like Richard Rose, frequently quoted by Catholic authorities, rejected this argument. The old issue had been resuscitated. Despite what John Darby has called 'the general woolliness' of the debate, key questions were certainly raised. The Presbyterians twice resolved in favour of integrated education in their General Assembly.[18] Methodists cautiously discussed the issue. The Church of Ireland, with more schools of its own in the Republic, faced a dilemma epitomised by Dr S.G. Poyntz, bishop of Cork, who admitted that integrated schools 'might be a panacea in Northern Ireland where there was a better spread of population. But in the Republic they could post the demise of the Church of Ireland.' The Catholic bishops were not prepared to go further than suggest some 'interaction' between schools rather than integration.[19] Cardinal Conway, however, in June 1971 reportedly considered that integrated education might some day be possible.[20] There was no follow-up of such cogitations, except perhaps in the qualified support given by Conway's successor, Cardinal O'Fiaich, who accepted the All Children Together Group's mixed Lagan College as a useful experiment.[21] Even Bishop Philbin had no objection to the traditionally non-segregated Hilden school in his diocese, no doubt realising that it could never become a precedent.[22]

The bishops did not, however, have it all their own way. Fr Michael Hurley, director of the Irish School of Ecumenics, Dublin, Fr Michael McGreil, lecturer in sociology, Maynooth, Professor Peter Connolly, also of Maynooth, Fr John Brady, director of the College of Industrial Relations, and Fr Desmond Wilson[23] all demanded educational rethinking. On the Church of Ireland side there was the outspoken Bishop Hanson who declared, 'I am still quite convinced that in Northern Ireland segregation of education is not merely mistaken. In the circumstances it is grossly immoral.'[24] A number of important organisations such as the Northern Ireland Civil Rights Association, the Catholic Renewal Movement, the Alliance Party, the Ulster Teachers Union (Protestant) and the Irish National Teachers Organisation (INTO) came out for integration.[25]

The pursuit of an integrated alternative: Lagan College

During the course of the Ulster Troubles integrated education has been a background issue rather than a front-runner. So far, the *status quo* has been generally maintained. This is a remarkable fact in view of the disappearance of Stormont, the dissolution of the monolithic Unionist Party, the rise of urban guerrillas, and all the other great changes of the decade. Will the upheaval of the 70s, 80s and 90s follow that of the 20s in leaving the segregated education system virtually untouched? At first change seemed possible. But despite Terence O'Neill's talk of educational integration,[26] the Stormont regime was as reluctant to interfere with Catholic education as its counterpart in the Irish Republic. Only after the abolition of Stormont and the establishment of the short-lived power-sharing regime did some abatement of educational divisiveness occur. As McAllister demonstrates, the mainly Catholic SDLP was, like most Irish nationalist organisations in the past, extremely wary about grasping the education nettle. Parental rights were always emphasised. However, in the power-sharing executive, some responsibility had to be taken for the policy statement *Steps Towards a Better Tomorrow* which timidly mooted pilot schemes in integrated education after consultation with interested parties. The non-SDLP education minister, Basil McIvor, duly introduced a proposal providing for shared schools with both traditions participating. The idea was attacked by the Roman Catholic Church authorities, allowing Paisley to make propaganda out of Canon Padraig Murphy's insistence that Roman Catholic children could only be taught by their co-religionists as these alone had the truth.[27] The executive fell before its nerve could be put to the test. McAllister argued that the SDLP, while claiming to be unanimous on the issue, lacked the stomach for a round with the Catholic hierarchy.

To a group of Catholic parents self-help seemed the only answer. Disillusioned by the collapse of the executive's effort, they attempted to establish, between the Catholic and the virtually Protstat public system, a third, integrated system. A new organisation, All Children Together, was formally established in 1977 with the assistance of A.C.W. Spencer, a Queen's University sociologist and English Catholic who had proved himself a redoubtable critic of the educational procedures of his Church. In the absence of a Northern Irish legislature the group used the good offices of Lord Dunleath, an Alliance supporter in the House of Lords, to secure the passage of a private member's bill through Westminster permitting the establishment of the integrated third system. The professed desire of the non-Catholic Churches for integration was put to the test. However, the bluff of the latter was soon called and none of the state institutions opted for the change, apart from the Throne school, about to be closed down. It became formally 'integrated' with no initial Catholic pupils. In 1981, Spencer and the All Children Together committee decided to act alone, though they lacked the finance to qualify for voluntary or endowed status under the 1978 Act. Nevertheless, in September 1981, Lagan College with 31 of the expected 60 children opened on a minimal budget. When it came to the crunch, it was mainly Protestant parents who withdrew at the last moment. Though the school survived its first years, and with luck and generous donations achieved a break-through into government aid, its advent was but a small outcome of many speeches and articles extolling the necessity of educational integration in Northern Ireland.[28]

Lagan College soon illustrated the basic ambivalence of unionist thought on the issue. Such dualism is manifest in the first years of Dr Paisley's *Protestant Telegraph*. In 1968 it roundly denounced Roman Catholic educational apartheid and asked why there was such hostility towards South Africa and Rhodesia.[29] On the other hand, the *Protestant Telegraph* noted the Church of Scotland General Assembly's rejection of integrated education. Again, in criticising an INTO pamphlet on education in Ulster, it maintained that few Protestants would allow their children to be taught by Roman Catholics, and that few of the latter would entrust their children to Orange instructors. Free Presbyterians and other Prot-stats knew well that the Roman Catholic hierarchy would never call their bluff, so they could continue to attack 'educational apartheid' with impunity. For this reason, the medieval historian Professor W.L. Warren denounced 'the fraud over integration on the Protestant side'. He suggested that middle-class Protestants saw integrated education for workers only. Warren's proclamation of Protestant evasion was not applicable to the Tara paramilitary organisation. Its policy was quite unambiguous: 'We must campaign now for integrated education. All Roman Catholic centres of education must be closed. Religious education must be provided only by Evangelical Protestants'. The Catholic Church, moreover, should be declared an illegal organisation.[30]

Paisley's separatism disturbs loyalists

Paisley, once a patron of William McGrath of Tara, was not prepared to go so far. Shortly after his election to Stormont in 1970, the doctor further clouded the issue in an interview with the *Ballymena Observer*. He denied that state schools were Protestant, insisting that the Catholics were entitled to run their own schools outside the state system, provided they paid for the privilege. He himself was building a school behind his church.[31] Other loyalists subsequently challenged Paisley on this issue. The UDA *Ulster* pointed out that insistence on sectarian schools was now characteristic of religious minorities in Great Britain. 'The experience of Northern Ireland in relation to segregated education should be a lesson to everyone.'[32] Similarly, the *Orange Standard*, edited by the Church of Ireland Canon S.E. Long, was critical, asserting that Paisley 'in one bold stroke has said more in justification of the continuance of Roman Catholic schools than any other loyalist politician has done since 1921.' Roman Catholic apologists would be rubbing 'their hands in glee' at the 'unambiguous, if unintentional, declaration in favour of segregated education'.[33] The *Protestant Telegraph* replied that 'the Free Church schools would be independent even of state aid and would be supported by voluntary donations'.[34] S.E. Long's own position was hardly more consistent. While he condemned Catholic 'education apartheid' for creating a 'ghetto mentality', he also attacked the 1947 Education Act which 'put back the clock making it possible for anyone as well as a Protestant, perhaps preferable to a Protestant, to teach Protestant children, parents and churches notwithstanding.' This was no less a justification for the Catholic system than Paisley's, unless it were accepted that Catholic children be taught by Protestants to free them of their 'ghetto mentality'. As Dervla Murphy said, this 'wonderful sentence' of Long's puts 'the Orange philosophy in a nutshell'.[35]

There was a difference of emphasis between the Free Presbyterians and the DUP. When the latter's conference in 1974 passed a resolution affirming the principle of integrated education, the *Protestant Telegraph* regretted, as Paisley had done in 1970, that the state schools, which delegated religious instruction to individual Churches, were not truly Protestant.[36] Ironically, in view of the old Bible-in-schools debate, Paisley threatened in 1973 to take the Free Presbyterian children out of state schools if the ecumenical *Common Bible* were used instead of the *Authorised Version*.[37]

This ultra-loyalist debate raises two important issues. First, the Free Presbyterian view of state education was easily exploited by Catholic separatists. Others rejected neutrality and asserted the Prot-stat right to impose their will on the youth of the country. This correlates with the Free Presbyterian 'zero sum' insistence on the total conversion of Ireland. The fact that Paisley rejected new, ecumenical, and accurate translations of the Bible as diabolical, underlines this principle. The discussion reverted to the nineteenth century when Archbishop Whately believed that the agreed book of scripture readings would undermine Catholicism. If, as Menendez has argued, the 'non-denominational' religion of the Northern Ireland State system was already saturated with the theology of the Thirty-nine Articles and the *Westminster Confession*, it is difficult to see what more Paisley could have demanded. But by the late 1980s, the Northern Ireland State schools were depicted as 'largely secularised'. Fundamentalists require insulation from evolutionary biology, liberal non-dogmatic theology and child-centred teaching without corporal punishment. Born-again teachers are required to 'save' the children.

The second related issue is the claim that Free Presbyterian schools differed from Catholic institutions in that they were self-financing. Could this really be the case? Like Lagan College, Free Presbyterian schools would eventually qualify for government aid. Would this be rejected? Experience throughout the world indicates the unlikelihood of such an outcome. In Australia, when aid for schools became general in the 1960s, even Seventh Day Adventists, ardent for the separation of Church and State, reconciled acceptance with their consciences. Could Free Presbyterians, when aid was available, emulate Australasian Catholics who maintained their schools for a hundred years without assistance? Most assuredly not, as the difficulty of self-financing education increased exponentially with soaring inflation. Moreover, Free Presbyterians with schools open in 1983 at Ballymoney, Newtownabbey, Bangor and Kilskeery, would have no celibate teaching orders which for generations reduced the cost of Catholic schools. By the mid-1980s there were about 120 pupils in the four Free Presbyterian schools. State inspectors worried about the unnaturally good behaviour of the children. As one teacher pointed out, 'in every subject the Bible is our chief reference book.'[38]

The ambiguity of loyalist secularism and republican separatism

Both the *Orange Standard* and the Free Presbyterians unconsciously converged with Catholic educational philosophy. The questions of self-finance and political indoctrination aside, separation from a general system, which leaves the responsibility for religious formation to parents, Churches and occasional religious instructors, must be based on 'permeation' theory. Permeation, regarded as essential to continuing faith, requires a persistent religious or doctrinal atmosphere. Without 'permeation', there is little reason why secular subjects, uninfluenced by particular doctrines, should not be taught. Could permeation go further than the Free Presbyterian provision for 'an academic institution in which teachers, pupils, teaching methods and subject matter are all subservient to the word of God, the Bible? Every book, every notion of man, every philosophy, will be evaluated by the principles and ideals of the Scriptures.'[39] Free Presbyterianism, by wishing to separate its children from the schools which others accepted as based on a fair Protestant consensus, was surely admitting that it had no right to speak for other non-Catholic Churches.

The loyalist paramilitary journals emphasised integrated education more than the Paisleyites whom they criticised. Thus in the South Belfast by-election of early 1982, it was only the UDA's John McMichael who featured integrated education strongly in his election leaflets: 'opposition to ... the senseless burden of having two separate school systems'. But had these loyalists anything further to contribute to the debate beyond the nineteenth-century Bible-in-schools state education with funds cut from private establishments? As critics they were on firmer ground. It was relatively easy to maintain that the divided communities which so shocked outside observers were not the doing of Prot-stats but the results of Roman Catholic policy.[40] They could also insist with some plausibility that it was 'naive and stupid' to prate about 'reconciliation when the problem of mixed education was left untouched'.[41] Loyalist papers painted a dramatic picture of the ill effects of segregated education. With children totally polarised at the age of five, confirmation denied by authorities like Bishop Philbin to state school Catholic children, and no subsequent social mix, was it surprising that violence should result? Children grew into teenagers, always attributing horns and tails to the other side.[42] In the Irish Republic, moreover, all was not sweetness and light. Many poor Protestants there suffered financial discrimination. The Church of Ireland Bishop Gilbert Wilson was quoted on the economic pressures forcing parents to send their children to Catholic schools.[43]

In a characteristic outburst, the UDA *Ulster Loyalist* placed the division of the community squarely on the shoulders of the Catholic bishops: 'they cannot be excused for teaching hatred. Few who have read Irish history as taught in RC schools, would fail to recognise the anti-British trends. Such patriotic writings do much to develop these young men and women who make and plant the bombs and murder with impunity. There is no doubt that the bulk of IRA activists have received their sectarian beliefs through the bigoted teachings of their RC schools.'[44] In her autobiography, Bernadette Devlin McAliskey portrays in Mother Benignus a highly opinionated anti-English principal, prepared to opt out of success at netball for fear that her children would be forced to stand for God Save the Queen. Her passion for Irish culture was, however, counterproductive.[45] Similar feelings to those of Mother Benignus lay behind the refusal of Catholic schools to grant the Queen's request for a jubilee holiday in 1977. Though many schools and individuals did take the holiday, Catholic authorities were accused of rejecting the monarch as head of State and deliberately inculcating dissidence into their pupils.[46] In his comparative study, Dominic Murray found excessive identification with the Irish Republic in a Northern Ireland Catholic school, but also a common Protestant-Catholic culture of pop music and certain sports. He did not recommend integration.[47]

Criticism of the political posture of minority education had some substance, if only because the Provisionals did, on balance, support the anti-imperialist character of Northern Irish Catholic schools. Menendez, a strong American advocate of the separation of Church and State in education, was surprised that publicly funded Irish schools could reject the Queen's jubilee, the flag (once so prominent in US education) and the national anthem.[48] Menendez noticed that Catholic schools in England closed for the jubilee. The problem was not Catholic education as such, but that the Irish Catholic parents considered the establishment of the Northern Irish State in 1921 as flagrantly unjust. The bishops could not neglect this if they were to preserve their influence. As a republican told a priest, if the Church had initially accepted integrated education, Roman Catholics would now be unionists at peace.[49] Catholic clergy naturally feared loss of religion more than loss of nationalism. Could the two be safely separated? The American system of complete secularism might, despite the fears of the

Catholic hierarchy, have left the religion of the Northern Irish minority relatively untouched but, as Menendez indicated, it would have disseminated unionism. As for the preaching of hatred, the Quakers Barritt and Carter argued in 1962 that there was very little definite evidence of it in Catholic schools. Bishop Cahal Daly insisted in 1979 that 'all recent Catholic catechetical syllabi and texts have a resolutely ecumenical orientation.'[50] Most observers, including Menendez, agree that there is little religious antagonism to Protestantism amongst Northern Irish Catholics.[51] The most extreme republican journals contain none of the racial-religious jokes, cartoons and invective so prominent in loyalist periodicals. On the other hand, Catholic schools fostering the songs, ballads, dances, and sports of the nationalist tradition, despite complaints by some republicans that Northern Ireland parochial schools are pro-British, were clearly a cultural necessity. If the Catholic schools used textbooks emphasising Ireland's spiritual quality, history books in state schools tended until recently to ignore Ireland altogether. Despite modernising of the historical curriculum, Provisional analysts still complain that the new textbooks teach revisionism.[52] Ironically, the ideas capable of permeating the system most effectively may have been those of Irish patriotism rather than Roman Catholic orthodoxy.

In Northern Ireland the religious ideals of educational separatists are identical to those in North America or Australasia, but opponents lack any firm ground for ideological counter-attack. This is well illustrated by the admissions of loyalist paramilitary journals unable to avoid the pitfalls they criticised in Paisley. Integrated education sounds excellent in theory but often its implications were not examined. As the 1973 white paper pointed out, not all Protestants (some Prot-ecums probably being associated with the Prot-stats) were happy at the thought of Catholic teachers for their children, especially when these were in orders.[53] In the United States there had been numerous controversies over the issue of banning public school teaching 'in costume'. Dervla Murphy tells of the horrified flight of a Protestant boy confronted by a nun in a Northern Ireland public examination.[54] In such situations polls supporting integrated education tend to be deceptive.

Law, ostensibly the journal of the loyalist workers, saw the problem as it appeared to the majority of non-Catholics in the Republic and for many Prot-stats and Prot-ecums in Northern Irish country areas. If there were 100 Protestants in a school of 1000 only ten were likely to marry into their own community and, under

Catholic marriage regulations, the community would be rapidly eroded.[55] Even more significant was the comment of the UDA *Ulster Loyalist* when it noted that a Sinn Féin (Provisional) Cumann, after four years of silence, had joined Catholics like Tony Spencer and Fr Des Wilson in advocating integrated education. Why were Provisionals now interested? The *Ulster Loyalist* found the answer in southern complaints that the IRA was infiltrating the educational system. Wilson and Spencer were therefore advised to tell their Provisional master 'that it was a good try, but the Protestant people of Ulster are not as stupid as he thought they were.' After all, 'what Protestant Father or Mother wants their child to be taught and brainwashed by IRA scum.' As the UDA commander, Andy Tyrie, pointed out in 1981, in its early years his organisation had considered all Catholics to be Provisionals.[56] Given that most Northern Ireland Catholic teachers were nationalists, integrated education, by implying Catholic teaching for Protestant children, might boomerang. In higher education, though republicans complained that only 2 per cent of the Queen's University staff was Catholic, the UDA's *Ulster* considered that the university was the only institution permitting association across the divide. Research in 1985 indicated that only 10 per cent of staff were Catholic. By 1993 the Catholic proportion had risen to 22 per cent.[57] But in 1992 the Fair Employment Tribunal forced Queen's University to pay £40,000 compensation and the university set aside a further £400,000 for pending cases of job discrimination against Catholics. On the other side, the UFF tried to assassinate a lecturer in 1991 on the ground that Queen's was a 'republican cesspit'. *An Phoblacht* on the other hand complained that the use of 'God Save the Queen' at academic functions was an insult to nationalists, and that the authorities had revealed their bigotry by selling off the University's hurling ground.[58] Antithetical interpretation was clearly at work.

Apart from integrated education's value as a propagandist weapon, loyalists had no real alternative policy to separate schools, other than the tacit suggestion that Catholics accept the Prot-stat state school system. According to Oliver Napier, Protestants 'use opposition to segregated schools as a convenient stick to beat Catholics, and not from any commitment to the principle of integrated education'.[59] Paisley went a step further than other loyalists in repudiating the state system as insufficient, but the same underlying problem required resolution: was a compromise desired and, if so, was it possible? To many unionists the response in both cases was negative. Even given goodwill, the search for compromise was difficult. The Catholic hierarchy and the Free Presbyterians were unhelpful. There was the question of bussing from segregated estates. Mere separation of Church and State was insufficient; education had to be separated from both Church and State. Proselytism, political and religious, had to be abandoned on both sides. Prot-stat complaints against the Roman Catholic Church were counter-productive as they increased group cohesion amongst Catholics. Could an initiative be expected from the republicans?

Republicans revive Davis: the Officials

As demonstrated above, the Irish republicans of the 1970s inherited an ambivalent tradition of educational philosophy. Despite the clarity of Thomas Davis's exposition of the dangers of classroom division, evasion of the issue had been the characteristic response. Would the Ulster Troubles repeat the Irish Revolution's evasion in view of the widespread publicity accorded to the issue? The answer seems to be no, not completely. However, if Davis is taken as a yardstick, there was still a revealing reluctance to quote his views on the problem. Not that Davis's comments on education were ignored. His truism, possibly derived from Voltaire, 'educate that you may be free', was frequently cited by Provisionals,[60] as was his emphasis on the need to maintain Gaelic culture. But the details of that education were left in a convenient Celtic twilight. Strangely enough, this failure to use Davis was equally characteristic of the Officials, who laid greater emphasis on the need for immediate integration than their Provisional rivals. The latter at least once acknowledged Davis's position, but only to refute Garret FitzGerald whom they accused of wrongfully invoking the names of Davis and Tone in his 1981 'crusade' for *de jure* recognition of the partition of Ireland. How dare he quote the integrationist Davis when refusing to allow Catholic children to travel by bus to a Protestant school in Wicklow?[61] As in loyalist rhetoric, however, this was a debating point rather than an indication of personal priorities. One reason for the neglect of Davis's educational integration was the indirect absorption of his ideas via Pearse's pamphlets rather than from his own words. Pearse had many radical educational ideas, but appears to have tactfully ignored integrated education.

Though as reluctant as the Provisionals to quote Davis, the Officials, from the split in late 1969, reiterated the need for common schooling. In 1973 Menendez, who had no love of Irish republicanism, was constrained to applaud the Officials for 'the best position of any party on education', thanks to their creditable endorsement of 'comprehensive integrated education and the secularisation of the educational system in Ulster'.[62] The Officials, in other words, were moving along North American lines of Church-State separation, which they praised.[63] Moreover, they were also concerned with the issue in the Irish Republic, joining the debate over community schools which dragged on for most of the 1970s. The *United Irishman* showed that the conversion of technical non-denominational schools to the new community institutions was unfair to Protestants as Catholic religious control was accepted by the government. Only lay, integrated education could prevent anti-Protestant bias.[64] The Officials also attacked the clerical managerial system of primaries in the south, which, they claimed, deprived parents of power over the education of their children. Such arguments undermined the insistence in the north that the separate systems were necessary to ensure parental rights. The Officials were not only concerned with Protestant rights but, like other socialists, feared that children moulded in a clerical environment would 'have little chance to develop a constructive political consciousness and instead of directing their hostility and frustration to the capitalist society which keeps them down, direct hostility to their own peer group and society in general'.[65] Separate education, they pointed out on another occasion, 'is by definition divisive and totally vicious'.[66] There was little use, the *United Irishman* argued in 1975, in the Roman Catholic and Church of Ireland bishops of Derry jointly condemning sectarian killings without recognising that their Churches' control of education had helped to perpetuate sectarianism.

The Officials rejected the Provisional counter-argument that conservatives, by attributing the division in Northern Ireland to separate education, denied the divisiveness of the British presence. 'The Republican Clubs have never claimed that separate educational institutions were the cause of sectarianism; rather they have pointed out that the schools are a result of the sectarian nature of the two States.'[67] Nevertheless, educational integration does mark an essential distinction between Provisional and Official policy in the 1970s. The former's insistence on British withdrawal as a prerequisite for national unity was opposed by the latter's desire for common education to achieve working-class solidarity before independence.

Were the Officials any more realistic about the prospects of developing common schools than their loyalist counterparts, with whom they sometimes co-operated? Certainly, Workers' Party or Republican Club candidates at elections, both local and parliamentary, urged the need for integration.[68] The issue was kept alive in comments on other events and at the political party's Ard Fheis.[69] A conference at Corrymeela on Ulster independence in 1976 was criticised, *inter alia*, because it resolved in favour of the right to private education.[70] Similarly, the Peace People were rebuked for their 'sentimental, public handholding exercises' which did nothing to improve housing, remove paramilitaries, or establish non-sectarian education.[71] In 1978 the *United Irishman* claimed that the Poleglass estate had achieved a victory over bigotry in that it was sufficiently close to loyalists to provide a unique opportunity for 'integrated comprehensive community schools under secular control'.[72] This suggestion indicates that the Officials and their Republican Clubs were a long way from an answer to those practical problems raised by loyalists when discussing common education. The difficulties were sufficient to daunt the American Menendez and Prot-ecums like Eric Gallagher and Stanley Worrall. Antithetical understanding was again present: if Prot-stats understood 'integration' to mean 'forcing Roman Catholic children to attend 'Protestant' schools',[73] the Republican Clubs undoubtedly wanted to force Prot-stat and Prot-ecum children into schools where they would learn socialism. People's Democracy (PD), a student-based group in the early Troubles and closer on education to the Officials than the Provisionals, insisted that 'the struggle against Capitalism requires a battle for integrated, comprehensive schools throughout Ireland. To achieve that requires tackling the vested interests who wish to maintain the present *status quo*'.[74] But, except when conversion is achieved by stealth or under a totalitarian regime, parents will accept only education in conformity with their own pre-existing ideals. The argument is thus circular, unless there are parents, equally fearful of Catholic or unionist authorities, who would prefer fair integration if not intimidated. We shall return to this question in considering the teacher-training debate of 1981-2.

Provisionals give two cheers for separatism

The Provisionals, who unlike the Officials were in constant strife with the Roman Catholic bishops, did understand the logic of integration. Their attacks on the bishops often used education as a weapon. They suggested, for example, that under the Stormont regime the Catholic hierarchy had been preoccupied with the control of schools and hospitals. Nothing had been done on housing or employment. Bishop Philbin, amongst his other offences, was denounced with the same heat—'a most despicable thing'—as in loyalist publications for his refusal to confirm state school children.[75] Nor were the Provisionals always pleased with Northern Irish Catholic schools and colleges. On internment in August 1971, the *Republican News* welcomed the protests of the lecturers at the two Catholic training colleges in Belfast, St Mary's and St Joseph's, but regretted that many other Catholic teachers were more concerned with their salaries. St Malachy's College refused to allow its staff to protest. St Mary's Grammar School rejected a child whose father was on the run; the staff of St Patrick's allegedly considered it a joke that the caretaker had been arrested. There was some justification for the criticism that 'with the present system of segregated education, the Catholic community provides a nice steady and safe position for a large number of teachers'.[76] A writer in the *Belfast Bulletin*, No. 8, complained that the teacher trainees in the Catholic colleges were 'blackmailed into acceptance' of denominationalism.[77] The *Republican News* complained that the hierarchy's 'rigid control of education has been responsible for the elimination of the Irish language and Irish history from the primary schools and their inferior status in secondary schools'. Instead, pupils were expected to believe 'a moronic repetition of British propaganda dressed up as moral teaching'.[78] Fr Des Wilson, moreover, argued in a thesis that the Roman Catholic Church did accept the dominant English, middle-class, academic culture, with little evidence of Irish content.[79]

However justified this criticism, the Provisionals were not completely consistent in maintaining it. In fact, their main educational argument insisted that, despite the manifest failings of the hierarchy, the Catholic system of separate education was the main buttress against imperialist indoctrination. Thus, while the *Republican News* lamented the unpatriotic attitude of many Catholic schools to internment, its stable-mate, *An Phoblacht*, suggested that the state education 'Murder Machine', denounced by Padraic Pearse early in the century, still existed. In the north 'segregated education, while serving to keep alive the national tradition in one section of that community, and preventing the complete imperial indoctrination of the whole population, nevertheless also serves to prolong the interweaving of religion with politics'.[80] This was a relatively realistic and frank appraisal of the situation, developed later in the Chilver debate of 1981-2.

For practical purposes it was difficult to maintain such a balance, especially in the face of loyalist criticism. Like their opponents, the Provisionals found it easier to attack the other side than to establish their own priorities. During the debate on the McIvor scheme of shared education, *An Phoblacht* denied that segregated education created conflict.[81] Earlier, the *Republican News* had published a letter from an American correspondent insisting that parochial schools in the United States were not divisive, and that the same system in Northern Ireland had not 'created bigotry or a segregated society. The British Government has created those conditions.' But another American correspondent some months later argued the opposite view that absolute secularity was as necessary in Ireland as in America where the system 'has been proven to eliminate religious bigotry' by educating children together and leaving religion to after-school agencies.[82] Cardinal Conway was seen as colluding with the British government.[83]

Loyalist attacks were easily parried. In 1975 the *Republican News* complained that the current onslaught on Catholic education demonstrated that the enemies of Irish freedom found even the limited independence from the state of Catholic schools unacceptable.[84] In 1980 the Provisionals' spokesperson on education, Una O'Neill, repudiated 'those liberal minds who have advocated integration of schools as a means to solve the troubles', as 'dangerously close in spirit to those who have built the H-blocks and encouraged loyalist murder-gangs into action'.[85]

Eire Nua and education

Good debating points must, however, be supported by positive policies. In 1971 the Provisionals published the Eire Nua proposals to establish their credibility as constructive thinkers. One of the chief influences on the draft was the Catholic author, Desmond Fennell.

While segregated education was seen as an antidote to imperialistic indoctrination, the linking of politics and religion was dangerous. As a result of this difficulty, a very limited form of integration was spelled out:

> Sinn Féin educational policy will aim to ensure the development of all the moral, intellectual and physical powers of our children so that they will become God-fearing and responsible citizens of a free and independent nation. The rights of the family as the primary and natural educator of the child and the spiritual interests of the various religious

denominations shall be acknowledged within the framework of an educational system whose philosophy shall be to unify the people with one national consciousness.

In rural areas, it was suggested, 'acceptance of inter-denominational schools' should present no problem in view of the goodwill between Protestants and Catholics in many Irish parishes.[86] In secondary schools 'the existing largely denominational structure will be encouraged to become inter-denominational in areas where minority facilities are absent'. Schools would 'range from fully secular through inter-denominational to fully denominational according to the historical background of the school'.[87] In the new Ireland it would be necessary 'to acknowledge the various religious denominations and to unite the [people] into one nation'. The only uniformity would be in the transmission of the national heritage and language.[88]

What did this programme mean? *An Phoblacht* in 1974 insisted that the Eire Nua policy was to integrate education after British withdrawal and the establishment of the nine-county subordinate Ulster government in a free Ireland. This, however, seems to exaggerate the effects of their policy, which came a great deal closer to the traditional Catholic position than to the integrationist viewpoint of Thomas Davis. Davis had, however, praised the nationalist teaching of the Christian Brothers. The Provisional education proposals, like those of the Irish revolutionary republicans of 1919-21, maintained the educational *status quo* to avoid unnecessary antagonism of the Roman Catholic hierarchy. The current system in the Irish Republic already provided a common Irish heritage and language instruction for Protestants and Catholics in separate schools. Some interdenominational institutions were painfully developing. In this respect the Officials were in theory far more advanced than their rivals. At the Provisional Sinn Féin Ard Fheis of 1975, a motion for a non-denominational system under local control was proposed, but appears to have been buried under other more dramatic issues.[89] By 1979 a booklet, *Eire Nua is Local Democracy*, advocated the 'integration' of schools at secondary level without apparently referring to religion. Eire Nua was dropped in the 1980s when Northern leaders like Gerry Adams took over from the more conservative Dublin-based Provisional establishment, but, as will be demonstrated later, there was no marked change in educational policy.

On this issue, as in other areas, the Irish Republican Socialist Party (IRSP), an apparently radical breakaway from the Officials, possessing its own aggressive Irish National Liberation Army (INLA), advanced little on PIRA policy, arguing for 'a completely secular education system with the active participation of teachers, parents, and students in the running of the schools'—but only in the context of a 32-county Republic. However, it was suggested in the *Starry Plough* that 'secularisation without integration would be a step in the right direction'.[90] Insofar as it alienated the Catholic hierarchy, the policy was unpractical.

The Chilver provocation—Catholic Church reaction

If the hunger strikes of 1981 intensified the conflict between the Provisionals and the Catholic Church, the long controversy over the *Chilver Report* plans for rationalising teacher education was the most pressing issue facing the Northern Ireland hierarchy in the educational debate of the 1970s and early 1980s. The separate training colleges (St Joseph's and St Mary's) were a crucial test case. In other countries separate education continued unscathed under a common system of teacher training. Unified teacher education sometimes encouraged a more tolerant approach in teachers of both systems. The *Loyalist News* in 1976 suggested that educational integration could begin with training colleges.

In February 1979 the British Labour government established the Chilver Committee on higher education. *Inter alia*, it investigated a sharp drop in vacancies for teachers. The UDA *Ulster* strongly supported the idea of amalgamating the Catholic colleges with Stranmillis, catering for Protestants. It regretted only that this should be brought about for financial reasons.[91] The committee duly published an interim report on 23 June 1980, suggesting the compromise siting of an amalgamated Catholic College as a separate unit on the Stranmillis location.[92] The Catholic hierarchy responded coolly, but an article in *Fortnight* predicted that the government would be able to appeal to Catholic parents over the heads of the Catholic bishops.[93] It no doubt assumed that the public opinion polls demonstrating Catholic support for integrated education would prove their efficiency. For a time an educational 'phony war' existed. There was occasional criticism of the Chilver Committee; in early 1981 a Roman Catholic pamphlet was published claiming that as 53 per cent of the Northern Ireland school population was being educated in their schools, Catholic facilities should be increased rather than restricted.[94] The hunger strikes of 1981 naturally attracted most of the attention of the nationalist community. However, the issues were linked by Frs Faul and Murray who praised two dead hunger strikers for 'a perfect fulfilment of the Catholic education received in Catholic schools'. In early November, about a month after their end, the educational campaign warmed up. The local minister for education, Nicholas Scott, appeared resolute in his replies to churchmen. Before Christmas, Bishop Philbin, relatively uninvolved in the hunger strike controversy, came out strongly against the Chilver proposals. In his final Christmas Day message the controversial bishop of Down and Connor condemned the unprecedented invasion of Catholic rights. The special position of Catholic education was now being ignored.[95] There was talk of applying to the European Court of Human Rights.

Though the incongruity of such a message in a period of peace and goodwill evoked some comment, the campaign reached its climax when 17 January 1982 was declared 'Education Sunday'. Circulars were distributed inside and outside churches and schools, while clergy addressed their congregations on the subject and a pastoral from the bishops was read. A petition containing 300,000 signatures was presented to the minister, attacking the amalgamation of the Catholic colleges, their resiting at Stranmillis, and the reduction of the quota in Catholic teacher training to 25 per cent, when, it was claimed, the Catholic school population was nearly twice as great.[96] The uncommitted population and the government were visibly shocked at so strong a reaction; the latter soon offered concessions.

In wider perspective, the whole issue was basically separable from Ireland. The arguments, apart from population statistics, were identical to those used in similar battles in New York, Sydney, Toronto, Cape Town and Wellington, New Zealand, not to mention the European continent and the Third World. Pride of place went to the 'permeation' or 'ethos' contention which demonstrated a desire not to avoid Prot-stat proselytism but to secure fundamental religious formation. As Fr P. Delargy put it, Catholic education was not just a matter of religious education classes: 'In fact, many Catholic students will find that subjects other than Religious Education are influential in making them think deeply about God'.[97] Bishop Philbin's secretary, Fr Thomas Toner, whom Bobby Sands had considered a potential opponent of the hunger strike,[98] pointed out that 'the Catholic view of life is something that is determined by the Catholic bishops and not by Mr Scott or Sir Henry Chilver'.[99] There were hints of the traditional 'double taxation' argument.[100]

Emotive parallels discovered an all-out attack on the Catholic school system. An *Irish News* editorial quoted the persecution of Henry VIII, the penal laws, and the suppression of religion in the Soviet Union.[101] Owen Carron, election agent to hunger striker Bobby Sands, MP, and the latter's parliamentary replacement after his death, also cited the penal laws. Carron brought the education issue up to date by insisting that it was an attack on civil rights comparable to the juryless Northern Ireland Diplock Courts and internment.[102] Indeed, Fr Brian Brady, once a St Joseph's lecturer, praised for his opposition to internment, extended the argument from 'ethos' to culture and heritage, just as the Provisionals themselves had done.[103]

The Provisionals and Chilver: a frank restatement

One reason for the success of the Catholic petition seems to have been the very polarisation created by the hunger strike. If so, it was bitterly ironical in view of the strife between the ecclesiastics and the Provisional and INLA resisters. The authorised reaction of Provisional Sinn Féin differed from that of Carron. Provisionals rejected Chilver, but not on religious grounds: 'In the North, the separate identity of the Catholic Schools and their policy of teaching Irish history and language have contributed towards keeping alive the flame of Nationalism.' In the future, however, republicans looked 'forward to the day when the Irish educational system is totally divorced from the control of any of the various religious denominations'.[104] This bald announcement was partly offset by an editorial in the *Andersonstown News*, which generally spoke for the Provisionals. It condemned the 'effrontery' of the hierarchy, which had for years connived at British cultural assimilation, now requiring the Catholics to man the barricades to 'defend their vested interest in the British school system'. Despite Brady, it complained that 'the orchestrators of the present anti-Chilver campaign have not been able to even mention the cultural aspect of education here, which is in our view, the only legitimate reason for having a separate system'. The *Andersonstown News* did not object to separate systems, 'not only two but maybe three or four', but wanted to take the opportunity to wrest control from the Anglicising Catholic Church.[105] The hierarchy's difficulty was evidently the republican's opportunity. Fr Des Wilson, a regular columnist for the *Andersonstown News*, speaking on the BBC's 'Good Morning Ulster',[106] condemned the hypocrisy of beginning what was to be 'Church Unity Week' with the highly divisive

'Education Sunday'. He lamented that Catholic educational attitudes had not changed in years. Almost alone amongst participators in the debate, Fr Wilson recognised that sharing was needed, not only between Protestants and Catholics, but also with Jews, Humanists and others. Radio talk-back programmes and some newspaper correspondence indicated that a number of Catholics resented the high-pressure tactics and emotional rhetoric of their clergy. Fr Anthony Ross of Edinburgh University, like Wilson, believed the segregated system counter-productive, citing surveys in proof. The ethos idea no longer worked in practice; mixed education which provided a challenge was more effective in the formation of Catholics.[107] Such opposition was ineffectual.

The Provisional case needed further clarification. Clerics like Frs Toner and Faul, believed to have worked against the hunger strike, were constantly berated. Faul's call to parents to give information to the authorities on their republican children was linked with the educational selfishness of the Catholic Church. But Una O'Neill provided a reasoned analysis of the education dilemma in an outspoken *An Phoblacht* article.[108] Ms O'Neill speculated that the hierarchy's 'unprecedented campaign' had succeeded by confusing a number of different issues: educational, religious, economic, and political. The problem was more complex than 'the pseudo-liberal waffle' of Minister Scott or the 'emotional sloganising' of the bishops. The Chilver committee had been established, with four Catholics out of eleven members, on the 'integrationist' view of the Troubles. O'Neill accepted the Catholic position that the committee was working towards a closure of the separate education system. She cited Cardinal O'Fiaich's contention that the Irish, rather than the Catholic character of teacher training, would suffer from amalgamation. Stranmillis, she claimed, was in the heart of Paisley-land and the college had its Orange Lodge and DUP branch. There had been sectarian assassinations of nationalists in the area.

Though she endorsed part of Cardinal O'Fiaich's argument, Una O'Neill was much harder on Bishop Philbin and Fr Brian Brady. The bishop's condemnation of the hunger strikers as a threat to Church authority was linked to his battle for Church authority in education. His understanding of 'Catholic' differed from the average nationalist concerned about economic deprivation, political emasculation, sectarian assassination, and harassment by security forces. O'Neill emphasised the indoctrination and fear for their jobs amongst Catholic college students. *The Belfast Bulletin*, No. 8, agreed. As for Fr Brady's *Catholic Education in Northern*

Ireland—the Chilver Challenge, the critic agreed that integrated education could not change the political fact of unionist domination, but this she felt was only a minor prop to the religious argument in an ambiguous statement. Like Fr Ross of Edinburgh and Fr Desmond Wilson, O'Neill rejected the 'ethos', or permeation, argument, denying that there was much effective Christianity in the system. In short, she summed up the Provisional position that 'the Chilver proposals must be resisted tooth and nail by republicans', not out of love of clerics like Fr Toner, the 'infamous Long Kesh chaplain', but because of the need for higher education and jobs in the Catholic area, and the fact that, despite the bishops, Catholic colleges refrained from teaching unionism and provided opportunities for Gaelic sport and dancing.

This article is worth quoting in detail as it contains one of the frankest expositions of the issue in the 1970s and 1980s. On the surface Una O'Neill's argument is cogently presented. Probing underneath, additional questions are raised. Is Stranmillis closer to the heart of Paisleyland than Queen's University itself? Nicholas Scott later offered an alternative site in the university region.[109] More important was the responsibility, occasionally recognised by the Provisionals, towards members of the unionist tradition deprived of their Irish cultural heritage.[110] If a Prot-ecum student wished to attend a céilí (dance), it would be much more difficult to reach West Belfast. The issue reverts to the difference between the Provisional belief that the British must initially be driven out by force, and the Official desire to unite the working classes first. The latter group tried to evade the undoubted strength of the argument for retaining higher education in West Belfast by suggesting that, while the proposed rationalisation presented no threat to the Catholic population, the West Belfast college sites should be kept open for the community, providing educational, social, recreational, and cultural resources.[111] This was a reasonable suggestion on paper, but without a higher educational role it is doubtful if the vigour of the institutions could be maintained. The SDLP had few constructive suggestions to add, apart from amalgamation of St Mary's and St Joseph's, without transfer to Stranmillis.[112] The educationally dissident SDLP representative, Rory McShane, like Thomas Davis in 1845, argued that transfer of the colleges could be an excellent experiment and that Catholic safeguards could be found. He resented the fact that there had been no real debate and insisted that there was evidence of many Catholics in favour of Chilver.[113]

Alliance, the colleges and general integration

On the moderate unionist side Alliance had long supported united teacher education in its gradualist approach to integrated education. Like the Provisionals, it rejected denominational education as the cause of the Ulster Troubles, but nevertheless considered it 'an obstacle to reconciliation'. Oliver Napier, himself a Catholic, accepted education permeated by religion as an ideal, but unsuitable for Northern Ireland: 'what may be desirable in Surrey may be a disaster in Fermanagh.' Why not, he asked in 1973, 'start by integrating Teachers' Colleges?' This suggestion was passed by the Alliance conference in 1975. Writing for *Alliance*, the Queen's University historian W.L. Warren was sceptical of the party's integration by consent, believing that eventually arms would have to be twisted. 'It cannot be emphasised too often that Protestants need integrated schooling as much as Catholics.' Like Napier, Warren was not opposed to denominational education but considered it a luxury which only an integrated society could afford. His experience of Catholic education products at Queen's University destroyed any faith in the permeation theory which 'left no discernible traces whatever'. Though Alliance policy had its weaknesses, its members endeavoured to break from traditional clichés.[114]

Loyalist Chilver confusion

In the Chilver debate the more conservative unionists failed to present a satisfactory alternative to nationalist confusion. Many spokespersons for the different groups used the opportunity to inveigh against Catholic separation. Dr Paisley, for example, declared that if the government backed down over the training colleges it was bowing 'to republican and Roman Catholic pressure' and discriminating against 'non-sectarian integrated education'.[115] Yet once again the nature of this so-called 'non-sectarian' education appeared in some doubt. The Rev. Bertie Park, a former Presbyterian moderator, explained how the Protestant Churches had refused to accept the initial removal of 'simple Bible reading' in the 1920s and gained representation on the board of the originally secular Stranmillis College.[116] Stranmillis itself rejected amalgamation with the secular Queen's University. The Church of Ireland primate, Archbishop John Armstrong, expressed his own concern that 'the traditional identity, ethos and moral and spiritual values' of Stranmillis be retained.[117] Thus the Church of Ireland argument was substantially that of the Roman Catholic, and made it more difficult for the Official Unionists to refute the 'ethos' argument by citing vandals and members of illegal organisations produced by the Catholic schools.[118] The DUP claimed to favour 'a system of non-sectarian integrated education and this includes support for the amalgamation of the colleges on the Stranmillis site'.[119] But the opinion of many of its Prot-stat members seems to have been summed up in the fears of Mr Williamson, a talk-back respondent to a radio debate on the subject.[120] His main object was to avoid Antichrist. He feared that undenominational schools might require association with the 'unclean thing'. In 1967 Paisley himself had recommended Bob Jones's university (where blacks, once totally excluded, can now enter on the undertaking not to date whites)[121] to 'escape the pollutions and poisons' of normal university life. Moreover, if Paisley was really determined to abolish Catholic training colleges, was it consistent for him to include a photograph of one in his collaborative book for American consumption as evidence against anti-Catholic discrimination?[122]

If the Chilver furore saw Catholic authorities in passionate defence of their system, the Western Education and Library Board imbroglio of 1985 placed loyalists in an equally beleagured position. Nationalist control of the Board after the May local elections, and the presence of three Sinn Féin representatives stimulated a predictable unionist panic. Though Free Presbyterian luminaries led the protest, the UDA's *Ulster* complained that the Protestant Churches were 'shilly shallying' as usual. Ironically recycling a perennial Catholic justification for separate schools, 'No Surrender' roared, 'All parents have the right to have the administration of their children's education in the hands of those they can trust.' Loyalist integrated education was intended clearly to place Catholics in schools administered by Protestants, not *vice versa*. As the moderate *Belfast Telegraph* pointed out, there was no evidence of discrimination by the new authority.[123]

Recent developments: ambiguity abounding

The Chilver controversy petered out in an anodyne report in 1982, with the Western Board affair, soon absorbed in unionist opposition to the Anglo-Irish Agreement of November 1985, epitomising the basic issues of the integrated education debate. Confusion existed on both the nationalist and unionist sides. The issue lay between Church leaders and dissident followers, rather than between Catholics and Protestants, a case of unconscious convergence. The 'ethos' argument was as popular with Free Presbyterians, and even the Church of Ireland primate, as with Catholic bishops. Certain recalcitrant educators, however, rejected it as divisive, unpractical and unnecessary.

As yet there was little hope of a positive solution, except from the experimental Lagan College, soon reinforced by other institutions.[124] In 1988, however, the government indicated a new concern to promote integrated education. The new common curriculum of 1989 included Education for Mutual Understanding (EMU) and Cultural Heritage among its compulsory programmes.[125] By 1990, when the Northern Ireland Education Minister Brian Mawhinney introduced a reform package, which included a boost to integrated education, Provisionals, Catholic bishops and loyalists were opposed. The bishops made an ultimately unsuccessful appeal to the High Court against alleged discrimination against the Catholic system which received 15 per cent less capital grants[126] than the integrated sector; Councillor Sammy Wilson, a former DUP Lord Mayor of Belfast, likewise complained that support for integrated education discriminated against the state system. Wilson feared that Protestants might be introduced to the Gaelic language and Catholic services. Joe Coggle, an independent unionist on the Belfast Education and Library Board, which refused co-operation with the Hazelwood Integrated School, was more forthright. He would not help 'Englishman Mawhinney' (in fact an Ulsterman) in his 'dirty work' against the two existing educational systems.[127] Yet some unionists denied their convergence with the Roman Catholic Church and condemned it for segregation while themselves rejecting integration. Thus in 1990 Councillor Rhonda Paisley attacked Cardinal Daly for telling Catholic parents that they were wrong to send their children to integrated schools. Daly, she said, denied freedom of choice to Catholics while shedding crocodile tears over community divisions. Ms Paisley rejected integration as a panacea: 'Ulster Protestants are not going to melt because integrated education is the "in thing" nor are they going to swallow Cahal Daly's advice—they spew him and his perversions out of their mouths.'[128]

The Provisionals emphasised Mawhinney's withdrawal of grants for the Irish language organisation, Glor na Gael, likely to threaten seven Irish nursery schools, providing for 140 children.[129] Educational convergence had now become conscious, rather than unconscious, as the two apparently antagonistic systems made common cause against a more threatening rival. The academic,

Frank Wright, also exhibited misgivings about the new emphasis on integration which had fallen foul of the Catholic hierarchy. He considered parental cultural choice more important than State promotion of integration which might be destroyed by counterproductive government zeal.[130] In another study, Una Agnew and her colleagues, however, believe that on balance integrated schools have forced changes in other institutions and in Northern Ireland 'have exercised an influence out of all proportion to their current strength.' Colin Irwin's study of Lagan College graduates revealed extremely positive advantages, such as a 44 per cent friendship ratio across the sectarian divide. Cardinal Daly, however, remained unconvinced.[131]

Thomas Davis might have discovered many similarities with the issues of 1845 in the 1982 and 1990 Northern Ireland disputes. However, instead of having the support of a number of Catholic bishops, it was left to clerics like Frs Des Wilson, Anthony Ross and, in his own way, the dissident Fr Buckley to argue that segregation was otiose. Davis, respecting the Christian Brothers for their patriotic teaching, would have had some sympathy with the Provisional arguments. It seems, however, that the Young Irelander's strong insistence on unity before independence would have brought him closer to the Workers' Party/Republican Clubs (Officials) in their desire for teacher training at Stranmillis. As a Prot-ecum himself, Davis was aware of the need to convert his own community to nationalism. The relations between the Provisionals and the Catholic bishops were extremely instructive. The Provisional justification of their stand was far more forthright and convincing than similar arguments during the Irish Revolution of 1919-21. Yet despite this increased sophistication, there remained a residual suspicion that the movement which could pillory the Roman Catholic bishops as British stooges and traitors to their people shrank from the ultimate step of challenging the bedrock of educational control. No one mentioned that the old Irish bardic schools, which continued into the seventeenth century, provided secular Gaelic instruction.[132] As in the Irish Revolution the need to justify violence left little energy for the potentially more treacherous educational debate.

Notes

1. *Alliance*, (A), Belfast, February 1973, for example.
2. See Davis, R. (1974), *Irish Issues in New Zealand Politics*, Dunedin: Otago University Press), 76 and 89 for New Zealand, and Davis, R.

(1980), *State Aid and Tasmanian Politics, 1868-1920*, Hobart: University of Tasmania, for Australia.

3.   See Davis, R. (1981), 'Catholic Education and Irish Nationalism: O'Connell to Community Schools', for a summary of these issues.

4.   Whyte, J.H. (1981), *Catholics in Western Democracies: a Study in Political Behaviour*, Dublin: Gill and Macmillan, 37. McKeague's *Loyalist News* (LN), 12 April 1975, published a detailed list of the canons on education from the *Codex Iuris Canonici*. See also Bouscaren, T.N. and Ellis, A.C. (1961), *Canon Law: a Test and Commentary*, Milwaukee: Bruce, 792-8.

5.   PT, 29 March 1975. He was attacked just as savagely by the Sinn Féin *Nation* [April] 1974 for a 'despicable ' action in refusing to confirm a boy educated at a state school.

6.   Anthony Spencer, a subsequent founder of Lagan. Napier, A, March 1973.

7.   PT, 11 November 1967.

8.   Archbishop Sir Guilford Young of Hobart, Tasmania. *Standard*, Hobart, 6 July 1962. He was, however, later prepared to accept a common religious education syllabus worked out in collaboration with the main Protestant churches.

9.   See Daly, Cahal, *Peace the Work of Justice*, 24-29. He cited studies by John Darby, John Salters and James Russell.

10. PT, 4 February 1967; LN, 10 April 1976.

11. From *Nation* leader 'Academical Education', 17 May 1845.

12. See Davis, R. (1987), *The Young Ireland Movement*, Dublin: Gill and Macmillan, 171-184.

13. Davis, 'Catholic Education and Irish Nationalism ' for summary.

14. Paisley, I., Robinson, P. and Taylor, J. (1982), *Ulster: The Facts*, Belfast: Crown, 67.

15. PT, 11 November 1967 and 6 January 1968 - nests of rebels.

16. Menendez, A.J. (1973), *The Bitter Harvest: Church and State in Northern Ireland*, Washington: R.B.Luce, 1973, 75-7.

17. See Davis, 'Catholic Education and Irish Nationalism '; U, September 1985.

18. Gallagher and Worrall, *Christians in Ulster*, 166-8.

19. Bishop E. Daly - Alf McCready interview, Radio Ulster, 21 February 1982.

20. Menendez, *The Bitter Harvest*, 86. Darby, J. (1976), *Conflict in Northern Ireland. The Development of a Polarised Community*, Dublin: Gill and Macmillan, 129. *The Ulster Debate: Report of a Study Group of the Institute for the Study of Conflict* (1972), London: Bodley Head, 131 (2 June 1971, Conway). See also Callaghan, *A House Divided: The Dilemma of Northern Ireland*, 79. Conway was prepared for 6th-form interaction.

21. See *Fortnight*, May-June, 1982, 15. (14 March 1982).

22. Davies, Janet (1982), 'Aspects of Community Interaction ', NUU Seminar, 8 January 1982.

23. Menendez, *The Bitter Harvest*, 86-88; Gallagher and Worrall, *Christians in Ulster*, 166.

24. *Community Forum*, 3, 3, 1973.
25. Menendez, 88.
26. O'Neill, *The Autobiography of Terence O'Neill*, 59, for controversial visit to Catholic School.
27. McAllister, Ian (1977), *The Social Democratic and Labour Party*, 135. PT, 11 May 1974.
28. Gallagher and Worrall, 162-4, and interview with A.E.W. Spencer.
29. PT, 27 July 1968.
30. PT, 20 December 1970. Warren, W.L., 'Other Thoughts on Integrated Education ', A, October 1973. For Tara see its undated *Ireland Forever*, Belfast.
31. PT, 9 May 1970.
32. U, December 1978.
33. OS, October 1978.
34. PT, December 1978.
35. Dewar, M.W., Brown, John and Long, S.E. (1967), *Orangeism, a new Appreciation*, Dromara: Slieve Croob Press, 183-4. Also quoted in Murphy, D. (1978), *A Place Apart*, Harmondsworth: Penguin, 115.
36. PT, 30 November 1974.
37. PT, 20 November 1973.
38. Bruce, Steve (1986), *God Save Ulster: The Religion and Politics of Paisleyism*, Oxford: Clarendon, 171-178; Moloney, Ed and Pollak, Andy (1986), *Paisley*, 172-8.
39. Spokesperson for Free Presbyterian Education Board, quoted in *Fortnight*, November 1983.
40. *Law*, (1,18) 1972.
41. *Ulster Loyalist* (UL), 2 March 1975; *Law*, (1,27) 1972.
42. *Combat* (C), May 1974; UL, 2 March 1975 and U, September 1981 (Quote).
43. C, (4,35) 1980 and U, December 1981.
44. UL, 2 March 1975.
45. Devlin, Bernadette (1969), *The Price of My Soul*, 62. It 'did drive lots of people away from it who couldn't take Irish culture for breakfast, dinner, and tea.'
46. *UDA News* (UDAN), (1,34) 1972.
47. Murray, Dominic (1985), *Worlds Apart: Segregated Schools in Northern Ireland*, Belfast: Appletree, 66 and 74.
48. Medendez, *The Bitter Harvest*, 72.
49. RN, 15 September 1972.
50. Carter, C. and Barritt, D. (1962), *The Northern Ireland Problem*, London: OUP, 92; Daly, *Peace the Work of Justice*, 22.
51. Menendez, 62.
52. Darby, John (1974), 'Miscellany: History in the Schools', *Community Forum*, 2, 1974, 37-42. AP, 8 September 1988 and 20 August 1992.
53. Menendez, 90.
54. Murphy, *A Place Apart*, 114.
55. *Law*, 4 February 1972.
56. UL, 16 December 1974. For Tyrie interview with *Washington Star*, AP, 6 June 1981.

57. *Fortnight*, March 1993.
58. RN, 10 August 1974; U, September 1981; For Queen's, Rupert Emerson, *Fortnight*, October 1985, July/August 1992 (*Irish News*, 4 June 1992), October 1991. AP, 18 February 1993, discussing leaked QUB report by David Gass and Ewart Bell on anti-Catholic and sexist bias, attacked QUB's 'appalling record of discrimination.' See AP, 24 September 1992, for anthem and hurling ground.
59. UL, 2 March 1975 suggests that hierarchy was responsible for anti-Catholic hatred. For Napier, A, March 1973.
60. RN, 5 March 1977; AP, March 1970, 29 June 1977, 18 November 1978, (Voltaire), 11 April 1981, 29 August 1981.
61. AP, 3 October 1981.
62. Menendez, *The Bitter Harvest*, 23.
63. UI, December 1974.
64. UI, December 1970.
65. UI, December 1972.
66. UI, August 1976.
67. UI, December 1975.
68. UI, May 1973, November 1973 and April 1979.
69. UI, February 1977 and February 1976.
70. UI, December 1976.
71. UI, January 1977.
72. UI, December 1978.
73. Gallagher and Worrall, 163, 171-2 and Menendez, 89.
74. *Unfree Citizen* (UC), 4 June 1973.
75. RN, 11 May 1974 and 25 September 1971 (housing etc.). *Nation*, April 1974. For a loyalist attack on Philbin's excommunication, see U, December 1981.
76. RN, 20 November 1971.
77. Belfast Workers Research Unit, *The Churches in Northern Ireland*, 11.
78. RN, 26 March 1972.
79. For Des Wilson's thesis, see *The Churches in Northern Ireland*, 8.
80. AP, November 1971. Sinn Féin (1971), *Eire Nua: The Social and Economic Policy of Sinn Féin*, Dublin, January 1971, 44.
81. AP, 17 May 1974.
82. RN, 20 October 1972.
83. RN, 14 April 1973.
84. RN, 7 June 1975.
85. AP, 10 May 1980.
86. RN, 18 June 1972. *Eire Nua*, 45.
87. RN, 30 June 1972.
88. RN, 20 April 1974.
89. AP, 24 October 1975.
90. AP, 26 May 1979. *Starry Plough* (SP), July 1975.
91. LN, 3 April 1976 and U, March 1979.
92. *The Chilver Interim Report* was published in June 1980.
93. *Fortnight*, July-August, 1980, 5.
94. An updated version was published as Brady, Brian (1982), *The Chilver Challenge: Catholic Education on Northern Ireland*, Belfast. See Law

(2,52) 1973 for Campbell McCormick complaining of 52 per cent in Catholic schools at a Vanguard meeting.

95. *Belfast Telegraph* (BT), 28 December 1981. Faul and Murray, *Irish News* (IN), 17 July 1981, quoted in *Church and State*, Cork, Autumn, 1981, 4.
96. IN, 16 March 1982.
97. IN, 19 January 1982.
98. AP, 13 June 1981. From Sands, Bobby (1981), *The Diary of Bobby Sands*, Dublin: Sinn Féin, 12.
99. IN, 14 January 1982.
100. Miller, A., BT, 9 January 1982.
101. IN, 13 January 1982.
102. IN, 14 January 1982.
103. Quoted by Mrs Mary Cosgrave. IN, 19 January 1982.
104. IN, 18 January 1982.
105. AN, 16 January 1982.
106. 18 January 1982.
107. Sunday Sequence 17 January 1982, Radio Ulster.
108. AP, 16 December 1982 and 1 February 1982.
109. *Irish Times* (IT), 5 March 1982.
110. AP, 5 June 1974 on the importance of using Irish traditional music and dance as a bridge to Protestant workers.
111. IN, 14 January 1982.
112. Paddy O'Donoghue, SDLP spokesperson on education insisted that Chilver must be dropped, IN, 20 January 1982.
113. Rory McShane on Good Morning Ulster, 18 January 1982. Alf McCreary lamented, 'even today it is astonishing how little we know of each other '. BT, 20 January 1982. M. Keegan (IN and BT, 20 January 1982) was concerned about the Catholic teachers educated at Stranmillis.
114. A, March and October 1973.
115. BT, 22 March 1982.
116. Sunday Sequence, 17 January 1982.
117. IT, 27 February 1982.
118. BT, 25 March 1982.
119. PT, 6 February 1982.
120. With John Rafferty, Radio Ulster 30 January 1982. Samuel Wilson, a DUP Councillor, objected to using public money for a chapel at Stranmillis. IN, 20 January 1982. The 'unclean thing' was a reference to Deuteronomy, 23, v. 14, quoted by the Rev. George Walker in a famous sermon preached after the siege of Londonderry, 1689. See Peter Robinson, *Their Cry was "No Surrender"*, 217-246.
121. PT, 2 September 1967; for Bob Jones and blacks, see 'Bob Jones wins Reprieve ', *Church and State* (February, 1982), Maryland, 16.
122. *Ulster the Facts*, 66.
123. *Protestant Blu Print* (PBP), 1, 11, 13 September 1985; U, November 1985; BT, 10 October 1985.
124. By 1992 there were fifteen primary and secondary integrated schools with a combined enrolment of 2840 pupils, about 1 per cent of the school population. A year later, the number had risen to 21, *Fortnight*, No. 32, September 1993, 33.

125. See Una Agnew et al., [1991], *Integrated Education: The Views of Parents*, School of Education, Belfast: Queen's University, 31, 39-40.
126. AP, 10 November 1988. Maire Nic Annaidh. *Fortnight*, July and August 1992.
127. See BT, 14 June 1989, 20 February 1990, 27 April 1990.
128. NPT, 24 March 1990.
129. AP, 6 September 1990.
130. Wright, Frank [1990], *Integrated Education and New Beginnings in Northern Ireland*, n.p.: The Corymeela Press, 19.
131. Agnew, Una, 40-41; Irwin, R., *Education and the Development of Social Integration in Divided Societies*, Belfast: Dept. of Social Anthropology, Queen's University, discussed in *Fortnight*, June 1991 and September 1991 (Daly).
132. For the secular tradition of the bardic schools, see Dowling, P.J. (1968), *The Hedge Schools of Ireland*, Cork: Mercier, quoted in Edwards, J. (1983), *The Irish Language: An Annotated Bibliography of Sociolinguistic Publications, 1772-1982*, New York: Gould, 65.

6 The propaganda of insurgency and counter-insurgency

Republicans, loyalists and the British Army

So far we have investigated the literature of conflict between loyalist and republican and between churchman and physical-force activist. Yet the Provisionals argued strongly that their war was not against loyalists but against Britain and her agents in Ireland. The focus must now shift in that direction. Was the strife between republicans and the British government a clear polarisation of interests, or did the two antagonists mirror each other?

The first Irish Revolution again gives perspective. To Robert Kee, in his popular history, the issue was clear. 'What was really happening was that the Volunteers [IRA] were goading the government into goading the people into rebellion—a process in which, much aided by the government itself, they were eventually to be successful.'[1] Naturally the Irish made no such admission. The most eminent Irish propagandist, Arthur Griffith, publisher of several newspapers as well as general overseer of the influential *Irish Bulletin*, had misgivings about Irish violence. He minimised republican force, counter-attacking where possible with stories of English atrocities. The advent of the Black and Tans and Auxiliaries in mid-1920 eased Griffith's task considerably. During the conflict his papers implied that a totally non-violent Irish movement was continually beset by homicidal maniacs in British uniforms. Griffith was adept at revealing British *agents provocateurs*. Ruthless actions by the Irish appeared either British lies or deliberate 'felon setting' by the alien government. Only reluctantly did Griffith even admit that the Irish retaliated against outrageous provocation by the Black and Tans.

The Amritsar precedent

Justification of such defensive arguments required a conspiratorial theory of some plausibility. Events in India proved invaluable. The Amritsar Massacre of March 1919 was ideal for Irish purposes. Though General R.E. Dyer received something of a hero's welcome from admirers in England, his shooting dead of nearly 400 unarmed Indian demonstrators appeared excessive punishment to all whose patriotic sympathies were not unconditionally engaged on the British side. Griffith denounced mini-Amritsars in Ireland. The incantation of names like Dyer and Amritsar was superb propaganda. Griffith's critics accused him of persistently retailing half-truths or downright lies even when the facts had been clearly established. Some of his tactics appeared dubious: on 'Bloody Sunday', 21 November 1920, a Griffith paper denounced the shooting of twelve members of a football crowd by British troops, but said nothing of the assassination of fourteen intelligence officers by the IRA earlier in the day, despite his private opposition to the latter.[2] Griffith undoubtedly realised that skilful propaganda was not simply an aid to physical-force rebellion, but rather the essence of revolution. Modern commentators argue that 'the guerrilla fighter is primarily a propagandist, an agitator, a disseminator of the revolutionary idea, who uses the struggle itself—the actual physical conflict—as an instrument of agitation'.[3] Griffith scarcely endorsed 'propaganda by deed', previously adopted in nineteenth-century Russia, but was well in advance of colleagues who still hoped that the IRA might eventually triumph over Britain in a set-piece battle, possibly armed with the traditional pike.[4]

By the 1970s there was more revolutionary theory to play with, some derived secondhand from Ireland itself. Although Griffith was repudiated by both branches of the IRA, Provisional Sinn Féin asserted its continuity with the movement he founded in 1905 and its 1918 objectives.[5] Griffith's tactics as a propagandist were tacitly followed. The emphasis on defence appeared at the start of the Provisional campaign; the Protestant incursions into Catholic areas after 1968 made it plausible. Similarly actions of the British Army after the Falls search in July 1970 enabled the Provisionals to assert their position as guardians of their community. Their opponents maintained, on the contrary, that PIRA, far from helping the Catholic community, was deliberately provoking the British violence they claimed to oppose. The papers of the security forces, the *Constabulary Gazette* and *Visor*, played a minor role in the debate. The latter did sometimes ridicule 'Seamus The Smear', PIRA's propaganda officer, and the contention that the Provisionals protected the lives of the general population. Thus PIRA and the security forces re-established the pattern of conflict between Arthur Griffith, denouncing Britain for goading the Irish into rebellion, and Lloyd George, repudiating a tiny murder gang deplored by the Irish people.

The issue is epitomised in the propagandist confrontation between Provisional spokesmen, such as Ruairí O'Brádaigh, Dáithí O'Conaill, and Seán MacStiofain, chief of staff before his arrest in 1972, on one side, and General Richard Clutterbuck on the other. In books like *Protest and the Urban Guerrilla* and *Living with Terrorism*,[6] Clutterbuck, eventually mutated into an academic, gave a coherent case for the British Army. He was reinforced by other writers such as Paul Wilkinson and Edgar O'Ballance. The rival intrepreters, as will be shown later, endeavoured to associate their opponents, like Griffith on General Dyer, with a frightening bogey. To the Provisionals the bogey was Clutterbuck's former student at the British Army Staff College, General Sir Frank Kitson, Commander-in-Chief United Kingdom Land Forces from 1982 to his retirement from the Army in 1985.

The contest of stereotypes: Kitson v. Marighela

Kitson, at forty-four the youngest British brigadier, commanded the 39th Brigade in Belfast from September 1970 to April 1972. In 1971 he published a controversial book on counter-insurgency, *Low Intensity Operations*. Copies were soon bought up by Irish republicans and the CIA.[7] Especially in the years 1974-77, republicans and others continually attacked Kitson as mastermind of internment, torture, brutal interrogation, subtle brainwashing, media control, black propaganda, incitement to sectarian murder, SAS assassination, and stealing felt from Thiepval barracks.[8] He became a propaganda code-word for all the most hated aspects of the British Army's service in Ulster. As late as 1993, eight years after Kitson had retired from the British Army, *An Phoblacht* published a photograph of Kitson in a standard denunciation of his influence.[9] On the loyalist side Kitson was sometimes praised—Professor Kennedy Lindsay told a Vanguard meeting that Northern Ireland needed more Dyers and Kitsons[10]—and sometimes reviled, as indeed by Lindsay himself some years later. One loyalist, in a classic example of antithetical interpretation, found Kitson a dupe of Catholic propaganda.[11] General Clutterbuck, however, did not mention his former student in the footnotes to his *Protest and the Urban Guerrilla*, which dealt with the early years of the second Irish revolution. He had more to say about the ideas of the Brazilian revolutionary, Carlos Marighela. Marighela's *Minimanual of the Urban Guerrilla* and *For the Liberation of Brazil*[12] were cited to demonstrate how urban guerrillas deliberately provoked government reprisals on their own communities to goad them into support of the revolution. The Provisionals portrayed a war in which Machiavellian fiends like Kitson brutally ill-treated the Catholic community to compel it to desert its natural leaders and defenders; the British Army, on the other hand, saw terrorists, steeped in Marighela, deliberately subjecting their own communities to bloodshed and brutality in the interests of a remote and extreme cause. MacStiofain's *Memoirs of a Revolutionary* has nothing to say about Marighela, only occasionally mentioned in republican literature, but a great deal on Kitson, 'our deadliest enemy in the north'.[13] These attitudes clearly mirror each other in patterned opposition.

Marighela, however, had no direct connection with Ireland, while Kitson commanded troops in Northern Ireland during the exceptionally important early years of the second Irish revolution. Is it possible, in the midst of such a welter of propaganda, to establish the basic facts about his Ulster mission? Very little official documentation is yet available on Kitson's precise work and influence in Northern Ireland, though Paddy Devlin, a member of the power-sharing executive, claims that 'it is clear from public records that his troops were instructed to put the boot into the Catholic section of the community'.[14] Brian Faulkner does not mention Kitson in his memoirs; indeed, most accounts of the Kitson period in Ulster give him little attention. Kitson himself does not include a description of his work in Northern Ireland in *Bunch of Five*, an autobiographical account, published in 1977, which indirectly answers some of his Irish critics. Clutterbuck ignores Kitson in his lengthy description of the build-up of terrorism from 1970 to 1972. The only significant hint of the Kitson influence from a semi-official source comes from Roy Bradford, a minister under

Faulkner in both the old Stormont regime and the later power-sharing executive. The fictional hero of Bradford's novel, *The Last Ditch*, is greatly impressed by Kitson's efforts to modernise the British Army against conservative opposition.[15]

Low-intensity theory and high-intensity practice

Generally Kitson kept a low profile until the publication of his *Low Intensity Operations* in the months following internment in August 1971. Then there appeared a direct connection between theory and practice. But this was not Kitson's first book. As early as 1960 he had published *Gangs and Counter-Gangs*, describing his experiences as an intelligence officer in the Mau Mau emergency.[16] His method had been to recruit loyal Kikuyu and Mau Mau prisoners, form them into pseudo-gangs accompanied by face-blackened British officers (sometimes himself), and send them into the forest to gather information or eliminate real Mau Mau formations. Though this book was subjected to intense Irish debate, it achieved notoriety only after the publication of *Low Intensity Operations*.

The new work was researched at University College, Oxford, 1969-70, under a defence fellowship. From academic cloisters Kitson was sent to apply his research in Northern Ireland. His second book developed his earlier experiences in Kenya, Malaya, Cyprus and Oman into a general theory. It suggested that the British Army, no longer able to rely on force of numbers, needed greater facility for psychological operations, irregular warfare, and co-operation with police at earlier stages in subversion.[17] Clearly the authorities were aware of these conclusions before sending him to Northern Ireland.

Kitson arrived in Belfast at a crucial juncture of the Troubles. The Conservatives replaced Labour in June 1970, and ended their so-called 'softly, softly' policy. The 'tea for soldiers' period concluded with the Falls arms search in July, after the first main Provisional action in the Short Strand. Even Clutterbuck considered the arms search 'ill-judged'.[18] It was, in fact, close to the force of numbers approach which Kitson criticised in his *Low Intensity Operations*. His appointment to Northern Ireland was clearly an attempt at greater subtlety. Kitson had the advantage of a lull before the Provisional urban guerrilla campaign began in earnest in February 1971. In the months before February, there were discreet meetings between officers and republican leaders.[19] Here Kitson's tactics should have worked most effectively. General Freeland had already established various community projects and clubs, ostensibly to enable the mixing of the different traditions. To Kitson such projects were extremely valuable as sources of information by the Army.[20] Total polarisation and no-go areas, on the other hand, made the type of intelligence hunting envisaged in *Gangs and Counter-Gangs* very difficult.

Kitson, however, did not succeed in checking the development of the Provisionals. In early 1971, General Harry Tuzo was appointed the new British Army commander in Northern Ireland. According to MacStiofain, there was tension between Tuzo, a conservative who favoured the establishment of a ring of steel round nationalist areas to provoke all-out confrontation with PIRA, and Kitson who sought fluidity enabling plain-clothes officers to infiltrate republican areas and emulate the counter-gangs in the Kenyan forest. Roy Bradford also suggested military opposition to Kitson who 'singlehanded, was attempting to drag the army through a revolution as great as Cardwell's'.[21]

Kitson and internment

By summer 1971 the Faulkner government decided on internment. Was Kitson, as subsequently alleged, the mastermind behind this strategy? Faulkner's memoirs mention Roy Bradford as a hardliner on internment.[22] Bradford approved of Kitson, so the latter may have been one of the military men in favour, especially if opposed to his sceptical superior Tuzo. Kitson's books hint approval of such tactics. In *Bunch of Five* he praises the massive use of internment in Kenya for saving many lives.[23] Republican critics quote Kitson's later comments in *Low Intensity Operations* that a large amount of low-grade evidence was more useful for subsequent development than a little high-grade information.[24] They also noted Kitson's approval of the pro-internment Robert Trinquier, a French general who endeavoured to suppress the Algerian Revolt.[25] Internment was an obvious means for obtaining low-grade information when informal contacts between soldiers and nationalist civilians were almost impossible. It therefore seems a fair deduction that Kitson did advocate internment more strongly than Tuzo. MacStiofain suggests an enormous 'shopping list' of information sought at this time.[26] If correct, it indicates just how little was known about the IRA.

The actual implementation of internment in Belfast was certainly Kitson's responsibility, yet he was clearly dissatisfied with the overall arrangements for 'Operation Demetrius'. The journalist

Simon Winchester points out that Kitson was on holiday when a dry-run practice internment was carried out on 23 July. He was, as a result, 'highly irritated' that surprise had been lost and dozens of suspects escaped. When the crucial day, 9 August, came there was further inefficiency. The RUC handed over the suspect list to Kitson, often with the wrong photographs, and the Army sent out three-man snatch squads.[27] This was clearly opposed to Kitson's view as his books insisted that Army and Special Branch should work together in building up information banks, rather than using soldiers simply as police agents.[28] But, as MacStiofain, PIRA chief of staff at the time, points out, Kitson was 'then little known to the public' and correspondingly less influential with his superiors.[29]

Clutterbuck is ambiguous on internment, admitting that it inevitably polarised opinion, but still claiming that it was the only alternative to the intimidatory tactics of vigilantes determined to create a backlash à la Marighela.[30] The arguments are another example of antithetical interpretation. Provisionals saw internment as part of a Kitsonian plot, British officers as an attempt to defeat a Marighela plot. What was the achievement? MacStiofain quotes Kitson's desire for low-grade information. Unlike other republicans attributing to Kitson all subsequent ill treatment, the PIRA chief of staff considered sensory deprivation, effective in eliciting confession, counter-productive for the brigadier. MacStiofain in fact suspects tension between officers wishing to obtain counter-insurgency leads and those who wanted experimental guinea-pigs. He points out that if one IRA member's name had been obtained from each of 700 detainees, the Provisionals would have been destroyed immediately. That they were not indicated either the inaccuracy of initial British information or the incompetence of their intelligence officers.

MacStiofain realised that Kitson's object was tactical information enabling the Army to build low-grade sources into contact leads for definite targets, instead of passively waiting for IRA units to appear in an exposed position.[31] This is a sensible reading of Kitson's work. The latter continually emphasised the need to develop background information into operational data capable of beginning a feedback process and 'chain reaction' which 'snowballs'.[32] The use of the latter word in the Parker Report on internment was attributed to Kitsonian influence.[33] But Kitson also talks of obtaining background information through soldiers and police 'in a friendly and civilised way'.[34] Moreover, he laid great stress on the efficient collating of overt information and even the reading of revolutionaries' memoirs available in the public libraries. A Belfast paper correctly asserted that he made war 'with a filing cabinet'.[35] A few years later it would have been a computer, introduced by MI5 in the mid-1970s.[36]

Kitson and interrogation

Republicans accused Kitson of organising the beating, electric shock treatment, psychological disorientation, and gross humiliation of internees at the Holywood Police Barracks. The Officials published a photograph of Kitson ('the face of a sadist') on their anti-internment pamphlet, *They came in the morning*.[37] Was this fabricated propaganda? Certainly, they could not deduce it from Kitson's books; he would hardly admit publicly to rough handling of suspects. There is one admission in *Counter-Gangs* of a night spent working over a prisoner 'as tough as nails and very unco-operative'. As Kitson and his assistants 'were not feeling particularly sympathetic' they succeeded in eliciting some useful information. In *Bunch of Five* Kitson repudiated brutality, distinguishing between formal interrogation for immediate tactical information and long-term, and ultimately more valuable, attempts to win a prisoner's friendship. Draughts, parties, horseplay, and a willingness to live without moralising in close proximity to a prisoner, were emphasised. The certainty of capital punishment for the unco-operative was a powerful incentive. Republican insistence that Kitson practised sleep deprivation might be deduced from his Kenyan habit of keeping initially hostile prisoners in chains. However, Joram Wamweya, a Kenyan guerrilla, ridiculed the naivety of special branch agents attempting to extract confessions by shackles. In formal interrogation Kitson emphasised confrontation with unexpected facts from background sources to 'break down' the prisoner.[38] As MacStiofain admitted, beating and torture were more useful in forcing confessions than obtaining information.[39]

Revolutionary propaganda lays considerable emphasis on torture which Hyams sees as standard practice for all counter-insurgents. Britain's 1978 condemnation by the European Court for inhuman and degrading treatment was a considerable victory for the Provisionals. They claimed that on TV Clutterbuck justified sensory deprivation[40] in *Living with Terrorism*. But despite emphasis on Pavlovian disorientation as more common than physical torture, he is at pains to insist that 'there is no real antidote to the loathsome techniques of modern interrogation—and they are equally loathsome whichever side uses them'.[41] Kitson's refusal to moralise in his books enabled republicans to invoke his name as a shorthand stereotype for cynical brutality. He became particularly useful, long after he had left Northern Ireland, in the period of Ulsterisation and prison protest.

The English debate Kitson

The publication of *Low Intensity Operations* in the months after internment began the demonisation process. The work caused a stir outside the ranks of Irish republicanism. Right-wing officers, lamenting the breakdown of authority in the permissive society, endorsed its views. It became the subject of correspondence in the London *Times*,[42] and a matter of concern to members of the Labour opposition in Westminster. It proved a propagandist godsend to Irish republicans. But what exactly caused the furore?

From the British viewpoint the significance of *Low Intensity Operations* lay not in its scenarios for developing counter-gangs against colonial insurgents, but its implications for the metropolis itself. Kitson defined 'insurgency' not simply as illegal measures, short of violence, to overthrow those in government, but even 'to force them to do things which they do not want them to do'. This came perilously close to suggesting army intervention in politics. Moreover, Kitson included 'pressure, strikes, protest marches, and propaganda' amongst such subversive activities. He envisaged a situation in which a 'genuine and serious grievance arose, such as might result from a significant drop in the standard of living'. The police failing to keep order, the army might have to restore it rapidly. 'The government should be in a position to keep the country running during a prolonged period of strikes and civil disturbance, and to this end either the police or the army should have men available who are capable of operating essential services such as power stations and sewerage systems with relatively little assistance from civilian experts.' Ironically, the UWC strike of 1974 suggested, incorrectly, that the British Army did not have this capacity. In 1971 Kitson had warned that the Ulster Troubles demonstrated that law and order could not be taken for granted even in the United Kingdom. 'It may be of interest to recall that when the regular army was first raised in the seventeenth century, "Suppression of the Irish" was coupled with "Defence of the Protestant Religion" as one of the two main reasons for its existence.'[43]

Such indiscretions were quickly seized on. In early 1972, when violence peaked in Northern Ireland, several Labour MPs, including Roy Hattersley, who as minister for defence had been involved in sending troops to Northern Ireland in August 1969, tabled parliamentary questions on Kitson's book. Kitson's views became particularly important after April 1972 when he left Ireland to become commandant of the school of infantry at Warminster. Were these views to be taught to young officers? Was *Low Intensity Operations* an official publication endorsed by the ministry of defence? The minister, Lord Balneil, tried to defuse the situation by stating that the book contained Kitson's private opinions only. It was, however, admitted that he had been given permission to publish. Kitson was now 'a figure of cult hatred on the further left'. In 1974 Colonel George Wigg, another Labour MP, opposed Kitson's view, operational in Northern Ireland, that soldiers should do police work. Roy Hattersley totally disagreed with some of Kitson's conclusions. Not even a right-wing Labour man could, in fact, do less. Hattersley insisted that political disputes must be decided by the elected government, not by soldiers.[44] Kitson touched on this issue in his 1971 book. He accepted that subversion in a good cause might sometimes be beneficial: the soldier in a democratic country was dependent on electors whose representatives 'will only make war when it is right to do so'.[45] However, the thrust of Kitson's suggestion seemed most appropriate to a Conservative or right-wing government. Indeed, by admitting that the government cause might sometimes be wrong, he almost insinuated that the soldiers should then take over.

Though Kitson's views were relevant in Britain where the Heath government soon fell after failing to resolve its dispute with the miners, they were even more applicable to Northern Ireland. The revealing reference to Cromwell's New Model Army and the suppression of Irish Catholicism, as a prelude to establishing the only military dictatorship in English history, was not allowed to pass unchallenged.[46] It was superb propaganda for both the Provisionals and the Officials, not to mention other groups. Nor was it mere propaganda. Some officers of MI5, which took over responsibility for Northern Ireland from MI6 in 1973, were engaged in a disinformation campaign against Prime Minister Wilson and several members of his cabinet, including the right-wing Hattersley, whom they imagined to be Russian communist spies. Colin Wallace, in the Information Policy unit in Lisburn barracks, was involved in disinformation, not only against PIRA, but also his own elected government.[47]

Authorities as eminent as Edmund Burke, Karl Marx and Friedrich Engels had warned that England's destruction of liberty overseas would undermine her own freedom. The Officials' *United Irishman* was one of the first to emphasise the idea of Northern Ireland as a laboratory for 'the spillover of repression' into England. Kitson, it claimed, intended to deal with English strikes by rubber bullets and CS gas. As a result, he was the darling of the middle classes.[48] The Provisionals also raised this issue, warning of a 'national plan' for drawing the fangs of the British working class. By 1990 they feared that British repressive techniques had been imported by Australia.[49] The socialist Bob Purdie, writing for *Republican News*, declared Kitson 'the submerged iceberg of British politics'. Purdie attributed to Kitson not only the use of the army in place of the police as a forthcoming threat to the British workers (thus agreeing with Wigg) but also an array of psychological and scientific techniques.[50] The message of warning to the British working classes was repeated in subsequent years; incidents such as police repression in Notting Hill (1976) and Lewisham (1977)[51] were cited as examples. The use of troops at London airport was also traced to the precedent of Northern Ireland accustoming the people to accept army urban activity. Subsequently, as *An Phoblacht* demonstrated, Kitson argued for low-level subversion to be dealt with by the police and not the Army.[52] The demand for the solidarity of the British working classes was well taken. Marx and Engels in the nineteenth century had continually emphasised the need for Irish self-government as a means to British emancipation. Marx's letter to Kugelmann, 29 November 1869, for example, not only insisted that the British workers take the initiative in dissolving the Union, but also warned that 'the English republic under Cromwell met shipwreck in—Ireland. Non bis in idem! (Not twice for the same thing!)'.[53] When Kitson was sent to command a BAOR division in Germany, a Provisional paper claimed that his system was being exported to EEC countries.[54] As if in reply, the *Constabulary Gazette: the Ulster Police Magazine* published an article from the *Daily Express* claiming that Northern Ireland was a Marxist 'laboratory for revolution'.[55]

Kitson and loyalism

Kitson's *Low Intensity Operations* infuriated republicans, but Paisley's *Protestant Telegraph* saw the book differently, complaining that officers like Kitson who had supported loyalist interests were soon recalled.[56] It thus agreed with opponents who argued that Kitson was in fact sacked when Whitelaw took over after the suspension of Stormont in March 1972.[57] The Kitson reference to the seventeenth-century British Army and its initial task of suppressing Irish Catholicism was more than relevant in this connection. Christopher Hill emphasises the significance of seventeenth-century Ireland in the Puritan hysteria against Antichrist.[58] Kitson was aware that 'certain sections of the unionist majority are trying to prevent their own government from giving concessions to the nationalist minority.'[59] As Kitson's success in Kenya and other places was based to a large extent on liaison with the local settlers or loyalist population, the *Protestant Telegraph* was probably correct in asserting Kitson's loyalist sympathies. Certainly, republicans were to argue that loyalist gangs in Northern Ireland had been set up by Kitson's agents. Whitelaw may well have felt that Kitson's continued presence after the publication of *Low Intensity Operations* would have been counter-productive, especially when he hoped to conciliate Catholics.

Kitson's theory

(1) *Law as a weapon*
Seán MacStiofain claimed that Kitson's counter-insurgency techniques were stepped up after his departure.[60] The Kitson references in republican papers increased sharply between 1974 and 1977. The current political situation required such propaganda. Sectarian assassination of Catholics and the use of undercover British agents were increasing but the threat to the Provisionals from a power-sharing SDLP and the emergence of the Peace People were potentially more threatening. The 'Kitson' issues can thus be grouped under the headings of British Army counter-insurgency, loyalist paramilitaries, SDLP on the power-sharing executive, Peace People, government control of the media, and the adoption of Kitson's methods in the Irish Republic.

A backdrop for all 'Kitsonism', and especially for the counter-insurgent British Army, was the treatment of law in *Low Intensity Operations*. According to Kitson, there were two alternative attitudes to law when dealing with subversion. First, it could be:

> just another weapon in the government's arsenal, and in this case it becomes little more than a propaganda cover for the disposal of unwanted members of the public. For this to happen efficiently, the activities of the legal services have to be tied in with the war effort in as direct a way as possible which, in effect, means that the member of the government responsible for law either sits on the supreme council or takes orders from the head of the administration.

Second, law could remain impartial while the government introduced tough legislation, and the legal officers maintained the distinction between the government, the enemy, and the uncommitted. Kitson accepted the second alternative was morally right and expedient for retaining the allegiance of the population, but speed or obstacles to strong legislation might require option number one.[61]

Such a vague and ambiguous passage was manna from heaven to the republicans.[62] As his other books show, Kitson criticised the delays of the Nairobi supreme court during the Mau Mau emergency, which sometimes released, on what seemed frivolous pretexts, guerrillas he had captured. Moreover, the Mau Mau committee members, who seem to have corresponded to overt Sinn Féin leaders, rarely did anything illegal.[63] The short, sharp proceedings of martial law were clearly more to his taste. Republicans, however, who stretch the meaning of admittedly chilling phrases like 'the disposal of unwanted members of the public' to cover wholesale assassination of opponents by plain clothes squads and torture of suspects, clearly exaggerate. Dillon and Lehane, in their *Political Murder in Northern Ireland* (1975) suggested that Kitson's book 'would seem to countenance under certain circumstances a campaign of assassination by the British Army undertaken by plain-clothes troops', but believe he would always insist on sanction at government level. To the fury of the Provisionals, they acquitted Kitson of demanding a wholesale campaign against the Catholic community and believed undercover assassination of Catholics by British Army units, as opposed to loyalist paramilitaries, infrequent.[64] The issue re-emerged after 1982 with the controversial 'shoot-to-kill' policy and the liaisons discovered between Protestant paramilitaries and the security forces at the end of the decade.

(2) Pseudo-gangs in Ulster

Despite the undoubted exaggeration of propagandists, 'Operation Motorman', which ended the no-go areas in July 1972, did make it easier to operate undercover squads which were the Northern Ireland equivalent of the pseudo-gangs simulating the Mau Mau. MacStiofain claimed, however, that they were badly organised and that Kitson's weakness was in defence. What if the guerrillas eliminated the special forces sent to eliminate them? MacStiofain ridicules the three-man Military Reconnaisance (or Reaction) Force Squads (MRF) of the early 1970s, who followed hit lists of Provisionals, posing with old Thompson guns as IRA or, transparently, as hitch-hikers. Certainly, the Provisionals were able to claim propagandist successes, equivalent to those of Arthur Griffith in the first Irish Revolution. The Four Square laundry service at Twinbrook, designed to obtain forensic evidence of gunshot stains on customers' clothes, and the Gemini Health Studio massage parlour on the Antrim Road were in 1972 put out of business by the Provisionals. These were 'deception operations' organised by operatives like Colin Wallace.[65] The Provisionals were also delighted in 1977 when they caught and eliminated Captain Robert Nairac, an SAS-associated officer posing as a republican sympathiser, complete with assumed Portadown accent. Nairac had led a group of Protestant extremists in assassinating John Green, a leading Provisional, in the Irish Republic. This operation was later assessed as a classic application of the Kitson pseudo-gang strategy.[66] The destruction of a helicopter by M-60 fire in 1978 allowed *An Phoblacht* to boast of the removal of another Kitson-trained intelligence officer.[67] It was not so much the precise score of MRF and SAS success measured against that of the Provisionals as the fact that the latter could exploit their efforts more effectively in propaganda. Another development, also attributed to Kitson, was the stakeout, resembling the Anglo-Indian tiger shoots under the Raj, when an SAS squad would lie in wait after locating an arms dump or other guerrilla resort. This rough and ready means of dealing with their opponents inevitably led to some mistakes, as in the case of the innocent John Boyle, killed by soldiers who were subsequently found not guilty of murder by the Lord Chief Justice, Lord Lowry. The verdict, declared an *An Phoblacht* writer, was judicial endorsement of stakeouts which broke every rule of the 'yellow card', supposed to determine the behaviour of the army.[68] SAS assassination policy, it was declared on another occasion, came straight from Kitson's textbook.[69] On the other hand, when the Provisionals wanted to justify their own assassination of Judge Rory Conaghan and Magistrate Martin McBurney in 1974 they cited Kitson's perversion of law as a weapon in the struggle.[70] An attempt to assassinate Lowry himself failed in 1982.[71]

The Provisionals were not only concerned to expose the security forces. They had also to find an explanation for loyalist assassination of Catholics, especially after Motorman. Given the Provisional philosophy of British troops out before community reconciliation, it was essential that they play down the possibility of a Protestant 'backlash' and civil war after withdrawal. Usually a backlash was simply rejected as government propaganda. It was asserted that the Prot-stats had never previously fought except under British auspices, that the paramilitaries engaged only in assassination, without emulating the IRA in facing the British Army, and that Prot-stats had no stomach for any physical force. Sometimes, however, it was admitted that there might have to be some fighting after British withdrawal. Again, the helpful Kitson showed a way out of any apparent inconsistency. Developing his counter-gang theory, it was argued that the loyalist assassination squads were actually organised or inspired by the British Army. Thus the withdrawal of the latter would automatically end sectarian killing.[72] The sinister UFF (Ulster Freedom Fighters), a cover for the UDA reluctant to admit illegality, might even mask British counter-insurgency.[73] Peter Dowling, the Kitson expert, writing a lengthy article in *Republican News* in 1977, classified the pseudo-gangs into three categories.[74] First, there were British units like the SAS which used various disguises but remained sections of the British Army. Second, came loyalist organisations such as the UVF, Red Hand Commandos, and Tara. These were generally independent, but their actions sometimes backfired on the British. Finally, mixed organisations like the UFF were infiltrated or set up by the British. Dowling referred to Kitson's book on Kenya, *Gangs and Counter-Gangs*, now increasingly publicised, for authority. The independence of groups like the UDA, UVF, and Red Hand Commandos was denied. Deliberate British strategy used them to terrorise the nationalist population into deserting the IRA, to divert IRA attention from British forces, to encourage the bloodbath theory, and to drive Catholics into larger and more easily controlled ghettoes.[75]

How much of this can be legitimately deduced from Kitson's *Gangs and Counter-Gangs*? On the general intimidation of the Catholic population, a remark attributed to Kitson in 1971 was quoted *ad nauseam*, 'I would squeeze the Catholic population until they vomit the gunmen out of their system'.[76] In *Low Intensity Operations* Kitson says more discreetly that 'conditions can be made reasonably uncomfortable for the population as a whole, in order to provide an incentive for a return to normal life and to act as a deterrent towards a resumption of the campaign.' Commenting on Mao's guerrilla fish swimming in the water of public support, Kitson ominously suggested that something might have to be done to the water.[77] Does this indeed imply that under a façade of minimum force, innocent Catholics would be gunned down by sectarian gangs, or death squads as republicans called them in the 1990s?[78] In *Gangs and Counter-Gangs* there is nothing quite so sinister, basically because Kitson is dealing with Mau Mau groups in the forest, not urban guerrillas. The counter-gangs, which mixed loyal Kikuyu, Mau Mau turncoats, local white settlers, and expatriate British officers, when they contacted real gangs for information or destruction, do provide some justification for the apparently far-fetched propaganda of the Provisionals. The single-man missions, which sometimes ended in the painful death of Kitson's accomplices, were more appropriate in Northern Ireland conditions. The Provisional argument, first put forward in the 1970s, that loyalist violence was not *sui generis* was later proved to have considerable plausibility, though difficult to attribute specifically to Kitson. The exposure of the bank robbers Eric and John Littlejohn, sentenced in 1973, as probable British agents, the scandal of Brian Nelson, UDA intelligence officer, revealed as a double agent in 1990, the aborted John Stalker investigation into RUC killings, and the revelations of insiders like Peter Wright, Colin Wallace and Fred Holroyd were all grist for the Provisional mill. In 1990 the Stevens Inquiry proved collusion between members of the security forces, who possessed lists of IRA suspects, and loyalist gangs who eliminated the latter.[79]

(3) Exploiting moderates: SDLP and Peace People
In 1974 and 1977 the Provisionals faced constitutional threats from power sharing and the Peace People. Kitson again provided a perfect propagandist answer to these advocates of constitutional reform and non-violence. *Low Intensity Operations*, in another well-quoted passage, outlined a strategy for exploiting the non-violent phase of subversion which precedes the outbreak of terrorism. Kitson believed that the movement was then at its most vulnerable. The simplest suppression was by 'naked force', but this was difficult for a British government. Instead, 'the judicious promise of concessions', while 'imposing a period of calm' and promising implementation of reform when normality was achieved, could separate leadership from rank and file. At such a time squeezing the potentially rebellious population becomes possible. The breathing space gained must be used to do:

> three further things quickly. The first is to implement the promised concessions so as to avoid allegations of bad faith which may enable the subversive leadership to regain control over certain sections of the people. The second is to discover and neutralise the genuine subversive element. The third is to associate as many prominent members of the population, especially those who have been engaged in non-violent action, with the government. This last technique is known in

America as co-optation ... and is described by Messrs Hoch and Schoenback as drowning the revolution in baby's milk.[80]

Though not used against the SDLP until after the power-sharing attempt had broken down, it was easy to portray that party, via the Kitson quote, as a British stooge dishonestly accepting co-optation from the Westminster government. This must have been particularly galling for the SDLP as it attacked Kitson as vigorously as others for provoking sectarian violence and putting the boot into the Catholic population. Ironically, Paddy Devlin, then an SDLP leader, accused Kitson of being the IRA's 'most powerful recruiting agent'.[81] Similarly, the Peace People, almost immediately after their emergence in 1976, were portrayed as Kitson's stooges.[82] Cartoons reinforced the verbal message. As all nationalists abhorred Kitson, reply was difficult.

(4) Black propaganda
Another major propagandist use of Kitson covered the whole range of media control and 'black propaganda'. This was the most vital area of the war itself which the Provisionals had to win to stay in business. As usual there were quotes apparently from *Low Intensity Operations*: the government 'must also promote its own cause and undermine that of the enemy by disseminating its view of the situation.... The countering of the enemy's propaganda and putting across of the government's point of view can be achieved by direct action, as for example the provision of leaflets, or the setting up of an official wireless or television network, or by trying to inform and influence the existing news media.... The real difficulty lies in the political price a democratic country pays in order to influence the ways in which its people think.' Kitson did indeed recommend the training of officers in psychological operations and media persuasion, but republicans elaborated on the implicit threat to free speech. There were a number of complaints in the 1970s about slanted pro-government reporting in the English press and revealing films like *A Sense of Loss* banned from television. Kitson's accommodating book helped to provide a suitably conspiratorial perspective.[83]

There was, however, the more positive side of Kitson's influence. 'Black propaganda' was depicted as the attempt to destroy the republican credibility in its own community and abroad through the Thiepval Barracks 'lie machine',[84] and even concocting outrages to attribute to PIRA. How far was it actually used in the second Irish revolution? Revelations by Colin Wallace, later found guilty of manslaughter in England after he had become a liability to MI5, show the extent of black propaganda operating in the early 1970s. Some gimmicks, such as the attempt to deter PIRA's female bombers by claiming that static electricity from their nylon undies would explode the bombs prematurely, were amusing, but others were clearly more sinister.[85] Such misinformation had a long history. During the first Irish Revolution the British disseminated a false issue of the *Irish Bulletin*, Dail Eireann's successful information sheet. On the other side, Arthur Griffith had effectively attributed to 'black propaganda' some counter-productive Irish actions. Such tactics are inevitable in war, formal or informal. In 1973 the *Andersonstown News* complained that the Sinn Féin fortnightly *Nation* had also been forged. *An Phoblacht* denounced Kitsonian influence when the UFF detonated a car bomb at Coalisland, apparently with the initial intention of blackening the reputation of the local Provisionals.[86] Kitson was also accused of originating his techniques of black propaganda in Kenya where he endeavoured to denigrate the African insurgents by mutilating beasts and like activities.[87] Needless to say, Kitson admits nothing so specific, yet there are interesting hints in *Gangs and Counter-Gangs*. The Mau Mau emergency certainly saw the extreme vilification of the Kikuyu, but Kitson's work is notable for its lack of emotion in this respect. He laughs at the obscene oaths that were imposed on new members of the 'Mau Mau', itself a term of contempt coined by its enemies. Nor does Kitson show any revulsion from leaders of the revolutionary movement. He had no compunction about using a witch doctor to discover, by some uncanny means, where a suspect had hidden money. 'The whole business was absolutely genuine.' On the other hand he considered that the Christian missionaries were 'discrediting the old without gaining acceptance for the new'. Most important of all, when participating in pseudo-gangs himself, Kitson admits to taking part in the administration of Mau Mau oaths and collecting money, ostensibly on their behalf.[88]

This admission is sufficient to give the Provisionals almost indefinite cover for black propagandist claims. When it is remembered how public revulsion for the primordial savagery of the Mau Mau oathing was disseminated to the world media during the Kenyan emergency, and that at least 222 Kikuyu were executed for administering illegal oaths, it is difficult to accept Kitson's off-hand announcement that 'sometimes our gang would have to administer the odd oath, or collect some money. Not to have done so would have seemed strange at the time.'[89] Irish republicans have always maintained, and Karl Marx fully agreed,[90] that the 1798 rising was deliberately provoked by the British government to justify the Union. The Presbyterian, William Orr, was not only hanged for administering the United Irish oath in 1797, but convicted on the unsupported word of an informer. 'The odd oath' in his case had grave consequences. Modern republicans, with their long tradition of denouncing 'perfidious Albion',[91] insisted that Kitson-inspired intelligence officers were guilty of every kind of misinformation and villainy. *Gangs and Counter-Gangs*, according to *An Phoblacht*, might provide the answer to the spate of inter-group killings, 'the result of diabolically clever action by enemy agents provocateurs' on Kitson's pattern.[92] Certainly, much 'Kitson' propaganda was made by Provisionals, led by Sinn Féin president, Ruairí O'Brádaigh, out of the 1975 splits between the Officials and the IRSP on one side, and the UDA and UVF on the other.[93] The Officials were also happy to attribute the IRSP to a Kitson plot.[94] The influence of this evil genius appeared so enormous that even great English universities, like Oxford, which gave him a defence fellowship, could be portrayed as the servants of counter-insurgency.[95] Though sustainable only by quotes out of context,[96] Kitson's malign potency in republican eyes mirrored those of the pope in Prot-stat demonology.[97]

The Irish republic and Kitson

Not only did Kitson's alleged influence extend to EEC countries but it incorporated the collaborationist government of the twenty-six counties. There army officers, said *An Phoblacht*, were trained according to a Kitson-style manual which taught anti-strike action. Justice Minister Cooney was accused of using Kitson's 'law weapon' argument to justify the atrocious treatment of political prisoners in Port Laoghise gaol. When several escaped in 1976, it was revealed that they had been stripped, handcuffed over chairs, and had cigarettes stubbed on their skin. This was regarded as vintage Kitson.[98] There appeared no object of Provisional invective unlinked with the bloodthirsty brigadier.

Clutterbuck and Marighela—do guerrillas provoke reprisal?

As mentioned, the use of Kitson by the Provisionals was mildly paralleled by Dr (General) Richard Clutterbuck's use of the Brazilian guerrilla, Carlos Marighela. The terrorist profile presented by Clutterbuck, and Kitson himself in parts of his books less emphasised by opponents, is clearly drawn. Though they pay lip-service to the possibility that subversives may sometimes be acting in a good cause, most government spokesmen are reluctant to accept this. They declare alleged grievances either imaginary or easily reformed by constitutional means. Thus Kitson places much emphasis on the views of the American J.J. McCuen who, like the brigadier's foreword writer, General Robert Thompson, assumed that revolution starts from nothing.[99] Kitson discussed the 'foco' theory of Castro, Che Guevara and Debray which enables a revolution to begin without the preliminary organisation of the people considered necessary by authorities like Mao Zedong.[100] Marighela, killed in late 1969 after a very brief career as a Brazilian guerrilla, became known in Britain in 1971 when his *Minimanual of an Urban Guerrilla* and *For the Liberation of Brazil* appeared in translation. His significance lies in his transfer of small revolutionary 'focos', gathering support in the country, to the cities, and to the popularisation of the term 'urban guerrilla'. Most established PIRA members have infinitely more practical experience than had Marighela. So far, only MacStiofain, in his underrated 1975 *Memoirs of a Revolutionary*, has produced a full-scale work of Provisional strategy. As indicated earlier, he has much to say about Kitson, but nothing on Marighela; Clutterbuck reversed this emphasis. Both sides were avoiding awkward subjects.

Clutterbuck's account of Northern Irish insurgency before 1973, notwithstanding his post at Exeter University, is clearly a defence of the British Army. He accepts that the 'Bloody Sunday' shootings of January 1972 were instigated by an IRA determined, despite the restraints of British soldiers, to keep tension high.[101] This contention is, of course, denied by MacStiofain who insists, on the contrary, that the Provisionals were ordered to stay away lest the British provoke them into a set battle where they would be destroyed.[102] Such accounts are as usual antithetical interpretations. Clutterbuck's other arguments are in like vein. He laments Provisional dirty tricks, such as anonymous phone accusations to instigate rough handling of sick, disabled or bereaved innocents, and attacks behind protective walls of children. Nevertheless, he insists that PIRA members are basically stupid, just as MacStiofain ridicules the inefficiency of the British. Clutterbuck, moreover, shows some bias in playing down the loyalists while admitting the UDA as a 'mirror-image' of the IRA. Loyalist tartan gangs are described with some sympathy, but their Catholic equivalents are 'hooligans'.[103]

The thrust of Clutterbuck's argument thus lies also in provocation. Bloody Sunday[104] is an excellent example. Here Marighela appears useful. According to Clutterbuck the basic terrorist strategy is openly admitted in his works. These are alleged to argue that the best way to ensure the people's support is to force the government to intensify repression: 'The police networks, house searches, arrests of innocent people and of suspects, closing off of streets, make life in the city unbearable. The military dictatorship embarks on massive political persecution. Political assassinations and police terror become routine.'[105] Middle-class constitutionalists clamour for free elections, but the masses will see that these are useless and join the revolution.[106]

Clutterbuck considers Marighela, whose comments certainly read like a preview of many aspects of the Ulster conflict, quite specific: 'As soon as a reasonable section of the population begins to take seriously the action of the urban guerrilla his success is guaranteed.' In a more revealing passage, also underlined by Clutterbuck, Marighela states: 'The basic principle of revolutionary strategy in a context of permanent political crisis is to unleash, in urban and rural areas, a volume of revolutionary activity which will oblige the enemy to transform the country's political situation into a military one. Then discontent will spread to all social groups and the military will be held exclusively responsible for failures.'[107] Clutterbuck associates these tactics with the efforts of Grivas in Cyprus, in Robert Taber's phrase, 'to create "the climate of collapse"'.[108] Thus Provisional bombing and other activities can all be seen as efforts to make life unbearable for the ordinary people, either directly or through anti-subversive repression. The ordinary people then vent their rage, not on the terrorists responsible, but on the established authorities.

This theory has often been applied by opponents of terrorism. Student rebels in the late 1960s were adept at provoking authorities into over-reaction and thus ensuring radical leadership of a formerly apathetic mass. It is a theory mirroring that of Provisional propagandists against Kitson. Indeed, if Colin Wallace, once an insider who later fell foul of the British authorities, is to be believed, Provisional propaganda was in fact close to the truth. According to Wallace, the counter-insurgency task was to 'wean the terrorists away from the population, set them against one another, disorientate them and make their leaders both unpopular with their supporters and the population at large.'[109] Clutterbuck argues against allowing insurgency to spread from Northern Ireland, just as his opponents developed a fear of counter-insurgency being used against British workers. Both are zero-sum conspiratorial theories; both believe in attack as the best means of defence; both maintain that ordinary people are being terrorised by unscrupulous opponents; both insist that they themselves work for the good of the masses, not their exploitation for ulterior ends. Can we dissipate this fog of rationalisation, and penetrate the real moral issues dividing the two sides?

Marighela out of context?

In analysing Kitson, it was found that, though some of his arguments and revelations gave reasonable cover to the Provisional propagandists, they grossly exaggerated both his powers and his malignancy. Was this equally true of Clutterbuck's treatment of Marighela, Grivas and others? Marighela in context certainly argued very strongly against the interpretation that he wished to revolutionise the masses by deliberately making their lives unbearable. He repeatedly insisted that 'revolutionary terrorist acts and sabotage are not designed to kill members of the common people, or upset or intimidate them in any way'. Even the passage cited by Clutterbuck on the guerrilla's need to be taken seriously by the masses was prefaced by declaring that guerrillas must win public support by identifying with popular causes. In a parallel passage, he says 'the stress the guerrilla lays on acting to help ordinary people is the best way of obtaining their support'.[110] This was very similar to the Provisional insistence that they always endeavoured to keep civilian casualties to a minimum by giving adequate warnings when bombs were detonated. What other guerrilla organisation in the world, they asked rhetorically, does that?[111] When eliminating the agents of the repressive government, and in Marighela's case American imperialism, there was little difference in the ruthlessness prescribed. As for economic warfare, Provisionals would have agreed heartily that 'the urban guerrilla is not afraid of dismantling and destroying the present economic, political and social system'. Marighela, moreover, had, like the Provisionals, broken with a Marxist non-violent party. He would also have appreciated the Provisional use of Kitson's remarks on making the legal system subservient to repression; that is precisely what he attributed to the repressive government in Brazil. His insistence on small urban 'focos', rather than regular formations with a clumsy chain of command is, probably coincidentally, close to the Provisional reorganisation of the late 1970s. Like Kitson and MacStiofain, Marighela emphasised the importance of good information sources, suggesting that insurgents, despite the need to retain everything in the head, would have an advantage here over government forces. MacStiofain and Marighela both underlined the importance of open media information,[112] which even Kitson did not disdain.

None of this constitutes an admission that the respective revolutionaries deliberately provoked reprisals against the civilian population. As pointed out in chapter three, this complaint was insinuated by some clerical opponents of the Provisionals and first Revolution IRA. The odd give-away passage can be culled from republican propaganda. The citation of O'Casey's 'you didn't want to die for Ireland' passage was one. In Provisional literature Marighela was mentioned vaguely as a martyr without much attempt to analyse his ideas, but his *Minimanual* seems to have circulated in Northern Ireland.[113] The UDA's *Ulster Loyalist*, on the other hand, was delighted to adopt Clutterbuck's interpretation and to claim that the Provisionals were studying Marighela and Grivas. A higher civilian death rate, it argued, was part of Provisional strategy. Violence would create a clamour for repression which would bear most heavily on the Catholic ghettoes. There PIRA's intimidation would be forgotten when it gave protection against soldiers and police.[114] This exposition invited a reply from the Provisionals, especially as Marighela might have been quoted against loyalist assassination. PIRA preferred to distract by emphasising Kitson. Clutterbuck was certainly attacked in republican journals, but usually alongside Kitson.

Grivas and the IRA

Grivas, however, could be disposed of less easily. In 1974 there was speculation in Dublin's *This Week*, quoted by the *Protestant Telegraph*, that Grivas's EOKA was one of the chief sources of Provisional strategy. Contact between IRA and EOKA in the 1950s at Wakefield prison was emphasised. MacStiofain confirmed this in *An Phoblacht* and in his memoirs. He admitted discussing common ideas but did not develop the Grivas strategy.[115] *An Phoblacht* published an article which showed that EOKA was prepared to kill British civilians, bomb, and execute collaborators and informers. Its stablemate, *The Republican News*, commenting on the *Grivas Memoirs*, declared that 'Grivas himself happens to be a rather unpleasant and arrogant old Fascist, however, it is instructive that the Brits have learned nothing'.[116] The Provisionals, moreover, reversed their opponents' argument by claiming that British squads had assassinated Turks and Cypriots to stir up inter-racial strife.[117] The Officials' *United Irishman* drew the anti-PIRA conclusion that in Cyprus as in Northern Ireland a 'kind of schizophrenia' operated; with both EOKA and the Provisionals, 'people knew that their policy was insane, but national hysteria made them tolerate it'. Ironically, Kitson himself would probably have disagreed with this verdict. Kitson admired Grivas's courage and determination and was happy to salute him in Cyprus when the brigadier, then 'peace keeping', saw him deliberately provoking the Turkish population.[118] Kitson and the Provisionals probably appreciated each other's strategy, but neither could afford to admit it. Sean Cronin, a former IRA chief of staff, is positive that Grivas's 'primitive warfare', also practised by Collins, was the model for the early Provisionals.[119]

PIRA's debt to Taber

Provisionals were less reticent on Taber. The defector, Maria Maguire, claims that not only were Cyprus and Aden direct models for the Provisionals but that Taber's *War of the Flea* (1969) was studied so closely that Ruairí O'Brádaigh bought copies for the seven members of the PIRA army council.[120] In 1982 it was still on sale in republican shops. The book is particularly appropriate in that it not only analyses Grivas's ruthlessness but relates modern guerrilla techniques to the Irish revolution, which sought 'to create an intolerable situation for the occupying power or its government'. Taber does not elaborate the strategy of provoking establishment repression to mobilise political support with the candour of Marighela's two passages, but he describes very clearly how even militarily ineffectual actions by the original IRA had powerful psychological results: 'Newspaper ink flowed more freely than blood'. The arrival of the Black and Tans was 'a godsend to the IRA'. Irish propagandists magnified each incident, the *Irish Bulletin* providing reports of ruthlessness with 'sufficient truth ... to make it credible'. This applied equally to PIRA's use of Kitson and Arthur Griffith's use of Amritsar. Taber is similarly perceptive in his analysis of *Grivas's Memoirs*. In Cyprus the British were goaded into one counter-productive action after another. He does not play down the more controversial aspects of Grivas's ruthlessness, such as the use of school-children as young as ten, for which the Provisionals have also been attacked. But Taber is sympathetic to revolution and insists that it can never be defeated while grievances and guerrillas remain. Grivas didn't simply blackmail the British out. As in Ireland, 'EOKA was an expression of the popular will, and, this being so, the British could have remained only by making war on the entire population'.[121]

Herein lies the real difference between Taber and writers like Clutterbuck. They may agree that revolutionaries use ruthless means to win the support of their communities and destroy the morale of the occupying power but they part company on whether grievances are real or artificially created. Hence the Provisionals openly praised Taber's *War of the Flea* as an 'excellent' work and related it to their guerrilla war. They fully endorsed his opinion that extermination was the only answer to insurgents who refused to surrender. Taber helped to educate at least one hunger striker of 1981. Ironically, Taber was also praised by the *Protestant Telegraph* which used his anatomy of revolution to classify Northern Irish events since 1969. However, it regarded him as a weapon to castigate the weakness of a British government apparently retreating from terrorism without a fight.[122] At any rate, all—Kitson, Marighela, Clutterbuck, Paisley, O'Brádaigh, and MacStiofain—could agree with Taber that guerrilla or revolutionary war 'is the extension of politics by means of armed conflict'.[123]

Loyalists and the propaganda of violence

So far this chapter has focused mainly on the mutually antagonistic attempts at self-justification by the Provisionals and the British Army. The loyalist paramilitaries were delighted to adopt British Army arguments against the Provisionals, while the latter endeavoured to make loyalist violence appear the result of Kitsonian provocation. But how did the loyalists justify their own actions? There was the usual inconsistency and division. Paisley, for example, approved of Kitson and regarded SAS stakeout killings as 'summary execution'. The assassination of the Provisional Sinn Féin president, Maire Drumm, was 'extermination', according to a letter published in the *Protestant Telegraph*. An article in the same paper accused the dead woman of never risking her neck but stirring up trouble with fiery speeches.[124] Similar criticism was applied to Paisley himself. Despite extremely divisive rhetoric, which hinted at ruthless measures against the Catholic population in association with the Third Force and the earlier UPV, and contacts with paramilitary leaders, nothing specifically illegal could be proved against him. On the contrary, it was insisted in the *Protestant Telegraph* that 'it is not part of the Protestant ethic or resistence mentality to engage in a murder campaign'.[125] Though

Roman Catholics were likely to commit genocide, Dr Paisley declared, 'Let Protestants not imitate Rome.' Killing Roman Catholics and burning their churches 'reduces Protestantism to the level of the Roman Church which the Bible states is drunk with the martyr's blood.'[126] Such a passage, ostensibly deprecating violence while simultaneously encouraging hatred, is typical of Paisley's rhetorical strategy. He could protect himself by claiming that it was their duty to evangelise not terrorise 'our Roman Catholic fellow countrymen'. Even John Knox himself had found it difficult to rein misguided Protestants of the 'rascal multitude'. In practice, however, the genocidal propensities of Roman Catholics impressed Prot-stats more than their convertibility to Free Presbyterianism. By maintaining his balancing act between verbal violence and incitement to action, Paisley evaded responsibility for the physical force which he always disavowed. His threats of independent action were designed to goad the security forces into more aggressive action rather than to take it himself. This was a variant of provocation akin to that attributed to his opponents. Yet Paisley's endorsement of the most ruthless action by the security forces was conditional. When counter-subversion was used on loyalists, Paisley reacted as vigorously as any Provisional.

Prot-stats' indiscretions

As indicated above, the Protestant paramilitaries were dissatisfied with Paisley. Unlike him, they needed to justify their undoubted violence. Like the republicans, they argued that it was minimal and defensive. The UDA used the UFF as a cover to evade the issue: its paper even published a letter from a Long Kesh prisoner insisting that the UFF was a Provisional organisation.[127] This was scarcely convincing propaganda. The UDA and UVF followed the Provisionals and emphatically denied making war on civilians. They rejected, however, each other's humane claims. Similarly, the Officials insisted that Provisionals attacked Protestant workers, not military targets. The UVF denounced 'the "romper room" where men, women and innocent teenagers have been brutalised and murdered in filthy secret UDA courts'. The UDA dismissed the UVF as delinquents who 'spent all night long polishing their leather jackets, and robbing milkmen, old-aged pensioners and kiddies' piggy-banks',[128] often in alliance with the OIRA. Neither Prot-stat paramilitary was as sophisticated in its defence of violence as the Provisionals. Presenting a petition against the power-sharing executive, the *Ulster Loyalist* roared; 'WHY THE HELL SHOULD WE

WORRY WHETHER WE ARE ACCUSED OF INTIMIDATION OR NOT'.[129] In May 1974, when the UVF blew thirty residents of Dublin and Monaghan into eternity, Sammy Smyth, the UDA spokesman, gloated on television that he was 'very happy about the bombings in Dublin'. Two years later he gave the most ferocious interview of the period to *Gown*. Legitimate targets, he said, were 'people who act against the state or give passive or active support to those who do'. As for innocent Catholics, 'war exists in Northern Ireland and in a war situation there are no innocent people'. No prisoners would be taken in the almost inevitable civil war. 'There will be no room for R.C.s in a new state.'[130] Paisley agreed that no neutrality was possible.[131] As late as 1981, the UDA Commander, Andy Tyrie, admitted that his organisation had originally killed Roman Catholics indiscriminately, believing them all to be Provisionals.[132] As for the UVF, 'We are not particularly concerned whether world opinion is on our side or not. We are not particularly concerned about the effects of the war effort on the economy—we would rather be paupers and free than rich men in chains.'[133] There was no need to seek indirect revelations from Brazil to demonstrate how loyalist paramilitaries treated the community.

The UVF, to a greater extent than the initially more reticent UDA, did sometimes try to justify itself. It presented at times an image of regular warfare, reminiscent of Pearse and the insurgents of 1916 on the republican side. Car bombs, booby traps and executions were out. UVF rifle platoons would decide the day. *Combat* was scandalised at the idea of killing teenage girls. 'No Protestant worthy of his high calling as a Soldier of the Faith would justify the slaughtering of an innocent girl and no Papist worthy of his Faith could justify a similar act of treason against God.' Two girls in a mobile shop at Craigavon in 1991 discovered otherwise. In theory the UVF was considerably more ecumenical than Paisley. *Combat*, however, agreed with the latter that the tactics of the enemy were not to be copied and that Protestant tradition from Calvin to William of Orange required ruthlessness against the enemy, but 'the greatest charity and compassion' towards non-combatants. Resistance was legitimate, retaliation (as the pope had said at Drogheda) unacceptable. But what were legitimate targets? Killing a young Queen's University student, Michael Adamson, for IRSP membership, was justified by the CIA's execution of Che Guevara, a hero to Provisionals and some loyalists. Besides, Adamson was an atheist, so the assassination was clearly non-sectarian. Nor was there anything wrong in bombing pubs frequented by the IRA. Innocent people should stay away. Furthermore, civilians inevitably suffered from aerial bombardment in war.[134] This argument, popular with Provisionals, was extended shortly afterwards when the UVF had to justify killing members of the Miami Showband, claiming at least two as Provisionals. The thrust of the previous argument on the humane Protestant tradition of warfare was blunted by the unconscious quotation from Connolly that 'there is no such thing as humane or civilised war.... Now I ask you, what is the difference between the UVF volunteer's bullet and the British soldier's bullet, what is the difference between a UVF man shooting a traitor or gunman and the executioner at Crumlin Road Gaol hanging his victim by the neck until dead?' More generally, 'what, may I ask, is the difference between the bombing of a public house in Belfast and the blockbusting pattern-bombing of German and British cities during the last war?'[135]

Kitson's cynicism?

Some loyalists thus argued like the British Army and the Provisionals. Was there any means of distinguishing between the moral arguments? Kitson is illuminating here. In the introduction to *Gangs and Counter-Gangs*, Kitson's commander in Kenya, General George Erskine, explicitly denied that rules were suspended to accommodate the special operations described. Only in the forest could the security forces 'act in unrestricted manner'. This proviso, instead of closing, opens up the whole debate. Are there in fact areas where normal laws and morality do not apply? Do the Ten Commandments lose validity in forests south of Suez and building sites west of the Lagan? In the book itself, Kitson admits that some people (he does not mention himself) took the law into their own hands. His comment could hardly be more ambiguous. 'Looking back, I am sure that this was wrong. Certainly this sort of conduct saved countless loyalist lives and shortened the Emergency.' Nevertheless, such conduct was frowned upon and rare. Britain's good name was lost for 'a few thousand Africans and a few million pounds of taxpayers' money.' Kitson's attitude converged with that of his Mau Mau opponents. He admits to thinking like a Mau Mau when operating in a pseudo-gang. Moreover, he virtually identified with Mau Mau who 'thought it would be fun to be a gangster and carry a pistol and kill their acquaintances. Their outlook was not far from many young men of spirit anywhere else in the world.' Opponents, perhaps sharing the same 'spirit', have not quoted this give-away passage. Kitson admitted disappointment when his most resourceful enemies were killed. He conceded himself beaten in argument by a young guerrilla, *en route* for the gallows. Accused of murdering white boys, the Mau Mau retorted that the youth of armed Kikuyu would not have secured mercy from the British Army. According to Kitson, 'I had already decided in my own mind that it was rebellion which was wrong. It is no use trying to be critical of the individual incidents which civil war brings in its wake. What is murder from one point of view may be unavoidable unpleasantness from another and even a triumph from a third.' This is the crux. Subsequently in *Bunch of Five* Kitson himself adopts the classic justification of the Provisionals, the UVF, and many other revolutionary organisations. From his Cyprus experience he admits that guerrillas must use any means available, even assassination. This, the future commander of British land forces declared, is more selective than the saturation and nuclear bombing of World War II; the assassin moreover runs more risk.[136]

Republican moralism?

The surprising conclusion that the Provisionals' worst enemy provided a final accolade for their actions is unavoidable. Kitson punctured the Marighela bogey raised by Clutterbuck. Why did the Provisionals fail to quote this passage with glee? Because, unlike Kitson, they could not afford to regard their operations as a 'game', though Dervla Murphy has emphasised their popular song, by Dominic Behan, 'The Patriot Game'.[137] They had to appeal always to the highest standards of morality. The contention that 'terrorists, like great powers, fight dirty' was inadmissible. Provisionals needed to use Kitson against the Catholic Church, and indeed asked the bishops why they did not condemn his views instead of Provisional actions.[138] Kitson had to be totally blackened to provide suitable propaganda. He assisted by asserting that the decline in official religion had relaxed moral standards. The individual soldier could therefore be guided only by legality or expediency.[139] When Kitson conceded that insurgency may sometimes be justifiable, the moral problem dissolved into individual conscience, in which revolutionary and government agent start at par. Who then has the right to cast the first moral stone?

Here Marighela suggests that the urban guerrilla has 'one enormous advantage' over conventional soldiers and police. 'He is defending a just cause, the cause of the people—whereas they are on the side of an enemy the people hate.'[140] This is to turn

Clutterbuck's argument on its head. Northern Ireland differs in many ways from South American dictatorships like Brazil. Nevertheless, there is a common factor, fully recognised by Marighela—nationalism. Provisionals were aided by separate schools, logically opposed by Clutterbuck,[141] instilling the nationalist tradition into the Catholic community. They were not left stranded in the wilderness of Columbia, like the left-wing 'focos' of their inspiration, Che Guevara, a hero even to some UDA men.[142] The notion that the Provisionals are simply a small 'murder gang' provoking an otherwise contented population in West Belfast, the Derry Bogside and the rural areas west of the Bann collapses on analysis. The people there are not, like Kitson, playing a 'game'. He has nothing with which to counteract their arguments, having himself rejected both moral and religious principles. Kitson appears to be a victim of what Taber has called the 'methods fallacy' of the American Army: 'the old-fashioned notion that guerrilla warfare is largely a matter of tactics and techniques, to be adopted by almost anyone who may have need of them, in almost any irregular warfare situation.'[143]

To sum up, we have seen how the British Army and the Provisionals did indeed confront each other with convergent mirror-image attitudes. Both were less than candid in their propaganda but agreed to a surprising extent. Both glossed over the delicate question of their own provocation and in their polemic tried to concentrate all attention on the foe's misdeeds, seen in both cases as a conspiracy likely to spread from Northern Ireland to England. The indiscretions of General Kitson's works gave the Provisionals a distinct advantage in the propagandist war, an advantage which could hardly be neutralised by raising the distant and less convincing spectre of the late Carlos Marighela. The latter was cited in 1984 by Sir John Biggs Davidson, Conservative spokesman on Northern Ireland, to justify an RUC rubber bullet killing.[144] Kitson's phrases were similarly twisted out of context, but he contributed sufficient revealing give-away passages to render even far-fetched assertions credible. The loyalists were no help to the British in view of their confusion over counter-insurgency, welcomed against the Provisionals but totally repudiated when 'Perfidious Albion' turned it on them. Other loyalist arguments tended to be clumsy versions of Provisional propaganda with too many revealing lapses. In the morality debate, Provisional propagandists have, surprisingly, more than held their own, mainly because of the weakness and errors of the opposition. Provisionals thus emerge a goal ahead in the great 'game' of psychological warfare. To keep their lead to the final whistle, however, they must win an even tougher contest over social and economic theory.

Notes

1. Kee, Robert (1972), *The Green Flag: A History of Irish Nationalism*, London: Weidenfeld and Nicolson, 657.
2. See Davis, Richard (1976), *Arthur Griffith*, Dublin: Dublin Historical Association, 30-33 and Davis, 'India in Irish Revolutionary Propaganda, 1905-22', 66-89. For an earlier version of this chapter, see Davis, R. (1986), 'Kitson versus Marigela: The debate over Northern Ireland Terrorism', 179-209.
3. Taber, R. (1972), *The War of the Flea: Guerrilla Warfare—Theory and Practice*, 23. Hyams, E. (1975), *Terrorists and Terrorism*, London: Dent, 165 and Lasswell, E. Dwight (1963), *Politics: Who gets what, when, how*, Cleveland: Meridian, 55.
4. Hayes-McCoy, G.A., quoted in Richard Davis, (1974) *Arthur Griffith and Non-Violent Sinn Féin*, 167.
5. RN, 30 April 1972, 'The Modern Sinn Féin of 1972 is the same organisation as was founded in 1905 and has the same objectives as it set itself in 1918.'
6. Clutterbuck, Richard (1973 and 1975), *Protest and the Urban Guerrilla*, London: Cassell; *Living with Terrorism*, London: Faber.
7. Kitson, Frank ([1971] 1975), *Low Intensity Operations: Subversion, Insurgency, Peace-keeping*, London: Faber.
8. UI, February 1976.
9. AP, 5 and 19 August 1993.
10. *Law* (2, 39) 1973.
11. Lindsay, K. (1980), *The British Intelligence Services in Action*, Dundalk: Dundrod Press, 84. The UDA's *Freedom Fighter*, June 1992, declared that truth had become a casualty in the British pursuit of Kitson's 'large scale persuasion'. Kingsley, Paul (1989), *Londonderry Revisited: A Loyalist Analysis of the Civil Rights Controversy*, Belfast: Belfast Publications, 204. Clutterbuck was also criticised for swallowing NICRA propaganda whole.
12. Marighela, C. (1971), *For the Liberation of Brazil*, Harmondsworth: Penguin.
13. MacStiofain, *Memoirs of a Revolutionary*, 72.
14. Devlin, P. (1975), *The Fall of the N.I. Executive*, Belfast: P. Devlin, 121.
15. Bradford, Roy (1981), *The Last Ditch*, Belfast: Blackstaff, 29.
16. Kitson, Frank (1960), *Gangs and Counter-Gangs*, London: Barry & Rockliffe.
17. *Low Intensity Operations*, 2, 68.
18. Clutterbuck, *Protest and the Urban Guerrilla*, 137.
19. Clutterbuck, *Protest*, 71.
20. *Low Intensity*, 92.
21. *The Last Ditch*, 29.

22. Faulkner, Brian (1978) *Memoirs of a Statesman*, (ed. John Houston), London: Weidenfield and Nicholson, 317, and for Tuzo's reluctance, 121.
23. Kitson, Frank (1977), *Bunch of Five*, London: Faber, 58-9.
24. *Low Intensity*, 72; RN, 6 August 1977; MacStiofain, 195.
25. *Low Intensity*, 5 and AP, 12 July 1974.
26. MacStiofain, 195.
27. Winchester, Simon (1974), *In Holy Terror: Reporting the Ulster Troubles*, London: Faber, 154-5 and 163. Noticed by RN, 8 March 1975.
28. *Bunch of Five*, 53 talks of the futility of the blind 'Dante' round-up in Kenya.
29. MacStiofain, 194.
30. *Protest*, 94-6.
31. MacStiofain, 195, 198 and 202-3.
32. *Low Intensity*, 98.
33. MacStiofain, 177. See Parker Report (Cmd. 4901) March 1972, 5. On the same page it claimed that the interrogator identified 700 IRA men.
34. *Low Intensity*, 130 and 117.
35. *Gangs and Counter-Gangs*, 126-7; *Low Intensity*, 199; *Bunch of Five*, 32 (filing cabinet), 47 (changing prisoners' allegiance by use of stick, carrot, and appeal to self-respect).
36. Wright, Peter (1988), *Spycatcher: The Candid Autobiography of a Senior Intelligence Officer*, Melbourne: Heineman, 358.
37. UI, 1.72.
38. *Gangs and Counter-Gangs*, 59 (unco-operative prisoner), 126 (chains), and 132 (horseplay etc.). *Bunch of Five*, 290. *Low Intensity*, 142 (breakdown prisoner). See Dowling, Peter, on 'Pseudo Gangs', RN, 5 November 1977. Wamweya, J. (1971), *Freedom Fighter*, Nairobi : East Africa Publishing House,185-6.
39. MacStiofain, 198.
40. RN, 19 January 1974.
41. *Living with Terrorism*, 68-70.
42. See Chris Walker, 'Senior Officers concerned about subversive faces', *Times*, 23 May 1972, and letters (Patrick Wall, MP, and James Lindsay pro Kitson; Denis Christian and Brian Stevens worried 26 May 1972. Kitson was also quoted in SP, 31 October 1971. See also Page, Bruce and Chester, Lewis (1972), 'The Guns of the New Model Army', ST, 14 May 1972, and Kelly, James (1976), *Genesis of Revolution*, Dublin: Kelly Lane, 26 and 35.
43. *Low Intensity*, 3, 25, 83, 24.
44. See *Times*, 10, 13, 23 June 1972 and 8 July 1972. AP, 5 June 1974 (Wigg).
45. *Low Intensity*, 8-9.
46. Peter Dowling in RN, 20 December 1975.
47. See Paul Foot, *Who Framed Colin Wallace?*, 37-114 (Foot, 78 cites Kitson as a source for the extreme right-wing disinformation strategy), 'The Clockwork Orange', and Peter Wright, *Spycatcher*, 363 and 368-72. It was suggested that Wilson, as a Soviet spy, may have murdered his predecessor as leader of the Labour Party, Hugh Gaitskell.
48. UI, June 1972., May 1973.

49. RN, 25 January 1975; AP, 24 May 1990.
50. RN, 20 September 1975.
51. RN, 4 September 1976 and AP, 24 August 1977.
52. While reviewing Anthony Babington (1990), *Military Intervention in Britian from the Gordon Riots to the Gibraltar Incident*, London: Routledge, Deidre Nic an tSaoir cited chapter four of Kitson's *Warfare as a Whole*, AP, 3 September 1992.
53. Marx and Engels, *Ireland and the Irish Question*, 394-5.
54. RN, 23 April 1977.
55. *Constabulary Gazette* (CG), May 1972.
56. PT, 21 June 1975.
57. McGuffin, J., *Internment*, 183, ft. 7 and Devlin, *The Fall of the NI Executive*, 119.
58. Hill, C. (1971), *Antichrist in Seventeenth-Century England*, London: CUP, 174 and 177.
59. *Low Intensity*, 88.
60. MacStiofain, 257.
61. *Low Intensity*, 69.
62. It was still making the point, complete with photograph, in AP, 5 August 1993.
63. *Bunch of Five*, 30-31; *Gangs and Counter-Gangs*, 44-5.
64. Dillon, M. and Lehane, D. (1973), *Political Murder in Northern Ireland*, 314 and 318. AP, 15 February 1974, regarded Dillon and Lehane as British propagandists, but RN, 24 November 1973, and 2 November 1974, found them useful, despite their criticism of PIRA, in demonstrating the extent of loyalist assassination. Farrell, *Northern Ireland: the Orange State*, 390, however, believes them 'sympathetic to loyalists'. Supergrasses, AP, 15 September 1983.
65. MacStiofain, 320, 317, 319-20. See also P. Dowling's article on Kitson, "'Special Operations' from Kiambu to Twinbrook", RN, 29 October 1977. MacStiofain believes the incident a demonstration of Kitson's weakness in defence. See also, Foot, *Who Framed Colin Wallace?*, 28.
66. RN, 21 May 1977; AP, 18 May 1977, and 29 June 1977. (Little to fear from such a vain and arrogant agent). For Nairac's assassination of John Green, see Duncan Campbell, 'Victims of the "dirty war"', *New Statesman*, 4 May 1984. Foot, *Who Framed Colin Wallace?*, 365. For Nairac assessment see AP, 27 May 1993, review by Art MacEoin of Anthony Bradley (1992), *Requiem for a Spy*, Mercier.
67. AP, 8 February 1978.
68. AP, 7 and 14 July 1979.
69. AP, 17 June 1978.
70. RN, 21 September 1974.
71. AP, 4 March 1982.
72. See Gerry Adams interview with the *Sunday World*, quoted by AP, 10 February 1979. He admitted the backlash a real possibility but the superior thought and action of the Provos would deter loyalists experienced only in assassination. See also comments on failure of Paisley's 1977 strike. AP, 18 May 1977. SP, December 1976: Loyalist bluff never called.

73. AP, 15 February 1974; RN, 18 June 1977.
74. RN, 7 May 1977.
75. RN, 3 April 1977. The English historian A.J.P. Taylor was quoted against the possibility of a bloodbath on Britain's withdrawal from Northern Ireland. See AP, 13 September 1970.
76. RN, 12 July 1975, 10 December 1977; AP, 25 January 1977, 7 September 1977, 2 November 1977.
77. *Low Intensity*, 87 and 49 (Mao's water), commented on by RN, 9 April 1977 and AP, 30 June 1988.
78. For Kitson associated with death squads, AP, 16 January 1992.
79. For Brian Nelson and Stevens Inquiry, AP, 4 July 1991; for Littlejohns, AP, 28 August 1993, Holroyd and Wallace, AP, 16 January 1992. Other important whistle blowers, David Seaman and Albert Walker Baker, AP, 27 May 1993. Howroyd, Fred (1989), *War Without Honour* (with Nick Burbridge), Hull: Medium, was reviewed 11 January 1990.
80. *Low Intensity*, 87. Attacked RN, 28 September 1974, 15 February 1975, 20 September 1975, 21 August 1976.
81. SDLP News, 5 October 1973, and Devlin, P., *The Fall of the N.I. Executive*, 121 and 123.
82. RN, 21 August 1976, 11 December 1976 and AP, 29 August 1991.
83. *Low Intensity*, 71 and 77, 'quoted' by RN, 19 March 1977 and Taylor, Peter [1979], 'Reporting Northern Ireland', *The British Media and Ireland*, London: The Campaign for Free Speech in Ireland, 22. See also 18. There is a considerable discrepancy in the different versions. Curtis, Liz, *Ireland: the Propaganda War*, 229-237, is useful on British policies.
84. RN, 21 May 1977.
85. Foot, *Who Framed Colin Wallace?*, 33.
86. AP, 14 December 1973. AN, 7 December 1973.
87. RN, 24 November 1973.
88. *Gangs and Counter-Gangs*, 166-9, 14 and 150. *Bunch of Five*, 42-3. Kitson kept guard while his African agents administered the oath.
89. *Gangs and Counter-Gangs*, 118. For executions see Clayton, Anthony (1976), *Counter-Insurgence in Kenya, 1952-60*, Nairobi: Transafrica Publishers, 15 and 54.
90. *Ireland and the Irish Question*, 214.
91. See C (4, 4) 1977; *UDA News*, November 1971; *Official UDA News* (1, 12,) 1972; RN, 5 December 1971, and 19 October 1974; PT, 12 June 1971, LN, 2 August 1975, etc.
92. AP, 9 May 1975.
93. AP, 11 April 1975, 2 May 1975.
94. UI, May 1975.
95. RN, 17 May 1975, 22 January 1977.
96. ST, 14 May 1972. Bruce Page and Lewis Chester refer to Kitson's image as 'a systematic and callous anti-democrat'.
97. PT, 27 May 1967 on the pope's visitation of famine on India.
98. AP, 1 March 1974; RN, 27 March 1976, 5 June 1976; AP, 12 January 1984.
99. Kelly, J., *Genesis of Revolution*, 112-114.

100. *Low Intensity*, 33. For Provisional discussion of focus see RN, 4 September 1977 (Debray's Critique of Arms) and AP, 23 February 1980 in O'Dowd, 'Cuba—"Tear away the mask"', which refers to Marighela.
101. *Protest*, 117.
102. MacStiofain, 226.
103. *Protest*, 98 (phone calls), 105 (stupidity), 127 (tartans).
104. For criticism of Clutterbuck on Bloody Sunday see AP, 6 April 1973, quoting G. Glennon in *Irish Press*, 6 March 1973.
105. Quoted by *Protest*, 248.
106. For Marighela (n.d.), *Minimanual of the Urban Guerrilla*, n.p.: Grassroots Publications, (39). In a more revealing passage (27) he explains how guerrillas can attack from a mass demonstration. Terrorism he regards (33) as 'armed propaganda'. For *Minimanual* passage see also *Community Forum*, February 1973, 6, which quotes it in full. A similar argument appears in 'Handbook for the Urban Guerrilla' quoted in Marighela, C., *For the Liberation of Brazil*, 94-5.
107. Marighela, *For the Liberation*, 46. Clutterbuck, *Protest*, 219.
108. *The War of the Flea*, 31.
109. Foot, *Who Framed Colin Wallace?*, 27.
110. *For the Liberation*, 112 and 94 and *Minimanual, Community Forum*.
111. RN, 9 June 1973.
112. *For the Liberation*, 63 (economic warfare), 127 (break with Marxists), 105-6 (legal system), 77-8 and 115 (good information). MacStiofain, 101-3.
113. AP, 2 and 23 February 1980. Two Marighela passages are quoted in Provisional Sinn Féin (1982), *Notes For Revolutionaries*, n.p.: Republican Publications, 24-5 and 35. These assert the priority of revolutionary action and the duty of revolutionaries to the revolution itself.
114. UL, 14 November 1974.
115. PT, 24 August 1974, 10 August 1974; UL, 22 March 1975; MacStiofain, 77-79. See also AP, November 1971.
116. AP, 12 April 1974; RN, 2 June 1973.
117. AP, September 1972.
118. UI, August 1974. *Bunch of Five*, 263.
119. Cronin, *Irish Nationalism*, 208.
120. McGuire, M. (1973), *To Take Arms: A Year in the Provisionals*, London: Macmillan, 74. For PIRA papers on Taber see *Tatler*, 4 1971, *Volunteer*, 50 and 59 1972.
121. Taber, 91. (intolerable situation), 95 (newspaper ink), 96 (Black and Tans), 107 (Grivas and children), 151 (war on whole population).
122. Nelis, Thomas, RN, 13 July 1974, 8 January 1977; AP, 19 September 1981; PT, 7 February 1976.
123. Taber, 26.
124. PT, 11 March 1978, 13 November 1976.
125. PT, 6 January 1973.
126. PT, 15 September 1973.
127. UL, 21 March 1974.
128. UDAN (1, 29) 1972; C, June 1975; UI, October 1971; UL, 22 March 1975.

129. UL, 31 January 1974. For Loyalist paramilitary rivalries, see Nelson, *Ulster's Uncertain Defenders*, 190, etc.
130. Fisk, R., 233. SP, 4/76. For *Gown* see RN, 14 February 1976.
131. PT, 18 September 1976.
132. AP, 6 June 1981, quotes *Washington Star* interview with Mary McGory.
133. C, October 1975.
134. C, (1, 33) 1974 and July 1975.
135. C, September 1975.
136. *Gangs and Counter-Gangs*, 46 (law in own hands), 179 (thinking like Mau Mau), 126 (fun to be gangster), 287 and 72 (disappointment), 174 (worsted in argument); *Bunch of Five*, 236. RN, 25 January 1975 quoted Frederic Raphael, reviewing Hyams, Edward (1975) *Terrorists and Terrorism*, in the *Observer*, 19 January 1975, that terrorists are feared because of their courage.
137. *Low Intensity*, 131. Murphy, D., *A Place Apart*, 190. RN, 4 June 1977, quotes 'game'. Fields, Rona (1977), *Society under Siege: A Psychology of Northern Ireland*, Philadelphia: Temple, 27, argues that Dominic Behan's poem is lived, not sung, by the children of Belfast and Derry.
138. AP, 12 April 1977 and RN, 2 November 1974.
139. *Bunch of Five*, 302.
140. Marighela, *For the Liberation*, 64.
141. *Protest*, 50.
142. RN, 24 August 1975 (UDA man with Che on cage locker). For several references to the RN, 6 March 1974 (linked with Pearse, etc.); 8 October 1977 (Juan Sosa's article uses him to justify violence) and 15 October 1977; UI, September 1971; AP, 5 July 1974.
143. Taber, 20.
144. For John Biggs Davidson, see interview with Janet Cohen on BBC Radio 4 World Tonight, 13 August 1984.

7 The convergence of orange and green socialism

The Marxist quagmire

As every Northern Ireland schoolchild knows, the Marxist debate in the Province is dominated by two basic antagonistic schools. The traditional Marxists see the essential problem as one of 'false consciousness'. Catholic and Protestant workers are misled by the British government, aided and abetted by Ulster employers, into sectarian disputes which prevent the formation of a powerful, united trade union movement capable of improving living conditions for all. It follows that 'false consciousness' keeps Ireland disunited. On the other hand, revisionist Marxists emphasise the 'uneven development' of the Northern and Southern Irish economies. This 'uneven development', which saw the North industrialise in the nineteenth century while the South lagged behind as a poor agrarian community, provides intellectual justification for Ulster workers to pursue their objectives in the context of the British economy. To recycle the tired old joke, assertion of communism in Northern Ireland is an insufficient descriptor: it is essential to declare whether one is a nationalist or a unionist communist.

The doyen of Northern Ireland interpretation, the late Professor John Whyte, considered that both schools of Marxism had contributed much to the ongoing debate. Michael Farrell's *The Orange State* and Eamonn McCann's *War and an Irish Town* were excellent examples of traditional Marxist interpretation, while the innovatory and well-researched BICO pamphlets and numerous works by scholars such as Paul Bew and Henry Patterson effectively expressed the revisionist Marxist viewpoint. Whyte ultimately rejected both interpretations as flawed explanations for the Northern Ireland conflict, demonstrating that the variety of opinion on each side made the perception of any coherent Marxist viewpoint difficult. Though Whyte was no friend to the Provisionals, the latter were delighted to quote his view that the work of writers such as Bew and Austen Morgan were 'porridge'. Tom O'Dwyer in *An Phoblacht* ridiculed 'the impossible task of dragging loyalism and Marxism together.' He saw these revisionists as middle-class academics attempting to assuage their guilt at the Northern Ireland conflict.[1] Indeed, the unwary analyst must pick his or her way through a minefield of rival ideologies, purporting to be based on Marx or Lenin, with the care required to negotiate a street lined with car-bombs. The problem is compounded by Marx and Engels themselves. In their numerous articles and historical fragments on Ireland they often fell short of the canons of classic Marxist-Leninism, being guilty of crudities such as 'adventurism', 'opportunism', and sometimes even green nationalism. The downfall of communism in Eastern Europe since 1989 suggests that the debate is now irrelevant. But the current world-wide popularity of 'economic rationalism' is not widely shared in Northern Ireland by either loyalists or republicans. They have converged in opposition to European integration and their attitude to capitalism is worth serious analysis, regardless of their capacity to adumbrate sophisticated economic theories.

Unlike the issues of violence and integrated education, the controversy over socialism has seen a less overt conflict between republicans and the Catholic hierarchy. This is surprising in that bishops have traditionally opposed socialism as strongly as violence or non-sectarian education. To some extent denunciations of violence in the current Ulster Troubles have automatically included socialism. Provisionals sometimes used liberation theology against clerical critics. Liberation theology, especially strong in South America, accepts force as necessary in the religious emancipation of mankind from secular injustice.

Though Marx died before the outbreak of Ulster unionist frenzy over Gladstone's first Home Rule bill, and Engels did not analyse the resistance aroused, their work on Ireland provides a mine of precedents which the Provisionals have been unwilling to tap. From their break with the Officials in 1969 to the 1980s, Provisionals kept Marx at arm's length. Similarly, the SDLP insisted on non-Marxist socialism.[2] The OIRA, PD, and IRSP, however, have been less dismissive. On the other side of the divide, the loyalist paramilitaries, though sometimes attempting to appear socially progressive, have repudiated Marxist influence. In most cases fear of religious authorities has been an important factor.

Marx and Engels on Ireland

As their collected Irish writings, made available in 1971 by courtesy of a then communist Moscow, clearly demonstrate, Marx and Engels were antipathetic to Ulster loyalists, rejecting many of their deeply cherished myths. The socialist pioneers saw the seventeenth-century Ulster plantations as the pernicious destruction of a co-operative society based on the Brehon laws, and denied the perennial loyalist contention that an appalling massacre of Protestants had taken place in 1641. Engels shed his initial anti-Irish prejudice and joined Marx in defending the Irish character from nineteenth-century English critics like Goldwin Smith. The Irish, Marx and Engels agreed, were far better revolutionary potential than the English. By the 1860s, Marx believed that English resistance would be triggered by initial revolution in Ireland, where the English ruling classes possessed great estates. In the First International they fought hard to destroy anti-Irish prejudice in English working-class leaders. Even more relevant to the 1970s and 1980s was their long battle on behalf of Fenian prisoners suffering atrocious gaol conditions. Marx's daughter, Jenny, played a significant role in securing the release of O'Donovan Rossa. In their treatment of the Catholic Church Marx and Engels were very close to the republican tradition. Marx emphasised the 'disgusting subserviency' of the Catholic bishops at the time of the 1800 Act of Union between Great Britain and Ireland. He was most impressed with the secularism of the Fenians and insisted that the English had driven the Irish people into the hands of the Catholic clergy. In *Capital I* he complained that one million Irish died in the famine, while 'to the wealth of the country it did not the slightest damage'. The Irishman, banished to the United States by the sheep and the ox, re-appeared as a Fenian. Like Arthur Griffith in his subsequent Sinn Féin programme, Marx insisted on Ireland's right to levy tariffs on British goods.[3]

The Connolly legacy

Though such arguments became commonplace in republican polemics, Marx himself filtered through the works of James Connolly. Was the latter ultimately a nationalist or a socialist? Was his final re-conversion to Catholicism before his execution as a 1916 Rising leader the key to his career? These issues have been much discussed. Inevitably current political polemic has treated Connolly like Thomas Davis, producing conveniently emasculated versions to suit the convenience of particular groups. Rather than enquiring whether Connolly was a true Marxist according to some current school of thought, it is essential to see whether Provisionals were justified in divorcing him from Marx in their own socialist tradition. 'Stop using James Connolly as a respectable crutch for Marx', complained the Officials.[4]

Connolly's *Labour in Irish History*, first published in 1910, provided a basis for a republican tradition of Irish socialism. Wolfe Tone he depicted as building his hopes 'upon the successful prosecution of a Class War, although those who pretend to imitate him today raise up their hands in holy horror at the mere mention of the phrase.' Connolly's biographer, Desmond Greaves, agrees that Tone's 'works are full of class judgements'. The Provisionals have persistently praised Greaves while denigrating subsequent 'revisionist' writers on Connolly.[5] It was Connolly who popularised Henry Joy McCracken's 'The Rich always betray the Poor' remark. He wrote on William Thompson, 'the first Irish socialist: a forerunner of Marx', without trying, as some republicans have done, to disparage the latter. Thompson, as Connolly argued, anticipated Marx by emphasising the importance of class war, but it was left to the latter as 'his chief and crowning glory' to see it 'as THE factor in the evolution of society towards freedom'. Connolly quoted extensively from Marx's *Capital*, 'his great work', to demonstrate that Irish wages failed to keep up with the cost of living. Like Marx, Connolly denounced the anti-labour attitude of Daniel O'Connell, but Marx and Engels appeared to have known little or nothing of William Thompson, James Fintan Lalor, and the Ralahine co-operative experiment, all emphasised by Connolly.[6] On Ulster, Connolly endeavoured to expose loyalist myths, as did Marx and Engels with a slightly different emphasis. Connolly pointed out that the battle of the Boyne was 'no demonstration of Protestant freedom as it led to the persecution of Presbyterians no less than Catholics'. Protestantism in the north of Ireland, he argued in 1913, was unique in that it equalled 'lickspittle loyalty' and 'servile worship of aristocracy', while Catholicism, elsewhere synonymous with these, was in Ireland associated with rebellion and democracy.[7] He saw Orangemen as slaves because they were reared amongst Catholics whose slavishness was greater than their own. Marx applied a similar analysis to the Irish and English working classes. Connolly, who had had some experience of organising the north-east, maintained that Orange workers were the product of false consciousness which prevented them from seeing the extent of their actual poverty. With Marx, he emphasised the divide and rule tactics of the British government.[8] On the whole, there is little essential difference between Connolly and Marx on the Ulster question.

Socialism, encyclicals and the first Irish Revolution

Every Churchman knew that Marx was an atheist, even if he understood nothing further of Marxism. Certainly the early Marx was much preoccupied in discovering in religion the alienation of man from his true nature. Modern exponents of liberation theology like J.P. Miranda, however, have found parallels between St Paul and Marx in the totality of their respective rejections of religious and secular sin.[9] In Connolly's time few Irish clerics were interested in such parallels. Leo XIII had spoken out against socialism in his great encyclical, *Rerum Novarum* (1891). While sympathetic to the working classes, he insisted, like Aquinas, that private property, though natural, be used for the general good. Leo allowed trade union association, but stigmatised socialism as dangerous to religion and family life. Connolly confronted *Rerum Novarum* in his answer to Fr Robert Kane, SJ, in 1910.

In the resultant *Labour, Nationality and Religion* Connolly defended Marx's materialist conception of history and theory of surplus value. The former idea, not essential to socialist thought, was also attributed by Connolly to Duns Scotus and William Thompson. Connolly provided ammunition for subsequent republican debate by citing St Clement, St Basil the Great, St Gregory Nic., St Ambrose, St Gregory the Great, and St John Chrysostom against absolute property rights. St Ambrose seemed particularly apt: 'It is nature itself that has given birth to the right of the community whilst it is only unjust usurpation that has created the right of private property.'[10] In fact *Rerum Novarum*, by quoting Aquinas's adaption of Aristotle's distinction between private property and the obligation to use it for public benefit, had undermined this type of interpretation.[11] Connolly was on stronger ground when he talked of the unjust usurpation which constituted the basis of Irish property rights. Much of his argument is in fact *tu quoque*. Are socialists anti-national? What about the Jesuits? As for atheism, Connolly seized upon an admission by Fr Kane that socialism was not logically incompatible with Christianity and left it at that. Connolly dismissed the likelihood of violence, considering capitalists as the most probable instigators. By associating the Reformation with capitalism he made Fr Kane appear the ally of Protestantism. Finally, Connolly reached the desired conclusion that 'Socialism is neither Protestant nor Catholic, Christian nor Freethinker, Buddhist, Mahometan, nor Jew: it is only HUMAN.'[12] This effective polemic answered clerical objections without addressing any of the deep issues. In the 1970s Provisionals could argue with equal conviction that either Connolly had refuted *Rerum Novarum* or that he had done no such thing. A probing loyalist critic considered Connolly's condemnation of the Church 'as strident as anything from the pages of the *Loyalist News*'.[13]

The issues were hardly clarified by Pearse's *Sovereign People,* which followed Connolly in exalting the maverick Young Ireland land reformer of the 1840s, Lalor. The latter was clearly no socialist in the modern sense but one who hoped to use would-be peasant proprietors as the driving force of the Irish Revolution. After Connolly's execution, there were many who shared Sean O'Casey's belief that Connolly had sold out socialism. Some modern academic interpreters have followed this tendency to see him as at best 'a green' socialist rather than a true 'red' internationalist.[14] However, even Marx argued that the Irish and the Poles 'are most internationalistic when they are nationalistic'. The Provisionals rejected 'revisionist' arguments that Connolly abandoned socialism in 1916 and maintained that even Marxists accepted 'a situation where an armed uprising can be a prelude to an awakening of the mass of the people.'[15] Nevertheless, the socialist element of the republican tradition was perceptibly attenuated after the Rising. The 1916 Proclamation hinted vaguely at the social ownership of Ireland and the 1919 Democratic Programme of Dail Eireann, which raised the hackles of some conservatives, were hardly incompatible with *Rerum Novarum*. The contemporary programme of the United States bishops, which permitted nationalisation on a fairly wide scale, was probably more advanced.

Subsequent republicans regarded the civil war prison letters of Liam Mellows as indicative of true socialism. But Mellows merely argued for the extension of the Democratic Programme to controlling, not owning, industry for the benefit of the working classes, and for banking to benefit industry and agriculture before profit.[16] This was little enough on which to build a tradition but in the 1920s and 1930s, attacked by both Catholic hierarchy and unionists, socialism was very much on the defensive in both the six and twenty-six counties.[17] The anti-Treaty IRA's attempts to register left-wing tendencies in offshoots like the Republican Congress and Saor Eire were soon stamped out. The abolition of proportional representation in the north-east made labour organisation difficult, if not impossible, in the face of the unionist monolith: Connolly's much quoted 'carnival of reaction' certain to follow partition. In 1931, Pius XI published the encyclical *Quadragesimo Anno*, which developed the ideas of Leo XIII. Private property was reaffirmed and even moderate socialism condemned for advocating a social welfare liable to destroy true liberty and true authority. However, it was argued that free competition had been effectively killed by huge industrial and financial complexes. A middle way between socialism and unbridled monopoly capitalism was seen in the establishment of semi-independent corporations as a buffer between the individual and the State.[18] The Irish constitution made some genuflections towards the encyclicals, and for a time, as John Whyte has demonstrated, the issue in the twenty-six counties appeared to be Catholic ideology versus British administration rather than anything of native Irish provenance.[19] Education throughout the period was based in theory on this principle of private initiative buttressed by public sustenance, despite Connolly's demand for control by secular authorities and lip-service to the advantages of common secular instruction.[20]

New alignments in the 1960s

By the late 1960s both Irish jurisdictions appeared to be moving towards a greater social awareness. Some intellectual socialists like David Thornley and Conor Cruise O'Brien entered the Dail to invigorate a defensive and ineffectual Irish Labour Party. In the north, after calling off its futile 'border campaign' of 1956-62, the IRA under Cathal Goulding studied Marxism and non-violence. Vincent Browne in his *Magill* exposure of the OIRA claims, however, that the radicalism achieved by 1968 has been much exaggerated. The IRA was still concentrating on relatively minor issues, such as protest 'fish ins', and was very confused in its social thought.[21] On the loyalist side, the anti-ecumenical movement which swept Paisley to the fore was a social rebellion of poorer loyalists against the upper-class 'fur coat' leaders like Terence O'Neill who had hitherto exacted unquestioning obedience. Meanwhile, an increase in the number of tertiary-educated Catholics provided the basis for the People's Democracy with its ambition to unite creeds behind a real secular socialism. While the IRA and old Nationalists disintegrated, PD briefly held the attention of the nationalist community. After 1970 the Provisionals and SDLP manoeuvred them into the position of a critical rump, generally supportive of PIRA.

The IRA split of 1969-70 has naturally been interpreted very differently by Provisional and Official propagandists. The former play down the economic issue. Seán MacStiofain insisted that all revolutions are naturally anti-capitalist, but the break-away group rejected Irish communist or Marxist dictatorship, which it regarded with the same anti-imperialist disdain as British colonialism or 'Free State' capitalism. 'Ours should be the democratic socialism that was preached and practised by the men of 1916.'[22] This formula begged a number of questions. The Officials branded their opponents as sectarian 'Green Tories' financed by the right-wing Fianna Fail government to prevent socialism spreading to the south.[23] This insistence had some initial plausibility but was complicated by other factors. The assumption that the Provisionals were Catholic bigots was partly derived from MacStiofain's earnest Catholicism. MacStiofain was outraged at Dr Roy Johnston, the IRA ideologist, who objected to the Rosary at republican commemorations. Such Marxism, MacStiofain maintained, was not anti-sectarian, but directed against religion as such.[24]

Popes and Provisionals: the aftermath of Vatican II

Also relevant to the Provisional stance were the ambiguities of Connolly himself and the publication of encyclicals like John XXIII's *Mater et Magister* (1961) and Paul VI's *Populorum Progressio* (1967), plus the latter's letter celebrating *Rerum Novarum*, *Octagesimo Adveniens* (1971). Though basically extending the earlier social encyclicals, Pope John appeared particularly liberal, while Paul was attacked in some quarters for approximating Marxism. Thus Avro Manhattan, writing in Paisley's *Protestant Telegraph*, used *Populorum Progressio* as proof of a secret deal between the Vatican and the Russian Communist Party. Like *Time* magazine, Manhattan was struck by the apparent reversal of traditional Catholic arguments insisting on absolute property rights. Their rejection of property rights placed the popes in the same category as Marx and Lenin.[25] Another of Paisley's columnists declared the encyclical an attempt to join the communists whom the Catholic Church had failed to destroy.[26]

Was this indeed a revolutionary assimilation of Roman Catholicism and socialism, ending a century of antagonism between Marx and the Vatican? Popes John and Paul stimulated the liberation theology of men like Archbishop Helder Camara, popular with the subsequent Provisionals, who believed socialism must be embraced with joy.[27] Paul attacked the profit motive and racism. He was even prepared to endorse conditional violence against 'manifest, long-standing tyranny which would do great damage to fundamental personal rights and dangerous harm to the common good of the country'. However, as his successor, John Paul II, pointed out in Drogheda, revolution usually produces other injustices and greater misery.[28] As in the past, the individual decided whether a situation justified revolt. To Paul VI, judging from his approbation of the RUC, Northern Ireland clearly did not.[29] These views appear little more than a restatement of the traditional Thomist doctrine that justifies revolution with a reasonable chance of success if supported by the majority against intolerable tyranny which can be countered in no other way.

But what of property? A careful reading of section 23 of *Populorum Progressio* demonstrates only a slightly updated version of the traditional papal argument that property must be used in the interests of all. This explains the apparently bald statement that 'private property does not constitute an absolute and unconditioned right'. Paul VI placed Connolly's quotations from the Fathers in perspective: St Ambrose had shown that in charity the poor merely received their own from the wealthy. 'The world is given to all, and not only to the rich.' Thus the Aristotelian distinction (commutative justice) between private property and public use was tacitly maintained.[30] A similar view was expressed in John XXIII's *Mater et Magister* which quoted another of Connolly's authorities, St Gregory the Great, on the need for personal charity, not, as Connolly's extract had implied, opposition to property as such. Arguably *Mater et Magister* is more progressive than *Populorum Progressio*.[31] In short, though accusations of communist sympathy are inappropriate, Paul VI and John XXIII did provide scope for a progressive, non-Marxist social programme.

Comhar na gComharsan: Connolly, Nyerere or Paul VI?

This is precisely what the new Provisionals endeavoured to create immediately after their break with the Officials. In the first issue of *An Phoblacht*, February 1970, they put forward a programme of moderate socialism, based on the *Comhar na gComharsan* ('Neighbours' Co-operation') philosophy, traced by Ruairí O'Brádaigh and Seamus O'Mongain to ideas developed by the IRA in a radio talk in 1939 and in their underground *War News* and *United Irishman* in 1940. Its originators were Sean McNeela, and Sean and Gearoid O'Mongain. Appropriately, in light of the discussion above, *Comhar na gComharsan* was based on Irish and Christian values. In the 1940s there had been discussion, clearly inspired by *Quadragesimo Anno*, of 'distributive ownership', the duty of the state to protect a limited private property, and the power of the community to appropriate the excess.[32] But the republican movement could not afford to be seen as a Catholic sectarian body, dependent on an encyclical-based policy formulated when the movement was dominated by the right-wing Sean Russell. The latter's advocacy of an English bombing campaign drove the future Nobel Peace Prize winner, Séan MacBride, and the great guerrilla leader, Tom Barry, out of the movement.[33] It was therefore declared that the ideas of *Comhar na gComharsan* were founded on moral law and 'an integral part' of Catholicism, Protestantism, Judaism, Islam, Gandhism. They were 'an extension of Marxism, insofar as they are opposed to the money dictatorship of the Capitalist system and the political dictatorship of communism in upholding the right and dignity of every human person.'

This flexible doctrine was set firmly in the republican tradition of Tone's men of no property. A passage from Thomas Davis in 1841 advocating cottage industry and peasant proprietorship was also quoted. Connolly had made relatively little use of Davis in his *Labour in Irish History*. As Sean Cronin, a pre-split IRA chief of staff argues, Davis was no radical, but a supporter of a type of distributism derived from Sismondi.[34] Ironically, the Protestant Davis, whose educational views were so unwelcome to the Catholic bishops, dovetailed neatly with the economic philosophy of the social encyclicals. After Davis, the usual representatives of left republicanism, Lalor, Pearse, Connolly, and Mellows were endorsed.

In its specific ideas, *Comhar na gComharsan* did not stray very far from the ideas of the great popes. Emphasis was laid on the nationalisation of the monetary system through the commercial banks and insurance companies. This was entirely in tune with *Quadragesimo Anno* which denounced capitalistic 'dictatorship … most forcibly exercised by those who, since they hold the money and completely control it, control credit also and rule the lending of money.'[35] It also followed the Douglas Credit movement, popular in the Great Depression of the 1930s, which appealed to many wishing to change the economic system without upsetting the class balance. In their desire to nationalise key industries, mines, building lands, and fishing rights, the Provisionals fell well within Catholic guidelines which permitted government ownership of particular enterprises where such were demonstrably in the public interest.[36] Ruairí O'Brádaigh, while generally condemning the 26-county government, praised its initiative in the establishment of the Shannon electricity scheme in 1926, Bord na Mona for turf, and the state sugar authority.[37] In fact, despite governmental rejection of socialism, the public sector of the Irish Republic has been extensive.

In rural areas, *Comhar na gComharsan* advocated the division of large ranches and the establishment of an upper limit for land ownership. This was an old idea ventilated by Arthur Griffith's papers early in the century. Limiting ownership could be based on the principle, derived by *Populorum Progressio* from the Fathers, that 'no one is justified in keeping for his exclusive use what he does not need, when others lack necessities.' The common good must come before 'acquired private rights'.[38] The programme also demanded agricultural co-operatives, developed by Sir Horace Plunkett and George Russell in the first decades of the twentieth century and recommended by John XXIII.[39] Nor was co-operation restricted to agriculture, but extended to large worker-ownership units in fishing, industry and the distributive trades. Ruairí O'Brádaigh hoped that by such means the economies of scale could be married to industrial democracy.[40] Such policies could be derived from old Irish precedents, but co-operation was also emphasised by the encyclicals which endeavoured thus to avert class war. It illustrates the 'principle of subsidiarity' limiting the power of the State. Other features of the Eire Nua programme, fully outlined in a 54-page pamphlet published by Provisional Sinn Féin on 28 June 1972, harmonise with subsidiarity.[41] The most obvious example was the federated four-province Ireland with tiers of authority ascending from powerful local bodies.

The co-operative system of *Comhar na gComharsan* was linked by Ruairí O'Brádaigh to Julius Nyerere's *Ujamaa* (Familyhood) socialism in Tanzania as well as to Fr James McDyer's co-operative experiment at Glencolumbkille in Donegal. *An Phoblacht* advised the Irish to get rid of their colonial attitude and learn from the Africans.[42] As Bob Purdie has pointed out, Nyerere's Catholicism was emphasised. Both his *Ujamaa* idea and Fr McDyer's community experienced difficulties in the late 1970s. The latter's views were praised as based on the monastic ideal, rather than the class struggle.[43] This was precisely the position of Nyerere, who appears to have been well versed in the encyclicals. He denied that African society had anything approximating European classes and wished to build his socialism, independent of Marx and Adam Smith, on the natural African sense of community, similar to that of ancient Ireland. He fully accepted the trusteeship ideal of property, as indicated in his declaration that a millionaire could be a socialist. This was precisely the type of socialism the early Provisionals sought.[44] It was also related to their Third World connection, which appeared in Ruairí O'Brádaigh's 1970 insistence that Irish trade would have to be diversified in directions like Africa where Irish teachers, doctors and missionaries had built up 'a great power-house of good will'.[45]

The *Comhar na gComharsan* programme was thus a cleverly argued attempt to link acceptable Catholic philosophy with Irish traditions dating back to the Brehon Laws. Ruairí O'Brádaigh insisted that it 'achieves a balance between the extremes of freedom and exploitation of man by man', inherent in the capitalism of the USA and EEC on one hand, and the 'much too severe curbs on personal freedom' of communist countries. 'I believe it to be an answer to the middle way sought by an eminent Churchman when he spoke within the past year of avoiding the 'bottomless pit' of Western permissive society and the 'concentration camp' of the Eastern bloc'.[46] This was plain speaking. The basic ideas were developed in the Eire Nua programme. The term 'Christian Socialism' was then appropriated for a movement regarded as the logical outcome of Christianity.[47] Connolly, *An Phoblacht* declared, had derided attempts to blame religious beliefs for social evils. Padraig O'Snodaigh suggested that Connolly might have accepted Catholic social teaching, had it been properly presented in Ireland.[48] This argument opposed Marx who saw religion as part of the superstructure of false consciousness which prevented the proletariate realising its economic interests, an essential issue in the Northern Irish debate. Such Provisional use of Connolly paralleled their insistence that denominational education was not the real cause of division.

The republican debate: encyclicals OK?

Their social philosophy did not make the Provisionals 'green fascists' as their enemies claimed. However, their position was confused. Occasionally, Marx was quoted favourably. Moreover, the party insisted that it stood for 'a free, democratic, socialist, secular Ireland.'[49] O'Brádaigh claimed that the Provisionals aimed at 'the separation of Church and State and the development of a pluralist society'.[50] Debate on these issues appeared in Provisional papers after 1974. Michael Farrell, one of the original PD leaders, took issue with Desmond Fennell, credited with drafting the Eire Nua programme and a regular columnist in *An Phoblacht* under the *nomme de plume* 'Freeman'. To Farrell and PD the object was a socialist way of life and not a Catholic or a Protestant tradition.[51] He was approaching the 'secular religion' which Cronin sees as Wolfe Tone's substitute for warring sects.[52] Some Provisionals evidently felt the same way. Niall Taylor, a Dublin Cumann PRO, insisted in 1977 that it was legitimate for Provisionals to advocate the Marxist struggle and atheism.[53] Fennell as 'Freeman' continued, however, to develop the case for Christian socialism.

In early 1975, Fennell, answering the question whether the Christian social principles were necessarily Catholic, frankly insisted that the overwhelming majority of the movement was Catholic. 'In practice' Sinn Féin 'commits itself to achieving an Ireland based on Catholic social principles. Sinn Féin, due to the inaction of the church authorities, was the only advocate of Christian social principles such as subsidiarity of function, pluralism, and the ultimate rights of the community over private property.'[54] Fennell was prepared to slaughter sacred cows such as the notion that Tone was a socialist.[55] The issue provoked controversy when Maoliosa O'Hanlon, speaking for the Provisionals in Armagh, claimed that the movement's philosophy was based on *Mater et Magister*. Dr Conor Cruise O'Brien, the Provisional *bête noir*, was accused of hinting, apropos O'Hanlon's speech, that the Provisionals were working for Rome. The editor of *An Phoblacht* quickly retorted that the party's ideology was based on the Brehon Laws which pre-dated Christianity. *Mater et Magister*, he said patronisingly, was progressive, in the perspective of Vatican conservatism, as it condemned monopoly capitalism and allowed the nationalisation of vital resources. The republican tradition was not simply Catholic but based on Lalor, Thompson (who anticipated the best of Marx), Jemmy Hope, Connolly, and Pearse.[56] Thus confusion was added to confusion. As

Purdie argued, Pearse obtained from Lalor, not socialism, but a theory basing property on an original social contract. This concept was easily reconciled with the encyclicals.[57] A working-class republican attacked Freeman (Fennell), claiming that Catholic social principles were contrary to republican philosophy. The Provisionals were fighting the Officials, not because they were Marxists or atheists but because 'they have become such died-in-the-wool Stalinists as to make democracy impossible.'[58]

Freeman defended the link with Catholic social principles. They were neither imperalist nor capitalist but supported policies secular in the sense of non-theocratic. There was no need to apologise for *Mater et Magister*; O'Hanlon's mistake was to give the impression that it was the only source. Connolly had quoted St Ambrose and demonstrated that it was possible to be both a Catholic and a socialist.[59] Fennell took up the same theme in 1979 when reviewing a book on Connolly by the French writer, Roger Faligot. Against Faligot and D.R. O'Connor Lysaght, Fennell insisted that Connolly was not a Marxist and that his final acceptance of the sacraments was more than 'the delusion of a dying man'.[60] The non-Marxism of Connolly was at that time virtually a Provisional dogma.[61] Part of the problem probably arose from the fact that, according to Deasun Breathnach, twice editor of *An Phoblacht*, the papal encyclicals, which attacked capitalism as vigorously as Marx, were almost unknown in Ireland.[62]

Provisionals north and south

In 1976 the issue created serious division between *An Phoblacht*, in Dublin, and the *Republican News*, published in Belfast. They disagreed first on the importance of the numerical superiority of the Protestant community in the north, played down by *Republican News*. *An Phoblacht* believed, secondly, that only a 'tiny minority' of Provisionals wanted a socialist objective. *Republican News* attributed this opinion to Fennell who had written recently for the *Irish Times* without mentioning socialism.[63] The debate continued through 1977 and 1978. Christine Elias, then an important spokesperson on Eire Nua, emphatically denied that the programme was Marxist, ridiculing Mairin de Burca, a former Official, for claiming to be both a Marxist and a Christian.[64] Elias, who professed democratic socialism, was countered by Jim Reilly. Marx, said Reilly, had demonstrated the alliance between religion and the establishment, and had also defended O'Donovan Rossa. De Valera, Griffith, Conway, Philbin, Paisley and Cromwell, he complained, were all good Christians.[65] Elias conceded Marxism to be a useful tool without economic determinism, but insisted on man's cultural and emotional nature, never in fact denied by Marx.[66]

Was there a class war? Deasun Breathnach, writing in 1978, pointed out that, although some Provisionals objected to the expression, younger members of the movement were talking of a boss class and a working class. He compromised by citing O'Brádaigh's view that names were irrelevant to the fact that Sinn Féin, alongside Tone, Connolly, and Pearse, stood with the have-nots.[67] More contentious was M. O'Callanain, who, devoted to the ideal of 'subsidiarity of function', insisted that Eire Nua was completely anti-Marxist. Kropotkin's decentralisation and co-operation were more to his liking.[68]

In 1979 *An Phoblacht* and *Republican News* were amalgamated. PD criticised this as stifling debate. The joint paper was edited by the northerner, Danny Morrison. To Sean Cronin it was a takeover by young Belfast Provisionals who were 'defiantly leftist'. Their ideas, he argued, were precisely those of the OIRA leaders in the 1960s that provoked the Provisional breakaway. The northern Provisionals could now condemn the Officials as reformists.[69] Cronin was correct in prophesying the rejection, by 196 out of 294 votes—a two thirds majority at the 1981 Sinn Féin Ard Fheis—of Eire Nua federalism. Northern delegates like Gerry Adams and Danny Morrison believed Eire Nua a sop to loyalists, but Ruairí O'Brádaigh and O'Conaill defended it.[70] The former Provisional chief of staff, Seán MacStiofain, under a cloud since breaking his hunger strike in 1973, resigned from Sinn Féin in protest at the chairman's handling of the debate.[71] However, it would be quite wrong to interpret the 1981 Ard Fheis as representing a move from the 'Christian socialism' of the encyclicals to some more left-wing or Marxist variant. Gerry Adams, leader of the northern Young Turks, was just as insistent in 1979 on avoiding the Marxist tag and grounding the movement's philosophy in the safe, if ambiguous, territory of Tone, Lalor, Connolly, and Mellows. Adams's economic thought developed little by 1986: 'I don't think socialism is on the agenda at all at this stage except for political activists of the left.'[72] Ironically, this was precisely the message of the original founder of Sinn Féin, Arthur Griffith, who insisted that national independence must come before all talk of social reform. Appropriately, at the Sinn Féin Ard Fheis in 1980 an attempt to replace 'Christian' principles with 'Social' principles in the party's objective failed. However, at the 1983 Ard Fheis 'Christian principles' were deleted from the objective and replaced with the republican socialist principles of the Easter Week Proclamation and the 1919 Democratic Programme.[73] A Derry republican summed up the situation very well in early 1982 when he declared that they must accept their roots in 'that contradictory confusing mixture of radical socialism and Catholic conservatism which are our historic elements'. He saw Lalor opposed to O'Connell, Connolly to Griffith, and Mellows to Collins.[74]

Griffith, O'Connell, and Collins should certainly be included in the tradition, despite the conventional republican strictures against them. Griffith, undoubtedly hysterical in his opposition to James Larkin and the 1913 lock-out, like the Provisionals showed many signs of encyclical influence. He sought a middle way between unrestricted capitalism and collectivist socialism, finding it in a type of corporatism. All, however, had to contend with the apparently unmentioned fact, laid down by *Mater et Magister*, that a Catholic is virtually obliged to follow this philosophy, unless they embark on the hazardous distinction between moral and social teaching.[75] On violence and sexual practice, many Irish Catholics follow their own consciences. A social policy acceptable to the Catholic authorities would, nevertheless, offset condemnations of violence, and indeed provide a basis for counter-attack. Total rejection of Catholic teaching and open espousal of Marxism might alienate many supporters and turn the clerical opposition into a crusade. But what of the Officials?

The Officials: real Marxists?

The Officials, after the split and their indefinite ceasefire of 1972, were less exposed to clerical condemnation. Nevertheless, their position was often ambiguous. They naturally capitalised on any weaknesses perceived in the Provisional position. They used O'Hanlon's reference to *Mater et Magister* to demonstrate that Provisional philosophy was a 'blend of sectarianism and anti-working-class power' with echoes of the brown- and blue-shirted 1930s.[76] This ascription of fascism to the production of John XXIII was extreme, but characteristic of the debate. Sometimes the Provisionals were depicted as Provo/Trots who saw a war of national liberation where there was none, and used 'socialist jargon to justify the bombing of children'.[77] Alternatively, they were 'Green Tories' seeking 'some sort of "jihad" or holy war'.[78]

Such attacks, to carry conviction, depended on an effective counter-strategy. Yet in many ways the Officials proceeded almost in tandem with the Provisionals. The former also emphasised the Third World dimension, dropping names like Frantz Fanon[79] and comparing the 'Christians for socialism' resolution of Santiago in 1972 with the failure of Irish Catholic clergy to emulate their South American counterparts.[80] At first the Officals, like the Provisionals, condemned the EEC as 'the biggest danger ever to face the Irish people'.[81] Later there was a complete *volte face* when the movement decided that the EEC could play a useful role in modernising Northern Ireland through multinational power. Full social revolution would then be possible with the prejudice of the Protestant working class eliminated. In the Workers' Party's *The Irish Industrial Revolution* (1977) the cult of small-scale industry from Griffith to Eire Nua was rejected. Pearse and the 1919 Democratic Programme were depicted as half socialist and half populist.[82] Originally, the Officials used the same nationalist stereotypes as the Provisionals. Henry Joy McCracken's rich betraying the poor,[83] probably obtained by Officials via Connolly, was also popular with some loyalists. Tone's 'men of no property' remark was regarded as an essential feature of his vision.[84] Pearse's *Sovereign People*, in which he extolled Fintan Lalor, and to a lesser extent Davis, was the 'touchstone of independence'.[85] When the Marxist Allende government in Chile fell to a right-wing coup, Cathal Goulding, the Officials' chief of staff, attributed the disaster to Allende's failure to emulate Pearse and Connolly by grounding revolution in the consciousness of the working classes, rather than in political institutions.[86] Attacking the control of multinationals in Ireland, an article in the *United Irishman* complained that 'Tone didn't fight so that Pfizer could pour its chemical muck into the Lee. Connolly didn't die so that Weston could push small shopkeepers onto the road and IBM operate without the irritation of American anti-trust laws.'[87] Southern Irish Labour politicans Noel Browne and Conor Cruise O'Brien were rebuked for condemning Connolly's participation in 'the united front of 1916'. The historian Owen Dudley Edwards was similarly reproved for his revisionist treatment of Connolly in *The Mind of an Activist*.[88]

The supposedly 'Marxist' Officials allowed a considerable amount of green ideology to seep into the pure springs of their socialist secularism. The deliberate confusion of thought engendered by such vague references to the republican canon was less necessary in view of the Officials' break with the Catholic Church. Under close scrutiny their opinions do not appear to have been very far to the left of the social theory which many

Provisionals wanted to keep in line with recent encyclicals. After 1977 it is arguable that they were to the right of PIRA.

What then was the real basis for the division in the IRA? The Officials heavily emphasised social policy as a natural and justifiable reason for the break. Sean Cronin, the former chief of staff, then in America, was repudiated for his insistence that the split was irrational.[89] In his subsequent book on Irish nationalism Cronin accepted the orthodox Official line that the split was based on divergence over socialism. He agreed that the Irish Fianna Fail government insisted on the IRA dropping its new radicalism as a precondition for receiving aid and hence stimulated the breakaway of IRA men like MacStiofain who were notoriously anti-red. This clear polarisation is difficult to sustain. Gerry Adams, as Provisional Sinn Féin president, insisted in 1983 that the real issue was the Officials' desire to recognise the Leinster House, Stormont and Westminster parliaments.[90]

Working-class unity: Officials woo loyalist toilers

One very important difference between the Officials and Provisionals (supported by the IRSP) was their respective attitudes to the Protestant working class. The lines here were not drawn with complete clarity. The Provisionals were occasionally divided. In 1976, for example, *An Phoblacht* emphasised consideration for northern loyalists against *Republican News*. The latter had more intimate contact with loyalist paramilitaries, and opposed such reasoning. The Provisional position, also adopted by the IRSP,[91] which claimed to be derived from Connolly, was that the British must be removed from Northern Ireland before any form of socialism could be implemented. From this proposition it followed that there could be no loyalist backlash after Britain's withdrawal and that any resistance by loyalists would be soon overcome. Though derided by intelligent observers like Fr Des Wilson and the eminent English historian, A.J.P. Taylor[92] as a piece of patent British propaganda, the 'backlash' proposition, whose most articulate upholder is Dr Conor Cruise O'Brien, is in fact neither self-evident nor contradictory. The nature of loyalist reaction if left without British support is the great question mark which has hung over Ulster since the days of Carson. No firm evidence exists either way. Even Prot-stats themselves are unlikely to know now how they would react in hypothetical circumstances.

Connolly, despite Provisional propaganda, is of little help. It is certainly true, as was argued in *Republican News*, that Connolly believed that workers should fight against partition, 'even to the death'.[93] It would, he believed, 'destroy the Labour movement by disrupting it. It would perpetuate in a form aggravated in evil the discords now prevalent, and help the Home Rule and Orange capitalists and clerics to keep their rallying cries before the public as the political watchwords of the day.'[94] This does not, of course, provide any blueprint for ending sixty years of partition. Connolly's participation in the Easter Week Rising shows that he was prepared then to place the ejection of Britain before socialism, but this, as already mentioned, was in line with Marx and Engels and secured the approbation of Lenin. The latter's insistence that factors like religion must be considered in assessing the total Irish situation can be used to justify working-class unity before British withdrawal or even unionist communism.[95] Conor Cruise O'Brien, moreover, believes Connolly inconsistent on the significance of the loyalist workers in Ulster.[96] It is certainly difficult to insist, as did the Provisionals, that Connolly would necessarily have required a rising of the nationalist working class against a totally alienated loyalist majority. Here the Official philosophy is important.

Goulding and other IRA leaders defended themselves from accusations of apathy towards Orange mobs in 1969 by insisting that they had feared further provocation. After the split this theme was developed. On the one hand they condemned the Provisional bombing campaign as being highly divisive and directed against civilian not military targets. Killing UDR men guiltless of terror, murder, or torture, was sectarian.[97] The Officials themselves had a few awkward actions to explain. The killing of Senator Jack Barnhill lost them the support of their radical ideologist, Roy Johnston, himself Prot-ecum.[98] While justifying the Aldershot bombing of February 1972 the *United Irishman* drew the lesson that no military solution was possible, and that working-class unity was essential. An indefinite ceasefire was proclaimed and by 1973 the Republican Clubs denied any connection with the Official IRA.[99]

The Officials, as this chapter will continue to call all bodies deriving from the Official IRA or Official Sinn Féin, began a 'long call' to the Protestants of Ulster.[100] This included acceptance of Stormont before its abolition. 'There can, of course, be no United Ireland worth talking about, or worth being part of, if the bulk of the Protestant working people is opposed to it.' Their fears of Rome had to be overcome; only after that could they be made aware of the cynicism with which British imperialism had exploited both north and south.[101] Direct rule in 1972 was rejected as no victory but a regression to the nineteenth century.[102] It was in keeping with this philosophy that the Officials subsequently supported the restoration of a Stormont Assembly, safeguarded for Catholics by a Bill of Rights. Efforts were made to appeal to the other side of the religious divide by praising loyalist worker 'radicalism on social issues'.[103] 'For all his faults, Paisley is an Irishman.'[104] This type of verbal cajolery is reminiscent of the efforts of Arthur Griffith and others before the first Irish Revolution to create the image of the Orangeman as a very good Irishman, despite religious bigotry.[105] It countered the popular claim expressed by the UDA that 'the Protestant in Northern Ireland is NOT Irish, does not regard himself as IRISH and objects most vehemently when he is allied with what, to him, is now a most obnoxious breed.' However, on one occasion at least, Paisley, praying for guidance against a Welsh heckler, was inspired to identify as Irish.[106]

The task of uniting the working class in the face of such ambiguous attitudes was clearly Herculean. It explains the Officials' great emphasis on integrated education. They expected no very rapid revolutionary progress. In 1971 a *United Irishman* article, 'The Way Forward', insisted that there could be no immediate socialism as the political development in the 26 counties was insufficient and in the north the 'overwhelming mass of Protestant workers are under Fascistic Paisleyite influence'. This was a far cry from recognising Paisley as a fellow Irishman. Yet it was still hoped that Paisley might come to realise that the British connection meant association with the EEC.[107] Paisley had also shown agreement with the other objective of the Officials at the time, fighting internment. A year later Thomas MacGiolla, the Official Sinn Féin president, still declared that 'the Irish revolution, which must continue and to which we pledge ourselves, demands the support of the Protestant working class'. Adapting Cardinal Conway, he insisted that they could not be bombed into the Republic or even a socialist republic.[108]

The Officials found some theory to back their position. Ruth First, later an anti-apartheid martyr, was quoted to demonstrate that in revolution socialism must be mobilised from below. An abrupt breach with the earlier regime made it easier for bourgeois groups to take over.[109] Sivanandan's Gramscist rejection of 'adventure by groups claiming to represent the masses' was commended.[110] It helped to explain how the IRSP split from the Officials in 1974 mirrored the right-wing Provisional split. The IRSP was an 'ultra-left instant revolutionary organisation' which forgot the fundamental premise of republicanism, Tone's uniting of Catholic, Protestant and Dissenter.[111] The Provisionals were also, somewhat inconsistently, depicted as supported by the Trotskyists of the Fourth International, who gave a modicum of intellectual respectability to their otherwise mindless violence.[112]

The plausibility of some Official arguments against violence must be balanced by their unreflective support for the Soviet Union. While Brezhnev was convinced that socialism and peace were indissoluble, the Officials saw Mao as insisting that a Third World War was inevitable. Such one-sided 'Stalinism' left the Officials vulnerable to Provisional counter-attack.[113] Moreover, the Officials were prepared to accept uncritically the value of nuclear energy, while their rivals were extremely sceptical.[114] Again, the Soviet influence seems the determinant. The USSR, despite its peace-loving nature, had offered to arm the OIRA in the early 1970s.[115] MacGiolla dismissed the Provisional ideology as 'viciously fascist', their American NORAID supporters as racist in their opposition to school bussing, and PIRA's existence as dependent on the CIA.[116] But the Officials' own deviation from socialism could also be charted.

The fundamental problem remained the conciliation of Protestant workers. The Officials had a strong case for their insistence that Provisional bombing made this virtually impossible. They could argue from a republican tradition. In his famous passage declaring his object to break the connection with England, 'the never-failing source of all our political evils', Tone's means were unity regardless of creeds. Thomas Davis agreed. He believed unity a precondition for independence: 'If you would liberate Ireland, and keep it free, you must have Protestant help—if you would win Protestants, you must address their reason, their interest, their hopes, and their pride.'[117] Ironically, it was the Provisionals who made the most of Davis, despite the *United Irishman's* occasional quotations from Davis's poetry linking the traditions.[118] In his repudiation of agrarian outrages in Munster and his endorsement of Catholic clerical denunciation, Davis was not a perfect precedent for the Provisionals, though he thought a just war productive of more heroism than 'almost any other human occupation'.[119]

But how could Protestant workers be conciliated in the 1970s and 1980s? Violence might be discouraged by Officials unilaterally abandoning their own. Officials could appeal to loyalist paramilitaries, as an approach to the Protestant working classes. Contacts were made in prison. The UVF man, Gusty Spence, gaoled for life for his participation in the 1966 Malvern Street murders, had by 1972 established prison connections with Officials interested in class-oriented socialist philosophy. In a gaol strike the

UVF flag was placed beside the republican tricolour. In April 1972 Spence created a stir by sending a letter of condolence to Mrs McCann, widow of Sean, an Official leader recently shot dead. Later in the year Spence may have tried to inject some of his enthusiasm into other UVF men when he secured what was ostensibly an enforced holiday after being given a short parole.[120] Several meetings between Officials and UVF men were held, and though publicly denied when the rival UDA exposed them, there seem to have been a number of instances of joint action. There were accusations that OIRA gave hit lists, containing names such as Seamus Costello, to UVF gunmen for elimination.[121] In about 1976, Fr McDyer, tactfully discarding clerical dress, hosted at Glencolumbkille a grand conference of paramilitaries: PIRA, OIRA, UDA and UVF. Advising his visitors to stop fighting and build bridges, McDyer 'was amused to observe the apparent comradeship and conviviality that developed.'[122]

The quest for loyalist radicalism

This fraternisation accompanied the Officials' search for hints of socialism by loyalist paramilitaries, including both UDA and UVF. In February 1974, during the brief attempt at a power-sharing executive, the UDA and UVF criticised the efforts of the rulers to divide the working classes. An editorial in the *United Irishman* welcomed such statements, arguing that the Officials had always insisted on the need to convince the Protestant working class that republicanism was the only way out of the present horror.[123] The uselessness of a six-county free state with Britain pulling the strings was asserted by the Officials. The Official Sinn Féin Ard Comhairle, or executive, took up the issue, agreeing with the UVF repudiation of the new Council of Ministers and Council of Ireland. It could 'recognise and appreciate [the] obvious class orientation of the UVF statement.'[124] The Officials also gave prominence to an interview with Sammy Smyth, editor of the UDA *Ulster Loyalist* and *Ulster Militant*. He clearly distrusted the middle classes, but his political philosophy was 'an area of confusion which is difficult to penetrate'. Smyth was bitterly opposed to BICO, a 'two nations' group, trying to infiltrate the UDA. He regarded James Connolly as 'a priest who joined the working-class movement as a socialist to ensure that the interests of the Vatican were always being looked after'. Socialism, Smyth maintained, meant simply looking after paupers, opposing profiteering, and winning fair wages. Trade unionism, said the *United Irishman*, was judged by Smyth according to the criteria of political nationalism, and he appeared haunted by the fear of a 32-county Ireland. The *United Irishman*, however, considered him educable, despite his muddled thinking.[125] So too did the radical Fr Des Wilson, who, regardless of savage personal abuse and an opprobious cartoon in Smyth's *Ulster Militant*, portrayed him as a unifying force in his 1982 novel, *The Demonstration*. Smyth also achieved 'great rapport' with Fr McDyer. Smyth told Sean Cronin that he could subscribe to the politics of the *United Irishman*, but that in contemporary Northern Ireland there were only Protestants and Catholics. However, when approached by Des O'Hagan on behalf of the Officials, Smyth told him to get stuffed. The IRSP, not without reason, ridiculed the Officials' efforts to discover vestiges of socialism in men like Smyth and Ken Gibson of the UVF, arguing that such people must be judged by their actions, not by their statements.[126] Smyth's 'socialism' was probably as developed as that of Tone or McCracken, but in taking it seriously the Officials were showing the desperation of their tactics, especially as Smyth was ferociously anti-Catholic, arguing that the only alternative to a united Ireland was the physical removal of all Catholics from Ulster. Smyth was assassinated in 1976, possibly by a loyalist who considered him too unpredictable.

Interviewing a number of Protestant paramilitaries, Steve Bruce heard them saying that they would be left of centre were it not for the partition issue. Socialism appeared impure for the very reason that it was an ideal professed by some Catholics. Working-class solidarity in itself was anathema because it required contact with Catholics. 'Anything even vaguely left-wing was vulnerable to conservative unionists playing the "red and green card": socialism equals nationalism.'[127] If these opinions were representative, there was little hope for the Officials' strategy.

Paisley's Prot-stat social encyclical

Dervla Murphy agreed with Bruce when arguing in *A Place Apart*, a book later extolled by the UDA, it was far easier for Catholics to make social gestures across the religious divide than for loyalists, who immediately earned the ferocious disapprobation of their co-religionists.[128] This was true of the Officials' unsuccessful attempt to woo the loyalist paramilitaries. The latter, with exceptions like Spence, were afraid of any apparent link with even the less violent OIRA. But it was not only tribal hostility. Prot-stats, like Catholics, had to face the challenge of socialism and religion. There was, by definition, no loyalist pope, issuing encyclicals to which all Prot-stats were supposed to submit. Or was there?

Paisley's *Protestant Telegraph* linked Romanism and communism in a single giant conspiracy, to be challenged effectively only by Bible Protestantism in its final Ulster redoubt.[129] But Paisley had originally challenged the wealthy unionist establishment on behalf of the working classes. His movement focused the energies of poorer loyalists likely to become diverted in dangerous directions unless properly channelled. John McKeague even had the impertinence, when accused of communism by Paisley, to suggest that the Doctor himself had 'a touch of the Comms'. Through the *Protestant Telegraph*, Paisley in 1971 decided to release an authoritative Prot-stat quasi-encyclical which could allay anxieties and restore the faithful to inner peace, serenity, and godly endeavour.

The encyclical, entitled 'Protestantism and Socialism', was republished for the continued edification of the elect in 1973 and 1978,[130] true Prot-stat social theory being relatively unchangeable. 'Protestantism', declaimed the encyclical, 'that is, Protestantism holding to the reformed faith, is completely incompatible with Socialism. The two are mutually antagonistic: they cannot coexist. Protestantism holding to the Reformed Faith believes in the innate corruptness of man [the doctrine of original sin]. Socialism believes in the innate goodness of man.' The encyclical defined socialism as requiring an equal distribution of property or state ownership. This meant the 'ultimate utopia of a temporal paradise. Without this heaven on earth philosophy there would be no impetus in Socialism.' For the Protestant, however, utopia was not on earth. The idea of 'Protestant Socialism' therefore 'carries the seeds of its own destruction in its inherent contradictions.'

The problem in Northern Ireland, according to 'Protestantism and Socialism', arose from the fifty-year rule of the landed gentry who had given the Protestant working class nothing but platitudes in return for their support. Now, the Protestant workers, wanting a voice of their own, had grabbed socialism as the first available philosophy. Some of the current working-class leaders were better known in the recent past for socialism than loyalism. The encyclical condemned the flirtation of the OIRA with the loyalist working class. There could be no Ulster without Protestantism. 'No atheistic socialism or atheistic loyalism, will save Ulster.' Such philosophy did not deny that Protestantism had a social conscience, far from it. The DUP existed to provide for reasonable loyalist working-class aspirations.

This was certainly one of the most forthright encyclicals on social questions in recent years. It clarified a number of issues left vague in the encyclicals disseminated by the rival establishment. However, 'Protestantism and Socialism' was in unconscious agreement with *Rerum Novarum* on the incompatibility of a socialism which aimed at 'transferring property from private individuals to the community' with Christianity. Connolly had debated Fr Kane on the equal distribution of property. As for original sin versus the perfectibility of man, despite Paisley's belief that popery rejected the former, it was well ventilated in the encyclicals of the Roman Catholic popes, Pius XI's *Divini Illius Magistri*, 1929, being a particlularly good example.[131] The assumption that socialism and atheism were indistinguishable was also found in Fr Kane's 1910 Lenten discourses but, as Connolly demonstrated, with some ambiguity. The Free Presbyterian encyclical, 'Protestantism and Socialism', thus agreed in essentials with the popes, and could no doubt have received an imprimatur from any competent Catholic authority.

Paisleyism and papalism: social agreement?

If there was no divergence in substance, there was certainly a difference in emphasis when compared with the later social encyclicals of Popes John XXIII and Paul VI. *Populorum Progressio* had been denounced in the *Protestant Telegraph*. As shown earlier, the statements of John XXIII and Paul VI retained the traditional idea of property as a trust, but were able to extend this sufficiently for advocates of liberation theology to draw startlingly new conclusions as to the duty of Christians in the modern world. Post-Vatican II encyclicals have played down the idea of an absolute contrast between Christianity and even 'moderate socialism' which is 'a concept of life ... bounded by time'. John XXIII certainly accepted the teaching of his predecessors in this regard, and, like Paisley, rejected 'the absurd attempt to reconstruct a solid and fruitful temporal order divorced from God'.[132] However, in *Pacem in Terris* Pope John made an important concession, allowing co-operation with movements whose ultimate philosophy is unacceptable. Cardinal O'Fiaich may have thought of this when he declared in early 1984 that it was not necessarily sinful to vote for Provisional Sinn Féin. The Irish theologian Professor Enda McDonagh of Maynooth summed up the current situation by accepting non-Marxist socialism as fully compatible with

Christianity, and even Marxism as worthy of Christian dialogue.[133]

In other words, Paisley's encyclical represented a particularly harsh nineteenth-century dichotomy between the other-worldliness of Christianity and the crude mundane materialism of socialism. It is the antithesis of liberation theology. In the early 1900s an Anglican bishop satirised what Enda McDonagh calls the 'pie-in-the-sky' argument: 'My dear brother, it is so hard. I have £10,000 and you ask me for a copper. It will be all right up there; just you wait.'[134] Paisley's attempt to lay down a consensus Protestant position on an issue so contentious must be seen as one of the most obvious examples of the unconscious convergence of the period. There is nothing clearly 'Protestant' in the thought displayed, but much that savours of Vatican I Catholicism. However, the second and less theoretical part of 'Protestantism and Socialism' sought a 'middle way' between the upper-class conservatism of the traditional unionists, and a full-scale left-wing alternative. This was in fact exactly what the Provisionals were attempting in their *Comhar na gComharsan* programme.

Prot-stat paramilitary 'Marxism'

What was the reaction of the loyalist workers to the 'Protestantism and Socialism' encyclical? The UDA, eventually the largest of all the loyalist organisations, was formally established in October 1971, nearly a year before Paisley's encyclical. Its rules established secularity, and rejected religious mentors.[135] Paisley was criticised by UDA publications.[136] In 1975 the *Ulster Loyalist* reported that eggs had been thrown at the Doctor by loyalist prisoners at Crumlin Road gaol.[137] Nevertheless, the UDA was prepared to co-operate with Paisley over the abortive strike of 1977. Generally the UDA retained something of a secularist image. In 1982 its leader, Andy Tyrie, ambiguously answered a BBC interviewer's questions on the movement's alleged atheism.[138] The UDA did not, however, omit to attack Paul VI's *Populorum Progressio*, not so much for its 'socialism' as its principle of a 'just war' which might be invoked by republicans who saw Ireland as one unit. The early *UDA News* also agreed with Paisley that the EEC was a tool of the Vatican.[139] By 1972 a number of UDA leaders had begun to take an interest in socialistic ideas, often with unpleasant consequences for themselves. On 14 October the class-conscious UDA men formed the Ulster Citizen Army. In the same month, 'Duke' Ernie Elliott, second in command of the Woodvale area, was arrested with books by Trotsky, Fanon, and Che Guevara on his person. Shortly afterwards he was shot by an opposing UDA faction. In early 1973, his Woodvale superior, the London-born ex-Army NCO David Fogel, defected and told his story to the *Sunday Times*. He also showed left-wing inclinations and hoped that the OIRA and UDA would come together.[140] Sammy Smyth has already been mentioned. Not only was the UDA, as Boulton pointed out, a direct borrowing mirror-image of the IRA in organisation but it nearly experienced its own version of the 1969 IRA split. To carry the parallel further, Andy Tyrie claimed that the UCA was a creation of British black propaganda.[141] In 1974 the UDA journal complained that the UVF, after intriguing with the Provisionals, had thwarted UDA efforts to talk to the Officials. However, the UDA did in that year send a mission under Glen Barr to Libya, which they insisted to the hostile UVF was not a communist country.[142] The UVF *Combat* regarded the mission as a betrayal of their efforts to defend the paramilitaries against accusations of communist influence. Worse still, the UDA delegates had talks with Provisionals, the Libyan government and other groups. People's Democracy regarded the episode in late 1974 as 'one of the oddest developments yet in the Irish struggle'.[143] The UDA, always well supplied with newspapers, was thus fairly reticent about its flirtations with the dreaded socialists. Dervla Murphy was told by 'a few brave UDA members' but 'behind closed doors', that they hoped the organisation would eventually become a genuinely socialist and non-sectarian political party.[144] Other observers have been more impressed by links with the English National Front.[145]

The UVF, which published *Combat* after 1974, was more openly, if just as ambiguously, involved in the Socialism and Christianity debate and also associated with the National Front. Gusty Spence, at large from June to November 1972, the UVF's great year as Bolton described it, endeavoured to spread the new socialistic philosophy. But what of Paisley's anti-socialist encyclical? The UVF, unlike the UDA, did not try to divorce itself publicly from Calvinist fundamentalism. Paisley and the Rev. Robert Bradford, it claimed, were revered in working-class homes. Yet a UDA man incautiously referred to the latter as a 'Bible thumping bigot'.[146] The first issue of *Combat* in April 1974 publicised an economic warfare campaign against big business and government departments to finance its war against the Provisionals. Yet two months earlier the UVF met with Provisional leaders such as Dáithí O'Conaill to work out a scheme for joint patrols. Clearly what Dervla Murphy has called the celebrated loyalist capacity for double-think was working overtime. A moderate UVF group opposing the populist right and seeking liaison with the Officials was overthrown in November 1974.[147] Thus both the UDA and UVF exhibited splits and divisions, often expressed in ideological terms.

The UVF mini-encyclical

In early 1974 to set the record straight, after allegations of communist influence from the United Ulster Unionist Council (UUUC) newsletter, an official statement, almost a mini-encyclical, was published over the name 'William Johnston (Capt.)', which provided the same UVF authentication as 'Captain Black' (in reality the mass killer John White) for the UFF, and 'P O'Neill' and 'Sean McGarrity' did for the Provisionals and Officials.

> Unlike the modernistic clergy and political protestant laity attached to the UUUC (Dr Paisley excluded), the Ulster Volunteer Force has never lent itself to support the ungodly and anti-christian doctrines of Arminianism, Modernism, Ecumenism, Humanism or 'new-light' pseudo-evangelism. Our Protestantism is based upon the Word of God and centres round the glorious doctrine of God's Sovereignty; our so-called socialism (a term which we reject) is based upon Christian benevolence and the teachings expounded by our Saviour in the Sermon on the Mount.
>
> For God and Ulster.[148]

For an organisation which admitted to greater ruthlessness than the Provisionals, an appeal to the Sermon on the Mount was a little bizarre, even by Ulster Prot-stat standards. It had the lofty intransigence of Pope Pius IX's refusal of reconciliation in the 1864 *Syllabus of Errors*, with 'progress, liberalism and modern civilisation'.[149] The 'Christian benevolence' on which the UVF officially based its 'so-called socialism' was of course the trusteeship notion of property built into all the papal encyclicals in response to Aquinas's adaptation of Aristotle. But more was to come. In the next *Combat* issue original sin was duly emphasised in 'Calvin's Column'. Furthermore, Claire MacDonald, in an article on 'The Money Manufacturers' National Front', wished to 'socialise the forces by which money emission is carried out'.[150] This was the quasi-Douglas Credit notion located earlier in *Quadragesimo Anno*. Lest there should be any doubt as to the UVF's convergence with the social theory of the encyclicals, an editorial several issues later explained that 'private entrepreneurs are simply the trustees holding the wealth on lease, as it were, from the nation'.[151] On social policy, the links between the Provisionals and the UVF were most appropriate. A *Combat* (UVF) editorial praised Desmond Fennell's 'community of communities' idea,[152] abandoned with Eire Nua in 1982.

Ideological shadow-boxing: the loyalists

Fortunately for the loyalists, they rarely read papal encyclicals, evincing more interest in tales of confessional debauchery and lascivious nuns. Moreover, the dust raised by accusations and counter-accusations of Marxist influence hid the real issue. In commenting on the IRSP break from the Officials, *Combat's* editor, Billy Mitchell ('Richard Cameron'), defended his own organisation from accusations of radicalism by asserting that it 'has always regarded the socialist-minded Republicans as the more dangerous in the long term'. He feared that the mindless bombings would 'one day give way to a serious revolutionary war engineered by idealists and backed by the International Socialists and Finance Capitalists'.[153]

Behind all this contradiction was an almost desperate search for a middle way which Catholics and Prot-stats might take, if necessary, without absolutely discarding either their traditions or Churches. The UVF realised that the old conservative allegiance had been the product of circumstances, and that they had been exploited by cynical politicians playing the Orange card. Ninety per cent of the loyalists interned in Long Kesh by 1974 were trade unionists. 'With friends like the Conservative Party, Ulster has no need of enemies.' Perhaps the British Labour Party should be given a chance? Communists, atheists and agnostics were not the Ulster loyalist's cup of tea.[154] These agonising reappraisals were the product of the apparent British treachery over the power-sharing assembly. After the successful UWC strike, which brought down the assembly, working-class loyalists gained very considerably in confidence. But bickering between the UDA and UVF on social issues continued into 1975.

The UDA journal in March 1975 insisted that the UVF motto should be 'For Karl Marx and Ulster'.[155] Worried by strife with the rival paramilitary, it believed in mid-1975 that the UVF Marxists still dominated in the Shankill while there were good relations between the UDA and UVF in East Belfast. A *Sunday News* article in 1974 had shown, it claimed, that the UVF's political thought was identical to that of both the Provisionals and Officials. As a result, a desperate Marxist leadership encouraged unpatriotic deeds and attacked the UDA as thugs to compensate for their falling subscriptions. On one occasion they were alleged to have hijacked a Provisional car on the Falls, released its Catholic owner and then shot a Protestant boy and pensioner. The UVF rank and file ought to be made aware of the actions of some named members.[156] Naturally, the UVF replied in kind, reasserting the communist links of the UDA men. Fogel's revelations to the *Sunday Times* of a UDA officer teaching him communism, Andy Tyrie's close links with the Queen's University BICO Marxist, Boyd Black, three UDA men found in IRSP company, and the condemnation to death of the former leader, Harding Smith, for threatening to expose the latter incident, were all mentioned.[157]

As suggested above, such arguments were ideological shadow boxing. Marxist intellectuals who see the Prot-stat paramilitaries as about to throw off their false consciousness and work towards a genuine non-sectarian socialism are too optimistic. It is very doubtful if any of the paramilitary leaders had a real understanding, apart from the ritual skimming of a few fashionable revolutionary texts, of the implications of Marxism. When challenged, *Combat* used the same loophole as *Pacem in Terris*. Though they attacked bad housing, unemployment, the cost of living, inadequate bus services, high fares, British Army brutality, internment, no-jury trials, and paid informers, that did not prove a UVF link with the OIRA which criticised the same things.[158] This response was a far cry from anything but the most Pickwickian socialism. One clear indicator of the failure to adopt a geniunely radical posture can be found in the strange silence of the Loyalist Association of Workers (LAW) on the subject. Recruited from the virtually all-Protestant Harland and Wolff shipyards, LAW represented a labour aristocracy. Before the formation of the UWC, LAW was the supposed union partner of the mainly petty-bourgeois UDA. LAW, like the Officials, emphasised integrated education, not socialism as a panacea. The Association was very much under the spell of Craig's Vanguard which Probert depicts as the old upper-class unionists in disguise. LAW approached class-consciousness only by identifying working-class Protestants as a buffer between 'better off' unionists and Catholic extremists. Northern Ireland was seen as a perennial 'pool of cheap labour for the British fly-by-night industrialists'. LAW was still basically concerned with sectarian issues, such as opposition to the Republic-based Irish Council of Trade Unions.[159]

A plethora of socialistic pundits

In this account emphasis has been placed on the main Prot-stat paramilitaries of which the UDA was by far the largest, though the UVF won the graffiti battle in Belfast streets, and the Provisional and Official republicans. A number of smaller groups with their own papers also participated in the debate. Did People's Democracy (PD) with the *Free Citizen*, the *Unfree Citizen*, and eventually the *Socialist Republic* purvey true Marxism? PD, however, had declined since the heady days of the 1969 Belfast to Derry march, and seemed, as the Provisionals claimed, to languish a few steps behind them. PD, moreover, appears to have had some difficulty in reconciling its belief in modified violence as essential to counter imperialism with their criticism of PIRA actions. PD eventually joined the Trotskyite Fourth International. BICO's *Comment* accepted the 'two nations' theory and sought salvation in the loyalist working class, which PD thought BICO had influenced during the 1974 UWC strike. The Communist Party of Ireland's *Unity* and *Irish Socialist* took the opposite line, criticising socialists who refused to accept nationalism, while also critical of the Provisionals. The CPI was accused by BICO of manipulating the Officials.[160] The IRSP lauded the Provisionals for their guerrilla war but in 1974 lamented their lack of working-class politics. Similarly, PD pledged support for the Provisionals but complained that their politics were 'lousy'. It cited Connolly against the Provisional and Official discussions with fascist loyalists. However, neither the IRSP nor PD were able to mobilise the working classes themselves. By December 1975 some IRSP members resigned because of its retreat to 'traditional republicanism'. The field was clearly dominated by the Provisionals. Even the sedate *New Statesman* in 1972 delighted the Provisional *Volunteer* by asserting that, like it or not, the Provisionals were the only real revolutionaries around.[161]

The basic idealogical conflict again centred on the Provisionals versus Paisley. But the UDA took a loyalist initiative in 1978 with proposals for Ulster independence from their New Ulster Political Research Group. Like the republicans they advocated consensus class-based politics instead of sectarianism.[162] The NUPGR scheme, though revived by the *Common Sense* proposal in 1987, was no more successful than the original Provisional plan for an Ulster assembly. In 1981 the UDA set up an Ulster Loyalist Democratic Party (in 1987 the Ulster Democratic Party), which, according to its philosopher, Ian Adamson, was based on the populist ideas of

Jemmy Hope, also revered by republicans.[163] In his book, *The Identity of Ulster*, Adamson favoured a co-operative democracy as a middle way between capitalism and socialism. His model was the Presbyterian poet and nationalist, also quoted by the UVF, George Russell (Æ).

All roads to Rome

An obvious conclusion emerges. Genuine class-consciousness in an appreciable body of workers is difficult to detect in Northern Ireland. On the contrary, all socio-economic roads lead to Rome, or to a passable imitation of the papal encyclicals from Leo XIII's *Rerum Novarum* of 1891 to Paul VI's *Populorum Progressio* of 1967. Whether the focus is the republican tradition of Tone, Davis, and Pearse, the recent economic arguments of Provisional Sinn Féin, the great Prot-stat encyclical of Paisley, the mini UVF formula of 'Capt. William Johnston', or Dr Ian Adamson, the philosopher of the sanitised UDA, the conclusion is the same. All agree with the popes on the need for some middle way between socialism and unrestricted capitalism, sometimes with a tinge of Douglas Credit philosophy. There seems in operation an 'invisible hand', à la Adam Smith, drawing Ulster contestants towards this censensus. Even the 'Marxist' Officials have found themselves swept inexorably into a middle-of-the-road compromise. It demonstrates clearly unconscious convergence between two seemingly irreconcilable traditions. In the heady days of socialist ideology, such a compromising common posture appeared a disastrous watering down of effective radical strategy; now, with the apparent dominance of economic rationalism, the philosophy of the papal encyclicals provides an important alternative economic viewpoint, especially in Northern Ireland with its horrendous unemployment rate often approaching 20 per cent.

Notes

1. Whyte, *Interpreting Northern Ireland*, 175-193. AP, 13 June 1991.
2. For discussion of Marxist criticism of Marx, see Connolly, James (n.d.), *Ireland upon the Dissecting Table: Connolly on Ulster and Partition*, Cork: Cork Workers' Club, 6. For SDLP see 'Publius' *Social Democrat* (SD), September 1976. Bew, P. Gibbon, P. and Patterson, H. (1979), *The State in Northern Ireland, 1921-72*, Manchester: Manchester University Press, 1-39, 'Marxism and Ireland', rejects the inadequacies of Marx, Engels and Connolly on Ulster.
3. Marx and Engels, *Ireland and the Irish Question*, 340 (Engels on Brehon Laws), 348 (Engels sees English provocation in 1641), 356

(Goldwin Smith), 394 (overthrow of English hierarchy in Ireland), 407 (more revolutionary than English), 417 (international), 249 (bishops and union), 399 (secularism of Fenians), 117 and 126 (Famine and Fenians). See also Sean Cronin, *Irish Nationalism*, 27.

4. *Teoric* (Official Theoretical Journal), 1, No. 2, 1971.
5. See for example, Tom O'Dwyer on Allen, Kieran (1990), *The Politics of James Connolly*, London: Pluto. Austen Morgan's work was dismissed as a diatribe, AP, 19 July 1990. AP, 30 August 1990, publicised Coughlan, Anthony C. *Desmond Greaves, 1913-1988: an Obituary Essay*, Irish Labour History Studies. Greaves had been a member of NICRA and participated at the PD march attacked at Burntollet. Greaves, C.D. (1961), *The Life and Times of James Connolly*, London: Lawrence and Wishart, was published before the Ulster Troubles began.
6. Connolly, J. (n.d.), *Labour in Ireland*, Dublin: Sign of Three Candles, (contains *Labour in Irish History* and *The Reconquest of Ireland*), 72 (Tone), 82 (McCracken), 96 (Thompson), 160-2 (Marx), 124 (O'Connell). See AP, 2.71. on Ralahine co-operative. *Volunteer*, 66, 1972 for Connolly on Thompson and Marx. See Greaves, *Tone and the Irish Nation*, 3.
7. *Ireland upon the Dissecting Table*, 28.
8. Connolly, J., *Labour in Ireland*, 184. Connolly's views on the Orangemen as slaves was quoted in the Provisional Sinn Féin (1982) *Notes for Revolutionaries*, 19-20. See also *Unfree Citizen* (UC), 5 August 1974.
9. Kirk, J. Andrew (1979), *Liberation Theology: An Evangelist View from the Third World*, London: Marshall, Morgan and Scott, 189.
10. Connolly, J. ([1910] 1962), *Labour, Nationality and Religion*, Dublin: New Books, 29-30.
11. Fremantle, A. (1959), *The Papal Encyclicals in their Historical Context*, New York: Mentor, 176. According to McKeague's *Loyalist News*, 19 July 1975, *Rerum Novarum* was 'so vague that its arguments could be successfully used for benevolent socialism or benevolent fascism'.
12. *Labour, Nationality and Religion*, 7-8, 51, 55, 61, 63.
13. AP, 16 May 1975 and 5 June 1975. LN, 10 August 1974 (Andy McCann).
14. See Morgan, Austen (1980), 'Socialism in Ireland—Red, Green and Orange', in Morgan, Austen and Purdie, Bob, eds, *Ireland: Divided Nation Divided Class*, 179. Connolly is today 'all things to all men (and women)'.
15. *Ireland and the Irish Question*, 450. AP, 28 March 1991: 'James Connolly the practical visionary'.
16. Cronin, S. (1971), *The Revolutionaries*, Dublin: Republican Publications, 186.
17. *An Phoblacht*, 20 January 1994, published the Democratic Programme in an article demonstrating how far Ireland, north and south, had deviated from its ideals, especially in relation to partition and the EC.
18. See Fremantle, 228-235.
19. Whyte, J.H. (1980), *Church and State in Modern Ireland, 1923-1979*, Dublin: Gill and Macmillan, 117.

20. Connolly, *Labour in Ireland,* 111 and 237 'an attempt to perform, by a mixture of bureaucracy and clericalism, what can only be accomplished by a full and complete application of democratic trust in the people'.
21. See 'Shadow of a Gunman', *Magill,* April 1982, 4-16 and 'The Secret World of the SFWP [Sinn Féin the Worker's Party]', *Magill,* May 1982.
22. MacStiofain, *Memoirs of a Revolutionary,* 135.
23. UI, October 1971, June 1972 (sectarian), October 1969 (FF finance for PIRA).
24. MacStiofain, 96 (Johnston), 139 (attacks UI re FF finance). Paul in *Octogesima Adveniens* (1971), criticised multinationals as being independent of public control and allowed a cautious approach to some aspects of socialism. Grenillon, O.J. (1975), *The Gospel of Peace and Justice: Catholic Social Teaching since Pope John,* New York: Orbis, 506 and 500. For general background, see 485-511.
25. PT, 15 April 1967.
26. PT, 2 September 1967 (Noel Smith).
27. Gerassi, J. (1971), ed., *Revolutionary priest: the Complete Writings and Messages of Camilo Torres,* 37. For an Irish theologian on Liberation Theology see McDonagh, Enda (1980), *The Demands of Simple Justice,* Dublin: Gill and Macmillan, 46-55.
28. Paul VI (1965), *On the Development of Peoples* (Populorum Progressio), Dublin: Catholic Truth Society, 21 (Section 31). *Ulster Militant* (UM) complains of justification for Just War, 14 1972.
29. RN, 15 October 1977.
30. *On the Development of Peoples,* 17-18. Fremantle (*Quadragesimo Anno*) 231.
31. *Mater et Magister* quoted in full (173-225). Guerry, E. (1961), *The Social teaching of the Church,* London: Saint Paul, 196.
32. AP, February and March 1970 and Ruairí O Brádaigh (Rory O'Brady) (1973), *Our People, Our Future: What EIRE NUA means,* Dublin: Sinn Féin, 7 (Irish Press [IP], 3 December 1970.)
33. Cronin, *Irish Nationalism,* 101.
34. Cronin, *Irish Nationalism,* 72; Davis, R., *The Young Ireland Movement,* 185. Jean Charles Sismondi (1773-1842).
35. Fremantle, 234.
36. Passage quoted by Patterson, *The Politics of Illusion,* 168.
37. O Brádaigh, *Our People, Our Future,* 37.
38. *On the Development of Peoples,* Section 23, 18.
39. Guerry, E., 202-3.
40. O Brádaigh, 8.
41. The original policy appeared in *Eire Nua: The Social and Economic Policy of Sinn Féin,* 1971.
42. AP, 25 January 1977.
43. Purdie, 'Reconsiderations on Republicanism and Socialism', *Ireland: Divided Nation, Divided Class,* 85. Purdie, 91, accepts that Catholic social thought, especially 'distribution' is a source of Provisional 'socialism'. AP, 1 February 1978 (D. Breatnach on McDyer). McDyer accepted a compromise between socialism and private enterprise. See

McDyer, James (1984), *Fr McDyer of Glencolumkille: An Autobiography*, Dingle: Brandon, 73-4.
44. Nyerere, Julius K. (1979), *Ujaama: Essays on Socialism*, New York: OUP, 1-12. Certain UDA leaders were also interested in Nyerere, see UM, October 1972.
45. O Brádaigh, 9.
46. O Brádaigh, 8.
47. RN, 17 November 1972.
48. AP, September 1972. See also Ransom, Bernard (1980), *Connolly's Marxism*, London: Pluto, 101-2. O Snodaigh, Padraig (1966), '1916—The Beginnings', *Christus Rex*, XX, 2, April, May, June 1966, 98-9.
49. AP, 1 February 1974.
50. O Brádaigh, 15.
51. AP, 26 April 1974.
52. Cronin, *Irish Nationalism*, 23.
53. AP, 17 August 1977.
54. AP, 28 March 1975 and 4 April 1975.
55. AP, 18 April 1975.
56. AP, 24 April 1975.
57. Purdie, *Divided Nation, Divided Class*, 85-6. He took the point from T.P. O'Neill.
58. AP, 30 May 1975.
59. AP, 6 June 1975.
60. AP, 6 and 13 February 1979 and 10 January 1979.
61. See Breatnach, D., AP, 8 March 1978.
62. AP, 29 April 1978.
63. RN, 31 July 1976.
64. AP, 7 September 1977.
65. AP, 28 September 1977.
66. AP, 12 October 1977.
67. AP, 8 February 1978.
68. AP, 26 October 1978 and 25 January 1978.
69. Cronin, *Irish Nationalism*, 211. PD's *Socialist Republic* (SR), Vol.1, No.7, 1978, considered it 'very dangerous' to stifle debate by amalgamation. See also Bishop and Mallie, *The Provisional IRA*, 310-12, etc.
70. AP, 5 November 1981.
71. AP, 3 December 1981.
72. Adams, Gerry (1986 and 1988) *The Politics of Irish Freedom*, Dingle: Brandon, 128-36, and *A Pathway to Peace*, Cork: Mercier, 79-83, appears to see socialism as an aspect of republicanism requiring control over the Irish economy in the interests of the people and the exclusion of foreign economic power. He cites Pearse and Fintan Lalor to this effect. In the context of the deregulatory 1990s this is in fact a potentially heady mixture. See also Patterson, *Politics of Illusion*, 185 and 189.
73. AP, 3 November 1979, 26 January 1980 and 17 November 1983; Purdie, 93. See also 'Adams on Republicanism and Socialism', *Fortnight*, September 1983.
74. AP, 14 January 1982.

75. Guerry, 19. A distinction must be made between obligatory Catholic teaching on faith and morals and the less compelling 'social teaching'.

76. UI, April 1975.

77. UI, September 1972.

78. UI, October 1971.

79. UI, September 1972 and August 1971.

80. UI, November 1974. *Teoric* (Official theoretical journal) No.1, Summer, 1971 carried a review in Gaelic of Fanon's *The Wretched of the Earth*.

81. UI, March 1972.

82. Cronin, *Irish Nationalism*, 213. Sinn Féin the Workers' Party (1977), *The Irish Industrial Revolution*, Dublin: Repcol, 28 and 55.

83. UI, September 1971 and April 1972.

84. UI, June 1973.

85. UI, December 1970.

86. UI, October 1973.

87. UI, November 1972.

88. UI, September and November 1971. Dudley Edwards was rebuked by the Official Sinn Féin in *The Irish Industrial Revolution*, 45, for participating in short-lived Marxist-Christian dialogue.

89. UI, June 1971.

90. Cronin, *Irish Nationalism*, 202-4. For Adams, *Fortnight*, September 1983.

91. SP, April 1975, July 1975, December 1975, July 1976, Nial Lenock's review of Michael Farrell, *The Orange State*.

92. AP, 22 March 1978. (Quotes Fr Wilson from *Dawn*), *Voices for Withdrawal*, n.d., 8.

93. RN, June 1970, (*Irish Worker*, 14 March 1914.).

94. *Ireland upon the Dissecting Table*, 49 (*Forward*, 21 March 1914.)

95. Lenin, V.I. (1966), *Collected Works*, Moscow, Vol. 31, 91. See 142 for white terror in India and Ireland (offsetting red terror).

96. See Davis, 'Ulster Protestants and the Sinn Féin Press, 1914-22', 60-85.

97. UI, May and June 1972.

98. Patterson, Henry, *The Politics of Illusion*, 139.

99. UI, March 1972. For dissociation see Malachy McGurrum, quoted in UC, September 1973.

100. UI, April 1971.

101. UI, June 1971.

102. UI, April 1972.

103. UI, April 1971.

104. UI, May 1970.

105. Davis, 'Ulster Protestants and the Sinn Féin Press, 1914-22', 60-85.

106. UL, 14 April 1974. For Paisley's Irish identification (adopting Irish practice of answering a question with another) see Paisley, Ian (1976) *Paisley the Man and His Message*, 135.

107. UI, September 1971.

108. UI, August 1972.

109. UI, December 1970.

110. UI, June 1976. Sivanandan, A. (1976), *Race, Class and the State: the black experience in Britain*, London: Institute of Race Relations, 247-9.
111. UI, January 1975.
112. UI, December 1978.
113. UI, July 196.
114. UI, October 1979 (nuclear), February-March 1980 (Afghanistan); AP, 20 May 1978 (against nuclear power) and 20 January 1979 (Whiddy dangers), 12 January 1980 (Afghan).
115. Cronin, *Irish Nationalism*, 236.
116. UI, August 1976, April 1977, August 1977.
117. *Nation* (N), 17 December 1842 (Protestant).
118. UI, November 1970.
119. Davis, Thomas (1914), *Selections from his Prose and Poetry*, with an introduction by T.W. Rolleston, London: Fisher Unwin, 282. See (Davis) 'The Mortality of War', *Nation*, 10 June 1843.
120. Boulton, 167-9.
121. UL, 13 April 1974, 5 May 1974, 21 November 1974, (talks with Provos), 26 April 1975; *Observer*, 6 June 1974; *Starry Plough* (SP) [July 1982].
122. *Fr McDyer of Glencolumkille*, 100-101. McDyer dates the conference 1977 but he claims that Sam Smyth, assassinated in 1976, was present.
123. UI, July 1974.
124. UI, February 1974.
125. UI, March 1974. For Smyth and BICO see *Volunteer*, No. 74, 1973, (two meetings held between certain leaders). For attacks on Wilson, who worked with him at Magee College, Derry, see UM, 30 September 1972: 'that liar and reprobate' and No. 18, 1973. For Smyth on Connolly, see UM, April 1972.
126. Cronin, *Irish Nationalism*, 243. See UM, 30 September 1972, for Smyth's 'If you want a Protestant Ulster then you are going to have to put the R.C.s out of it.' For IRSP, SP, April 1975 and April 1976 (Smyth). Smyth's approach, UM, 19 (3 February 1973). See also *Fr McDyer of Glencolumkille*, 100-101. McDyer dates the conference at 1977 but Smyth was assassinated in 1976. Foot, Paul, *Who Framed Colin Wallace?*, 147-50.
127. Bruce, Steve (1992), *The Red Hand: Protestant Paramilitaries in Northern Ireland*, Oxford: OUP, 243.
128. Murphy, D., *A Place Apart*, 110.
129. PT, 25 January 1969 -- 'last bastion'.
130. PT, 23 September 1972, 27 October 1973, 15 April 1978.
131. Fremantle, 168. Pius XI ([1929] 1963), On the Christian Education of Youth, London: Catholic Truth Society, paras 67 and 69. For Paisley (1964), *Why I am a Protestant*, Belfast: Puritan, 9-10.
132. *Mater et Magister*, Guerry, 178 and 217. John XXIII (1963), *World Peace*, London (Australian Catholic Truth Society) 58 (para. 187).
133. McDonagh, Enda (1980), *The Demands of Simple Justice*, 53.
134. McDonagh, 49. Anglican Bishop J.E. Mercer of Tasmania.
135. *UDA News* (UDAN), 17 October 1971.
136. UDAN, 17 October 1971.
137. UL, 10 February 1975.

138. See 'Heartland' with Margaret Derry on Belfast Dundonald area, broadcast, Radio Ulster 14 April 1980.
139. UDAN, 27 October 1971, 19 October 1971.
140. Boulton, 178 and 182-3.
141. Foot, *Who Framed Colin Wallace?*, 147.
142. UL, 21 November 1974.
143. *Combat* (C), (1, 32) 74. UC, 25 November 1974.
144. Murphy, D., *A Place Apart*, 151.
145. Interview, 6 August 1982, on 'good Morning Ulster' with Virginia Ware, editor of *Seachlight* who alleged a meeting between an NF leader and Tyrie in 1981 and plans for joint military training in Wales. John McMichael for the UDA denied specific links.
146. C, 8 April 1974 and UL 26 September 1974.
147. UL, 21 November 1974 and *Observer*, 6 June 1974. Probert, *Beyond Orange and Green*, 141.
148. C, (1, 22) 1974. For John White, see Holland, Jack (1982), *Too Long a Sacrifice: Life and Death in Northern Ireland since 1969*: Harmondsworth: Penguin, 101.
149. Error 80, Fremantle, 152.
150. C, (1,23) 1974.
151. C, (1, 26) 1974.
152. C, 5 (1,8) 1974.
153. C, (2,1) 1975.
154. C, 8 April 1974.
155. UL, Easter 1975.
156. UL, 13 April 1975.
157. C, June 1975.
158. C, 1 May 1974.
159. *Law*, (2,53) 1973, (2, 52) 1973, (2,38) 1973. For analysis, see Probert, *Beyond Orange and Green*, 136-141.
160. UC, 8 July 1974 (BICO and UWC strike and Boyd Black advisers). AP, 27 November 1979, 19 April 1980.
161. SP, April 1975 and May 1975. *Volunteer*, 49, 1972 and UC, 30 September 1974 (for PD) and 29 September 1972 for David George's NS article.
162. U, January 1979, quotes *Magill*.
163. Adamson, I. (1981), *The Identity of Ulster*, Belfast: the Author, 68-9. Bruce, *God Save Ulster: The Religion and Politics of Paisleyism*, 259 and 261, sees 'elements of socialism' in the UDA programme for an independent Ulster which he considers counterproductive in the Northern Ireland context.

8 The propaganda of the third and fourth world

The anti-imperial front

Previous chapters have shown republicans and some loyalists striving to appear progressive in the eyes of the world. In ideological conflict with both British government and Catholic Church republicans often draw on overseas examples and precedents. Nineteenth-century Irish nationalist did likewise: Thomas Davis and other Young Irelanders endeavoured to raise Irish consciousness by attacking British imperial misrule in countries such as India, New Zealand, Canada, South Africa and Australia.[1] The Fenians carried on the tradition by exulting in the heroics of the insurgent Maoris[2] in the 1860s, while Sinn Féin in the early twentieth-century identified with Indian nationalism.[3] The rights of indigenous people were generally asserted, though some leading nationalists like John Mitchel and Arthur Griffith believed in white superiority.

This pattern of support continued during the Ulster Troubles after 1968. The breakaway Provisionals originally ridiculed the 'long-distance revolutionaries' who sought justice everywhere except their own country. Soon the Provisionals were competing with the Officials and other radical groups for identification with popular struggles overseas, but not with low-status terrorist gangs, despite the insistence of their opponents. The new assertiveness of Fourth World minorities such as Maoris, Australian Aborigines, and Amerinds in Canada and the USA were well-advertised in republican newspapers. Contacts were encouraged between local Irish republicans and such indigenous groups. Kenya was associated with the misdeeds of Kitson. The transformation of Jomo Kenyatta, the evil manager of Mau Mau, to President Sir Jomo, the welcome guest at Buckingham Palace, made excellent Provisional propaganda.[4] During the 1981 hunger strikes several Indian newspapers drew parallels between Sands and Jatin Das, a former supporter of Gandhi who turned to physical force and died on hunger strike when imprisoned for manufacturing explosives.[5]

Southern Africa, however, provided the overseas ideological battleground for Northern Ireland. In the 1970s the focus was Rhodesia. There Ian Smith's white minority regime, which had made a Unilateral Declaration of Independence (UDI) from Britain in 1965, was fighting for survival against local Patriotic Front guerrillas and weakly applied United Nations sanctions. A Commonwealth-supervised election in early 1980 resulted in the landslide victory of Robert Mugabe's ZANU[6] and the establishment of an independent Zimbabwe. Attention then shifted to South Africa, where increasing assertion by the black majority after the Soweto uprising of 1976 led to an explosive mix of repression and reform which culminated in the release of Nelson Mandela and the legalisation of his African National Congress (ANC) in 1990. In both Rhodesia/Zimbabwe and South Africa, loyalist/republican debate provided a remarkable example of calculated opposition, with some hints of unconscious convergence and antithetical interpretation.

The ideological battle for Zimbabwe/Rhodesia

The *Protestant Telegraph* was established a year after Smith's UDI. Dr Paisley and his American ally, Dr Bob Jones, strongly supported the white regime. Eric Fromm has argued that Calvinist predestination was revived in Nazism which similarly asserted the basic inequality of man. Yet Geoffrey Bell sees Paisley's support for Ian Smith as based on a common religious attitude, rather than racism as such.[7] This must be tested. The *Protestant Telegraph* certainly claimed to be solidly behind Rhodesia, not because of its 'alleged racism', but because of its constitutional government, hemmed in by communist puppets. Moreover, the Rhodesian ecumenists and five Roman Catholic bishops were opposed to the

Smith regime. This identification was strengthened by the expulsion in 1977 of the Northern Ireland-born Bishop Donal Lamont for refusing to order his clergy to inform on guerrilla activities.[8] The Roman Catholic Church, said Dr Paisley's paper, could always be relied on to oppose democracy and righteousness. 'Democracy' in this context presumably referred to the rule of the elect, rather than a mere majority. When Lamont was put on trial by the Rhodesian government in 1976 the *Protestant Telegraph* drew an analogy with Bishop Edward Daly who had attacked the British Army for its actions on Bloody Sunday, 1972. Lamont's sentence showed that the pope disliked the Smith government and wanted full negro power: 'He envisages a papist state with blacks in the ascendancy whose superstitious nature can more easily assimilate the errors and idolatry of Romanism'.[9] As the *Protestant Telegraph* maintained on another occasion, a franchise based on different rolls was perfectly acceptable and practised by leaders such as President Ayub Khan in Pakistan.[10] On the other side, although Lamont was a firm believer in non-violence, the Provisionals used his example as positive propaganda against supporters of the Northern Ireland security forces.[11]

The *Protestant Telegraph* was delighted that UDI Rhodesia had defied both communism and the Roman Catholic Church, whose Rhodesian periodical, the *Southern Cross*, had been banned for opposing the *status quo*. Far from believing intelligence to reside in both races, a correspondent from the United States, Dr Billy John Hargis, who had met Ian Smith, provided first-hand evidence that 'before Prime Minister Smith and the white Rhodesian government came along, the Africans were savages. These white leaders have civilised them.' Bob Jones, whose racially segregated university had honoured Paisley with a doctorate, applauded the 'great sacrifice'[12] of English settlers in Rhodesia, partly compensated, no doubt, by the Land Apportionment Act which reserved the best areas for the tiny white minority while the vast majority of the population lived well below the poverty line.

Paisley and his colleagues were thus totally opposed to any action against Rhodesia. They denied that a 'rebellion' had taken place or that the Smith regime was 'illegal'. Loyalists deplored sanctions; the very attempt of the United Nations to impose them demonstrated, as Jones said, the sickness of modern society. The hanging of rebels against the regime was commended. Denunciations of apartheid in Rhodesia and South Africa were turned by Paisley against the Catholic Church which enforced religious (but not racial) apartheid in its schools.[13] The importance of Rhodesia to loyalists antedated the Northern Ireland Troubles, and indeed the rise of an effective African guerrilla resistance.

The Ulster/Rhodesia majority/minority argument

The outbreak of violence in Ulster, anticipating that of Rhodesia in 1972, and thus giving some justification to the republican claim that Zimbabwe guerrillas had been inspired by the Irish,[14] intensified the debate. The *Republican News*, later finding it 'astonishing to see how similar the two areas (Rhodesia and Northern Ireland) are', castigated Harold Wilson for inconsistency. In Rhodesia he wanted majority rule for the blacks, but in Ireland he accepted minority rule for the 'Ulster Protestants'.[15] This majority-minority contention, reversed, became a stock argument with loyalists after the suspension of Stormont in March 1972. In his speech on the 'black day for Ulster', Bill Craig used the loyalist version of the Rhodesian majority-minority theory. The British, he said, in an excellent example of antithetical interpretation, were inconsistent in demanding majority rule in Rhodesia, while denying it to the majority in Northern Ireland.[16] To republicans the whole of Ireland was the unit; to the loyalist the six counties were self-sufficient. Craig talked vociferously for a time of a UDI for Ulster and his Vanguard party received considerable support from Prot-stat paramilitaries, but Paisley, despite his admiration for the Smith regime, was opposed to Ulster UDI from the start. Realistically, he saw that Rhodesia, rhetoric aside, was very different from Northern Ireland. By 1980, the UDA, which had been working on a plan for an independent Ulster, emphasised that a UDI like that of Rhodesia, about to become independent Zimbabwe, would be disastrous.[17]

The majority-minority argument depended on whether the 'majority' referred to the Irish people as a whole (republican) or to the Northern Ireland population (loyalist). It was circular in that it rested on the individual's belief in the justice or otherwise of the partition of Ireland. The argument was, however, used by Paisley's paper and other loyalists till at least 1977.[18] Interpretation of the Downing Street Agreement of December 1993 depended on this majority-minority contention. The republicans always rejected the six counties as a unit. As a prisoner in Long Kesh pointed out, the loyalist 'majority' was based on an area artificially created by the British.[19] The argument could be turned back on Paisley. He and his colleagues had shown that they were not in favour of majority rule everywhere; how then could they demand majority rule in

Northern Ireland?[20] As *An Phoblacht* said in 1980, it was absurd for the reactionary Paisley to compare himself with the then electorally victorious Mugabe.[21] Nationalists deliberately exploited this loyalist association with the Smith regime. On 'Bloody Sunday' the *Republican News* quoted the *Protestant Telegraph* against the principle of one man one vote, which had been declared 'simply a gimmick for a few black people with a few "A" and "O" levels who feel they can exploit the natives of Rhodesia better than the white'.[22] Was this exploitation to be the prerogative of 'the white civilised minority' or a few blacks 'able to read a book'? This, declared the Provisional journal, was similar to the Northern Irish civil rights issue in 1968 when the minority declined to accept the honour 'of being exploited by your civilised Unionist gangsters'. In both the six counties and Rhodesia the exploited people had now decided to look after themselves.[23] After 'Bloody Sunday' a republican verse incorporated the Rhodesian analogy:

> They talk about the sacred vote
> And bid us all take careful note
> That numbers in the North hold sway
> That Unionists must have their way
>
> But on Rhodesia's sunny swards
> The vote breeds no such just rewards
> Here they have a change of heart
> The few may rule the greater part.

The same issue reinforced the lesson with a cartoon showing a grinning Ted Heath with arms around Brian Faulkner and Ian Smith, gloating over their respective massacres at Derry and Gwelo.[24] The link between the DUP and the Smith regime was asserted again by both Provisionals and Officials. According to the *United Irishman*, 'the two Ians would certainly have a lot to talk about, niggers, Teagues, commies, perfidious Limeys and democratic rights. Well maybe not about democratic rights.'[25] The *Republican News* publicised a Portadown DUP member who called on Ian Smith to visit Ulster to discuss common problems.[26] Ian Smith thanked the DUP branch for its support. The fact that the Smith regime by 1977 was growing less secure, despite its bravado, enabled republicans to take full advantage of their opponents' identification with a cause rejected by liberal opinion and supported by some unfortunate friends. This was demonstrated in the UVF's *Combat*. In 1974 the UVF was flirting with the British neo-fascist National Front, publicising its views in a National Front pamphlet on Rhodesia. The pamphlet denied that South Africa and Rhodesia were guilty of any act of injustice to the African majority. A *Combat* correspondent suggested that loyalists draw closer to both the National Front itself and the white regime in South Africa and Rhodesia. Was the National Front fascist? *Combat* thought not. Dr Paisley was associated with the Rev. Brian Green, once an NF parliamentary candidate. 'Is it likely that Ian Paisley—and we all know how he makes sure that his doorstep is clean—would associate with known fascists and nazis?'[27] Such logic appeared irrefutable. By 1978 the UDA journal *Ulster* seemed alive to the dangers of this settler association. It denounced the people in high places who had run Northern Ireland on the 'apartheid' lines of South Africa and Rhodesia. *Combat* also loosened the link with settler racism. The *Loyalist News*, of Paisley's enemy McKeague, accepted that the southern African blacks must have majority rule. This increasing awareness did not prevent two UDA leaders visiting South Africa in the 1980s and praising the defences of the white regime.[28]

Other Ulster/Rhodesia links and precedents

The violence of the Rhodesian struggle provided an excellent opportunity for republican/loyalist antithetical interpretation, spiced with calculated antagonism. Horrific massacres, sometimes of missionaries, were confidently attributed by the Provisionals, not to the Patriotic Front, but to the Rhodesian Army's Selous Scouts, believed to be the equivalent of the SAS in Northern Ireland.[29]. Loyalists with equal fervour denounced the Patriotic Front for the killings and attacked the World Council of Churches (WCC) which, to Paisley's annoyance, had given £6,355 to organisations like Mugabe's ZANU. The WCC members now had missionary blood on their hands.[30] The Orange Grand Master, Martin Smyth, also opposed to WCC assistance to African nationalists, complained of the double standard by which Africans were dubbed guerrillas, while the IRA were terrorists.[31] In 1980, the year of Zimbabwe independence, loyalist Presbyterians, no friends of Mugabe, finally voted the Northern Ireland Presbyterian Church out of the WCC.[32]

In fact the *Protestant Telegraph's* idea of what security forces should do in southern Africa was very similar to what republicans accused them of actually doing. Praising young Britons who emigrated to Rhodesia to join its army instead of serving in Northern Ireland, 'more power to them', the Paisley journal enthused on how they could pursue anti-terrorism without the shackles imposed on soldiers in Ulster. In Rhodesia there was no yellow card imposed on soldiers.[33] Six-county Catholics had for years complained that British soldiers never abided by their yellow card which allowed them to shoot only in very restricted circumstances.[34]

Numerous far-fetched parallels between Northern Ireland and Rhodesia were suggested by republicans. The UDA's idea of an independent Ulster was rejected on the basis of Rhodesian analogies.[35] Bishop Abel Muzorewa, who collaborated with Ian Smith before Mugabe's election victory, was compared to Arthur Griffith and Michael Collins who had sold Ireland out in the 1921 Anglo-Irish Treaty. Officials and Provisionals vied with each other in attempting to establish fraternal relations with the Patriotic Front.[36] The victory of Mugabe in 1980 was undoubtedly a boost to republicans in general, soured somewhat for Provisionals when post-independence Zimbawe newspapers continued to describe them as terrorists.[37]

Irish republicanism's historical links with South Africa

In both Rhodesia and South Africa, attempts were made by Irish republicans to forge personal links with black African leaders. There was ample precedent for this. As early as the 1840s and 1850s Young Ireland nationalists Thomas Davis and William Smith O'Brien sympathised with the 'Kaffirs' in their resistance to white settlers.[38] Davis rejected British aggression and conquest all over the world; O'Brien in his Tasmanian penal exile, after the failure of the 1848 Rebellion, was more circumspect. Though supporting the Kaffirs, and other native peoples oppressed by invaders, O'Brien could not, however, accept the right of a few uncivilised tribes to lock up vast acres of land on which Europeans could live profitably. Moved, perhaps by the horrors of the Irish Famine of 1845-49, O'Brien suggested a modified 'apartheid'. Natives who wished to preserve their own culture could live apart in their own areas. O'Brien was sceptical of the value of European civilisation to other peoples. In marked contrast to modern apartheid, he insisted that a native wishing to live amongst Europeans be accorded full rights in their society. O'Brien's scheme presupposed the existence of ample land for all.

By the turn of the nineteenth century the roots of a very different segregation policy were already discernible in South Africa. Black Africans had in many cases been restricted to ownership of poor, inadequate lands, while denied political rights, except partly in Cape Colony. Nevertheless, Irish nationalists then directed their sympathies towards white Afrikaners struggling for self-determination against the British Empire. Two Irish brigades fought on the Afrikaner side in the second Boer War. Major John McBride, second-in-command of one of these units, was later executed for his part in the Irish Rising of 1916. John McBride's friend, Arthur Griffith,[39] founder of Sinn Féin and Irish President in 1922, lived from 1896 to 1898 in South Africa where he used his journalistic skill to advance the Boer cause. His total identification with the Afrikaner ignored the plight of the 'Kaffir'.[40] McBride's wife, the famous Maud Gonne, not only tried to organise the sinking of a British troopship *en route* to South Africa, but was personally thanked by the exiled Transvaal President Kruger for Irish assistance during the War.[41] The MacBrides' son, Séan, won the Nobel Peace Prize in 1974, not for supporting the Afrikaners, but for his efforts to persuade them to evacuate Namibia.

During the Anglo-Irish War, 1919-21, politically conscious Irish residents in South Africa supported the more advanced Afrikaner nationalists who looked for leadership from General Barry Hertzog, rather than the now British-oriented General Jan Christian Smuts. Smuts's efforts to intercede with Irish leaders to persuade them to accept dominion status were not appreciated by the South African Irish.[42] Afrikaner nationalism, not the infant and still ultra-moderate ANC, became the natural focus for the embattled Irish. Meanwhile, some early ANC leaders, as had Smith O'Brien, accepted racial segregation as potentially beneficial.[43]

Memories of Afrikaner-Irish amity endured into the 1970s. In 1974, Provisional Sinn Féin's *Republican News*, edited by the old-guard republican Sean McCaughey, denounced British Boer War atrocities, when the women and children were rounded up in disease-ridden internment camps.[44] It also demonstrated, apropos British intentions in Northern Ireland, that attempts at Anglicising South Africa after the 1902 Treaty of Vereeniging, which ended the Boer War, had failed dismally.[45] Moreover, *Republican News* cited Liam Mellows, executed by the Irish Free State Government in 1922. Mellows had compared the former Boer War generals J.C. Smuts and Louis Botha with his Irish opponents, Collins and Griffith. Both groups had signed treaties with Britain and, according to Mellows, led governments subservient to British interests. Like many Irish South Africans of that period, Mellows supported more extreme Afrikaner nationalists.[46] When younger Northern Ireland republicans Danny Morrison and Gerry Adams took over *Republican News* in 1975 and the whole Provisional movement some years later, they worked hard to identify with the emergent black Africans, increasingly oppressed since the 1910 grant of independence. The development of full-scale apartheid in South Africa after 1948 naturally attracted attention in Ireland. As in Rhodesia Ulster loyalists identified with the Afrikaners, previously supported as freedom fighters by Irish republicans, while the latter now sympathised with the black majorities, hitherto ignored. The majority/minority argument, developing in Rhodesia, was applied also in South Africa. The loyalist version suffered an unintentional setback in 1986 when the South African ambassador to the United Kingdom, Dr Denis Worrall, visited Northern Ireland. Worrall shocked the Unionists, the only group willing to receive him, by maintaining that as majority rule was inappropriate in Northern Ireland power-sharing was necessary.[47]

In the 1970s Officials and Provisionals, as with Rhodesia, took up issues such as the Sharpeville (1960) and Soweto (1976) massacres of blacks and the death in 1977 at white police hands of the charismatic Black Consciousness leader, Steve Biko. Greetings were exchanged where possible with exiled ANC leaders. Until the 1980s white repression, unlike that of neighbouring Zimbabwe, was relatively effective in South Africa.

Loyalists and South Africa

Several recent writers have constructed elaborate comparisons between the Ulster Protestants and Afrikaners.[48] To Adrian Guelke, formerly a Northern Ireland political scientist with a South African background, both states lack democratic legitimacy: South Africa because of its minority rule, Northern Ireland because of its artificial boundary giving Protestants a local majority.[49] He thus disposed of one apparent difference between the two areas, that Northern Ireland Protestants can legitimately claim majority rule in their six counties. Guelke also documented liaison between Ulster Protestants and Afrikaners. Michael Macdonald, an American political scientist, accepted that Ulster Protestants and Afrikaners represent settlers dealing with hostile natives; both depend on the degrading of their opponents to forge their own identities. In each country, Macdonald maintained, the intransigents of the dominant group hold a veto over attempts by liberal politicians to reform the system. Robert Crawford, a Presbyterian cleric and academic, further suggested a similarity between the reforms of P.W. Botha, Prime Minister and President of South Africa in the 1980s, and the unsuccessful liberalisation of

Terence O'Neill in Northern Ireland. Like Macdonald, Crawford saw conservative Calvinism, common to both Ulster Protestants and Afrikaners, encouraging the idea of a chosen race. Moreover, the historical consciousness of Afrikaner and Ulster Protestant ran parallel in their covenanting zeal and emphasis on the defeat of the Zulus and Catholics at Blood River (1838) and the Boyne (1690) respectively. The once dominant Afrikaner secret Broederbond was roughly equated with the Orange Order in Northern Ireland. Such identification of Ulster Protestants as colonists endorsed Provisional ideology.

Paisley and his followers did little to refute such arguments. They insisted that South Africa was the victim of a worldwide attempt to destroy Christian civilisation and the capitalist system. The Free Presbyterian Church in 1963 became a member of the International Council of Christian Churches, assisted by South Africans to counteract the WCC. The *Protestant Telegraph* considered the prohibition of cricket tours to South Africa equivalent to banning the Orange twelfth of July processions in Northern Ireland. Republicans, on the contrary, strongly opposed sporting tours to South Africa.[50] Free Presbyterians were concerned when the Dutch Reformed Church in the Netherlands, supportive of African nationalism, broke with its counterpart in South Africa. Paisley accused the Roman Catholic Church of undermining the established order in Southern Africa as a whole.[51] Afrikaner opinion, remembering traditional links with Irish nationalism, was ambivalent on Ulster. In 1981 many Afrikaans papers sympathised with the republican hunger strikers, but in 1982 the South African defence journal *Scope* praised the counter-insurgency of the SAS in Northern Ireland.[52] In the same year a letter from Leon Van Wyk, press officer of the Reformed Nationalist Party, Durban, used the argument of inconsistency on majorities and minorities in Ulster and South Africa against Mrs Thatcher. He requested Ulster Protestant solidarity with the Afrikaners' attempt to maintain the Protestant Reformed Faith. An Ulster-South African Solidarity Campaign was established in Durban, and South African arms appear to have gone early to Protestant paramilitaries like Tara, small but very aggressive.[53] Some Northern Irish Protestants joined the white Southern African security forces. Paisley's former close associate, Noel Doherty, who established the Puritan Printing Press and the *Protestant Telegraph*, became a South African publicist after serving a two-year gaol sentence for explosives' offences in Northern Ireland.[54] The UDA not only praised the South African Defence Force for its pursuit of terrorists, but when the paramilitary establised its own élite unit, the Ulster Defence Force, to deal with a potential Doomsday situation in Northern Ireland, a UDA member claimed in 1983 that it had been instructed in South Africa, Israel and the Lebanon. Next year the Provisionals cited two UDA men training in South Africa.[55] Most dramatically, in 1989 an attempt to trade missile secrets from the Belfast Short Brothers' aircraft factories for South African arms for the Ulster Resistance, a paramilitary group sponsored, then disavowed, by Paisley, was foiled in Paris. The South African Government admitted the proffered arms deal but denied that it had been officially sanctioned. Paisley showed his concern by arranging to fly to Paris, but was later accused by the UDA of abandoning the 'Paris Three'. The Provisionals considered it appropriate that the neo-Nazis from Northern Ireland should co-operate with their fascist counterparts in South Africa.[56] In their own efforts to identify with the more apparently acceptable black anti-colonial 'Freedom Fighters', the Provisionals, as in the case of Rhodesia, experienced considerable initial competition in their own community.

From protest to tactical co-operation

South African repression became a valuable Provisional weapon. Loyalist identification with racist minority regimes suited the republicans. Some UDA spokesmen indicated awareness of this fact.[57] According to a senior British Conservative backbench MP, Andrew Hunter, what had been mere contact within protest movements in the 1960s and 1970s evolved into tactical co-operation between the Provisionals and the ANC in the 1980s. Momentum certainly increased after the Northern Ireland hunger strikes of 1981. In 1982 Fr Enda McDonagh found young Soweto blacks coupling Bobby Sands and Steve Biko 'in their list of contemporary heroes'.[58] The *Republican News* quoted without denial another republican paper's suggestion that Provisionals were fighting alongside blacks in Zimbabwe and South Africa.[59] Some young black South Africans believed in 1981 that the ANC was being advised by the PIRA.[60] Joe Cahill, a former leader of the Belfast Provisionals, claimed in 1984 that South African blacks had sought aid from his movement. In June of the same year a South African newspaper quoted a former ANC operative to the effect that the ANC bombing campaign was 'deployed and supplied' by the PIRA and its smaller republican rival, the Irish National Liberation Army (INLA).[61] The Provisionals showed a paternal interest when the ANC in 1980 sabotaged three widely separated state oil and gas plants. This appeared a turning point as the ANC units had hitherto been inhibited by frontier security and the break-up of their cells within South Africa itself. Now they were able, according to *An Phoblacht*, to move through the protective screen with impunity.[62] Until 1983 few lives were lost in ANC campaigns. But the retaliatory Pretoria car bomb of that year, which killed nineteen, was reminiscent of the Provisionals. Robert Crawford suggests that a split occurred in the ANC, similar to that in the IRA, which led to the striking of soft, civilian targets which the original organisation refused to touch.[63] Nelson Mandela, when gaoled for life in 1963, supported only sabotage against installations, not personnel. In his speech from the dock he declared that the new ANC militant wing, Umkonto we Sizwe, was on no account 'to kill or injure people', though provision was made for guerrilla training which might be necessary in the future.[64] From prison he lamented the 1983 Pretoria car bomb as 'a tragic accident', accepting the occasional possibility of injuries or deaths as a by-product of sabotage, but rejecting the policy of assassination.[65] This distinguishes Mandela from the Provisionals, who take full responsibility for the assassination of British military or governmental personnel, while maintaining that bomb warnings are normally given to civilians. Mandela was not in a position to speak for all ANC or Umkonto members, to many of whom Provisional tactics clearly had considerable appeal.

In 1988, Andrew Hunter publicly claimed 'irrefutable evidence' that ANC and Namibia's South West African People's Organisation (SWAPO) were meeting PIRA representatives. He repeated the assertion in 1990, citing a meeting at Downpatrick on 4 April between ANC representatives and Provisionals, led by the IRA South Down commander. Though the ANC, later endorsed by Mandela himself, 'utterly and unequivocally' repudiated 'this preposterous fabrication', such contacts, even if unauthorised at higher levels, are distinctly possible. Unabashed, Hunter insisted that the PIRA and ANC had held twenty meetings in the three years leading to July 1990. Furthermore, the ANC and PIRA had co-operated on a plan to assassinate Margaret Thatcher in Zimbabwe.[66]

The ANC leadership in the 1990s has no propagandist advantage to gain from identification with the Provisionals, while the latter have every reason to identify with such a popular cause as the ANC. When South African black activists wanted Irish advice on hunger strike tactics, they approached the Irish Anti-Apartheid Movement (IAAM), not the Provisionals. Nevertheless, to the chagrin of Irish Taoiseach Garret Fitzgerald, who resigned from IAAM, Provisional Sinn Féin was affiliated with the movement. As IAAM's leader, Kader Asmal, a law lecturer, is an important ANC officer, Sinn Féin has obtained, through IAAM, a tenuous link with the ANC.[67] With observer status at the UN and acceptance as a signatory to the protocol accepting the Geneva convention in its war of national liberation the ANC had a clear advantage over the PIRA, even before the release of Nelson Mandela and the removal of the four-year-old state of emergency in 1990. PIRA had never achieved such international respectability. Guelke demonstrates the existence of a terrorist 'pecking order' where less acceptable organisations seek association with more prestigious counterparts, who keep the former at arm's length. Thus PIRA, which Guelke locates in the middle range, scorns liaison with Italian Red Brigades, while vainly pursuing the ANC and PLO.[68] Protestant paramilitaries and fringe republican organisations rank even lower than PIRA.[69] Hence Provisionals insisted that their only allies were the Black Freedom Fighters, while the ANC admitted links with the PLO but repudiated any with the IRA.[70]

SWAPO, originally of lower status than the ANC, and Namibia appeared more forthcoming. Official Sinn Féin in 1976 sponsored the Irish tour of George James, a SWAPO representative based in London; SWAPO sent greetings to the Provisional Sinn Féin Ard Fheis in 1980. In 1981 the Provisionals publicised support for Owen Carron, Bobby Sands's election agent and replacement as MP for Fermanagh-South Tyrone, from the exiled Anglican bishop of Namibia, Colin Winter. The Namibian cause obtained considerable coverage in *An Phoblacht*.[71] After SWAPO in 1990 assumed the government of independent Namibia, open support for PIRA does not appear on its agenda.

Though the Provisionals have never been unambiguously endorsed by ANC leaders like Oliver Tambo and Nelson Mandela (compared by Provisionals to Bobby Sands), *An Phoblacht* long endeavoured, by frequent quotation, to demonstrate the ANC's ideological affinity with Irish republicanism.[72] Gerry Adams often cites Mandela, and has suggested the ANC's moderate, mildly socialist Freedom Charter of 1955 as a model for Ireland.[73] Mandela's release by President F.W. de Klerk in February 1990 was celebrated with a full front-page photograph in *An Phoblacht*: 'walking free, Nelson Mandela brings our freedom that much closer.'[74] Mandela's refusal to discountenance the continuing armed struggle of Umkonto we Sizwe was taken as an endorsement of PIRA tactics. The new breakaway Republican Sinn

Féin disapproved of the Provisionals' 1986 decision to take their seats if elected to the Irish Dail. To Republican Sinn Féin, Mandela's greatness lay in his refusal to compromise his principles. Their contemptible 'Free State Sinn Féin' rivals had exhibited no similar consistency.[75] On the extreme unionist side Paisley continued to snipe at African leaders such as Archbishop Desmond Tutu and the Rev. Alan Boesak.[76] The extremist groups, however, had no monopoly of the South African debate.

Irish constitutionalists and the ANC

Irish constitutionalists and political moderates had long exhibited concern over South Africa. The eminent writer, diplomat and Irish Labour politician Conor Cruise O'Brien had been an early member of the Irish anti-apartheid movement when it was 'open and liberal'. He resented attempts by the IAAM to prevent him breaking the academic boycott by lecturing at Cape Town University in 1986. As Irish minister for Posts and Telegraphs in the 1970s, O'Brien had incurred perennial Provisional ire for banning them from broadcasting. The Provisionals were accordingly overjoyed when O'Brien was challenged in Cape Town by demonstrators carrying banners combining pro-IRA and pro-ANC logos.[77]

Other Irish constitutional politicians, North and South, particularly resented the Provisional attempt to appropriate Mandela. In February 1990 the Belfast constitutional nationalist *Irish News* sounded out Billy Masethla, deputy chief spokesman for the ANC in Britain, on links with the IRA and received a categorical denial. The ANC rejected such unfounded rumours and emphasised the IAAM as its sole Irish contact.[78] Such repudiation emboldened Councillor Seamus Lynch of the Workers' Party (formerly Official Sinn Féin) to attempt, unsuccessfully, to persuade the Belfast City Council to grant Mandela its Freedom.[79] To a member of the SDLP, the majority constitutional nationalist grouping in Northern Ireland, the Provisionals resembled the Nicaraguan Contras rather than the ANC.[80] Barry White, biographer of SDLP leader and influential IAAM member[81] John Hume, saw Mandela as achieving an excellent balance between force and conciliation; to White, some of Mandela's statements were remarkably relevant to Northern Ireland.[82]

In a debate in the Irish Senate, two non-party senators, David Norris and Joe O'Toole, representing the University of Dublin and the National University of Ireland respectively, repudiated Sinn Féin. Sinn Féin was attempting, after Mandela's release, to 'carpet bag' the ANC's principle of continued armed struggle to justify its totally different policies.[83] Senator Brendan Ryan, another National University member, was concerned that both South African and Irish Churchmen, plus Irish people in general, believed that the ANC's armed struggle lacked moral justification. Ryan contrasted repudiation of the ANC with belief in the '(apparently) impeccable moral credentials' of the Irish Rising of 1916.[84] If indeed most Irish clergy and laity venerated the 1916 insurgents while rejecting the ANC, the Provisional attempt to gain credit by identification with the latter may have backfired in Ireland.

An Phoblacht, however, endeavoured to make capital from the visit of their critics, Senators John A. Murphy and Shane Ross, to South Africa and their subsequent recommendation of the lifting of sanctions.[85] The Provisionals, who rejected the possibility of a serious Protestant backlash on British withdrawal from Northern Ireland, continued to support sanctions as demanded by Mandela in contrast to the members of the Irish liberal establishment. Murphy's concern that continued sanctions might encourage a white backlash against de Klerk was relevant to another Irish visitor's belief that de Klerk in February 1990 resembled the reforming Northern Ireland Prime Minister Terence O'Neill in 1968, shortly before a Protestant backlash overthrew him. To some extent the March 1992 white referendum, which endorsed de Klerk's negotiations with black leaders, makes comparison with O'Neill less apt, but difficulties still remained from white militants. The power of the South African white resistance and the precariousness of Mandela was confirmed by Adrian Guelke, who, like Robert Crawford, also considered that 'the circumstances in which de Klerk's less radical predecessor, P.W. Botha, and O'Neill embraced reform were remarkably similar in a number of respects'.[86] Far from the ANC position justifying the IRA, the latter's actions at this time may have made Irish opinion sceptical of force in the South African context.

Black South African opinion and the Provisionals

While the Irish debate on South Africa raged, ANC leaders had tasks more pressing than academic analysis of Irish parallels. Yet African leaders clearly had some conception of the Irish situation. The ANC theoretical position on Northern Ireland may be partly deduced from interviews. Meeting Seamus Martin of the *Irish Times*, the released Mandela asked if his interviewer was a member of the IRA. On Martin's denial of membership, Mandela said 'good, very good'.[87] A clue to his attitude was provided in Archbishop Desmond Tutu's interview with the same reporter, Seamus Martin. The South African situation, declared the archbishop, 'is different from the Northern Ireland situation in that our guys did not have the possibility of parliamentary procedures and channels which the IRA do have.' A leading SDLP member and former Irish senator, Bríd Rodgers, agreed: 'We aren't a country like South Africa.... People looking for justice and equality for Catholics in Northern Ireland have a political route open to them.' In a different but similar context, Mandela explicitly endorsed this argument.[88] As Tutu demonstrated, the originally non-violent ANC only adopted the armed struggle when banned. Justifying the South African bishops' call for a moratorium on violence, Tutu suggested that the ANC's armed struggle was 'rhetorical and almost an academic issue.'[89] Joe Slovo, the veteran communist and Umkonto we Sizwe leader, agreed when he declared that the AK 47 would be redundant when democratic politics were open to all.[90]

While tension exists in the ANC, as in the Provisional movement, between advocates of vigorous armed struggle and supporters of progress by political means, President de Klerk's liberal policies have given an initial advantage to the latter. Mandela's early writings show that he abandoned with considerable diffidence the non-violence of his former leader, Chief Albert Luthuli. Though passive resistance seemed impossible after 1960, Mandela was sometimes unhappy with Umkonto we Sizwe after 1983. Martin's interview with Mandela's released colleague, Walter Sisulu, provided another clue when Sisulu referred to the distant achievements of Eamon de Valera. To Provisional Sinn Féin leader Gerry Adams, de Valera was a 'non-republican'.[91] Though a hero of the 1916 Rising, de Valera as Taoiseach from 1932 to 1948 had dealt firmly with the IRA of that period, many of whom had been imprisoned, interned or executed. *An Phoblacht*, justifying the IRA's far from rhetorical violence in 1990, did not report the comments of South Africa's black leaders. Gerry Adams, launching his *Cage Eleven* in London shortly after the Provisionals had gunned down two Australian tourists at Roermond in the Netherlands, still maintained the South African analogy: 'My view is the same as Nelson Mandela's: we need negotiations to lead to cessations [of armed force], not cessations to lead to negotiations.'[92] It was clear that when Mandela visited Ireland in person he would come under considerable pressure to define clearly his opinion on Ireland.

Mandela in Ireland: reactions

Mandela arrived in Ireland on 2 July 1990 to receive the Freedom of Dublin. His speech in Dail Eireann appeared impeccable. Mandela committed the ANC to the 1916 Proclamation's intention to 'cherish all the children of the nation equally', while quoting W.B. Yeats's warning in Easter 1916: 'Too long a sacrifice/ Can make a stone of the heart'. At a dinner, hosted by the IAAM and the Irish Congress of Trade Unions, Mandela acknowledged the 'tremendous inspiration' to South Africa of Irish heroes and heroines, but pointed out again that the ANC armed struggle developed only when the government stopped all peaceful protest. Umkonto had been scaled down since 1986.[93] The implications were clear, but most attention focused on his response to questions on modern Ulster. Pressed by journalists, Mandela suggested peace talks between the IRA and the Thatcher Government: 'What we would like to see, is that the British government and the IRA should adopt precisely the line we have taken in regard to our internal situation. There is nothing better than opponents sitting down to resolve their problems in a peaceful manner.' He pointed out that Britain had negotiated in the past without demanding that its opponents lay down their arms and instanced the Rhodesian settlement. Britain should take the line adopted in South Africa. The minority status of the Provisionals was not the issue, but the ineffectiveness of force in such situations. Mandela, however, categorically denied ANC meetings with the IRA.[94] Gerry Adams and Provisional Sinn Féin seized on Mandela's general statement as an endorsement of their armed struggle in Northern Ireland. *An Phoblacht* again devoted its front page and much of its contents to Mandela the 'Peacemaker', revelling in 'the acute embarrassment' which the ANC Deputy President's comments had caused the British and Irish establishments: 'TWO DAYS THAT SHOOK THE SYSTEM'.[95] On the following day, Mandela was forced to qualify his remarks at a meeting of the House of Commons Southern African Committee, explaining that he had not commented on the IRA or the British Government but expressed the ANC view that all world conflicts should be solved peacefully.[96]

Other reactions to Mandela varied. The unionist Belfast *News Letter*, like a number of English papers, considered Mandela's 'clumsy and insensitive' intervention had 'done his cause a great disservice'. It raised the majority-minority inconsistency argument again by quoting a leading MP's insistence that the ANC was fighting for democracy while the IRA was fighting against democracy.[97] The rival constitutional nationalist *Irish News*, however, supported Mandela. Negotiations, in the context of a ceasefire and on the understanding that Provisional Sinn Féin represented only 2 per cent of the population of the Irish Republic and 11 per cent of that of Northern Ireland, were welcomed. Violence should not give Sinn Féin a disproportionate voice in a settlement. Earlier the *Irish News* had criticised Mandela for omitting to declare for non-violence on his release.[98] Kader Asmal, of the IAAM, rejected as patronising the complaints of the *Irish Times* and other papers that Mandela knew nothing of Northern Ireland. However, Asmal drew the customary distinction between South Africa without black voters and Northern Ireland with a democratic franchise: 'there are no parallels.'[99] But, as *An Phoblacht* correctly pointed out, there was nothing new in the idea of negotiating with an IRA in arms; the British government had already during the Ulster Troubles dealt directly with Sinn Féin and the IRA itself. The *News Letter* insisted, however, that the 1972 negotiation, when the British government flew to London an IRA delegation, which included Gerry Adams, was politically naive.[100] It was subsequently maintained by Sinn Féin that the British government began secret negotiations with them in October 1990, the year of Mandela's visit.[101]

The belief, voiced by a South African government representative, that Mandela had 'put his foot in it again',[102] was offset by an ANC spokesman. The latter claimed that Mandela's support of negotiations with the IRA was intended to preempt Margaret Thatcher's subsequent efforts to persuade the ANC to drop its armed struggle to aid de Klerk against his white extremists. This partly justified *An Phoblacht's* insistence that Sinn Féin was no more capitalising on the ANC than the latter on the IRA.[103] Mandela was under pressure, not only from some of his own supporters but from organisations like the Pan African Congress. Though the PAC receives little attention from Provisional Sinn Féin, its members were probably more willing to emulate IRA tactics than the officials of the ANC. Mandela later admitted that the black on black violence in one province originated in antagonism between the ANC and PAC.[104]

Loyalists did not entirely escape Mandela's spell. The UDA's *Ulster* characteristically attacked Margaret Thatcher for welcoming Mandela's release, despite his continued acceptance of the armed struggle. The Iron Lady's 'metal fatigue' was equated with her earlier willingness to negotiate with Rhodesian rebels. British talks with the IRA now appeared unpleasantly possible to the UDA. Two months later, however, an *Ulster* columnist, perhaps with tongue in cheek, reversed the traditional loyalist arguments by commending Mandela and identifying the white South African minority, not with the Ulster unionists, but with the nationalists. Under the 1985 Anglo-Irish Agreement, loyalists appeared to the columnist a rightless majority, like the black South Africans. Mandela, the article argued, had demonstrated that force, rather than conventional constitutional unionist politics, was the only effective strategy for gaining a hearing for loyalist demands.[105] Like the Provisionals, some UDA members seemed to be talking of resistance to British colonialism, empathising now with the colonised, not with the settlers. By 1992, however, the UDA's *Warrior* was again identifying with the South African white community and emphasising links between PIRA and the ANC.[106] Such a debate could not continue long at its initial intensity, but it did not evaporate completely as new developments in South Africa reinforced Irish parallels.

The Provisionals had every reason to keep the controversy alive. A correspondent on the Provisional's *An Phoblacht* rejected the 'spurious argument' that Northern Ireland differed from South Africa in its franchise. The ballot-box was not the only criterion of democracy; with the current denial of free speech and other disabilities, Northern Ireland, like South Africa, was 'a British-controlled, undemocratic, irreformable state'.[107] *An Phoblacht* continued to give space to South Africa, emphasising the rising violence of Chief Buthelezi's Inkatha movement, which it regarded as an agent of the South African government, against the ANC. The paper demonstrated that the MacBride principles for fair employment in Northern Ireland had been based on the American Sullivan principles in South Africa.[108] But on 7 August 1990 the ANC called a ceasefire to facilitate negotiations with de Klerk. Though this clearly distinguished the organisation from the Provisionals who in 1990 stepped up their assassinations in Europe, Britain and Northern Ireland, *An Phoblacht* accepted the change philosophically: the ANC was 'on the road to victory' as de Klerk had compromised by promising to avoid collusion with Inkatha.[109] Mandela was now less often mentioned, though great emphasis was placed on the iniquities of Buthelezi. In a theoretical debate on the stages of revolution, an *An Phoblacht* correspondent asserted, unrebuked, that the forms of imperialist control differed considerably in Ireland and South Africa.[110]

Mandela's Irish experience made him especially cautious when he visited Australia in late October 1990. He was forced to repudiate an attempt to organise a radio debate with Buthelezi and the latter contrived to publish in Rupert Murdoch's *Australian* a letter claiming his total blamelessness for South African black on black violence.[111] More embarrassing was the demand for endorsement by Australian Aboriginal leaders. Mandela, to the irritation of some, refused to comment on the internal affairs of Australia, while sympathising with the Aboriginal problems and meeting certain leaders. More important, Mandela firmly asserted the priority of democracy argument, so much used in the Northern Ireland context: however bad their conditions, Australian Aborigines, unlike the South African majority, had the vote.[112] Ironically, *An Phoblacht* had celebrated the Australian bicentenary in 1988 by an article, 'Two Centuries of Australian Racism', succinctly detailing, as South African government publications have frequently done, some of the worst atrocities of the past and present. It concluded with a comparison between the spate of Aboriginal deaths in custody and the demise of Steve Biko at the hands of his white South African gaolers.[113] In an interview with Bob Geldof in October 1992, Mandela appeared to abandon his earlier cautious approach when he declared that 'the IRA is conducting a struggle for self-assertion. They do not want Britain—a foreign country—to run a colony. We don't want any form of colonialism and, wherever that colonialism is, we support those who fight it because people should have self-expression.' *An Phoblacht* naturally made capital out of this apparent admission that Northern Ireland was a colonial struggle, but the ANC hastily denied that Mandela's remarks implied support for the IRA.[114]

More capital for the Provisionals had been made earlier in 1992 when the *Independent* newspaper revealed that South African agents had attempted, with the assistance of Ulster loyalists, the assassination of Dirk Coetzee, a former South African policeman who had deserted to the ANC. The South African Defence Force denied orders to attempt the assassination, but claimed that their agents were investigating links between the ANC and PIRA. This was good copy for the Provisionals, who emphasised the admission by the exposed British double agent, Brian Nelson, sentenced to ten years for working with the UDA, that arms for loyalists had been exported from South Africa. According to *An Phoblacht*, before 1988 loyalist death squads had only home-made sub-machine-guns, sawn-off shotguns and revolvers. From South Africa they obtained rocket launchers, rocket warheads, assault rifles, fragmentation grenades, Browning pistols and ammunition. This made it easy for the loyalists to launch their increased attacks on Catholics after

1991. *An Phoblacht* made less of an admission by the ANC that there had been shared military training camps with PIRA, but no other connection. The Northern Ireland Secretary of State, Sir Patrick Mayhew, was forced to dismiss as 'rubbish' Gerry Adams's claim that British military intelligence had connived at the import of loyalist arms from South Africa.[115]

Amidst a welter of far-fetched parallels and established connections, what are the essential issues? It has been demonstrated above that the Provisionals in their Northern Ireland campaign have fought hard for identification with the ANC. Their main object has been association with the most highly estimated national liberation cause in the modern world, at the top of Guelke's 'pecking order'. Success has been fitful. Community rivals with the same objectives, like the SDLP and the WP, have drawn very different analogies and applied them to the Provisionals' detriment, as often as *vice versa*. The Provisionals have been helped by the fairly consistent support of many unionists, especially Paisley, for the white minority regimes in Southern Africa. The two groups mirrored each other with arguments, sometimes unconsciously convergent, and sometimes demonstrating antithetical interpretation. There have been some interesting attempts at direct contact, ranging from joint propaganda to interchange of men and weapons for violent conflict. Official leadership has usually repudiated the contacts or dismissed them as unauthorised, but rank and file liaison does seem to have taken place. In the second half of 1990 Nelson Mandela became the focus of most attention. He engaged in a most precarious balancing act, attempting to preserve the loyalty of supporters, win over enemies, and gain the approbation of the outside world by appearing simultaneously strong and conciliatory. The ANC was a much broader coalition than the Provisionals, embracing accommodationists, willing to accept the continuance of some white power, as well as militants demanding immediate majority rule.[116] The Irish issue has underlined the dilemma of armed struggle versus non-violent resistance. When does force become necessary? To many it appears justified in South Africa but not Northern Ireland, yet in practice distinctions are not easy to draw. Is the franchise the bottom line? Guelke would agree with some Provisionals in suggesting that neither Northern Ireland nor South Africa have democratic legitimacy. Is the quality of violence the bedrock? Sabotage against installations might be acceptable, but not assassination. However, as Mandela admits, innocent people may die in attempted sabotage. The ANC at grass roots, if not at leadership level, has been unable to distance itself from 'necklace' murders. Again, can South African black on black violence, which makes the Northern Ireland death rate appear puny,[117] really be attributed exclusively to Inkatha, the white government's proxies, as *An Phoblacht* insists? Such contemporary debate is valuable when it opens up awkward questions, even before reliable data is available, and inhibits the tendency to see contemporary events in comfortable stereotypes. The success of the ANC and Mandela at the South African non-racial election of April 1994 negated comparison with the IRA and UDA. *An Phoblacht* responded coolly. Like Mahatma Gandhi, who tried to wean Indian opinion from the violence of the original Irish Revolution,[118] President Mandela may be forced to live with opponents convinced that ruthless, rather than academic, force is the ultimate source of political power.

Four propagandist criteria

To conclude, we have seen how important, for both loyalists and republicans, were the Third and Fourth Worlds in the Ulster propagandist debate of the 1970s, 1980s and 1990s. We may for convenience categorise the general use of overseas examples under demands for *universal human rights, solidarity* with particular movements, *consciousness raising* by emotive parallels or emulation, and finally the *distraction of the enemy*. Britain not being directly engaged in any other major colonial conflict, apart from the Falklands, only indirect distraction was possible. This took the form of protests at British embassies and demonstrations against visiting members of the royal family. At the other end of the scale, *human rights* were asserted strongly by republicans who dropped the Mitchel-Griffith tradition of élitist insular nationalism in favour of the frank universalism of Thomas Davis. Griffith had demanded an Irish share of the British Empire. The loyalists, especially Paisley, were far closer to Mitchel and Griffith, though the UDA and UVF fitfully saw the disadvantage of being closely linked with crude racism. The Paisleyite argument played exactly into the hands of the republicans. By showing himself the friend of white settler reactionaries, Paisley almost established the case for Irish republicans as anti-imperialist insurgents. When siding with opponents of majority rule, Prot-stats neutralised what should have been their strongest argument, their local Northern Ireland preponderance. To some extent, their argumentative position has been retrieved by Prime Minister Mugabe's post-independence discovery of his own 'Ulster' in Ndebele country. On the second point, the establishment of specific *relations with other groups*, the Provisionals played their game skilfully. Their opponents linked them with European terrorist gangs like the Baader Meinhof, the Red Army Faction, and the Angry Brigades. The Provisionals rejected such links, claiming that their only allies were the blacks.[119] We have shown their efforts to make personal contact with representatives of 'acceptable' national causes like those of Zimbabwe and South Africa, plus Fourth World oppressed groups such as the Aborigines, Maoris, and American Indians. On the loyalist side, contact with white regimes was more dramatic.

The third criterion, *consciousness raising*, led to a diversity of arguments. British atrocities in India and Kenya were associated with more recent examples in places like Cyprus and Aden, and then in a grand anti-imperialist sweep with South Africa and Rhodesia. Men such as Kenyatta, Mugabe, Nkomo, and Mandela were depicted as heroes whose words and actions invited emulation. The SDLP was denounced according to overseas analogies. Works like Fanon's *Towards the African Revolution* and *The Wretched of the Earth* were of 'immense interest',[120] justifying violence and helping Northern Irish republicans to see themselves as genuine members of the physically and psychologically oppressed Fourth World, rather than as a slightly less privileged section of the First. Some of the economic analogies derived from overseas helped to establish this most convincingly. The Paisleyite and other loyalist attacks, which portrayed Irish Catholics as savages, reinforced republican arguments. When identifying as anti-imperialists, the Provisionals could avoid the consequences of their vagueness on socialism—shared with the ANC[121]—and score another propagandist goal against loyalist opponents entangled in 'politically incorrect' patterned opposition and antithetical interpretation. The Provisionals had many rivals, such as the Officials and PD, who were equally outspoken in their anti-imperialism. But PIRA was particularly concerned to scrap the 'green fascist' tag. The Provisional writers often achieved this with greater finesse than that of their opponents.

Notes

1.   See Davis, *The Young Ireland Movement*, 200-14.
2.   See Davis, Richard, 'The Shamrock and the Tiki: Irish Nationalists and Maori Resistance in the 19th century', *Journal of Intercultural Studies* (Melbourne), Vol. 1, No. 3, December 1980, 16-27.
3.   Davis, *Arthur Griffith and Non-Violent Sinn Féin*, 92-3.
4.   RN, 6 March 1976 and 4 January 1975.

5. *Hindu*, Madras, 7 May 1981. See also, *Amrita Bazaar Patrika*, Calcutta, 7 May 1981 and *Pioneer*, Lucknow, 7 May 1981.

6. The Zimbabwe African National Union had been part of the Patriotic Front.

7. Bell, *The Protestants of Ulster*, 46. Fromm, Eric (1963), *Fear of Freedom*, London: Routledge and Kegan Paul, 76.

8. Lamont, Donal (1977), *Speech from the Dock*, London: Catholic Institute for International Relations. For Lamont's earlier opposition to the white Rhodesian Government, see Linden, Ian (1980), *The Catholic Church and the Struggle for Zimbabwe*, London: Longman, passim.

9. PT, 16 October 1976, 27 November 1976.

10. PT, 14 June 1969, 3 December 1966.

11. AP, 26 October 1976; V, Vol. 2, No. 3 1976. Lamont was cited against Cardinal Conway and Dr Garret FitzGerald. The two latter upheld Lamont's refusal to give information to the Rhodesian authorities, but denied the principle in Northern Ireland.

12. PT, 11 November 1967 and 13 April 1968.

13. PT, 3 and 17 December 1966, 24 August 1968, 11 May 1968, 27 July 1968.

14. AP, 13 July 1977.

15. RN, 5 December 1971.

16. UDAN (1, 4) 1972.

17. U, March 1980.

18. PT, 9 August 1975 (C. Smith), 26 February 1977; C, May 1976 and (4, 7) 1977.

19. RN, 5 November 1977.

20. RN, 10 July 1976.

21. AP, 22 March 1980.

22. RN, 22 January 197.

23. RN, 30 January 1972.

24. AP, April 1972.

25. RN, 26 February 1977; UI, 5.77.

26. RN, 26 February 1977.

27. C, (1, 15) 1974, (1, 12) 1974 and (2,2) 1975.

28. U, December 1978; LN, 14 August 1976 and 25 September 1976. See also James McKnight in *Fortnight*, April 1984.

29. RN, 14 May 1977; AP, 8 June 1977 and 8 July 1978. See McDonagh, 152-3, for the dilemma of the Church in dealing with these measures. Tim Sheehy and Eileen Sudworth, of the London-based Catholic Institute for International Relations, point out in their introduction to Lamont's 'Speech from the Dock' that the Selous Scout issue was particularly controversial: 'They often masquerade as guerrillas and exact retribution from those Africans who co-operate with them in this guise. By committing atrocities in the guise of guerrillas they aim to confuse and alienate the local people and to test their loyalty.' At Dabwa Kraal 16 women, 6 girls, and 7 men were slaughtered. Seven Catholic missionaries suffered a like fate, and a year later it was the turn of eight Pentecostalists. The *Republican News* pointed out that Major Richard Stannard, formerly serving in Northern Ireland, was Ian Smith's public relations officer and that General Carver, who wrote

a foreword for Kitson, had been sent to Rhodesia as a peace-keeper (12 February 1977 and 24 September 1977). *Fortnight*, No. 192, March 1982, showed more pertinently that Alan Gingles, formerly of the loyalist paramilitary Tara, had joined the Selous Scouts.

30. PT, July 1978.
31. OS, February 1979.
32. 1980, see Gallagher and Worrall, *Christians in Ulster, 1968-1980*, 149.
33. PT, 28 May 1976.
34. AP, 8 July 1978.
35. AP, 2 August 1974 and 20 November 1976; RN, 26 November 1977.
36. Officials: condolences to Joshua Nkomo (Zimbabwe African Politican Union) and Ivy Nkala (Patriotic Front delegate to Ard-Fheis), UI, February 1977 and May 1980. Provisionals: ZANU representative at Queen's University and Ruairí O Brádaigh on solidarity, AP, 19 May 1979 and RN, 13 March 1976.
37. AP, 10 May 1980.
38. W.S. O'Brien, Tasmanian Journal, National Library of Ireland, Ms 449, 12 February 1850; *Nation*, 5 November 1842.
39. A 'non-republican' according to Provisional Sinn Féin President Gerry Adams. See Adams, *The Politics of Irish Freedom*, 39.
40. See Davis, *Arthur Griffith and Non-Violent Sinn Féin*, 7, 12, 14, 92, 107-8.
41. MacBride, Maud Gonne ([1938] 1983), *A Servant of the Queen: Reminiscences.* Woodbridge, Suffolk: Boydell Press, 304-6, 341-2. According to *An Phoblacht*, 24 August 1989, Derrick McBride, grandson of John and Maud Gonne, was imprisoned for 12 years on Robben Island for ANC activities, and their great-grandson, Robert John was condemned to death, but reprieved, in South Africa as a member of the ANC's Umkonto we Sizwe.
42. Davis, R. (1977), 'The Self-Determination for Ireland Leagues and the Irish Race Convention in Paris, 1921-22', *Tasmanian Historical Research Association: Papers and Proceedings*, 24, 3 (September, 1977), 88-104. See also, Daniel, T.K. (1986), 'Erin's Green Veldt: The Irish Republican Association of South Africa, 1920-22', *The Journal of the University of Durban—Westville*, New Series 3, 1986, and McCracken, Donal P. (1983), 'The Irish in Nineteenth Century South Africa', *Journal of the University of Durban—Westville*, Vol. 4, No. 2, 1983.
43. Davenport, T.R.H. (1987), *South Africa: A Modern History*, 3rd ed., London: Macmillan, 261. The South African Natives National Congress (later the ANC) leaders were divided on the merits of segregation, while there was 'a widespread conviction among prominent liberal thinkers that segregationism should be given a chance to show that it could be fairly applied.'
44. RN, 25 May 1974.
45. RN, 3 August 1974.
46. RN, 7 June, 1975.
47. Guelke, Adrian (1991), 'The Political Impasse in South Africa and Northern Ireland', *Comparative Politics*, January 1991, 145 and 146-7. Worrall was interested in the application of 'consociationalism', or

power-sharing, of Arend Lijphart in South Africa and presumably
Northern Ireland. Lijphart, A. (1980) *Democracy in Plural Societies: a
Comparative Exploration*, New Haven: Yale University Press, 137 and
236-7 on Northern Ireland (unfavourable) and South Africa (the only
democratic solution, though difficult).

48. See MacDonald, Michael (1986), *Children of Wrath: Political Violence
in Northern Ireland*, Cambridge: Polity Press, 134-147. See also
Crawford, Robert G. (1987), *Loyal to King Billy: a Portrait of the Ulster
Protestants*, Dublin: Gill and Macmillan, 106-117, and Guelke, A. (1988),
Northern Ireland: the International Perspective, Dublin: Gill and
Macmillan, passim.
49. Guelke, 5.
50. See, for example, AP, 10 January 1981 and 25 January 1990: 'Cricket
Racists Caught Out', dealing with the abandonment of the English
Mike Gatting tour.
51. PT, 26 February 1977 (capitalism), 13 June 1970, (12th), 15 April 1978,
(Dutch Reformed), 15 December 1972, (Gray review). *Fortnight*,
December 1982 - Andrew Pollack (UCCC).
52. RN, 7 August 1976. See also Adrian Guelke, 'Desperation in Pretoria',
Fortnight, No. 274, June 1989.
53. *Belfast Newsletter*, 2 January 1982. *Fortnight*, December 1982 (arms to
Tara) and April 1984 (Ulster solidarity).
54. Moloney and Pollack, *Paisley*, 141.
55. Guelke, *Northern Ireland: the International Perspective*, 76, quotes
Ulster, March 1985 and *Belfast Telegraph*, 14 December 1983. See also
AP, 2 February 1984.
56. For an excellent analysis of the wider implications, see Guelke, Adrian
(1989), 'Desperation in Pretoria', *Fortnight*, No. 274, June 1989, *News
Letter*, Belfast, 5 and 10 May 1989, and *Irish News*, 5 May 1989. £10
million was offered for Starstreak, Britain's newest surface to air
missile. U, October/November 1989. AP, 27 April 1989.
57. *Ulster* (UDA), February 1979. *Ulster* complained that the bulldozing of
houses in Northern Ireland to enforce segregation was comparable to
apartheid techniques in South Africa.
58. *Fortnight*, May 1983.
59. *Starry Plough* (IRSP), 15 February 1977, quoted in RN, 26 February 1977.
60. Writer's interview with Dr Nthatho Motlana in Johannesburg, 20
January 1981.
61. Quoted in Bishop and Mallie, *The Provisional IRA*, 308. For *The
Citizen*, 23 June 1984, see Hunter, Andrew (1989), 'IRA and
ANC/SWAPO Cooperation', *European Freedom Review*, London,
Vol. 1, No. 2, Winter 1989, 9-13.
62. AP, 21 June 1980.
63. Crawford, *Loyal to King Billy*, 114.
64. Mandela, Nelson (1973), *No Easy Walk to Freedom*, London:
Heinemann, 172 and 177.
65. The Commonwealth Group of Eminent Persons (1986), *Mission to
South Africa*, Harmondsworth: Penguin, 70.

66. *News Letter*, Belfast, 15 and 16 July 1988. *Belfast Telegraph* (BT), 20 April 1990; SWAPO *News Letter*, 3 July 1990. Hunter is preparing a book on the relationship between the Provisionals and the ANC.
67. AP, 30 November 1989. The IAAM sent medical advice and a book by Peadar O'Donnell, a radical republican and novelist of a previous generation. Provisional Sinn Féin is, however, affiliated to the IAAM. See Steve MacDonogh introduction to Adams, Gerry, *The Politics of Irish Freedom*, xiv. For Kader Asmal, see *Irish Times* (IT), 29 June 1990.
68. Palestine Liberation Organisation.
69. Guelke, A., *Northern Ireland: the International Perspective*, 15.
70. AP, 11 August 1979. *Irish News*, 23 February 1990, Henry McDonald.
71. UI, April 1975 and October 1976. AP, 26 January 1980. and 26 November 1981.
72. RN, 6 March 1976; Sinn Féin's pamphlet, *Notes For Revolutionaries*, 8, 30 and 32. The Irish Sean Hosey was imprisoned in South Africa for ANC activities, AP, 2 September 1978.
73. Adams, Gerry, *The Politics of Irish Freedom*, 5, 22 (Vorster in 1963 on Northern Ireland Special Powers Act), 44 and 130-1 (long-distance revolutionaries who support revolution in South Africa but not Ireland), 113 (South African blacks can only obtain equality at the expense of whites), 144 (Biko an argument for maintaining Irish culture); Adams, Gerry (1988), *A Pathway to Peace*, 80-81. Mandela also figured prominently in Adams' presidential address to the Sinn Féin 1990 Ard Fheis, see AP, 8 February 1990 and IT, 5 February 1990. For Freedom Charter, see Karis, Thomas G. (1983), 'Revolution in the Making: Black Politics in South Africa', *Foreign Affairs*, 62, 2, 394: 'a mildly socialist but not anti-capitalist bourgeois democracy'.
74. AP, 15 February 1990.
75. *Saoirse*, New Jersey, March 1990. Mandela, it was demonstrated, could have had freedom in 1975 had he renounced the armed struggle.
76. *Protestant Blu Print*, Vol. 1, Nos. 10 and 14, 6 and 29 September 1985. The UDA's *Ulster*, February 1986, diverted by demanding sympathy for blacks massacred by black regimes. Boesak was forced to resign his ministry after the exposure of his second adultery in 1990.
77. O'Brien, C.C. (1988), *Passion and Cunning and Other Essays*, London: Weidenfeld and Nicholson, 170 and 185. The banners declared support for the IRA and the UDF, an ANC support coalition. For Gerry Adams on episode, see AP, 23 October 1986: they chanted, 'Victory to the ANC! Victory to the IRA! We share their contempt for Dr O'Brien and we share their solidarity in our common struggles.' Quoted by Hunter, 'IRA/ANC Cooperation', *European Freedom Review*, 11.
78. IN, 23 February 1990.
79. IN, 26 February 1990.
80. IN, 20 January 1987.
81. Hume was the main speaker at an Irish rally to celebrate Mandela's release, IN, 12 February 1990.
82. BT, 15 February 1990.
83. IT, 23 February 1990.
84. IT, 1 March 1990.

85. AP, 14 June 1990.
86. For J.A. Murphy's articles, see *Sunday Independent*, Dublin, 10 and 17 June 1990. For comparison between O'Neill and de Klerk, see BT, 17 February 1990, and Guelke, Adrian (1990), 'More than an easy walk', *Fortnight*, No. 286, July/August, 15. See also, Guelke (1991) 'The Political Impasse in South Africa and Northern Ireland', 157.
87. IT, 24 February 1990, in *Fortnight*, No. 283, April 1990, James McKnight quotes from *Irish Times*.
88. Quoted in Shannon, Elizabeth (1989), *I am of Ireland: Women of the North Speak Out*, Boston: Little Brown, 99. For Mandela, see refusal to take up Aboriginal cause in Australia, *Australian*, 25 October 1990.
89. IT, 2 March 1990.
90. IT, 30 June 1990 (Profile of Mandela).
91. IT, 21 February 1990. Adams, *The Politics of Irish Freedom*, 39.
92. Yallop, Richard (1990), 'The Armalite that is Adams', *Age*, Melbourne, 6 June 1990 and the Australian Broadcasting Corporation's AM programme, 5 June 1990.
93. Mandela, Nelson (1990), *Walk the Last Mile with us: Nelson Mandela's Speeches in Ireland*, Dublin: AAM, 7, 15-16.
94. *News Letter*, 3 July 1990. I am indebted to Clare Murray for research in Belfast, July 1990.
95. AP, 5 July 1990.
96. IN, 4 July 1990. The committee's chairman, Conservative Ivor Stambrook, angered Labour members by regretting that Mandela had not condemned IRA violence. The leader Neil Kinnock rejected any parallel between South Africa and Northern Ireland. Mandela himself complained that 'it saddens me that as we leave Ireland we find ourselves dragged into a controversy that was not of our making and which we never intended.' He claimed that he had simply replied to a question on the IRA with a reiteration of the ANC position on ending violence. *Walk the Last Mile*, 33. When Archbishop Tutu visited Newcastle, Northern Ireland, for an Anglican Primates' Conference on 14 April 1991, he declared, like Mandela, that Sinn Féin should be included in the suggested peace talks.
97. *News Letter*, 4 July 1990.
98. IN, 3 July and 12 February 1990.
99. IN, 4 July 1990.
100. *News Letter*, 4 July 1990.
101. AP, 20 January 1994.
102. Tothill, David (1990), 'Ambassador to Australia', *Australian*, 7-8 July 1990.
103. AP, 5 July 1990, contains much of the detail on Mandela's Irish visit cited above.
104. *Mercury*, Hobart, 25 October 1990.
105. U, March and May 1990.
106. *Warrior*, May 1992 - It recommended a white South African journal, the *South African Patriot*.
107. AP, 26 July 1990.

108. AP, 4 January and 2 August 1990; Guelke, *Northern Ireland: the International Perspective*, 149.
109. AP, 9 August 1990.
110. AP, 6 September 1990 (Seán Mac Brádaigh).
111. *Australian*, 23 October 1990. Buthelezi claimed 1.8 million paid up Inkatha members compared to the ANC's less than 200,000. In early 1991 Mandela and Buthelezi met for the first time since the former's release.
112. *Australian*, 24 October 1990: 'They have the vote. They also have rights of assembly and movement.' There was a grave denial of land rights; the ANC would support indigenous rights which were coming before the United Nations.
113. AP, 4 February 1988.
114. AP, 22 October 1992, *Fortnight*, December 1992.
115. *Fortnight*, September 1992; AP, 23 July and 10 September 1992. For Brian Nelson, 4 February 1993. The journalist Brian Rowan provided this information, attributed to the security forces, which conflicted with official denial at Nelson's trial that he had been in South Africa in 1985. See also, AP, 5 August 1993.
116. Guelke, 'The Political Impasse in South Africa and Northern Ireland', 159.
117. Guelke, however, argued in early 1991 that proportionately to population Northern Ireland violence is worse than South Africa's. He cites a calculation originally made in 1988. See Guelke, 'The Political Impasse in South Africa and Northern Ireland', 145.
118. See Davis, R. (1986), 'The Influence of the Irish Revolution on Indian Nationalism: The Evidence of the Indian Press, 1916-22', *South Asia*, New Ser., IX, 2 (December 1986), 55-68.
119. AP, 11 August 1979.
120. AP, 13 September 1980.
121. See Karis above, 'Revolution in the Making: Black Politics in South Africa', *Foreign Affairs*, 394. An earlier version of much of the material in this chapter appeared as Richard Davis, "Nelson Mandela's Irish Problem: Republican and Loyalist Links with South Africa, 1970-1990", *Eire-Ireland*, Vol. XXVII, No. 4, Winter 1992, pp.47-68.

Conclusion – Alice through the looking-glass?

This land we stand on holds a history
so complicated, gashed with violence,
split by belief, by blatant pageantry
that none can safely stir and still feel free
to voice his hope with any confidence.

Slave to and victim of this mirror hate,
surely there must be somewhere we could reach
a solid track across our quagmire state,
and on a neutral sod renew the old debate
which all may join without intemperate speech.

John Hewitt[1]

Tweedledum and Tweedledee
    Agreed to have a battle;
For Tweedledum said Tweedledee
    Had spoiled his nice new rattle.
Just then flew down a monstrous crow,
    As black as a tar-barrel;
Which frightened both the heroes so,
    They quite forgot their quarrel.

Lewis Carroll

Unity in enmity

The foregoing chapters have endeavoured to examine the truth of John Hewitt's view that both 'traditions' in Northern Ireland are 'slave to and victim of this mirror hate'. Their paper war has been shown to be as significant as their shooting and bombing war. Atrocious and irrational deeds have been defended by sophisticated and plausible dialectics. Sometimes good cases have been ruined by crude and obtuse rationalisation. Paramilitaries, especially the Provisionals, have admitted the importance of the paper war and that it requires as much intelligence, self-discipline, and determination to succeed.

Triangular determinism: the Hindu-Muslim

In the foregoing chapters the paper war has been primarily between loyalists (or Prot-stats) and republicans, though the third party, the British Army and its political directors, has been a constant presence, and at the centre of the stage in chapter six. Comparing Ireland in the first Revolution with the partition of India, Nicholas Mansergh developed a theory of triangular determinism in which a nationalist majority, by asserting its authority when the ruling authority relaxes its grip, drives the minority towards separatism.[2] A similar triangle operated in the North of Ireland in the 1970s, 1980s and 1990s. Ironically, Catholic population growth might some day result in a replay of 1921, with a Prot-stat rejection of majority rule, not against a Catholic majority in the whole island, but in their own selected six counties. This would be unfortunately appropriate as much of the propaganda on both sides analysed above is but a development of ideology fully formed by 1921. It is therefore essential to discover how far the polemic of two internally fragmented factions represents an unbridgeable gap and how far antagonism is the product of artificial conflict.

All community conflicts are to some extent artificial. In 1947 some Hindus and Muslims who had lived together in amity, sometimes sharing each other's festivals,[3] cut each other to pieces, not because of any local dispute, but because they had heard of similar slaughter thousands of miles away. Thus propaganda triumphs over humanity and common sense. Genuine differences in tradition and culture can be a source of delight when not exploited for political ends. Economic rivalry in a depressed area encourages the use of differences for personal advantage. The basic issue in Northern

Ireland may be whether 'the Prot-stat tradition' is sufficiently different from that of its neighbour to justify a second partition to preserve its local majority.

Catholic increase: Prot-stat militancy

It was frankly admitted in the 1930s by leaders like Lord Brookeborough[4] that unionists strove to maintain their two-to-one majority against a higher Catholic birthrate by making life sufficiently uncomfortable for the latter that they were persuaded to emigrate. For nearly fifty years the ratio remained virtually unchanged. Despite the horrendous unemployment rate, shown to be 2.5 per cent higher for Catholics in 1971, it seems that the Catholic population has in the last decade begun to catch up rapidly, increasing by 5 per cent. Over 50 per cent of schoolchildren are Catholics. The census of 1991 suggested that a Catholic majority is possible in the foreseeable future. Catholics now number 43 per cent of the population, with 45 per cent in Belfast.[5] The abolition of Stormont has dismantled part of the discriminatory apparatus favouring Prot-stats. Moreover, the Provisional campaign has made life sufficiently unpleasant to persuade Prot-stats to join the emigration queues in larger numbers. Time is not on their side, especially as economic depression in a world of multinationals knows no sectarian boundaries. There are indications of loyalist desperation in their demands for regression to the Stormont era, which some imagine might stem the Catholic flood. The assassinated Sammy Smyth exhibited a ghastly logic when he declared the sole alternative to a united Ireland to be the removal of all Catholics before they reached 51 per cent of the population. 'Bumping off a few Roman Catholics, Provos, IRA, call them what you will is not the answer to our problem.... The only way to eliminate the IRA/Provos is not to waste time trying to separate them from their passive but willing supporters, but to draw our swords and decapitate the lot of them. That way, the problem is solved.'[6] In 1993, a *News Letter* poll suggested that 42 per cent of its admittedly unionist readers agreed with loyalist paramilitary violence.[7] A ray of hope lies in the five councils, with unionists and nationalists evenly balanced, where power sharing between unionists and the SDLP has taken place. Another promising sign is the Northern Ireland opinion poll claiming 56 per cent general support, and strong approval of Sinn Féin voters, for the December 1993 Joint Declaration of John Major and Albert Reynolds.[8] If such figures are realistic, many on both sides of the political divide may be prepared to abandon ideology in return for a peaceful settlement.

Is it a mirror-image?

At this critical stage serious propaganda analysis is essential. What precisely is the Prot-stat case, and how does it differ from its opponents? If the ideology of one side is the mirror-image of the other, then it is more difficult to argue that there are two 'nations', not a single tradition of symbiotic antagonism. 'We resemble what we hate'. The psychologist, Edward de Bono, sees a tug-of-war as an apt metaphor for Northern Ireland: 'none of the parties involved dares relax its hostility towards the other parties for a single moment because at that moment the party would instantly be condemned by its supporters as having "gone soft".'[9] The metaphor can be extended: the contestants, by pulling against each other, provide mutual support. If one team releases the rope, the other collapses in confusion. Michael Macdonald, arguing the colonial Northern Ireland theme, also sees the conflict as benefiting both parties: 'because Protestant loyalty was salient only in contrast to Catholic disloyalty, Protestant settlers had an incentive to maintain the disloyalty of Catholic natives. If Catholics were reconciled to colonialism, Protestants would have become superfluous and lost their claim to special privilege.'[10] The same depressing conclusion appears in the American satirical *Report from an Iron Mountain on the possibility of Peace*, published on the eve of the Ulster Troubles. The *Report* maintained that as 'allegiance requires a cause, a cause requires an enemy.'[11] Thus war becomes 'the principal basis of organization on which all modern societies are constructed.' The Bristol University political scientist, Henri Tajfel, whose 'social identity theory' appealed to Professor John Whyte, came to a similar conclusion. Humans need self-esteem, best achieved within a group asserting superiority over another group.[12]

Such interpretations suggest that extremist papers help to provide social cement by stirring the antagonisms that achieve group and hence social cohesion. Are the sources cited in this book typical of most people in Northern Ireland? We have assessed the claims that such papers do indeed speak for large numbers in the community. Ten per cent of Northern Ireland voters consistently support Sinn Féin. Most Catholics are opposed to force, but many members of the SDLP voting majority have been reluctant to hand over a Provisional to the RUC, even without fear of reprisal. Similarly, many moderate unionists reject and ridicule Paisley, but in a crisis, or a European election, large numbers rally to him as the strongest voice of unionism. The Northern Ireland extremist press, moreover, must appear as ideology in its Sunday best presenting a favourable image to the outsider, as well as gathering in the faithful. The analyst must be continually on the alert for give-away indications of bigotry and hatred masked by a smooth, smiling outward face. Loyalists, as we have seen, were more addicted to incautious revelation than republicans and often treated the opinion of uncommited outsiders with contempt. On both sides the papers contain arguments frequently expressed by a much greater number. Otherwise, the organisations represented would soon be out of business.

(1) Patterned opposition
Initially, we gave a broad interpretation to the mirror-image metaphor, covering patterned opposition, the borrowing of symbols or organisational techniques, calculated antagonism, masked or unconscious convergence and antithetical interpretation. The lines between these usages are fluid. As for patterned opposition, there is a discrepancy between republican and loyalist periodicals, less often found on wall graffiti. Loyalists, when attacking nationalists, used racial and religious derision in argument, cartoon, and verse. Republicans retaliated with savage representations of the British monarch, royal family, army, and government in general. Their polemic asserted an imperialist plot, while some loyalists attributed all troubles to the machinations of the Vatican. Paisley's paper also attacked the royal family. There was little uniformity on either side. Loyalist paramilitaries denounced their own middle classes, while republicans vented much anger on community rivals. But a similar general pattern was maintained. Only the treatment of religion was different.[13] Catholics rarely traded religious insults. Here this 'patterned' mirror-image metaphor is less apt.

(2) Symbol borrowing
The borrowing of symbols and organisational techniques was widespread. The Protestant paramilitaries were modelled on the IRA down to details such as the issuance of statements by eponymous leaders such as 'Capt. William Johnston' and P. O'Neill. Both sides delighted in satirical verse, sometimes set to the music of opposition songs. This was particularly noticeable on the loyalist side and indicated relative cultural deprivation. An *Andersonstown News* correspondent complained, 'now I know the Loyalists are

lacking in cultural heritage but would you lay off our lovely rebel tunes'.[14] Orange and Hibernian banners are revealing. At a distance Patrick Sarsfield is indistinguishable from William III, hardly surprising in that the banners are sometimes made by the same firm. Black Preceptories are immune from the usual Protestant inhibition against carrying images of Jesus in procession.[15] There seems a type of loyalist superstition regarding the symbols of their opponents. Paisley believed that the pope possessed the magical, if diabolical, power to send famine to India.

(3) *Calculated antagonism*

The third mirror-image usage, calculated antagonism, generally applied to action rather than theory. In chapter six, on insurgency and counter-insurgency, we dipped gingerly into the murky pool of provocation and violence. All three groups of participants, British Army, republicans, and loyalists, vociferously accused others of 'dirty tricks', or atrocities fabricated to discredit the enemy. These were clearly used by all contestants when it suited them. Indeed, as was sometimes blurted out, especially by loyalists and General Kitson, war is by definition a game without rules.

(4) *Unconscious convergence*

'Calculated antagonism' when transmuted into periodical propaganda often became unconscious convergence. This represents the real heart of the essay. In the rival interpretations of history, in the actions of the respective Churches, in the pursuit of educational efficiency, in the treatment of violence, in the quest for social justice, and in the attitudes to colonial revolution, conventional wisdom has ascribed vast differences between the Catholic and 'Protestant' mentality. Early in the account, however, we replaced the word 'Protestant', suggestive of a consensus not evident in non-Catholic churches after Vatican II, with the term 'Prot-stat'. The latter is not a term of abuse, but a word covering all who believe that political or physical means are required to deal with the threat of the Roman Catholic Church. Between 'Prot-stats' and Catholic republicans we found continual convergence. Only in historical mythology was there a type of patterned opposition where republicans sanctified a basically secular tradition, and Prot-stats secularised a religious fundamentalism. Catholic nationalists turned the Bodenstown commemoration of an anti-papal secularist into a religious duty; Prot-stats converted the celebration of Calvinist victory into a pagan festivity. However, an updated UDA loyalism seeks a pre-Christian racial myth of ancient

Ulster unity to counter religious traditionalism. Another exception to convergence was discovered in the conflict over imperialism. Here the example of calculated antagonism was perfect. Paisley, and other conservative unionists, despite the eventual reluctance of some Prot-stat paramilitaries, stood four-square behind the settler minority regimes, while Irish republicans to a man identified with black majority liberation. This, as has been suggested, meant the virtual propagandist capitulation of loyalists, some of whom withdrew in time from such an isolated position. Post-independence Zimbabwe problems and continued South African strife, however, could be used for loyalist vindication.

On ecclesiastical influence, education, violence, and socialism, concurrence was obvious. Catholics, on revolutionary issues, were no more restricted by religious authority than Prot-stats. Both loyalists and republicans faced clergy equally determined to maintain the educational *status quo*, and, partly as a result, failed to progress towards integrated schooling, apparently so rational and necessary. On violence we discovered loyalists, republicans, and British soldiers justifying their actions on identical grounds, thus creating a moral stasis. As for economics, both loyalists and republicans, with a few exceptions, were inexorably drawn to a middle way between capitalism and socialism, in full accord with the philosophy of the papal encyclicals.

(5) Antithetical interpretation
Antithetical interpretation was an interesting variant of convergence. The actions of Catholic bishops in particular were interpreted in such a ludicrously divergent manner as to achieve a quasi-convergence. No bishop could simultaneously be a promoter of revolutionary violence and an agent of the British government. The latter's actions were often themselves subjected to such widely divergent assessments. Another form of antithetical interpretation was demonstrated by DUP and republican reactions to the hopeful Downing Street Declaration of Major and Reynolds in December 1993. To Ian Paisley the British government had 'jettisoned the union' and 'rolled out the red carpet for the IRA.' His lieutenant Peter Robinson saw in the Declaration 'a dagger in the heart of Ulster'. On the other side Hilda MacThomas in *An Phoblacht* denounced 'Major's unionist agenda.'[16]

What is the meaning of all this? On the religious flank the Prot-stats seem addicted to an authority system usually associated with Catholicism. Observers since the Rev. James Armour have contended that conventional Protestant liberty is notably absent from Ulster. But Irish Catholicism may also be a borrower. Accusations of 'Jansenism' have long been levelled at the Irish majority religion. Though popularly associated with rigorous sexual morality, shared with northern Prot-stats, technical Jansenism approximates Calvinist theology. If such Jansenism does permeate Irish Catholicism, it creates mirrored convergence at the very heart of the religious division.

A gloomy prognosis?

Perhaps, as the traditions of Northern Ireland so obviously mirror each other, their conflict is easily resolved? Unfortunately, the reverse is true. History demonstrates that minute deviations of religious or political principle can cause extremely bitter strife. Psychology shows that hatred is often most intense between close relatives. Sociologists like Tajfel maintain that an endangered identity requires an external enemy to ensure group cohesion. The latter applies particularly to Northern loyalists, generally rejected by British Protestants. Sarah Nelson demonstrated that many unionists, despite their bluster, feel acute inferiority towards the Catholic minority. Nationalists have appeared more culturally secure, but analysis shows that their problems parallel those of the unionists. Southern Catholics have scarcely more sympathy for the plight of the Northern Ireland minority than British Protestants for the fate of the majority. Northern nationalism, cultural and political, is therefore more strident than that of the south. The Provisional IRA is but an extreme response to this threatened identity. Deprived of external approbation, the two northern communities turn angrily back on each other. As in the tug-of-war, the collapse of one contestant brings disaster to the other.

The aftermath of the Anglo-Irish Agreement provides excellent illustrations. A cessation of PIRA assassination would undermine unionist opposition by suggesting that the Accord had increased general security; unionist acceptance of the right, enshrined in the Agreement, of both communities to their own identity and symbols would embarrass the Provisionals. Similarly, if the Catholic hierarchy announced total acceptance of undenominational education, Prot-stats would be forced to campaign for separate schools. Fortunately, both sides can count on predictable behaviour across the divide. The liberal demand for mutual concessions thus becomes wildly unrealistic.

The Northern Ireland problem does not, of course, involve the two local communities alone. It is as naive to contend, despite the insistence of the 1993 Downing Street Declaration, that the British government has always been a disinterested umpire, as it is to adopt the antithetically interpreted belief that the British presence is the sole obstacle to community harmony. Regardless of the findings of British opinion polls the stability of the island of Ireland has international implications. A Provisional-dominated united Irish Republic, or a maverick UDI 'Ulster', selling itself to the highest bidder, would affront Anglo-American global interests. Britain, as chapter six demonstrated, is herself an integral part of the Northern Ireland symbiosis.

It is possible to discern positive advantages for all participants in the current Ulster Troubles. The unionist and nationalist communities use their structured opposition to evade long-term questions about their identity and future; the British government controls a ritual antagonism better than other possible scenarios; Irish ministers present the northern stalemate as a distraction from economic disaster, while avoiding the overwhelming problems posed by a united Ireland. Life in the collusively antagonistic world of Tweedledum and Tweedledee may have positive attractions.

Is a solution really required to end such a creative stalemate? Though all groups may gain from the impasse, its continuance depends on the mobilisation and fine tuning of passions notoriously difficult to control. In both national and personal histories, the unforseen can destroy overnight a long-standing equilibrium. The more imaginative alternative is to convert John Hewitt's 'mirror hate' into mutual understanding by quietly abandoning the crazy logic of the zero-sum game which ensures that victory will go to unionists or nationalists, but not both.

Notes

1. 'The Anglo-Irish Accord' in Frank Ormsby, ed. (1981), *The Collected Poems of John Hewitt*, Belfast: Blackstaff, 537-8.
2. Mansergh, Nicholas (1978), *Prelude to Partition: Concepts and Aims in India and Ireland*, Cambridge: CUP, 13 for summary.
3. See Zinkin, Taya (1962), *Reporting India*, London: Chatto and Windus, 47, on riots swinging backwards and forwards like a pendulum. 29 for the strife stirred up by Bengali newspapers. She quotes a French landlord, Pierre Delauney, who maintains that, despite the propaganda, East (Muslim) and West (Hindu) Bengal really shared the same culture. The same argument is put forward by Asim Roy (1973 and 1983) who demonstrated ('The Social Factors in the Making of Bengali Islam', *South Asia*, Perth, No. 3. August 1973, 23-35, and *The Islamic Syncretistic Tradition in Bengal*, Princeton: Princeton

University Press, 69, passim) that, despite the efforts of their leaders, Bengali Muslims were traditionally drawn to Hindu culture.

4. Brookeborough, then Sir Basil Brooke, was frank that if employers did not act properly 'we shall find ourselves in the minority instead of the majority'. (March 1934). Quoted by Farrell, *Northern Ireland: The Orange State*, 91.

5. McKittrick, David (1992), 'Catholics to be the Majority in Ulster', *Independent on Sunday*, 1 November 1992. 11 of the 26 district councils now have a Catholic majority. Ten years earlier the issue was debatable. For the view that Catholic population was then between 40-42 per cent see Frank Curran, *Fortnight*, November 1983. He disagreed with Dr Paul Compton, see *Fortnight*, March 1983. Compton believed 37.5 per cent closer to the mark but agreed that the Catholic population is growing slowly.

6. UM, 4, 1972.

7. For *News Letter* poll, 31 March 1993, see *Fortnight*, May 1993.

8. Ulster Marketing Survey Ltd for ITN, quoted in Liam Ferrie, *The Irish Emigrant* [US email Journal], No. 364, 24 January 1994.

9. De Bono, Edward (1985), *Conflicts: A Better Way to Resolve Them*, London: Harrap, 102.

10. Macdonald, *Children of Wrath: Political Violence in Northern Ireland*, 22.

11. Trewin, Leonard C. (1968), *Report from Iron Mountain on the Possibility of Peace*, London: Macdonald, 76 and 111.

12. Whyte, John (1982), 'An Interpretation of the Northern Ireland Problem', Paper prepared for the 7th Annual Conference of the Political Studies Association Work Group on United Kingdom Politics, Belfast, 20-24 September 1982. Quotes Tajfel, Henri (1981), *Human Groups and Social Categories: Studies in Social Psychology*, Cambridge: CUP, and Whyte, *Interpreting Northern Ireland*, 97.

13. *A Place Apart*, 111. Bell, Geoffrey, *The Protestants of Ulster*, 62: Republican newspapers 'do not contain the bigotry and sectarianism of the Protestant papers .... There is no mention in them of wishing to kill Prod scum, no caricature of Protestants as dirty, smelly and idle'.

14. AN, 14 December 1974, commenting on LN, 30 November 1974, which had converted 'The Boys of the Old Brigade' to 'The Boys of the Y.C.V. Brigade'. The latter suggested other possible variations to the loyalists. Other examples can be found in the Kerr, Ken, ed. (n.d.), *UDA Song Book*, n.p.: 'Come all ye Young Protestants' to the tune of 'The Patriot Game'; 'The Junior I.R.A.' to the tune of 'Behind the Wire'; 'They've banned the wearing of the Sash' (UDAN, 14.1971); 'Who Fears to Speak of '72' (UDAN, 15.1972); 'I'd love to go to Belfast' ('Off to Dublin in the Green') OUDAN 1.31.1972; 'Ulster won' Die' (The Patriot Game), UL, 15 November 1973; 'The Sash that once through Belfast Streets' (The Harp that Once through Tara's walls), UL, 13 January 1974; 'I met with Orange Willie' (The Wearing of the Green), UL, 21 February 1974; 'An Ulster Soldier' (The Soldier's Song) UL, 1 August 1974.

15. On several RBP banners the depicted ascension of Christ seems based on a painting by Raphael, patronised by the very pope, Leo X, against

which Luther revolted! For an excellent analysis of the Royal Black Institution's symbolism see Buckley, Anthony P. (1985-86), 'The Chosen Few: Biblical Texts in the Regalia of an Ulster Secret Society', in *Folk Life*, Vol. 24, 5-24. Buckley demonstrates that Biblical texts are used as symbols of the Ulster Protestants as a chosen people defending themselves in an alien land.

16.   AP 13 and 20 January 1994.

Glossary of terms and parties

Gaelic terms

Cuman	Association or society
Taoiseach	Prime Minister
Dail	Parliament
Ard Comharle	High Council
Ard Fheis	National Convention
Comhar na gComharsan	Neighbours' Co-operation
TD	Teachta Dála (Dail Deputy)

Some paramilitary affiliations

Constitutional Parties
- Democratic Unionist Party (Paisley), DUP
- Official Unionist Party (technically 'Ulster Unionist Party'), OUP
- Social Democratic and Labour Party (Constitutional Nationalists), SDLP

Protestant Paramilitaries
- Ulster Defence Association, UDA
- Ulster Freedom Fighters (terrorist cover for UDA), UFF
- Ulster Volunteer Force, UVF
- Protestant Action Force (cover for UVF), PAF
- (Also Red Hand Commandos, Tara, etc.)

Republican Paramilitaries

- Provisional Irish Republican Army (or the IRA after 1969 when not otherwise stated), PIRA
- Provisional Sinn Féin (open movement for PIRA)
- Official IRA (fades after 1972), OIRA
- Official Sinn Féin (open movement for OIRA)
- Workers' Party (a later designation for the Officials), WP
- Irish Republican Socialist Party (split from Official Sinn Féin), IRSP
- Irish National Liberation Army (terrorist wing of IRSP), INLA
- Irish People's Liberation Organisation (breakaway from INLA), IPLO

Irish Paramilitaries and their Propaganda Organs

A Crescent Mirrors Convergence and Divergence

Select bibliography

Newspapers and abbreviations

Alliance [A]
Amrita Bazaar Patrika (Calcutta) [APB]
An Phoblacht [AP]
An Siol (1932-36)
An Solus (Official) [AS]
An t-Oglach (1940-44)
Andersonstown News [AN]
Barricades Bulletin [Ba]
Belfast Newsletter [BN]
Belfast Telegraph [BT]
Church and State, Maryland
Church and State: A Forum of Irish Secularist opinion, Cork
Combat (UVF) [C]
Constabulary Gazette: The Ulster Police Magazine [CG]
Fortnight, Belfast
Free Citizen (PD) [FC]
Ireland: International News Briefing,
Ireland (Provisional: free to foreign subscribers).
Iris (Provisional: a glossy for overseas readers).
Irish Catholic [IC]
Irish News [IN]
Irish People (weekly)
Irish Republican Information Service bulletin
Irish Times. [IT]
Irishman, Belfast (Presbyterian).

Law (Loyalist Association of Workers)
Loyalist News (UVF-Red Hand Commandos) [LN]
New Protestant Telegraph [NPT]
New Statesman [NS]
New Times
Northern People (Official) [NP]
Northern Star
Official UDA News [OUDAN]
Orange Standard [OS]
Peace by Peace (Peace People) [PP]
Protestant Blu Print (Paisley) [PBP]
Protestant Telegraph [PT]
Republic of Ireland (Anti-Treaty) [RI]
Republican News [RN]
Resurgent Ulster (1951-55)
Saoirse, New Zealand Irish Post
SDLP News [SDLPN]
Social Democrat (SDLP) [SD]
Socialist Republic (PD) [SR]
Starry Plough (IRSP) [SP]
Sunday Press [SP]
Sunday Times [ST]
Tattler (Provisional) [Ta]
Teoric (Official).[Tl]
The Nation (Young Ireland) [N]
The Observer [O]
Tir Gradh (1963-5)
UDA News [UDAN]
Ulster (UDA) [U]
Ulster Loyalist (UDA) [UL]
Ulster Militant (UDA) [UM]
Unfree Citizen (PD) [UF]
Unionist Clarion (OUP) [UC]
United Irishman (Official) UI
Vanguard Bulletin [Va]
Visor (British Army) [Vi]
Voice of Ulster (DUP) [VU]
Volunteer (Provisional) [V]
Women's View (bi-monthly)
Workers Life (monthly)
Young India

Books

Adams;, Gerry (November 1986). *Presidential Address by Gerry Adams to the 82nd Annual Sinn Féin Ard-Fheis, Mansion House,* Dublin: Sinn Féin Publicity Department.
_____ (1987), *The Politics of Irish Freedom,* Dingle: Brandon.
_____ (1988), *A Pathway to Peace,* Cork: Mercier.

_____ (1990), *Cage Eleven*, Dingle: Brandon.

Adams, James, Morgan, Robin and Bambridge, Anthony (1988), *Ambush: The War between the SAS and the IRA*, London: Pan.

Adams, Michael (1968), *Censorship: the Irish Experience*, Dublin: Scepter.

Adamson, Ian (1974), *Cruthin: The Ancient Kindred*, Newtownards: Nosmada.

_____ (1982), *The Identity of Ulster: the Land, the Language and the People*, [Belfast].

Alexander, Yonah & O'Day, Alan, eds (1984), *Terrorism in Ireland*, London: Croom Helm.

Armstrong, David, with Hilary Saunders (1985), *A Road too Wide: The Price of Reconciliation in Northern Ireland*, Basingstoke: Marshalls.

Arthur, Paul (1974), *The People's Democracy, 1968-1973*, Belfast: Blackstaff.

_____ (1980), *Government and Politics in Northern Ireland*, London: Longman.

Arthur, Paul, and Jeffrey, Keith (1988), *Northern Ireland Since 1968*, Oxford: Blackwell.

Aughey, Arthur (1989), *Under Siege: Ulster Unionism and the Anglo-Irish Agreement*, Belfast: Blackstaff.

Babington, Anthony (1990), *Military Intervention in Britain*, London: Routledge.

Barkley, J.M. (n.d.), *The Roman Church: A Handbook for Parents and Teachers*, Belfast: Presbyterian Church in Ireland.

Barzilay, David (1973), *The British Army in Ulster*, Belfast: Century Services Limited.

Belfast Workers Research Unit (1980), *The Churches in Northern Ireland*, Belfast Bulletin No. 8, Belfast.

Belfrage, Sally (1987), *The Crack: A Belfast Year*, London: André Deutsch. Also published as (1987), *Living with War: A Belfast Year*, New York: Elisabeth Sifton Books.

Bell, Desmond (1990), *Acts of Union: Youth Culture and Sectarianism in Northern Ireland*, London: Macmillan.

Bell, Geoffrey (1976), *The Protestants of Ulster*, London: Pluto.

Bell, J. Bowyer (1987), *IRA Targets and Tactics: The Gun in Politics. An Analysis of Irish Political Conflict, 1916-1986*, Oxford: Transaction Books.

Bell, Robert, 'Directory of N. Ireland Political Periodicals', *Fortnight*, Belfast, No. 229, 18 Nov. 1985, pp. 11-17.

Beresford, David (1989), *Ten Dead Men: The Story of the 1981 Hunger Strike*, New York: Atlantic Monthly Press.

Bew, P., Hazelkorn, H., Patterson, H. (1979), *The Dynamics of Irish Politics*, London: Lawrence and Wishart.

Bew, P., Gibbon, P. & Patterson, H. (1979), *The State in Northern Ireland, 1921-72*, Manchester: M U.P.

BICO (1974), *'Hidden Ulster' Explored: A Reply to P. O'Snodaigh* , Belfast: BICO.

Bishop, Patrick, & Eamonn Mallie (1988), *The Provisional IRA*, London: Corgie.

Boal, F.W. & Douglas, J.N. (1982), *Integration and Division: Geographical Perspectives in the Northern Ireland Problem*, London: Academic Press.

Boland, Kevin (1988), *Under Contract with the Enemy*, Cork: Mercier.

Bolton, Roger (1990), *Death on the Rock and other stories*, Great Britain: W.H. Allen.

Boulton, David (1973), *The UVF 1966-73: An Anatomy of Loyalist Rebellion*, Dublin: Gill and Macmillan.

Bouscaren, T.N. and A.C. Ellis (1961), *Canon Law: a Test and Commentary*, Milwaukee: Bruce.

Bowen, Desmond (1983), *Paul Cardinal Cullen and the Shaping of Modern Irish Catholicism*, Dublin: Gill & Macmillan.

Boyd, Andrew (1972), *Brian Faulkner and the Crisis of Ulster Unionism*, Tralee: Anvil.

Boyle, Kevin and Hadden, Tom (1985), *Ireland: A Positive Proposal*, Harmondsworth: Penguin.

Bradford, Roy (1981), *The Last Ditch*, Belfast: Blackstaff.

Bradley, Anthony (1992), *Requiem for a Spy*, Cork: Mercier.

Brady, Brian (1982), *The Chilver Challenge: Catholic Education on Northern Ireland*, Belfast.

Brady, Ciaran, ed. (1989), *Worsted in the Game: Losers in Irish History*, Dublin: Lilliput.

Brewer, T.D. with Kathleen Magee (1991), *Inside the RUC: Routine Policing in a Divided Society*, Oxford: Clarendon.

Bromley, Michael (1989), 'War of Words: The *Belfast Telegraph* and Loyalist Populism' in Yonah Alexander and Alan O'Day, eds, *Ireland's Terrorist Trauma: Interdisciplinary Perspectives*, Hemel Hempstead: Harvester Wheatsheaf, pp. 213-233.

Brooke, Peter (1987), *Ulster Presbyterianism*, Dublin: Gill & Macmillan.

Bruce, Steve (1986), *God Save Ulster: The Religion and Politics of Paisleyism*, Oxford: Clarendon.

Buchanan, R.H. (1982), 'The Planter and the Gael: cultural dimensions of the Northern Ireland Problem', in F.W. Boal and J.N.H. Douglas, *Integration and Division: Geographical Perspectives on the Northern Ireland Problem*, London: Academic Press.

Buchanan, R.H. and Walker, B., eds (1987), *Province, City and People*, Antrim: Greystone Books.

Buckley, Anthony D. (1985-86), 'The Chosen Few: Biblical Texts in the Regalia of an Ulster Secret Society', *Folk Life*, Vol. 24, pp. 5-24.

Budge, Ian and O'Leary, Cornelius (1973), *Belfast: Approach to Crisis: A Study of Belfast Politics, 1613-1970*, London: Macmillan.

Buijtenhuijs, R. (1973), *Mau Mau: Twenty Years After; the Myth and the Survivors*, The Hague: Mouton.

Burke, Edmund (1872), *Burke's Works*, 111, London: Bell and Daldry.

Burton, Frank (1978), *The Politics of Legitimacy: Struggles in a Belfast Community*, London: Routledge & Kegan Paul.

By'eeeee The Right ... Laugh! British Army Cartoonists Describe their View of Army Life in Northern Ireland, Belfast: CSL, 1973.

Callaghan, James (1973), *A House Divided: The Dilemma of Northern Ireland*, London: Collins.

———— (1987), *Time and Chance*, London: Collins.

Carlson, Julia, ed. (1990), *Banned in Ireland: Censorship and the Irish Writer*, London: Routledge.

Carter, Charles and   Barrit, D. (1962), *The Northern Ireland Problem*, London: OUP.

Caul, Leslie, ed. (1990), *Schools under Scrutiny: The Case of Northern Ireland*, Basingstoke: Macmillan Education.

Clarke, A.F.N. (1984) *Contact*, London: Pan.

Clarke, Liam (1987), *Broadening the Battlefield — the H-blocks and the Rise of Sinn Féin*, Dublin: Gill & Macmillan.

Clayton, Anthony (1976), *Counter-Insurgence in Kenya, 1952-60*, Nairobi: Transafrica Publishers.

Clifford, Brendan, ed. (1984), *The Life and Times of Thomas Moore (Ireland's National Poet)*, London: Athol Books.

Clutterbuck, Richard (1973), *Protest and the Urban Guerrilla*, London: Cassell.

_____ (1975), *Living with Terrorism*, London: Faber.

Collins, Tom, ed. (1985), *Ireland after Britain*, London: Pluto.

_____ (1986), *The Irish Hunger Strike*, Dublin & Belfast: White Island Book Company.

Comerford, R.V. (1979), *Charles J. Kickham: A Study in Irish Nationalism and Literature*, Co. Dublin: Wolfhound.

Connolly, James (1962), *Labour in Ireland*, Dublin: Sign of Three Candles, (contains *Labour in Irish History* and *The Reconquest of Ireland*).

_____ (1954), *Labour, Nationality and Religion*, Dublin: New Books.

_____ (1976), *Ireland upon the Dissecting Table: Connolly on Ulster and Partition*, Cork: Cork Workers' Club.

Coogan, T.P. (1980), *On the Blanket*, Swords: Ward River Press.

Coughlan, Anthony (1986), *Fooled Again? The Anglo-Irish Agreement and After*, Cork & Dublin: Mercier.

Cronin, S. (1971), *The Revolutionaries*, Dublin: Republican Publications.

Crossman, Richard (1975, 1976, 1977), *The Diaries of a Cabinet Minister*, London: H. Hamilton and Cape.

Crozier, M., ed. (1989), *Cultural Traditions in Northern Ireland*, Belfast: Institute of Irish Studies.

Curtis, Liz (1984), *Ireland: The Propaganda War: The Media and the 'Battle for Hearts and Minds'*, London: Pluto.

Daly, Cahal B. (1973), *Violence in Ireland and the Christian Conscience*, Dublin: Veritas.

Daly, Cahal B. (1979), *Peace the Work of Justice: Addresses on the Northern Tragedy, 1973-79*, Dublin: Veritas.

Darby, John (1974), 'Miscellany: History in the Schools', *Community Forum*, 2, pp. 37-42.

_____ (1976), *Conflict in Northern Ireland. The Development of a Polarised Community*, Dublin: Gill and Macmillan.

_____ (1983), *Dressed to Kill: Cartoonists and the Northern Ireland Conflict*, Belfast: Appletree.

Darby, John, Dodge, Nicholas and Hepburn, A.C. (1990), *Political Violence: Ireland in a Comparative Perspective*, Belfast: Appletree.

Davey, Ray (n.d.), *Take Away this Hate*, Corymeela Press.

Davis, R.P. (1974), *Arthur Griffith and Non-Violent Sinn Féin*, Dublin: Anvil.

_____ (1974), *Irish Issues in New Zealand Politics*, Dunedin: Otago University Press.

_____ (1976), *Arthur Griffith* Dublin: Dublin Historical Association.

_____ (1977), 'The Advocacy of Passive Resistance in Ireland, 1916-1922', *Anglo-Irish Studies*, III, Cambridge, pp. 48-9.

_____ (1977), 'The Self-Determination for Ireland Leagues and the Irish Race Convention in Paris, 1921-22', *Tasmanian Historical Research Association: Papers and Proceedings*, 24, 3, pp. 88-104.

_____ (1977), 'India in Irish Revolutionary Propaganda, 1905-1922', *Journal of the Asiatic Society of Bangladesh* (Dacca), Vol. XXII, No. 1, April, pp. 66-89.

_____ (1980), 'The Shamrock and the Tiki: Irish Nationalists and Maori Resistance in the 19th century', *Journal of Intercultural Studies* , Melbourne, Vol. 1, No. 3, December, pp. 16-27.

_____ (1980), *State Aid and Tasmanian Politics, 1868-1920*, Hobart: (University of Tasmania).

_____ (1980), 'Ulster Protestants and the Sinn Féin Press, 1914-22', *Eire-Ireland*, St Paul, Winter, pp. 60-85.

_____ (1981), 'Catholic Education and Irish Nationalism: O'Connell to Community Schools', *ANZHES Journal*, Adelaide, Vol. 10, No. 1, Autumn, pp. 1-12..

_____ (1982), 'Robert Lynd: A Man for all Seasons', *Pace*, Belfast, Vol. 41, No. 2, Summer/Autumn, pp. 20-22.

_____ (1986), 'Kitson versus Marighela: The debate over Northern Ireland Terrorism', in Yonah Alexander and Alan O'Day, eds, *Ireland's Terrorist Dilemma*, Martinus Nijhoff, Dordrecht (Neth.), pp. 179-209.

_____ (1986), 'The Influence of the Irish Revolution on Indian Nationalism: The Evidence of the Indian Press, 1916-22', *South Asia (Australia)*, New Ser., Vol. IX, No. 2, December, pp. 55-68.

_____ (1986), 'The Manufacture of Propagandist History by Northern Ireland Loyalists and Republicans', in Yonah Alexander and Alan O'Day, eds, *Ireland's Terrorist Dilemma*, Martinus Nijhoff, Dordrecht (Neth.), pp. 145-177.

_____ (1987), *The Young Ireland Movement*, Dublin: Gill and Macmillan.

_____ (1989), 'Irish Republicanism v. Roman Catholicism: The Perennial Debate in the Ulster Troubles', Alan O'Day and Yonah Alexander, eds, *Ireland's Terrorist Trauma: Interdisciplinary Perspectives*, London: Harvester Wheatsheaf, pp. 34-74.

Davis, Thomas (1914), *Selections from his Prose and Poetry*, London: Fisher Unwin.

De Baróid, Ciarán (1989), *Ballymurphy and the Irish War*, Dublin: Aisling.

De Bono, Edward (1985), *Conflicts: A Better Way to Resolve Them*, London: Harrap.

De Paor, Liam (1990), *Unfinished Business: Ireland Today and Tomorrow*, London: Hutchinson Radius.

Deutsch, R. and Magowan, V. (1974-5), *Northern Ireland, 1968-74: A Chronology of Events* (3 vols.), Belfast: Blackstaff.

Deutsch, Richard (1977), *Mairead Corrigan/Betty Williams*, New York: Baron.

Devlin, Bernadette (1969), *The Price of My Soul*, London: Pan.

Devlin, P. (1975), *The Fall of the N.I. Executive*, Belfast: P. Devlin.

Dewar, M.W., John Brown and S.E. Long (1967), *Orangeism, a new Appreciation*, Belfast.

Dillon, Martin and D. Lehane (1973), *Political Murder in Northern Ireland*, Harmondsworth: Penguin.

Dillon, Martin (1988), *The Dirty War*, London: Hutchinson.

_____ (1989) *The Shankill Butchers: A Case Study of Mass Murder*, London: Hutchinson.

Doherty, Frank (1986), *The Stalker Affair: including an account of the British Secret Service*, Dublin: Mercier.

Dowling, P.J. (1968), *The Hedge Schools of Ireland*, Cork: Mercier.

Downey, James (1983), *Them and Us: Britain-Ireland and the Northern Question, 1969-1982*, Dublin: Ward River Press.

Dunne, Derek (1988), *Out of the Maze: The True Story of the Biggest Jail Escape Since the War*, Dublin: Gill and Macmillan.

Dunne, Tom (1984), *Theobald Wolfe Tone: The Colonial Outsider: An Analysis of his Political Philosophy*, Cork: Tower Books.

Durham, Earl of (1905), *The Report of the Earl of Durham, Her Majesty's High Commissioner and Governor-General of British North America*, London: Methuen.

Easthope, Gary (1986), 'Religious War in Northern Ireland', *Sociology*, Oxford, Vol. 10, No. 3.

Edwards, J. (1983), *The Irish Language: An Annotated Bibliography of Sociolinguistic Publications, 1772-1982*, New York: Gould.

Edwards, Ruth Dudley (1977), *Patrick Pearse: The Triumph of Failure*, London: Faber.

Egan, Bowes and McCormack, Vincent (1969), *Burntollet*, Belfast: LRS.

Eire Nua (1971): *The Social and Economic Policy of Sinn Féin*, Dublin: Eanair.

Evans, Estyn (1984), *Ulster: The Common Ground*, Mullingar: Lilliput.

Evelegh, Robin (1978), *Peace-Keeping in a Democratic Society: The Lessons of Northern Ireland*, London: Hurst.

Faligot, Roger (1983), *Britain's Military Strategy in Ireland: the Kitson Experiment*, London and Dingle: Zed and Brandon.

Farrell, Brian (1971), *The Founding of Dail Eireann: Parliament and Nation Building*, Dublin: Gill and Macmillan.

Farrell, Michael(1980), *Northern Ireland: The Orange State*, London: Pluto.

Faul, Denis and Murray, Raymond (1978), *The Castlereagh File: Allegations of RUC Brutality, 1976-1977*, n.p.

_____ [1980], *H-Block and its Background* (from *Doctrine and Life*, November), Belfast.

_____ [1980], *Moment of Truth for Northern Ireland* (from *Doctrine and Life*, March), Belfast.

Faulkner, Brian (1978), *Memoirs of a Statesman*, (ed. John Houston), London: Weidenfield and Nicholson.

Feehan, John M. (1983), *Bobby Sands and the Tragedy of Northern Ireland*, Dublin: Mercier.

Fennell, Desmond (1985), *Beyond Nationalism: The Struggle against Provinciality in the Modern World*, Swords: Ward River Press.

_____ (1988) *The Revision of Irish Nationalism*, Dublin: Open Air.

Fields, Rona (1977), *Society under Siege: A Psychology of Northern Ireland*, Philadelphia: Temple.

Fisk, Robert (1975), *The Point of No Return: The Strike which broke the British in Ulster*, London: André Deutsch.

Fitzgerald, Billy (1990), *Father Tom: An Authorised Portrait of Cardinal Tomas O Fiaich*, London: Collins.

Flackes, W.D. and Elliott, Sydney (1989), *Northern Ireland: A Political Directory, 1968-88*, Belfast: Blackstaff.

Forde, Ben [with Chris Spencer] (1979), *Hope in Bomb City*, Basingstoke: Lakeland.

Foster, R.F. (1988), *Modern Ireland*, London: Penguin.

Foster, Thomas C. (1989), *Seamus Heaney*, Dublin: O'Brien Press.

Fremantle, Ann (1963), *The Papal Encyclicals in their Historical Context*, New York: Mentor.

Fromm, Eric (1963), *Fear of Freedom*, London: Routledge and Kegan Paul.

Gaffikin, Frank and Morrisey, Mike (1990), *Northern Ireland: The Thatcher Years*, London: Zed.

Gallagher, E. and Worrall, S. (1982), *Christians in Ulster, 1968-1980* OUP.

Galliher, John and DeGregory, Jerry L. (1985), *Violence in Northern Ireland: Understanding Protestant Perspectives*, Dublin: Gill & Macmillan.

Galway, James (1978), *An Autobiography*, London: Chappell.

Garvin, Tom (1981), *The Evolution of Irish Nationalist Politics*, Dublin: Gill and Macmillan.

Gerassi, J., ed. (1971), *Revolutionary Priest: the Complete Writings and Messages of Camilo Torres*, London: Jonathan Cape.

Gibson-Harris, D. (1990), *Life-Line to Freedom: Ulster in the Second World War*, Lurgan: Ulster Society.

Goldring, Maurice (1987), *Faith of Our Fathers: The Formantion of Irish Nationalist Ideology, 1890-1920*, Dublin: Repsol.

_____ (1991), *Belfast: From Loyalty to Rebellion*, London: Lawrence & Wishart.

Gordon, David (1989), *The O'Neill Years: Unionist Politics: 1963-1969*, Belfast: Athol Books.

Gray, John (1989), Introduction to *Northern Ireland Political Literature on Microfiche: Catalogue and Indexes: Phase 1—Periodicals 1966-1987*, Belfast: Linen Hall Library, pp. i-ii.

Greaves, C. D. (1963), *Tone and the Irish Nation*, London: Connolly Assn.

Greer, G. (1971), *The Female Eunuch*, London: Paladin.

Grenillon, O.J. (1975), *The Gospel of Peace and Justice: Catholic Social Teaching since Pope John*, New York: Orbis.

Grey, Lord, ed. (1990), *Banned in Ireland: Censorship and the Irish Writer*, London: Article 19.

Guerry, E. (1961), *The Social teaching of the Church*, London: Saint Paul.

Gwynn, D. (1948), *O'Connell, Davis and the Colleges Bill*, Cork UP.

Hall, Michael (1988), *20 Years: A Concise Chronology of Events in Northern Ireland from 1968-1988*, Newtownabbey: Island Publication.

Hanson, Richard (1963), *The Bible as a Norm of Faith*, Durham: Durham University Press.

_____ (1980), 'It is a Religious Issue', *Encounter*, Vol. XV, No. 4, October, pp. 11-20.

_____ (1983), *The Life and Writings of St Patrick*, New York: Seabury Press.

Harbinson, Robert (1987 [1960]), *No Surrender: An Ulster Childhood*, Belfast: Blackstaff.

Heaney, Seamus (1975), *North*, London: Faber.

Hesketh, Tom (1990), *The Second Partition of Ireland: The Abortion Referendum of 1983*, Dun Laoghaire: Brandsman Books.

Heslinga, M.W. (1971), *The Irish Border as a Cultural Divide*, Netherlands: Van Gorcum.

Hewitt, John (1986), *Freehold and Other Poems*, Belfast: Blackstaff.

Hickey, John (1984), *Religion and the Northern Ireland Problem*, Dublin: Gill & Macmillan.

Hill, M. and Barber, S. (1990), *Aspects of Irish Studies*, Belfast: Institute of Irish Studies.

Hill, C. (1971), *Antichrist in Seventeenth-Century England*, Oxford: OUP.

Hofstadter, Richard (1966), *The Paranoid style in American Politics*, London: Cape.

Holland, J. (1981), *Too Long a Sacrifice: Life and Death in Northern Ireland since 1969*, New York: Dodd, Mead.

Howroyd, Fred [with Nick Burbridge] (1989), *War Without Honour*, Hull: Medium.

Hull, Roger H. (1976), *The Irish Triangle: Conflict in Northern Ireland*, Princeton: Princeton University Press.

Hyams, E. (1975), *Terrorists and Terrorism*, London: Dent.

Inglis, Brian (1973), *Roger Casement*, London: Hodder & Stoughton.

Inglis, Tom (1987), *Moral Monopoly: The Catholic Church in Modern Irish Society*, Dublin: Gill & Macmillan.

Insight (1972), *Ulster*, Harmondsworth: Penguin.

International Year Book and Statesman's Who's Who (1989), E. Grinstead: Reed Information Services.

Irvine, Maurice (1991), *Northern Ireland: Faith and Faction*, London: Routledge.

Jeffrey, K., ed. (1985), *The Divided Province: The Troubles in Northern Ireland, 1969- 1985*, London: Orbis.

John XXIII, (1961) *Mater et Magister*, London: Catholic Truth Society.

_____ (1963) *World Peace*, London: Catholic Truth Society.

Kamen, H. (1967), *The Rise of Toleration*, London: Weidenfeld & Nicholson.

Kee, Robert (1986), *Trial and Error*, London: Hamish Hamilton.

Keena, Colm (1990), *Gerry Adams—A Biography*, Cork: Mercier.

Kelley, Kevin (1982), *The Longest War: Northern Ireland and the IRA*, Dingle: Brandon.

Kelly, James (1976), *Genesis of Revolution*, Dublin: Kelly Lane.

Kennedy, Liam (1986), *Two Ulsters: A Case for Repartition*, Belfast: [author].

Kensit, J.A. (1921), *Rome behind Sinn Féin?*, London: Protestant Truth Society.

Kerr, Ken, ed. (n.d.),*UDA Song Book*, n.p.

Kilfeather, T.P. (1969), The Connaught Rangers Tralee: Anvil.

Kingsley, Paul (1989), *Londonderry Revisited: A Loyalist Analysis of the Civil Rights Controversy*, Belfast: Belfast Publications.

Kirk, Andrew (1979), *Liberation Theology: An Evangelist View from the Third World*, London: Marshall, Magin and Scott.

Kitson, Frank (1960), *Gangs and Counter-Gangs*, London: Barry & Rockliffe.

_____ (1975), *Low Intensity Operations: Subversion, Insurgency, Peace-keeping*, London: Faber.

_____(1977), *Bunch of Five*, London: Faber.

Kormski (1985), *Dog Collars*, Belfast, *Fortnight*.

Lamont, Donal (1977), *Speech from the Dock*, London: Catholic Institute for International Relations.

Lasswell, H. (1963), *Politics: Who gets what, when, how*, Cleveland: Meridian.

Lecky, W.E.H. (1910), *History of the Rise and Influence of Rationalism in Europe*, Vol. 2, London: Longman.

Lenin, V. I. (1966), *Collected Works*, Moscow, Vol. 31.

Leonard, G. (1976), *Light on Archbishop LeFebvre*, London: Catholic Truth Society.

Lewin, L.C. (1968), introduction, *Report from Iron Mountain on the Possibility and Desirability of Peace*, London: Macdonald.

Lindsay, K. (1980), *The British Intelligence Services in Action*, Dundalk: Dundrod Press.

Longford, Lord and McHardy, Ann (1981), *Ulster*, London: Weidenfeld & Nicholson.

Lyons, F.S.L. (1960), *The Fall of Parnell, 1890-91*, London: Routledge.

_____ (1982), *Culture and Anarchy in Ireland, 1890-1939*, Oxford: OUP.

_____ (1979), *The Burden of Our History*, W.B. Rankin Memorial Lecture, Belfast: Queen's University.

Lyons, F.S.L. (1973), *Ireland Since the Famine*, London: Collins/Fontana.

MacDermott, Frank (1939), *Theobald Wolfe Tone*, London: Macmillan.

MacDonagh, Oliver (1983), *States of Mind: A Study of Anglo-Irish Conflict, 1780-1980*, London: Allen & Unwin.

Macdonald, Michael (1986), *Children of Wrath: Political Violence in Northern Ireland*, Cambridge: Polity Press.

MacNeill, J.T. (1962), *The History and Character of Calvinism*, New York: OUP.

MacStiofain, Seán (1975), *Memoirs of a Revolutionary*, Great Britain: Gordon Cremonesi.

Madden, D.O. (1843), *Ireland and its Rulers, since 1829*, London: T.C. Newby.

Mandela, Nelson (1990), *Walk the Last Mile with us: Nelson Mandela's Speeches in Ireland*, Dublin: Irish Anti-Apartheid Movement.

Manhattan, Avro (1971), *Religious Terror in Ireland*, London: Paravision.

Mansergh, Nicholas (1978), *Prelude to Partition: Concepts and Aims in India and Ireland*, Cambridge: CUP.

Marighela, Carlos (1971), *For the Liberation of Brazil*, London: Penguin.
_____ (n.d.), *Minimanual of the Urban Guerrilla*, n.p.: Grassroots Publications.
Marrinan (1973), *Paisley: Man of Wrath*, Tralee: Anvil.
Martin, F.X. (1968), 'The 1916 Rising—coup d'état or a bloody protest'?', *Studia Hibernia*, no.8, pp. 106-137.
Marx, K. and Engels, F. (1978), *Ireland and the Irish Question*, London: Lawrence and Wishart.
Masrui, Ali (1967), *On Heroes and Uhuru Worship*, London: Longman.
McAllister, Ian (1977), *The Northern Ireland Social Democratic and Labour Party*, London: Macmillan.
McCabe, Leo (1939), *Wolfe Tone and the United Irishman: For or Against Christ?* London: Heath Cranton.
McCafferty, Nell (1981), *The Armagh Women*, Dublin: Co-op Books.
McCann, Eamon (1981), *War and an Irish Town*, London: Pluto.
McCarthy, Michael J.F. [1922], *The British Monarchy and the See of Rome: the Tragedy of Ireland*, London: Protestant Truth Society.
McCartney, Donal (1968), 'The Church and the Fenians' in M. Harmon, ed., *Fenians and Fenianism*, Dublin: Scepter.
McCrea, William (1980), *In His Pathway: The Story of the Rev. William McCrea as told to David Porter*, London: Lutterworth Press.
McCreary, Alf (1980), *Corrymeela—The Search for Peace*, Belfast: Christian Journals Ltd.
McDonagh, Enda (1980), *The Demand of Simple Justice*, Dublin: Gill and Macmillan.
McElroy, Gerard (1991), *The Catholic Church and the Northern Ireland Crisis, 1968-86*, Dublin: Gill and Macmillan.
McGuffin, John (1973), *Internment*, Tralee: Anvil.
_____ (1974), *The Guineapigs*, Harmondsworth: Penguin.
McGuire, M. (1973), *To Take Arms: A Year in the Provisionals*, London: Macmillan.
McKeown, Ciaran (1984), *The Passion of Peace*, Belfast: Blackstaff.
McKittrick, David (1989), *Despatches from Belfast*, Belfast: Blackstaff.
McVeigh, Joseph (1989), *A Wounded Church: Religion, Politics and Justice in Ireland*, Cork: Mercier.
Menendez, A.J. (1973), *The Bitter Harvest: Church and State in Northern Ireland*, Washington: R.B. Luce.
Millar, D.W. (1978), *Queen's Rebels: Ulster Loyalism in Historical Perspective*, Dublin: Gill & Macmillan.
Mitchel, John (n.d.), *Ireland from the seige of Limerick*, London: Washbourne.
_____ [1914], *Jail Journal*, Dublin: Gill.
Moloney, Ed and Andy Pollack (1986), *Paisley*, Dublin: Poolbeg.
Morgan, Austen and Bob Purdie, eds (1980), *Ireland—Divided Nation Divided Class*, London: Ink Links.
Morrison, Danny [1979], 'Censorship at Source: The raids on *Republican News*', Campaign for Free Speech in Ireland, *The British Media and Ireland*, London, pp. 45-6.
_____ (1989),*West Belfast*, Cork: Mercier.

Morrison, H. (1983), *Betty Sinclair: A Woman's Fight for Socialism*, Belfast: AT and GWU.

Murphy, David (1991), *The Stalker Affair and the Press*, Boston: Unwin.

Murphy, Dervla (1980), *A Place Apart*, Harmondsworth: Penguin.

Murray, Raymond (1990), *The SAS in Ireland*, Cork: Mercier.

Namier, L. (1963), *Vanished Supremacies: Essays on European History, 1812-1918*, New York: Hayer.

Nelson, Sarah (1984), *Ulster's Uncertain Defenders: Protestant Political, Paramilitary and Community Groups and the Northern Ireland Conflict*, Belfast: Appletree.

Newman, J. (1977), *The State of Ireland*, Dublin: Four Courts Press.

Northern Ireland Economic Development Office (1986), *Demographic Trends in Northern Ireland, Report 57:*, Belfast.

Nyere, Julius K. (1979), *Ujaama: Essays on Socialism*, Oxford: OUP.

O'Snodaigh, Padraig (April, May, June 1966), '1916—The Beginnings', *Christus Rex*, XX, 2.

O'Brádaigh, Ruairí (1973), *Our People, Our Future: What EIRE NUA means*, Dublin: Sinn Féin.

O'Brien, C.C. (1957), *Parnell and his Party, 1880-90*, Oxford: Clarendon.

_____ (1972), *States of Ireland*, London: Hutchinson.

_____ (1978), *Herod: Reflections on Political Violence*, London: Hutchinson.

_____ (1980), *Neighbours: The Ewart-Biggs Memorial Lectures 1978-1979*, London: Faber.

_____ (1988), *Passion and Cunning and Other Essays*, London: Weidenfeld & Nicholson.

O'Brien, Jack (1989), *British Brutality in Ireland*, Cork: Mercier.

O'Casey, Sean (1973), *Drums under the Windows*, London: Pan.

O'Clery, Conor (1987), *The Dictionary of Political Quotations on Ireland, 1886-1987: Phrases make History Here*, Boston: G.K. Hall.

O'Donnell, E.E. (1977), *Northern Irish Stereotypes*, Dublin: Research Branch of College of Industrial Relations.

O'Dowd, Liam, Rolston, Bill and Tomlinson, Mike (1980), *Northern Ireland Between Civil Rights and Civil War*, London: CSE Books.

O'Faolain, Sean, ed. (1937), *Autobiography of Theobald of Wolfe Tone*, London: Nelson.

O'Fiaich, Tomas (February 1968), 'The Clergy and Fenianism', *Irish Ecclesiastical Record*, Vol. CIX, No. 2, pp. 81-103.

O'Malley, Padraig (1990), *Biting at the Grave: the Irish Hunger Strikes and the Politics of Despair*, Belfast: Blackstaff.

_____ (1990), *Northern Ireland: Questions of Nuance*, Belfast: Blackstaff.

O'Neill, Terence (1972), *The Autobiography of Terence O'Neill*, London: Rupert Hart Davies.

Oram, Hugh (1983), *The Newspaper Book: A History of Newspapers in Ireland, 1649-1983*, Dublin: MO Books.

Paisley, I.R.K. (1964), *Why I am a Protestant*, Belfast: Puritan.

_____ (n.d.)*Three Great Reformers*, Belfast: Puritan.

_____ (1972), *United Ireland: Never!* Belfast: Puritan.

_____ (1976), *Paisley: the Man and His Message*, Belfast: Martyrs Memorial Publications.

_____ (1982), *No Pope Here*, Belfast: Martyr Memorial Publications.

Paisley, I.R.K., P. Robinson and J. Taylor (1982), *Ulster: The Facts*, Belfast: Crown.

Patrick, Derrick (1981), *Fetch Felix, The Fight against the Ulster Bombers, 1976-77*, London: Hamish Hamilton.

Patterson, Henry (1989), *The Politics of Illusion: Republicanism and Socialism in Modern Ireland*, London: Hutchinson Radius.

John Paul II, Pope (1979), *The Pope Teaches—including Speeches made in Ireland*, September, 1979, London: Catholic Truth Society.

Paul VI, Pope (1965), (Populorum Progressio). *On the Development of Peoples*, Dublin: Catholic Truth Society.

_____ (1971), *Octogesima Adveniens*.

Pius XI, Pope (1963), *On the Christian Education of Youth*, London: Catholic Truth Society.

Probert, Belinda (1978), *Beyond Orange and Green: The Northern Ireland Crisis in a New Perspective*, Dublin: Academy Press.

Purdie, Bob (1990), *Politics in the Streets: The Origins of the Civil Rights Movement in Northern Ireland*, Belfast: Blackstaff.

Purdy, Anne (1989), *Molyneux: The Long View*, Antrim: Greystone.

Ransom, Bernard (1980), *Connolly's Marxism*, London: Pluto.

Rees, Merlyn (1985), *Northern Ireland: A Personal Perspective*, London: Methuen.

Robinson, Peter (1988), *Their Cry was "No Surrender": An Account of the Siege of Londonderry, 1688-89*, Belfast: Crown.

Rolston, Bill and Tomlinson, Mike (1988), *Unemployment in West Belfast; the Obair Report*, Belfast: Obair.

Rolston, Bill, ed. (1991), *The Media and Northern Ireland: Covering the Troubles*, London: Macmillan.

Rosberg, G.G., Jr. and Nottingham, J. (1966), *The Myth of 'Mau Mau'; Nationalism of Kenya*, New York: Praeger.

Roy, Asim (1983), *The Islamic Syncretistic Tradition in Bengal*, Princeton: Princeton University Press.

Ryder, Chris (1989), *The RUC, a Force under Fire*, London: Methuen.

Sands, Bobby (1981), *Prison Poems*, Dublin: Sinn Féin.

_____ *The Writings of Bobby Sands*, Dublin: Sinn Féin.

_____ (1982) *Skylark Sing your Lonely Song: An Anthology of the Writings of Bobby Sands*, Dublin: Mercier.

_____ (1984) *One Day in My Life*, Dublin: Mercier.

_____ (1990) *The Diary of Bobby Sands: The first seventeen days of Bobby's H-Block hunger strike to the death*, 2nd ed., Dublin: Republican Publications.

SFWP (1977), *The Irish Industrial Revolution*, Dublin: Repcol.

Shaw, Fr Francis (1972), 'The Canon of Irish History—a Challenge', *Studies*, Summer.

Shearman, Hugh (1942), *Not An Inch*, London: Faber.

_____ (1972) *27 Myths about Ulster*, Belfast (Ulster Unionist pamphlet).

324   *Mirror Hate*

Sinn Féin Publicity Department (1985), *The Good Old IRA: Tan War Operations*, Dublin: Sinn Féin.
Sinn Féin (1982), *Notes For Revolutionaries*, Dublin: Sinn Féin.
Smyth, Clifford (1987), *Ian Paisley: Voice of Protestant Ulster*, Edinburgh: Scottish Academic Press.
Stalker, John (1988), *Stalker: Ireland, 'Shoot to Kill ' and the 'Affair'* London: Penguin.
Steinbeck (1973), John, *Of Mice and Men* and *Cannery Row*, Harmondsworth: Penguin.
Stewart, A.T.Q. (1967), *The Ulster Crisis*, London: Faber.
_____ (1977) *The Narrow Ground: Aspects of Ulster, 1609-1969*, London: Faber.
Swift, Jonathan (1967), *Gulliver's Travels*, Harmonsdsworth: Penguin.
Sykes, Norman (1959), *The Crisis of the Reformation*, London: Geoffrey Bles.
Taber, R. (1972), *The War of the Flea: Guerrilla Warfare—Theory and Practice*, London: Paladin.
Taylor, Peter (1980), *Beating the Terrorists?*, Harmondsworth: Penguin.
Taylor, Peter (1989), *Families at War: Voices from the Troubles*, London: BBC Books.
Teague, Paul (1987), *Beyond the Rhetoric: Politics, the Economy and Social Policy in Northern Ireland*, London: Lawrence and Wishart.
The Ulster Debate: Report of a Study Group of the Institute for the Study of Conflict (1972), London: Bodley Head.
Trewin, Leonard C. (1968), *Report from Iron Mountain on the Possibility and Desirability of Peace*, London: Macdonald.
UDA/NUPGR (29 March 1979), *Beyond the Religious Divide* , Belfast UPGR.
UDA/UPGR (1987) *Common Sense Belfast: UPGR.*
Unionist Joint Working Party, The (1986), *Unionism: a Policy for all the People*, Belfast.
Violence in Ireland: A Report to the Churches, (1976), Belfast and Dublin: Christian Journals Limited and Veritas.
Waciuma, Charity (1969), *Daughter of the Mumbi*, Nairobi: East Africa Publishing House.
Ward, Margaret (1990), *Maud Gonne: Ireland's Joan of Arc*, London: Pandora.
Westminster Confession of Faith, (1978), Glasgow: Free Presbyterian Publications.
White, Barry (1984), *John Hume: Statesman of the Troubles*, Belfast: Blackstaff.
White, Jack (1975), *Minority Report: the Protestant Community in the Irish Republic*, Dublin: Gill and Macmillan.
Whyte, J.H. (1980), *Church and State in Modern Ireland, 1923-1979*, Dublin: Gill & Macmillan.
_____ (1981), *Catholics in Western Democracies: a Study in Political Behaviour*, Dublin: Gill & Macmillan.
Whyte, J.H. (1990), *Interpreting Northern Ireland*, Oxford: Clarendon.
Wilkinson, Paul (1981), *British Perspectives on Terrorism*, London: Allen and Unwin.

Wilson, Bryan (1970), *Religious Sects: A Sociological Study*, London: Weidenfeld & Nicholson.

Wilson, Des [1982], *The Demonstration*, [Belfast].

_____ (1985), *An End to Silence*, Cork: Mercier.

Wilson, Des, and Kearney, Oliver (1988), *West Belfast—The Way Forward*, [Belfast].

Wilson, Dorothy & Dunn, Seamus (1989), *Integrated Schools: Information for Parents*, Coleraine: Centre for Conflict, University of Ulster.

Wilson, Sam (1981), *The Carson Trail*, Belfast: Crown.

Winchester, Simon (1974), *In Holy Terror: Reporting the Ulster Troubles*, London: Faber.

Winter, Gordon (1981), *Inside Boss*, Harmondsworth: Penguin.

Wright, Joanne (1991), *Terrorist Propaganda: The Red Army Faction and the Provisional IRA, 1968-86*, London: Macmillan.

Zinkin, Taya (1962), *Reporting India*, London: Chatto and Windus.

Index